R-UPS &
SECRETS

The Complete Guide to
Government Conspiracies,
Manipulations & Deceptions

Nick Redfern

VISIBLE
I N K
PRESS

Detroit

ABOUT THE AUTHOR

Nick Redfern works full time as an author, lecturer, and journalist. He writes about a wide range of unsolved mysteries, including Bigfoot, UFOs, the Loch Ness Monster, alien encounters, and government conspiracies. His many books include *The Zombie Book, The Bigfoot Book, The Monster Book, Secret History, Secret Societies,* and *The New World Order Book.* He writes regularly for *Mysterious Universe.* He has appeared on numerous television shows, including the History Channel's *Ancient Aliens, Monster Quest,* and *UFO Hunters;* VH1's *Legend Hunters;* National Geographic Channel's *The Truth about UFOs* and *Paranatural;* BBC's *Out of This World;* MSNBC's *Countdown;* and SyFy Channel's *Proof Positive.* Nick lives just a few miles from Dallas, Texas' infamous Grassy Knoll and can be contacted at his blog:

http://nickredfernfortean.blogspot.com.

ACKNOWLEDGMENTS

I would like to offer my very sincere thanks to my tireless agent and friend, Lisa Hagan, and to everyone at Visible Ink Press, and particularly Roger Janecke and Kevin Hile.

OTHER VISIBLE INK PRESS BOOKS BY NICK REDFERN

Area 51: The Revealing Truth of UFOs, Secret Aircraft, Cover-ups & Conspiracies
ISBN 978-1-57859-672-0

The Bigfoot Book: The Encyclopedia of Sasquatch, Yeti, and Cryptid Primates
ISBN: 978-1-57859-561-7

Control: MKUltra, Chemtrails, and the Conspiracy to Suppress the Masses
ISBN: 978-1-57859-638-6

The Monster Book: Creatures, Beasts, and Fiends of Nature
ISBN: 978-1-57859-575-4

The New World Order Book
ISBN: 978-1-57859-615-7

Secret History: Conspiracies from Ancient Aliens to the New World Order
ISBN: 978-1-57859-479-5

Secret Societies: The Complete Guide to Histories, Rites, and Rituals
ISBN: 978-1-57859-483-2

The Zombie Book: The Encyclopedia of the Living Dead
With Brad Steiger
ISBN: 978-1-57859-504-4

PHOTO SOURCES

Gray Barker: p. 94.
Cassowary Colorizations: p. 193.
CBS-TV: p. 146.
Cryotank (Wikicommons): p. 402.
Cryptocone (Wikicommons): p. 37.
Deutsches Bundesarchiv: p. 297.
David dos Dantos: p. 389.
W & D Downey: p. 54.
Dudeanatortron (Wikicommons): p. 161.
Erik1980 (Wikicommons): p. 322.
Executive Office of the President of the United
    States: pp. 80, 382.
Peter Facey: p. 294.
Federal Bureau of Investigation: pp. 249, 359, 370.
Herbert Frank: p. 345.
Nicolas Genin: p. 306.
Jane Gitschier: p. 296.
Milton H. Greene: p. 246.
Bobak Ha'Eri: p. 328.
Juhauski72 (Wikicommons): p. 59.
Roy Kerwood: p. 262.
Kunsthistorisches Museum Wien, Bilddaten-
    bank: p. 53.
Lazarusx (Wikicommons): p. 49.
Library of Congress: p. 5.
Alan Light: p. 406.
Michiel1972 (Wikicommons): p. 229.
Ministry of Defense (The Netherlands): p. 342.
Jeff Mock: p. 361.
Ave Maria Mõistlik: p. 76.
Marcelo Montecino: p. 172.
Mary Ann Moorman (Mary Krahmer): p. 168.
National Aeronautics and Space Administra-
    tion: pp. 180, 203, 205.

National Archives and Records Administration:
    pp. 257, 394.
National Library of Australia: p. 254.
Serouj Ourishian: p. 123.
Paphrag (Wikicommons): p. 299.
Nick Parfjonov: p. 320.
Keenan Pepper: p. 22.
Luis Perez: p. 63.
Laura Poitras / Praxis Films: p. 386.
Andreas Praefcke: p. 51.
Roswell Daily Record: p. 240.
Abbie Rowe: p. 178.
Camilo Sanchez: p. 271.
A. Secoy: p. 287.
Robert Sheaffer: p. 157.
Shutterstock: pp. 3, 11, 13, 15, 20, 25, 31, 34,
    41, 44, 67, 73, 78, 83, 86, 102, 117, 120, 133,
    141, 149, 154, 184, 190, 194, 197, 198, 210,
    213, 216, 233, 268, 273, 275, 278, 284, 288,
    304, 308, 311, 313, 315, 352, 408.
Abi Skipp: p. 325.
Brad Steiger: p. 96.
Sweeneyr (Wikicommons): p. 362.
Roberto Tenore: p. 85.
Transpoman (Wikicommons): p. 397.
U.S. Air Force: pp. 92, 110, 162, 243.
U.S. Congress: p. 130.
U.S. Department of Defense: p. 138.
U.S. Department of State: p. 181.
U.S. Senate: p. 348.
Taras Young: p. 376.
Z22 (Wikicommons): p. 107.
Public domain: pp. 89, 100, 114, 128, 171, 211,
    222, 224, 225, 236, 260, 366, 375.

COVER-UPS & SECRETS
THE COMPLETE GUIDE TO GOVERNMENT CONSPIRACIES, MANIPULATIONS & DECEPTIONS

Visible Ink Press®
43311 Joy Rd., #414
Canton, MI 48187-2075

Visible Ink Press is a registered trademark of Visible Ink Press LLC.

Most Visible Ink Press books are available at special quantity discounts when purchased in bulk by corporations, organizations, or groups. Customized printings, special imprints, messages, and excerpts can be produced to meet your needs. For more information, contact Special Markets Director, Visible Ink Press, www.visibleink.com, or 734-667-3211.

Managing Editor: Kevin S. Hile
Art Director: Mary Claire Krzewinski
Typesetting: Marco DiVita
Proofreaders: Larry Baker and Shoshana Hurwitz
Indexer: Larry Baker

Cover images: Shutterstock.

10 9 8 7 6 5 4 3 2 1

Printed in the United States of America.

Library of Congress Cataloging-in-Publication Data

Names: Redfern, Nicholas, 1964- author.
Title: Cover-ups & secrets : the complete guide to government conspiracies, manipulations, and deceptions / by Nick Redfern.
Other titles: Cover-ups and secrets
Description: Canton, MI : Visible Ink Press, [2019]
Identifiers: LCCN 2019000825 | ISBN 9781578596799 (pbk. : alk. paper)
Subjects: LCSH: Conspiracies—History.
Classification: LCC HV6275 .R449 2019 | DDC 001.9—dc23
LC record available at https://lccn.loc.gov/2019000825

ALSO FROM VISIBLE INK PRESS

Alien Mysteries, Conspiracies, and Cover-Ups
by Kevin D. Randle
ISBN: 978-1-57859-418-4

Angels A to Z, 2nd edition
by Evelyn Dorothy Oliver, Ph.D., and James R Lewis, Ph.D.
ISBN: 978-1-57859-212-8

Armageddon Now: The End of the World A to Z
by Jim Willis and Barbara Willis
ISBN: 978-1-57859-168-8

The Astrology Book: The Encyclopedia of Heavenly Influences, 2nd edition
by James R. Lewis
ISBN: 978-1-57859-144-2

Conspiracies and Secret Societies: The Complete Dossier, 2nd edition
by Brad Steiger and Sherry Hansen Steiger
ISBN: 978-1-57859-368-2

Demons, the Devil, and Fallen Angels
by Marie D. Jones and Larry Flaxman
ISBN: 978-1-57859-613-3

The Dream Encyclopedia, 2nd edition
by James R Lewis, Ph.D., and Evelyn Dorothy Oliver, Ph.D.
ISBN: 978-1-57859-216-6

The Dream Interpretation Dictionary: Symbols, Signs, and Meanings
By J. M. DeBord
ISBN: 978-1-57859-637-9

The Encyclopedia of Religious Phenomena
by J. Gordon Melton
ISBN: 978-1-57859-209-8

The Fortune-Telling Book: The Encyclopedia of Divination and Soothsaying
by Raymond Buckland
ISBN: 978-1-57859-147-3

The Government UFO Files: The Conspiracy of Cover-Up
By Kevin D. Randle
ISBN: 978-1-57859-477-1

Hidden Realms, Lost Civilizations, and Beings from Other Worlds
by Jerome Clark
ISBN: 978-1-57859-175-6

The Horror Show Guide: The Ultimate Frightfest of Movies
by Mike May
ISBN: 978-1-57859-420-7

The Illuminati: The Secret Society That Hijacked the World
by Jim Marrs
ISBN: 978-1-57859-619-5

Real Aliens, Space Beings, and Creatures from Other Worlds
by Brad Steiger and Sherry Hansen Steiger
ISBN: 978-1-57859-333-0

Real Encounters, Different Dimensions, and Otherworldly Beings
by Brad Steiger with Sherry Hansen Steiger
ISBN: 978-1-57859-455-9

Real Ghosts, Restless Spirits, and Haunted Places, 2nd edition
by Brad Steiger
ISBN: 978-1-57859-401-6

Real Miracles, Divine Intervention, and Feats of Incredible Survival
by Brad Steiger and Sherry Hansen Steiger
ISBN: 978-1-57859-214-2

Real Monsters, Gruesome Critters, and Beasts from the Darkside
by Brad Steiger and Sherry Hansen Steiger
ISBN: 978-1-57859-220-3

Real Vampires, Night Stalkers, and Creatures from the Darkside
by Brad Steiger
ISBN: 978-1-57859-255-5

Real Visitors, Voices from Beyond, and Parallel Dimensions
by Brad Steiger and Sherry Hansen Steiger
ISBN: 978-1-57859-541-9

Real Zombies, the Living Dead, and Creatures of the Apocalypse
by Brad Steiger
ISBN: 978-1-57859-296-8

The Religion Book: Places, Prophets, Saints, and Seers
by Jim Willis
ISBN: 978-1-57859-151-0

The Sci-Fi Movie Guide: The Universe of Film from Alien to Zardoz
by Chris Barsanti
ISBN: 978-1-57859-503-7

The Spirit Book: The Encyclopedia of Clairvoyance, Channeling, and Spirit Communication
by Raymond Buckland
ISBN: 978-1-57859-172-5

Supernatural Gods: Spiritual Mysteries, Psychic Experiences, and Scientific Truths
by Jim Willis
ISBN: 978-1-57859-660-7

UFO Dossier: 100 Years of Government Secrets, Conspiracies, and Cover-Ups
By Kevin D. Randle
ISBN: 978-1-57859-564-8

Unexplained! Strange Sightings, Incredible Occurrences, and Puzzling Physical Phenomena, 3rd edition
by Jerome Clark
ISBN: 978-1-57859-344-6

The Vampire Book: The Encyclopedia of the Undead, 3rd edition
by J. Gordon Melton
ISBN: 978-1-57859-281-4

The Werewolf Book: The Encyclopedia of Shape-Shifting Beings, 2nd edition
by Brad Steiger
ISBN: 978-1-57859-367-5

The Witch Book: The Encyclopedia of Witchcraft, Wicca, and Neo-paganism
by Raymond Buckland
ISBN: 978-1-57859-114-5

Introduction

If there is one thing that all of us can say with certainty, it's that we are living in a world of definitive uncertainty. Fake news, alternative facts, outright lies, fears of nuclear war, widespread surveillance of the population, mass shootings, the rise of a totalitarian state, and more have led millions of us to distrust the word of government. And with good reason, too. There are countless conspiracy theories in circulation that suggest the world as we see it is not as it really is.

At a global level, more and more people are beginning to realize that we are being manipulated and lied to. We are denied access to secrets that shouldn't be secrets. Our politicians obfuscate, deny, and outright lie. No-one knows who to trust. The nightly news is being replaced by carefully orchestrated propaganda. Our iPhones are monitored as are our laptops and our landlines. As for social-media, that too is ripe for spying by men in black suits. No wonder, then, that the last few years have seen an incredible rise in conspiracy theories, deceptions, and cover-ups. They range from the controversial to the shocking, and from the nightmarish to the downright terrifying. And you can find all of them in the pages of this book.

Highlights of *Cover-ups & Secrets: The Complete Guide to Government Conspiracies, Manipulations, and Deceptions* include dark agendas to restrict our access to the Internet and even plans to ban books that our politicians view as undesirable; the decision to suppress cancer cures as a means to ensure the pharmaceutical industry continues to reap gigantic profits; the new technologies that can control our minds at the flick of a switch; the ever-controversial Roswell UFO affair; the murder of politicians, scientists, world leaders, and even Princess Diana, all in the name of national security; the theories that the truths behind 9/11 still elude us; secrets concerning controversial issues like UFOs and time travel; abominable plans to decrease the human population by orchestrating a limited nuclear war in the near future; and the overall goal to have us all living in states of fear, ignorance, and unending subjugation.

Truly, we live in a world of cover-ups and conspiracies.

Contents

Introduction   [vi]

"REAL NIGHTMARES" E-BOOKS BY BRAD STEIGER

Book 1: *True and Truly Scary Unexplained Phenomenon*

Book 2: *The Unexplained Phenomena and Tales of the Unknown*

Book 3: *Things That Go Bump in the Night*

Book 4: *Things That Prowl and Growl in the Night*

Book 5: *Fiends That Want Your Blood*

Book 6: *Unexpected Visitors and Unwanted Guests*

Book 7: *Dark and Deadly Demons*

Book 8: *Phantoms, Apparitions, and Ghosts*

Book 9: *Alien Strangers and Foreign Worlds*

Book 10: *Ghastly and Grisly Spooks*

Book 11: *Secret Schemes and Conspiring Cabals*

Book 12: *Freaks, Fiends, and Evil Spirits*

PLEASE VISIT US AT VISIBLEINKPRESS.COM

The U.S. Government's Secret UFO Project

Shortly before Christmas 2017, startling news surfaced that caught the attention of conspiracy theorists just about here, there, and everywhere. The reason why so much attention was given to the story was simple: it all revolved around the existence of a secret UFO program within the U.S. government. It was a program that ran from 2007 until 2012 and which was secretly funded to try to determine the true nature of the UFO phenomenon. Not only that, the story was blown wide open by none other than the *New York Times*. Before we get to the heart of the matter, it's important to note the history of secret UFO programs within the government. Such programs date back to the late 1940s, when the UFO phenomenon began and UFOs were termed flying saucers and flying discs.

It was in summer 1947 that the UFO controversy began. On June 24, 1947, a pilot named Kenneth Arnold encountered a squadron of strange-looking, boomeranglike aircraft flying near Mount Rainier, Washington State. As an experienced pilot, Arnold was puzzled by the fact that he was unable to figure out what, exactly, the craft were. On landing, Arnold shared his story with the media and told them that the objects, like saucers, skimmed across a body of water in a kind of up-and-down motion. In literally only hours, the term "flying saucer" was coined. The big irony is that the "saucer" part came from Arnold's observation of how the object flew, not their shape.

The U.S. military quickly moved to investigate the case as well as a wave of quite literally hundreds of additional sightings throughout the remainder of 1947 and into 1948. Thus was born the government's first UFO program, Project Sign. Interestingly, the Project Sign staff concluded that a UFO phenomenon really did exist, but they were unable to state with any degree of accuracy what the objects actually were. Theories posited by Sign personnel included Russian craft and the creations of a secret group within the U.S. government. Some of the Sign staff favored the extraterrestrial hypothesis. In 1948, Project Sign was replaced with Project Grudge. Just like Sign, Grudge had its personnel who championed the alien angle, while others suggested military aircraft of some kind—either the product of Uncle Sam or the Soviets.

Certainly, the most ambitious of all the UFO programs (or, at least, the ones we know of) was Project Blue Book. It's worth noting the content of the U.S. Air Force's fact sheet on Blue Book, which provides a brief history of the program. As the Air Force notes:

> On December 17, 1969, the Secretary of the Air Force announced the termination of Project BLUE BOOK, the Air Force program for the investigation of UFOs. From 1947 to 1969, a total of 12,618 sightings were reported to Project BLUE BOOK. Of these 701 remain "Unidentified." The project was headquartered at Wright-Patterson Air Force Base, whose personnel no longer receive, document or investigate UFO reports. The decision to discontinue UFO investigations was based on an evaluation of a report prepared by the University of Colorado entitled, "Scientific Study of Unidentified Flying Objects"; a review of the University of Colorado's report by the National Academy of Sciences; past UFO studies and Air Force experience investigating UFO reports during the '40s, '50s, and '60s.

The Air Force continues:

> As a result of these investigations and studies and experience gained from investigating UFO reports since 1948, the conclusions of Project BLUE BOOK are: (1) no UFO reported, investigated, and evaluated by the Air Force has ever given any indication of threat to our national security; (2) there has been no evidence submitted to or discovered by the Air Force that sightings categorized as "unidentified" represent technological developments or principles beyond the range of present-day scientific knowledge; and (3) there has been no evidence indicating that sightings categorized as "unidentified" are extraterrestrial vehicles.

> With the termination of Project BLUE BOOK, the Air Force regulations establishing and controlling the program for investigating and analyzing UFOs were rescinded. Documentation regarding the former BLUE BOOK investigation has been permanently transferred to the Military Reference Branch, National Archives and Records Administration, Washington, DC 20408, and is available for public review and analysis.

This is also from the Air Force:

Since Project BLUE BOOK was closed, nothing has happened to indicate that the Air Force ought to resume investigating UFOs. Because of the considerable cost to the Air Force in the past, and the tight funding of Air Force needs today, there is no likelihood the Air Force will become involved with UFO investigation again.

There are a number of universities and professional scientific organizations, such as the American Association for the Advancement of Science, which have considered UFO phenomena during periodic meetings and seminars. In addition, a list of private organizations interested in aerial phenomena may be found in Gayle's *Encyclopedia of Associations*

The term "flying saucer" originated from a description of alien craft provided by pilot Kenneth Arnold in 1947.

(edition 8, vol. 1, pp. 432–433). Such timely review of the situation by private groups ensures that sound evidence will not be overlooked by the scientific community.

A person calling the base to report a UFO is advised to contact a private or professional organization (as mentioned above) or to contact a local law enforcement agency if the caller feels his or public safety is endangered.

The last word from the Air Force is this: "Periodically, it is erroneously stated that the remains of extraterrestrial visitors are or have been stored at Wright-Patterson AFB. There are not now nor ever have been, any extraterrestrial visitors or equipment on Wright-Patterson Air Force Base." This last piece, of course, being a nod to the notorious "Roswell UFO crash" of July 1947, which claims that the strange bodies found outside of Roswell were secretly sent to Wright-Patterson for analysis and autopsy.

It should also be noted that it wasn't just the U.S. military that created UFO researcher programs. The CIA did likewise.

On December 2, 1952, the CIA's assistant director H. Marshall Chadwell noted in a classified report on UFO activity in American airspace: "Sightings of unexplained objects at great altitudes and traveling at high speeds in the vicinity of major U.S. defense installations are of such nature that they are not attributable to natural phenomena or known types of aerial vehicles."

Believing that something really might be afoot in the skies of America, Chadwell prepared a list of saucer-themed recommendations for the National Security Council:

1. The Director of Central Intelligence shall formulate and carry out a program of intelligence and research activities as required to solve the problem of instant positive identification of unidentified flying objects.

2. Upon call of the Director of Central Intelligence, government departments and agencies shall provide assistance in this program of intelligence and research to the extent of their capacity provided, however, that the DCI shall avoid duplication of activities presently directed toward the solution of this problem.

3. This effort shall be coordinated with the military services and the Research and Development Board of the Department of Defense with the Psychological Board and other governmental agencies as appropriate.

4. The Director of Central Intelligence shall disseminate information concerning the program of intelligence and research activities in this field to the various departments and agencies which have authorized interest therein.

Forty-eight hours later, the Intelligence Advisory Committee concurred with Chadwell and recommended that "the services of selected scientists to review and appraise the available evidence in the light of pertinent scientific theories" should be the order of the day. Thus was born the Robertson Panel, so named after the man chosen to head the inquiry: Howard Percy Robertson, a consultant to the agency, a renowned physicist, and the director of the Defense Department Weapons Evaluation Group.

Chadwell was tasked with putting together a crack team of experts in various science, technical, intelligence, and military disciplines and have them carefully study the data on flying saucers currently held by not just the CIA but the Air Force, too—who obligingly agreed to hand over all their UFO files for the CIA's scrutiny—or, at least, the Air Force *said* it was all they had.

Whatever the truth of the matter was regarding the extent to which the USAF shared its files with Chadwell's team, the fact that they had a significant body of data to work with was the main thing, so the team—which included Luis Alvarez, physicist and radar expert (and, later, a Nobel Prize recipient); Frederick C. Durant, CIA officer, secretary to the panel, and missile expert; Samuel Abraham Goudsmit, Brookhaven National Laboratories nuclear physicist; and Thornton Page, astrophysicist, radar expert, and deputy director of Johns Hopkins Operations Research Office—quickly got to work.

The overall conclusion of the Robertson Panel was that while UFOs, *per se*, did not appear to have a bearing on national security or the defense of the United States, the way in which the subject could be used by unfriendly forces to manipulate the public mindset and disrupt the U.S. military infrastructure *did* have a bearing—and a major one, too—on matters of a security nature. According to the panel's members: "Although evidence of any direct threat from these sightings was wholly lacking, related dangers might well exist resulting from: A. Misidentification of actual enemy artifacts by defense personnel. B. Overloading of emergency reporting channels with 'false' information. C. Subjectivity of public to mass hysteria and greater vulnerability to possible enemy psychological warfare."

It was also recommended that a number of the public UFO investigative groups that existed in the United States at the time, such as the Civilian Flying Saucer Investigators (CFSI) and the Aerial Phenomena Research Organization (APRO), should be "watched" carefully due to "the apparent irresponsibility and the possible use of such groups for subversive purposes."

The panel also concluded that "a public education campaign should be undertaken" on matters relative to UFOs. Specifically, agreed the members:

> The debunking aim would result in reduction in public interest in "flying saucers" which today evokes a strong psychological reaction. This education could be accomplished by mass media such as television, motion pictures, and popular articles. Basis of such education would be actual case histories which had been puzzling at first but later explained. As in the case of conjuring tricks, there is much less stimulation if the "secret" is known. Such a program should tend to reduce the current gullibility of the public and consequently their susceptibility to clever hostile propaganda.

The CIA continued:

> In this connection, Dr. Hadley Cantril (Princeton University) was suggested. Cantril authored *Invasion from Mars* (a study in the psychology of panic, written about the famous Orson Welles radio broadcast in 1938) and has since performed advanced laboratory studies in the field of perception. The names of

Well-known radio and TV broadcaster Arthur Godfrey was considered by the CIA for enlistment in the effort to communicate effectively to the American public about UFOs.

Don Marquis (University of Michigan) and Leo Roston were mentioned as possibly suitable as consultant psychologists.

Also, someone familiar with mass communications techniques, perhaps an advertising expert, would be helpful. Arthur Godfrey was mentioned as possibly a valuable channel of communication reaching a mass audience of certain levels. Dr. [Lloyd] Berkner suggested the U.S. Navy (ONR) Special Devices Center, Sands Point, L. I., as a potentially valuable organization to assist in such an educational program. The teaching techniques used by this agency for aircraft identification during the past war [were] cited as an example of a similar educational task. The Jam Handy Co. which made World War II training films (motion picture and slide strips) was also suggested, as well as Walt Disney, Inc. animated cartoons.

In other words, the Robertson Panel was less about determining what UFOs were, and more concerned with addressing how the Soviets might manipulate the phenomenon as a means to create mass hysteria in the United States. All of which brings us back to the modern era.

It was on December 16, 2017, that the *New York Times* broke the news that despite years of assurance from the U.S. government to the effect that its UFO investigations were shut down in 1969, the Pentagon was still in the UFO game; in fact, it was up to its neck in it. It's hardly surprising that the story became not just nationwide news but worldwide, even. The official title of the project was the Advanced Aviation Threat Identification Program (AATIP). The program began quietly in 2007 in the offices of the Defense Intelligence Agency, with a budget of $22 million, and was encouraged into existence by Democratic senator Harry Reid, who had a personal interest in the subject of UFOs. The AATIP program was run by a man named Luis Elizondo and generated a 490-page-long report on various UFO encounters that the group studied. At the time of this writing, that report is still not in the public domain. When the news broke in December 2017, the UFO research community quickly waded into the heart of the controversy, as did the media.

Politico stated the following, which is highly thought provoking: "The revelation of the program could give a credibility boost to UFO theorists, who have long pointed to public accounts by military pilots and others describing phenomena that defy obvious explanation, and could fuel demands for increased transparency about the scope and findings of the Pentagon effort, which focused some of its inquiries into sci-fi sounding concepts like 'wormholes' and 'warp drives.'"

On December 20, writer Paul Seaburn stated:

Just days after the *New York Times* and Politico reported on the existence of a Pentagon program called the Advanced Aviation Threat Identification Program and the To The Stars Academy (TTSA) releasing what it calls "The first official UAP footage ever released by the USG," Luis Elizondo, a member of TTSA after resigning from the Pentagon, revealed on CNN that he believes in the existence of extraterrestrials, and that belief is not just a gut feel but based on scientific evidence.

Indeed, Elizondo said: "These aircraft—we'll call them aircraft—are displaying characteristics that are not currently within the US inventory nor in any foreign inventory that we are aware of. Things that don't have any obvious flight services, any obvious forms of propulsion, and maneuvering in ways that include extreme maneuverability beyond, I would submit, the healthy G-forces of a human or anything biological."

Elizondo told the *Daily Beast*: "Objectivity is an imperative when dealing with a subject as unknown as and contentious as UFOs. However, there are still those observations that defy explanation. Observations by highly trained individuals such as fighter or airline pilots who would recognize aircraft shapes and aircraft movements."

Even more is to come. UFO investigator Anthony Bragalia stated:

The program's director, intelligence official Luis Elizondo, also confirmed the existence of contracts to Bigelow Aerospace for the construction modification of facilities in Las Vegas, NV to house strange metal-like materials recovered by military personnel as UFO residue, flotsam, shot-off pieces, or crash items. This admission to the retrieval of UFO debris by the US military is historic. Details are scant on the precise nature of the material. But *New York Times* reporter Ralph Blumenthal, when pressed for details by MSNBC earlier this week, replied: "They have, as we reported, some material from these objects that is being studied so that scientists can find what accounts for their amazing properties ... it's some kind of compound that they don't recognize."

In April 2018, Bragalia said the following:

This author filed a Freedom of Information Act (FOIA) request with the US Defense Intelligence Agency seeking details on the Pentagon's UFO-related Advanced Aerospace Threat Identification Program, as reported in the *New York Times* in December. In January, a FOIA was filed to compel the release of test results of purported UFO alloys held by Bigelow Aerospace in Nevada under the federal program. The extraordinary reply to the request included a litany of "reasons" why the government wants at least two and a half years to reply to my request.

In May 2018, yet another development occurred. Writer-researcher Paul Seaburn said:

> The latest 13-page document was obtained by George Knapp, the award-winning investigative reporter at KLAS-TV in Las Vegas and a frequent host on *Coast to Coast AM*. The announcement by KLAS doesn't reveal how it obtained the information but it has been working with former Senator Harry Reid who has said many times that there is considerable information available about military UFO encounters. That includes those seen in 2004 by crew members on the U.S.S. *Nimitz* aircraft carrier, the U.S.S. *Princeton* and a number of F-18 pilots who provided the video feeds and shocking commentary.

> Knapp reports on lasvegasnow.com that this was not a single UFO incident but a series of encounters lasting two weeks. The report refers to them as Anomalous Aerial Vehicles (AAV) but social media today calls them the Tic Tac UFOs because of their white elongated oval shape. Among the key findings in the report—the AAV is not something that belongs to the U.S. or any other nation. It was so advanced, it rendered U.S. capabilities ineffective. It showed velocities far greater than anything known to exist, and it could turn itself invisible, both to radar and the human eye. Essentially, it was undetectable, and unchallenged.

Right now, this is where things stand: the current UFO program of the U.S. government remains steeped in secrecy and controversy, despite the revelations of the *New York Times* in December 2017, and Anthony Bragalia is being stonewalled on key issues pertaining to the project and the data and evidence its staff acquired. Time will tell whether we get to learn more about the Advanced Aviation Threat Identification Program.

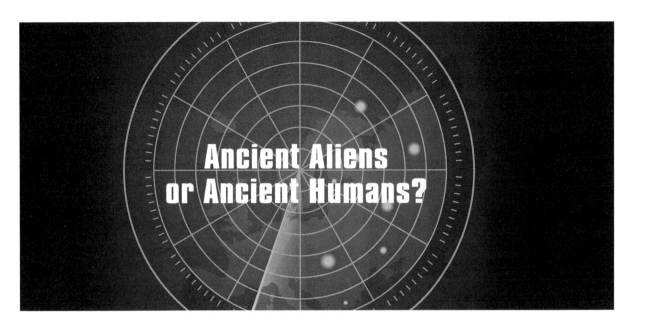

Ancient Aliens or Ancient Humans?

Ever since the beginnings of recorded history, people have reported seeing strange and incredible vehicles in the skies of our planet. Millennia ago, they were perceived as phenomena of a supernatural kind: namely, the work of a god or multiple gods. Today, the extraterrestrial hypothesis is all-dominating. Also, a faction within the UFO research community believes that the UFO phenomenon is demonic in nature. Others suspect that our aliens might actually be time travelers from the future. However, what if an even stranger—and far more controversial—theory existed than all of those combined? What if the U.S. government knows all about it and has chosen to keep us all in the dark? It's a theory that many dismiss or haven't given much thought to—if, indeed, any thought. It's a theory that suggests that the UFO phenomenon has at its heart not aliens—modern, ancient, or both—but an offshoot of the human race, which exists in distinct stealth. Sounds too bizarre to be true? Maybe not.

Over the course of millions of years, countless types of humans have existed—some of a proto-nature, others savage, hairy, and primitive, and more than a few highly evolved. Among the list are the Neanderthals, the Cro-Magnons, and, of course, us: *Homo sapiens*. What if another group of humans existed, however, one that has successfully managed to remain hidden—and off the grid, so to speak—for countless millennia, and to protect their real identities, they present themselves as space-faring aliens from faraway worlds—distant galaxies, even. Is such a theory possible? Does the U.S. government have a secret awareness that we share the planet with an ancient aspect of the human race? The evidence suggests that the government does indeed know.

One person who strongly suspected that the UFO phenomenon has its origins right here on Earth was the late Mac Tonnies, who, in 2009, tragically died—at the age of just thirty-four—from heart disease. At the time of his death, Tonnies was busily putting the final touches to his book on the subject, which he titled *The Cryptoterrestrials* and which was published posthumously in 2010. Tonnies concluded that alien abductions, the abilities of the assumed E.T.s to breathe our air, and their concerns about nuclear war were all due to one fact: the aliens were from right here, and they always have been. I was fortunate enough to interview Tonnies just a few months before his passing, and he shared with me a wealth of fascinating data on his thoughts, suspicions, and conclusions. Let's see what he had to say:

> After devouring countless books on the UFO controversy and the paranormal, I began to acknowledge that the extraterrestrial hypothesis suffered some tantalizing flaws. In short, the "aliens" seemed more like surreal caricatures of ourselves than beings possessing the god-like technology one might plausibly expect from interstellar visitors. Like [UFO researcher] Jacques Vallee, I came to the realization that the extraterrestrial hypothesis isn't strange enough to encompass the entirety of occupant cases. But if we're dealing with humanoid beings that evolved here on earth, some of the problems vanish.

Tonnies continued:

> I envision the cryptoterrestrials engaged in a process of subterfuge, bending our belief systems to their own ends. And I suggest that this has been occurring, in one form or another, for an extraordinarily long time. I think there's a good deal of folkloric and mythological evidence pointing in this direction, and I find it most interesting that so many descriptions of ostensible "aliens" seem to reflect staged events designed to misdirect witnesses and muddle their perceptions.

During the course of his research into the cryptoterrestrial theory, Tonnies spent a great deal of time addressing the matter of alien abductions. For those who aren't fully aware of the nature of the phenomenon, a bit of background data is required.

Regardless of whether people believe or don't believe in the reality of the alien abduction phenomenon, undoubtedly, the vast majority of people have heard of it. It was, however, a phenomenon that was pretty much unknown until September 19, 1961. Yes, a few earlier cases existed, but for the most part, they were not publicized until after September 19, so what, exactly, is so significant about that particular date? The answer is that it was the date of a now historic UFO event that occurred to a married couple from New Hampshire. They were Betty and Barney Hill.

At the time in question, the Hills were driving home from a vacation in Canada when the journey suddenly took on strange and unearthly proportions. It was on a dark stretch of road that the Hills caught sight of a curious light in the sky; it even seemed to be monitoring or shadowing them. They watched it for a while and then, something really strange happened: The Hills became confused, experienced a sense of missing time—of several hours, no less—and after getting home suffered from weird and traumatic dreams; they were dreams that suggested that they may have been taken onboard the craft and even experimented on by weird-looking, humanoid figures. In no time at all, the dreams became definitive nightmares. Something had to be done, and it was.

When things got really bad for the Hills and the nightmares and stress began to overwhelm them (Barney, for example, developed stomach ulcers), they sought help; it was a very good idea, as that same help led to answers for what happened on that mystery-filled drive

New Hampshire couple Betty and Barney Hill asserted they were abducted by aliens in 1961. At first, their memories came only in nightmares, but the nightmares were actually suppressed memories.

back to New Hampshire. They were put in touch with a neurologist and psychiatrist who operated out of Boston, Massachusetts, named Benjamin Simon. Clearly aware that the Hills were in deep states of anxiety, he elected to subject them to regressive hypnosis—with the permission of Betty and Barney, of course. What followed next can only be described as incredible. Both husband and wife told near-identical stories of being taken from their vehicle onto what can only be described as an unidentified flying object and subjected to a series of medical procedures—most of which were very intrusive and stressful. Frightening, even. The encounter went on for roughly two hours. The memories of Betty and Barney were so detailed that the amount of time Benjamin Simon worked with the Hills ended up being months.

Such was the phenomenal reaction to the story of Betty and Barney Hill that it prompted author John Fuller to write a book on the subject, titled *The Interrupted Journey*—an appropriate title, indeed—which was published in 1966. Since then, the alien abduction phenomenon has grown and grown and spread like wildfire. We may never know for sure how many people believe they may have been kidnapped and experimented on by black-eyed, dwarfish beings from faraway galaxies. After all, not everyone wants publicity—particularly so not publicity of a very controversial type. In that sense, it's possible that just as many silent abductees as publicly visible ones exist. To demonstrate the sheer level of experiences on record, though, it is worth noting that after Whitley Strieber's 1987 alien abduction-themed book *Communion* was published, Strieber and his late wife, Anne, received letters from the public in no fewer than six figures. Other books, such as Budd Hopkins's *Missing Time* and Dr. John Mack's *Passport to the Cosmos*, have added to the controversy and given it more publicity.

As for what may be behind the abductions, certainly, the most controversial and widespread belief is that alien entities are engaged in a massive, covert program to create what may amount to untold numbers of alien–human hybrids. Some researchers and abductees believe that the outcome of the rise of the hybrids will be a positive one: the dawning of a new world, filled with prosperity and peace. Dr. David Jacobs, though, in his books *The Threat* and *Walking Among Us*, concludes that the hybrid issue is downright dangerous and that we are being infiltrated by aliens who, bit by bit, are infiltrating us with one goal in mind: complete control. The fact that many abductees believe they have been implanted with devices that have an unclear agenda adds weight to the theory that the alien abduction issue is a threat to both national security and the people of Earth.

What if a far more down-to-earth explanation existed for the alien abduction phenomenon, though? That question brings us back to Mac Tonnies:

> I regard the alleged "hybridization program" with skepticism. How sure are we that these interlopers are extraterrestrial? It seems more sensible to assume that the so-called aliens are human, at least in some respects. Indeed, descriptions of intercourse with aliens fly in the face of exobiological thought. If the cryptoterrestrial population is genetically impoverished, as I assume it is, then it might rely on a harvest of human genes to augment its dwindling gene-pool. It would be more advantageous to have us believe we're dealing with omnipotent extraterrestrials rather than a fallible sister species. The ET–UFO mythos may be due, in part, to a long-running and most successful disinformation campaign.

Tonnies then turned his attention to the claims of Antonio Vilas-Boas, a Brazilian lawyer who claimed that, in 1957, as a young man living on his family's farm, he was abducted onto a UFO and had sex with a surprisingly hot-looking space babe. Tonnies said of Vilas-Boas's story:

> After intercourse, the big-eyed succubus that seduced Antonio Vilas-Boas pointed skyward, implying a cosmic origin. But the mere fact that she appeared thoroughly female, and, moreover, attractive, belies an unearthly explanation. Further, one could argue that the clinical environment he encountered aboard the landed "spacecraft" was deliberately engineered to reinforce his conviction that he was dealing with extraterrestrials.

If cryptoterrestrials are using humans to improve their genetic stock, it stands to reason they've seen at least a few of our saucer movies. As consummate anthropologists, they likely know what we expect of "real" extraterrestrials and can satisfy our preconceptions with a magician's skill. Their desire for our continued survival, if only for the sake of our genetic material, may have played a substantial role in helping us to avoid extinction during the Cold War, when the UFO phenomenon evolved in our skies, much to the consternation of officialdom.

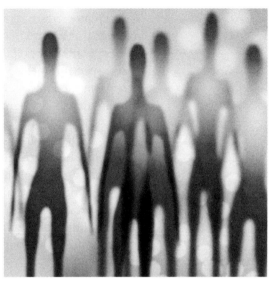

Since the 1960s, testimonials about alien abductions have been on the rise.

It is indeed a fact that in the early to late 1950s, countless people across the planet claimed close encounters with very human-looking aliens, who demanded that we lay down our atomic weapons lest we turn our planet into a radioactive wasteland, all but bereft of life. Of course, this begs an important question: why would aliens from a planet in a star system who-knows-how-many light years away even care about what might happen—of a cataclysmic nature—on our world? Well, a good argument can be made that they *wouldn't* care. Why should they? However, if, as Tonnies suspected and suggested, the "aliens" are really cryptoterrestrials from right here, then their fears that we might destroy the Earth become far more understandable; they are forced to share the planet with the most violent and destructive species on the entire planet: us, the human race. Tonnies says of what became known as "the Space Brothers":

> Commentators regularly assume that all the Contactees [a term for those who claimed encounters with human-like aliens, chiefly in the 1950s] were lying or else delusional. But if we're experiencing a staged reality, some of the beings encountered by the Contactees might have been real and the common messages of universal brotherhood could have been a sincere attempt to curb our destructive tendencies. The extraterrestrial guise would have served as a prudent disguise, neatly misdirecting our attention and leading us to ask the wrong questions; which we're still asking with no substantial results.

When, in 2008, Tonnies began to talk and write publicly about the cryptoterrestrial theory, he got mixed responses from UFO researchers, as Tonnies himself admitted to me:

The cryptoterrestrial theory has met with mixed reactions. Some seem to think that I'm onto something. Most UFO researchers are, at best, extremely skeptical. Others think I'm parroting John Keel's "superspectrum" [Keel was the author of the acclaimed 1975 book, *The Mothman Prophecies*], a variation on the "parallel worlds" theme that in turn shares memes with Jacques Vallee's "multiverse." Both ideas suggest that we somehow occupy dimensional space with our "alien" visitors, doing away with the need for extraterrestrial spacecraft while helping explain the sense of absurdity that accompanies many UFO and occupant sightings. Keel and Vallee have both ventured essentially "occult" ideas in cosmological terms; both the "superspectrum" and the "multiverse" require a revision of our understanding of the way reality itself works. But the cryptoterrestrial hypothesis is grounded in a more familiar context.

Tonnies expanded:

I'm not suggesting unseen dimensions or the need for ufonauts to "downshift" to our level of consciousness. Rather, I'm asking if it's feasible that the alleged aliens that occupy historical and contemporary mythology are flesh-and-blood human-like creatures that live right here on Earth. Not another version of Earth in some parallel Cosmos, but on Earth. While I can't automatically exclude the UFO phenomenon's "paranormal" aspects, I can attempt to explain them in technological terms. For example, I see no damning theoretical reason why "telepathy" and "dematerialization" can't ultimately be explained by appealing to cybernetics, nano-technology and other fields generally excluded from ufological discourse.

He concluded: "The cryptoterrestrial hypothesis manages to alienate champions of the extraterrestrial hypothesis and those who support a more esoteric, 'inter-dimensional' explanation. It offers no clear-cut reconciliation. It does, however, wield explanatory potential lacking in both camps."

Echoing Tonnies's words are those of longtime UFO investigator Timothy Green Beckley, who has his own tale of the cryptoterrestrial kind to share:

Some people might suggest that because the Space-Brothers look so much like us that they could be from somewhere right here on Earth—an ancient race, maybe. There are a lot of cultural legends about advanced beings living underground: UFOs coming out of the oceans, lakes, caverns. The whole hollow-Earth thing is a little hard for me; but the caverns theory I can take.

I remember one incident, 1970s, where I was lecturing and a gentleman—a professor at the college where I was lecturing—came up to me and told this story about how he was driving outside of a town in Michigan. It was rather late at night, and he saw these lights in the woods. He pulled over, and there was no other traffic coming in either direction; but there was already another car parked at the side of the road.

He described seeing some sort of ship in the distance—a UFO. A group of human-like aliens got out, walked to the car, which was a Cadillac, or something like that. He watched them and could see they looked human. They just got in the car and drove off. But then, a couple of weeks later, he sees one of the same guys in a supermarket. These reports sound far-fetched; but there's so many of them of what seem to be aliens being able to move among us. But, if they're really from here, that might explain it.

Now we get to the issue of a U.S. government cover-up concerning the cryptoterrestrials.

While Mac Tonnies's admittedly intriguing theory was simply that—a theory—this story has an even more intriguing aspect, one that comes from a former employee of the U.S. government. He writes under the pen name of E. A. Guest. His real name, however, is Walter Bosley, who served in both the U.S. Air Force Office of Special Investigations (AFOSI) and the Federal Bureau of Investigation (FBI). He has revealed a startling story told to him by his father, who was also a respected figure within the U.S. military.

The theory put forth by Mac Tonnies about "aliens" is that they are truly cryptoterrestrials, a species that evolved along the same path as humans but is now much more advanced than *Homo sapiens*.

In the 1950s, Bosley's father worked on various projects that would ultimately have a significant bearing upon the manned space program, including "training pilots in altitude chambers" and "flight medicine training." At one point in his career, Bosley's father was ordered to attend a briefing at Wright-Patterson Air Force Base in Dayton, Ohio. It was a briefing on none other than the legendary UFO crash outside of Roswell, New Mexico, in early July 1947. Despite what UFO researchers—and a sizeable amount of the public— think, Bosley says his father told him that nothing of an extraterrestrial nature crashed in Roswell on that fateful—and, for the crew, fatal—day. In Bosley Jr.'s very own words: "According to my father, these vehicles came from inside the planet. The civilization … exists in a vast, underground system of caverns and tunnels beneath the southwest and is human."

He continues: "Occasionally, they come and go, emerging in their vehicles and occasionally they crash. They are human in appearance, so much so that they can move among us with ease [and] with just a little effort. If you get a close look, you'd notice something odd, but not if the person just passed you on the street."

Significantly, Walter Bosley says: "I believe that the ET hypothesis has been used by the 'aliens' themselves, because it is most readily embraced by people who have had encounters with them."

Bosley's words bring us back to Mac Tonnies and his theories on the conspiracy-filled Roswell affair of July 1947.

In his 2009 book *The Cryptoterrestrials*, Tonnies speculated on the possibility that the Roswell craft was balloonlike and built, flown, and disastrously crashed by ancient humanoids that lurk in the depths of the planet. Controversial? Yes, but he made some interesting observations on this possibility. In Tonnies's own words:

> The device that crashed near Roswell in the summer of 1947, whatever it was, featured properties at least superficially like the high-altitude balloon trains ultimately cited as an explanation by the Air Force. Debunkers have, of course, seized on the lack of revealingly "high-tech" components found among the debris to dismiss the possibility that the crash was anything but a case of misidentification; not even Major Jesse Marcel, the intelligence officer who advocated an ET origin for the unusual foil and structural beams, mentioned anything remotely resembling an engine or power-plant.

Tonnies continued in a fashion that emphasized that the cryptoterrestrials may not be as scientifically and technologically advanced as they might prefer us to think they are: "The cryptoterrestrial hypothesis offers a speculative alternative: maybe the Roswell device *wasn't* high-tech. It could indeed have been a balloon-borne surveillance device brought down in a storm, *but it doesn't logically follow that it was one of our own.* Upon happening across such a troubling find, the Air Force's excessive secrecy begins to make sense."

Regardless of what you, me, or, indeed, any number of the well-known Roswell researchers/authors—such as Bill Moore, Kevin Randle, Stan Friedman, or Don Schmitt—might think or conclude, the fact is that Tonnies's cryptoterrestrial theory is probably the only one that allows for the Roswell crash site to have been comprised of very unusual non-*Homo sapiens* but, at the same time, incredibly simplistic technology.

The alien theory should, of course, require highly advanced technology to have been recovered—yet, we hear *very* little on this matter aside from talk of fields full of foil-like material with curious properties. Accounts of the military coming across alien-created "power plants" and "engines"—as Tonnies described them—are curiously absent from the Roswell affair. It's that aforementioned foil and not much else.

Perhaps, Tonnies was indeed on the right track when it came to Roswell. Maybe, Walter Bosley, who still pursues the story, is still on the right track. Just perhaps, it was the Roswell affair that—quite out of the blue—led the U.S. military to realize, to both its amazement and its fear, that we are not the only species of human on the planet and, in the process, a huge cover-up was initiated to ensure that the world never gets to know the true story of Roswell's cryptoterrestrials.

The Strange Tale of a Time Traveler

From 2000 to 2001, the world of conspiracy theorizing was rocked when a man using the name of John Titor came forward claiming to be a time traveler from the future, specifically from 2036. Such was the fascination with Titor's story, conspiracy researchers took deep notice of what he had to say to the point that what began as an interesting series of claims quickly became a veritable phenomenon. Was Titor all that he claimed to be? Was his story of being a member of the U.S. military true? Was he really a man from the future, or was the whole thing a strange hoax? Before we get to the matter of answering those questions, let's first take a look at the history of time travel in both reality and fiction.

Within the specific genre of science fiction, fantastic tales of time travel to the far-flung future or to the distant past are hardly rarities. Take, for example, H. G. Wells's epic novel of 1895, *The Time Machine*. The book tells the story of a brilliant, London, England-based scientist, inventor, and adventurer who journeys to the year 802,701 C.E., where, to his complete and utter dismay, he finds that the human race (in the form that we understand it, at least) no longer exists. In its place are the Eloi and the Morlocks. The former are relatively human-looking beings (albeit of smaller stature), yet they utterly lack vitality, imagination, and any desire to learn or advance. The Morlocks, meanwhile, are fearsome, savage, and nightmarish beasts who dwell in darkened underground lairs and who use the Eloi as we use cattle: namely, as a source of food.

In the 1968 movie *Planet of the Apes*, Charlton Heston's character, Taylor, a NASA astronaut, arrives on a nightmarish world run by a ruthless race of talking apes. Only at the film's climax, as he stumbles upon the broken remains of the Statue of Liberty, does Taylor realize with horror that he has not set foot on some far-off planet after all. Rather, he is home, two thousand years in the future, after a worldwide nuclear holocaust has destroyed human civilization and given rise to the world of the apes.

The Philadelphia Experiment is an entertaining Hollywood film allegedly based on real events, which tells the story of two sailors—David Herdeg and Jim Parker—who are propelled through time from 1943 to the Nevada Desert, circa 1984. The BBC show *The Flipside of Dominick Hide* is also about time travel: the main character travels through time from 2130 C.E. to London, England, in 1980. Ostensibly there to observe the transportation systems of the past, Hide subsequently finds himself on a quest to locate one of his distant ancestors. Let's not forget Michael J. Fox's character, Marty McFly, who in the 1985 Hollywood comedy blockbuster *Back to the Future* travels through time to 1955, where he almost makes out with his then teenaged mom, comes perilously close to wiping out his own existence as a result of his time-traveling antics, and single-handedly invents rock 'n' roll. *Déjà Vu* is a 2006 movie with Denzel Washington that told the story of U.S. government agents trying

There have been numerous movies about time travel, of course. This is the Delorean time machine from the movie *Back to the Future* on display at a Germany car expo. The concept of time travel is intriguing, but could it really work?

to solve a terrorist attack by using secret time-travel technology to look into the past. Also, who can forget *12 Monkeys*, starring Bruce Willis? In other words, at least as far as megabucks movies and literary classics are concerned, the theme of time travel is a spectacularly successful one.

Tales of fictional time-traveling heroes and strange futures aside, what of the real world? Is it possible that one day we might travel through time in much the same way that today we hop on a plane to take our yearly vacation?

"Time travel is not theoretically possible, for if it was they'd already be here telling us about it," British physicist Professor Stephen Hawking famously said a number of years ago. Even if time travel did one day become a possibility, it would be beset by major problems, as Hawking notes: "Suppose it were possible to go off in a rocket ship, and come back before you set off. What would stop you [from] blowing up the rocket on its launch pad, or otherwise preventing you from setting out in the first place? There are other versions of this paradox, like going back and killing your parents before you were born."

Mac Tonnies, the late author of the book *After the Martian Apocalypse*, which is a study of the controversial "Face on Mars" mystery, believed that he had the answer to the potential problems cited by Hawking: "Stephen Hawking condemned time travel because, in his opinion, it should enable a constant stream of visitors from our own future. He assumes, perhaps unwisely, that we'd be aware of these visitors, when in truth it's remarkably easy to think of reasons our ancestors might choose not to visit at all."

Tonnies continued:

Other physicists are at work refuting the paradox of going back in time and killing your parents before you are born. If they're right, a time traveler from the future could interact with others, including his or her past self, so long as no action was taken that would endanger the traveler's own continued existence. It's difficult to visualize how this might work, although the idea makes logical sense. Maybe the best analogy would be a physical system that relies on a principle of least action, such as a ball rolling inexorably downhill.

He further noted: "The fascinating upshot of this is that there's a chance we're indeed being visited by advanced beings from our own future, but their interactions with us would be necessarily limited lest they doom themselves to nonexistence."

Tonnies also wonders if the many UFO sightings that have been reported for decades may not be due to the actions of aliens from the other side of the galaxy but the result of time-traveling humans masquerading as E.T. to keep secret their real point of origin.

"If time travel is possible," said Tonnies, "the behavior of UFOs may be at least partially explained: formal contact with us would result in a causality violation of some sort, so they must remain content with maintaining their presence behind a curtain of subterfuge."

If we are indeed being visited by time travelers from the future, then surely, the biggest question is: How are they getting here? One possibility is by what is known in physics as wormholes, a term coined in 1957 by theoretical physicist John Wheeler.

The wormhole is basically a shortcut through both space and time; although firm evidence for the existence of these so-called "time tunnels" has not yet been firmly proven, they do not fall outside of the boundaries presented in Einstein's theory of general relativity. Indeed, in 1988, Kip Thorne, a gravitational theorist at Caltech, demonstrated that wormholes, if they existed, could be kept open by using what is known as Casimir Energy, or exotic matter. The Casimir Effect is based upon a force that is exerted as a result of the energy fields that exist in the space between objects. Of course, if such exotic matter could be harnessed and controlled, then for our time traveler of the future, taking a trip into the past via a wormhole may be relatively commonplace.

Jenny Randles, the author of a number of books on time travel, including *Breaking the Time Barrier*, *Time Storms*, and *Time Travel: Fact, Fiction & Possibility*, offers a cautionary view on traveling through time: "The ability to manipulate time would provide a dictator with the ultimate doomsday device: allowing one to change the past or adapt the future until it suited his or her own ends."

Nobel Prize-winning physicist Kip Thorne believes there could be wormholes, and that they can be kept open by taking advantage of the Casimir Effect.

Also, as Randles perceptively notes: "Human society will face many difficult questions when that first time machine is switched on. Like the first moon landing, the discovery of time travel will change our world."

The idea of time travel fascinates us because it offers us the possibility, however remote, of revisiting and recapturing a moment from our youth: the very first time we had sex, the day we bought our first car, that special night when we first got the chance to chug down a long, cold one. If time travelers from our future are secretly visiting us already, as Mac Tonnies suggests as a possibility, at least it shows that we have a future!

Let's now take a look at a few claims of time travel in the real world.

One of the most famous examples of what some researchers think may have been a definitive time slip involved two British women: Charlotte Anne Moberly and Eleanor Jourdain, who, it has been suggested, traveled through time while visiting the gardens of the Petit Trianon in Versailles, France. It was August 10, 1901, when the pair paid a trip to the Palace of Versailles. While walking through the grounds, both Moberly and Jourdain were overcome by distinctly oppressive feelings of gloom and uneasiness. They would later claim to have met with a wide variety of individuals, all garbed in eighteenth-century clothing and who they came to believe had been members of the court of none other than Marie Antoinette. More controversially, the pair said they saw a figure they thought may very well have been Marie Antoinette herself.

> Did Moberly and Jourdain really cross the time barrier into centuries past? To this day, the story has as many believers as it does detractors....

Did Moberly and Jourdain really cross the time barrier into centuries past? To this day, the story has as many believers as it does detractors, but we need to take careful note of one important factor: their amazing story does not stand alone. Indeed, numerous reports are on record of people apparently passing through time—entirely at random and without the benefit of any form of out-of-this-world technology.

A key event of the First English Civil War, the Battle of Hopton Heath (a small village in south Shropshire) was fought on Sunday, March 19, 1643, between Parliamentarian and Royalist forces. The battle ended at nightfall, with the actual victory and outcome still remaining matters of very much personal opinion. The Royalists, for example, had succeeded in capturing eight enemy guns, while the Parliamentarians believed that their successful killing of the enemy commander, the Earl of Northampton, was of equal—if not even greater—significance.

However, without doubt of even more significance was a startling event that occurred at some point in winter 1974. It was late at night, and then-thirty-six-year-old John "Davy" Davis, a Lichfield, Staffordshire-based house painter at the time, was driving near Hopton Heath when he began to feel unwell: an ominous tightness developed in his chest, he felt light-headed, and, as he succinctly put it, "my left ear hurt and felt hot."

Quickly pulling over to the side of the road, Davis was amazed to see the night sky suddenly transform into daylight, while the road in front of him no longer existed: instead, it had been replaced by a mass of fields, heathland, and tangled trees. In front of him, countless soldiers adorned in what was clearly Civil War clothing waged harsh war upon one another. Notably, Davis said that although at one point, he was "nearly bloody surrounded" by the soldiers, it was almost as if they could neither see him nor his vehicle. This afforded Davis a degree of relief, as he was practically frozen to the spot and "couldn't have run if I had wanted to." As it transpired, Davis didn't need to run anywhere: just a few seconds later, the bizarre scene suddenly vanished, and Davis found himself sitting at the edge of the road with his car squashed against a large line of hedge and with complete and utter normality returned.

Horning is an old village in Norfolk, England, situated between Wroxham and Ludham on the River Bure. The village's Ferry Inn is typical of the many old taverns that dominate the area, and the thirteenth-century church of St. Benedict can be found half a mile to the east of the village. On a summer's afternoon in either 1978 or 1979, the Margolis family was enjoying a stroll around the picturesque village when, like so many before them and since, they were overcome by a feeling of distinct uneasiness and unreality as well as total silence and a slight dizziness.

That uneasiness quickly mutated into concern, fright, and overwhelming disorientation as the landscape became "fuzzy" ("like a big heat-haze"), the houses were replaced by ancient cottages, and the road ahead of them became little more than a muddy track. As for the cars that had been in sight, they were no more. Instead, a battered and bruised cart appeared that was being pulled by a large cart-horse. A thin man dressed in brown walked alongside the horse, yet appeared not to notice any of the family in the slightest.

Suddenly, however, the modern-day sounds of cars and voices began to echo all around them, and the strange spectacle was now utterly gone. Notably, it seems that Mrs. Margolis may very well have been exposed to the odd scene for slightly less of a period of time than was her now late husband and their eleven-year-old son. "I looked at them when I came out of it," recalled Mrs. Margolis in a 1997 interview, "and it was like they were in a trance: their mouths were hanging down, and their eyes looked funny. Then they looked like they woke up and we were all back together again."

Interestingly, odd and unsettling feelings and sensations, such as those referenced in each of the cases above, were also referred to by author Andrew Mackenzie in his book *Adventures in Time: Encounters with the Past*. Such events, reported Mackenzie, are "often accompanied by feelings of depression, eeriness and a marked sense of silence, deeper than normally experienced." Similarly, Jenny Randles's book *Time Storms: Amazing Evidence for Time Warps, Space Rifts, and Time Travel* firmly demonstrates that whatever we may think we know about the nature of time, in reality, we may not even know the half of it.

All of which brings us back to the matter of John Titor and his extraordinary claims of traveling from the future to the year 2000.

Undoubtedly, John Titor's claims stretch credulity to the absolute max—particularly so because many of his claims did not come to pass. For his supporters, though, that's not a problem: they suspect that multiple alternative timelines may exist rather than just one—which, admittedly, provokes even more controversy. It all began at the dawning of the twenty-first century. It was just one year before 9/11 that John Titor turned up on various online forums, claiming to be one of Uncle Sam's warriors—but from thirty-six years in the future. The story that Titor told was not a good one. In fact, it was downright grim and disturbing. Some might even say it was bone chilling.

It's important to note that we don't even know whether "John Titor" was the man's real name. Initially, his claims that were posted online went nameless. That changed when, in early 2001, Titor began posting extraordinary stories to the late Art Bell's BBS forums. Since the site required users to provide a name, our alleged time traveler chose "John Titor." According to his story, Titor lived and worked in Tampa, Florida, in 2036. He had a mission to travel back in time to 1975—ostensibly to access certain computer-based technologies that could, in some unclear fashion, help the people of the future with their very own computers.

It is hardly surprising that Titor's claims became big news—and very quickly, particularly so at the late Art Bell's site. When Titor's claims and pre-

According to John Titor, there was supposed to be a violent civil war in the United States in the 2000s, followed by nuclear war with Russia in 2015, but none of that actually came to pass.

dictions were made in the 2000–2001 period, they understandably shook up a lot of people. After all, he was talking about nuclear war, the collapse of much of civilization, a future that was both dangerous and dark, and a world very different from ours—in many respects, even unrecognizable. Let's see what, exactly, Titor had to say.

John Titor loudly proclaimed that a civil war would begin in 2004, which would progress until it really blew up big-time in 2008. Such was the scale of the civil war, said Titor, that the United States fragmented into five separate regions. Things got worse: in 2015, Russia launched a number of nuclear missiles at the United States, which caused massive death, destruction, and turmoil. Titor said that the people of 2036 referred to this brief, terrible exchange between the United States and Russia as "N Day."

Of course, it's important to note that none of this ever happened, and, more significantly, Titor made no mention of 9/11—without doubt the worst attack ever on the United States next to the events of Pearl Harbor in December 1941. Titor, however, had a get-out clause for this highly problematic part of his overall story: namely, he explained that the future was not set in stone: traveling back and forth in time could result in the creation of multiple timelines. In other words, Titor implied, his future and our future might be radically different. In his world, a brief Third World War occurred but no 9/11.

On this very matter, Mike Suave, in his 2016 book *Who Authored the John Titor Legend?*, says: "For skeptics this represents too easy of an out, placing John's story in the loathsome category of 'unfalsifiable,' leading many to dismiss the story out of hand the moment they come across what Wikipedia lists as John's 'predictive failures.'"

Titor himself acknowledged this problem with his story:

When the day comes for my "prediction" to be realized it will either happen or not. If it does happen, then your ability to judge your environment is crippled by your acceptance of me as a "knower of all things" and gifted with the ability to tell the future. If I am wrong, then everything I have said that might possibly have made you think about your world in a different way is suddenly discredited. I do not want either. Although I do have personal reasons for being here and speaking with you, the most I could hope for is that you recognize the possibility of time travel as a reality. You are able to change your world line for better or worse just as I am. Therefore, any "prediction" I might make has a slight chance of being incorrect anyway and you now have the ability to act on it based on what I've said. Can you stop the war before it gets here? Sure. Will you do it? Probably not.

John Titor mysteriously vanished in 2001; his claims, however, still intrigue and entertain thousands of dedicated followers. They believe that he is not the hoaxer that many believe him to be but someone whose claims of multiple timelines in our future can explain the inconsistencies in Titor's tales.

When Aliens Become Deadly

The following report titled *Research Findings on the Chihuahua Disk Crash*, originally from "JS" to "Deneb Team Members" and dated 23 March 1992, was mailed to researcher Elaine Douglass in July 1993 and postmarked Santa Ana, CA. Elaine mailed the original to Leonard Stringfield, who later published it. The report appears to have been written by a source or sources with intimate knowledge of the incident at issue, who desired the release of the evidence to interested parties. The report reads:

> On 25 Aug. 74, at 2207 hrs., U.S. Air Defense radar detected an unknown approaching U.S. airspace from the Gulf of Mexico. Originally the object was tracked at 2,200 knots (2530 mph) on a bearing of 325 degrees and at an altitude of 75,000 feet, a course that would intercept U.S. territory about forty miles southwest of Corpus Christi, Texas. After approximately sixty seconds of observation, at a position 155 miles southeast of Corpus Christi, the object simultaneously decelerated to approximately 1700 knots (1955 mph), turned to a heading of 290 degrees, and began a slow descent. It entered Mexican airspace approximately forty miles south of Brownsville, Texas. Radar tracked it approximately 500 miles to a point near the town of Coyame, in the state of Chihuahua, not far from the U.S. border. There the object suddenly disappeared from the radar screens.
>
> During the flight over Mexican airspace, the object leveled off at 45,000 feet, then descended to 20,000 feet. The descent was in level steps, not a smooth curve or straight line, and each level was maintained for approximately five minutes. The object was tracked

by two different military radar installations. It would have been within range of Brownsville civilian radar, but it is assumed that no civilian radar detected the object due to a lack of any such reports. The point of disappearance from the radar screens was over a barren and sparsely populated area of Northern Mexico. At first it was assumed that the object had descended below the radar's horizon and a watch was kept for any re-emergence of the object. None occurred.

At first it was assumed that the object might be a meteor because of the high speed and descending flight path. But meteors normally travel at higher speeds, and descend in a smooth arc, not in "steps." And meteors do not normally make a thirty-five degree change in course. Shortly after detection, an air defense alert was called. However, before any form of interception could be scrambled, the object turned to a course that would not immediately take it over U.S. territory. The alert was called off within twenty minutes after the object's disappearance from the radar screen. Fifty-two minutes after the disappearance, civilian radio traffic indicated that a civilian aircraft had gone down in that area. But it was clear that the missing aircraft had departed El Paso International with a destination of Mexico City, and could not, therefore, have been the object tracked over the Gulf of Mexico. It was noted, however, that they both disappeared in the same area and at the same time.

With daylight the next day, Mexican authorities began a search for the missing plane. Approximately 1035 hrs there came a radio report that wreckage from the missing plane had been spotted from the air. Almost immediately came a report of a second plane on the ground a few miles from the first. A few minutes later an additional report stated that the second "plane" was circular shaped and apparently in one piece although damaged. A few minutes after that the Mexican military clamped a radio silence on all search efforts.

The radio interceptions were reported through channels to the CIA. Possibly as many as two additional government agencies also received reports, but such has not been confirmed as of this date. The CIA immediately began forming a recovery team. The speed with which this team and its equipment was assembled suggests that this was either a well-rehearsed exercise or one that had been performed prior to the event. In the meantime, requests were initiated at the highest levels between the United States and Mexican governments that the U.S. recovery team be allowed onto Mexican territory to "assist." These requests were met with pro-

UH-1 Hueys like the ones seen here were used to seek out the missing airplane in Mexico that was lost around the same time as a UFO sighting occurred.

fessed ignorance and a flat refusal of any cooperation. By 2100 hrs, 26 Aug. 74, the recovery team had assembled and been staged at Fort Bliss. Several helicopters were flown in from some unknown source and assembled in a secured area.

These helicopters were painted a neutral sand color and bore no markings. Eyewitness indicates that there were three smaller craft, very possibly UH-1 Hueys from the description. There was also a larger helicopter, possibly a Sea Stallion. Personnel from this team remained with their craft and had no contact with other Fort Bliss personnel.

Satellite and reconnaissance aircraft overflight that day indicated that both the crashed disk and the civilian aircraft had been removed from the crash sites and loaded on flat bed trucks. Later flights confirmed that the convoy had departed the area heading south. At that point the CIA had to make a choice, either to allow this unknown aircraft to stay in the hands of the Mexican government, or to launch the recovery team, supplemented by any required military support, to take the craft. There occurred, however, an event that took the choice out of their hands. High altitude overflights indicated that the convoy had stopped before reaching any inhabited areas or major roads. Recon showed no activity, and radio contact between the Mexican recovery team and its headquarters ceased. A low altitude, high speed overflight was ordered.

The photos returned by that aircraft showed all trucks and jeeps stopped, some with open doors, and two human bodies lying on the ground beside two vehicles. The decision was immediately made to launch the recovery team, but the actual launching was held up for the arrival of additional equipment and two additional personnel. It was not until 1438 hrs. that the helicopters departed Fort Bliss. The four helicopters followed the border down towards Presidio then turned and entered Mexican airspace north of Candelaria. They were over the convoy site at 1653 hrs. All convoy personnel were dead, most within the trucks. Some recovery team members, dressed in bioprotection suits, reconfigured the straps holding the object on the flatbed truck, then attached them to a cargo cable from the Sea Stallion. By 1714 hrs the recovered object was on its way to U.S. territory. Before leaving the convoy site, members of the recovery team gathered together the Mexican vehicles and bodies, then destroyed all with high explosives. This included the pieces of the civilian light plane which had been involved in the mid-air collision. At 1746 hrs the Huey's departed.

The Hueys caught up with the Sea Stallion as it re-entered U.S. airspace. The recovery team then proceeded to a point in the Davis Mountains, approximately twenty-five miles north east of Valentine. There they landed and waited until 0225 hrs. the next morning. At that time they resumed the flight and rendezvoused with a small convoy on a road between Van Horn and Kent. The recovered disk was transferred to a truck large enough to handle it and capable of being sealed totally. Some of the personnel from the Hueys transferred to the convoy.

All helicopters then returned to their original bases for decontamination procedures. The convoy continued non-stop, using back roads and smaller highways, and staying away from cities. The destination of the convoy reportedly was Atlanta, Georgia. Here the hard evidence thins out. One unconfirmed report says the disk was eventually transferred to Wright-Patterson A.F. Base. Another says that the disk was either transferred after that to another unnamed base, or was taken directly to this unknown base directly from

Atlanta. The best description of the disk was that it was sixteen feet, five inches in diameter, convex on both upper and lower surfaces to the same degree, possessing no visible doors or windows. The thickness was slightly less than five feet. The color was silver, much like polished steel. There was [sic] no visible lights nor any propulsion means. There were no markings.

There were two areas of the rim that showed damage, one showing an irregular hole approximately twelve inches in diameter with indented material around it. The other damage was described as a "dent" about two feet wide. The weight of the object was estimated as approximately one thousand five hundred pounds, based on the effect of the weight on the carrying helicopter and those who transferred it to the truck. There was no indication in the documentation available as to whether anything was visible in the "hole."

It seems likely that the damage with the hole was caused by the collision with the civilian aircraft. That collision occurred while the object was traveling approximately 1700 knots (1955 mph). Even ignoring the speed of the civilian aircraft, the impact would have been considerable at that speed. This is in agreement with the description of the civilian aircraft as being "almost totally destroyed." What was being taken from the crash site were pieces of the civilian aircraft. The second damage may have resulted when the object impacted with the ground. The speed in that case should have been considerably less than that of the first impact.

No mention is made of the occupants of the civilian aircraft. It is not known if anybody or bodies were recovered. Considering the destruction of the civilian light aircraft in mid-air, bodies may well not have come down near the larger pieces.

Unfortunately, what caused the deaths of the Mexican recovery team is not known. Speculation ranges from a chemical released from the disk as a result of the damage, to a microbiological agent. There are no indications of death or illness by any of the [U.S.] recovery team. It would not have been illogical for the recovery team to have taken one of the bodies back with them for analysis. But there is no indication of that having happened. Perhaps they did not have adequate means of transporting what might have been a biologically contaminated body. Inquiries to the FAA reveal no documents concerning the civilian aircraft crash, probably because it did not involve a U.S. aircraft nor did it occur over U.S. airspace. It should be noted that the above facts do not tell the complete story. Nothing is known of the analysis of the craft or its contents. Nothing is known about the deaths associated with the foreign recovery team. Nor is it known if this craft was manned or not.

Other questions also remain, such as why would a recovered disk be taken to Atlanta? And where did the disk come from? It was first detected approximately 200 miles from U.S territory, yet U.S. air defenses extend to a much greater distance than that. If the object descended into the atmosphere, perhaps NORAD space tracking has some record of the object. Alternate possibility is that it entered the Gulf of Mexico under radar limits then "jumped" up to 75,000 feet. Considering prior behavior exhibited by disks of this size, it is probable that the entry was from orbital altitude. The facts that are known have been gathered from two eye witness accounts, documentation illegally copied, and a partially destroyed document. This was done in 1978 by a person who is now dead. Only in February of this year did the notes and documents come into the hands of our group.

While the description of the crash and recovery of the unknown object broadly conforms to the data presented in other reports, the reference to an apparently lethal biological agent present at the scene is somewhat unusual. However, it is not without precedent. For example, the so-called (and unofficially released) *Majestic 12, 1ˢᵗ Annual Report* document refers to what appear to have been similar biological agents present at UFO crash sites in New Mexico in 1947. According to one extract from the allegedly real top-secret U.S. government document titled *Biological Warfare Programs*:

The 1974 incident of a small plane disappearing in Mexico somehow being involved with a UFO incident was, according to official statements after the fact, an overblown incident involving drug traffickers in a Cessna.

BW programs in U.S. and U.K., are in field test stages. Discovery of new virus and bacteria agents so lethal, that serums derived by genetic research, can launch medical science into unheard of fields of biology. The samples extracted from bodies found in New Mexico, have yielded new strains of a retro-virus not totally understood, but, give promise of the ultimate BW weapon. The danger lies in the spread of airborne and bloodborne outbreaks of diseases in large populations, with no medical cures available.

The document continues:

The Panel was concerned over the contamination of several SED personnel upon coming in contact with debris near the power plant. One technician was overcome and collapsed when he attempted the removal of a body. Another medical technician went into a coma four hours after placing a body in a rubber body-bag. All four were rushed to Los Alamos for observation. All four later died of seizures and profuse bleeding. All four were wearing protective suits when they came in contact with body fluids from the occupants…. Autopsies on the four dead SED technicians are not conclusive. It is believed that the four may have suffered from some form of toxin or a highly contagious disease. Tissue samples are currently being kept at Fort Detrick, Md…. In the opinion of the senior AEC medical officer, current medical equipment and supplies are wholly inadequate in dealing with a large scale outbreak of the alien virus.

Similarly, the unauthenticated *Interplanetary Phenomenon Unit Summary* of 1947 states with respect to individuals present at a UFO crash site in New Mexico that same year: "Ground personnel from Sandia experienced some form of contamination resulting in the deaths of 3 technicians. The status of the fourth technician is unknown. Autopsies are scheduled to determine cause of death."

Another point is worthy of note: the location to which the disk was apparently taken, namely Atlanta, Georgia. It transpires, somewhat intriguingly, that Atlanta is home to the headquarters of the Centers for Disease Control and Prevention. The CDC is at the forefront of helping to lessen, and ultimately stop, any and all threats posed by hostile forces that may wish to unleash deadly viruses upon the United States and its people. "Category A" viruses, for the CDC, are considered to be the most serious of all.

They are those specific viruses that, says the CDC, "can be easily spread or transmitted from person to person," that "result in high death rates and have the potential for major public health impact," that "might cause panic and social disruption," and that would "require special action for public health preparedness." It practically goes without saying that all four of those criteria that fall into the CDC's "Category A" could more than easily apply to the outbreak of a virus that returns the dead to some psychotic semblance of life.

Moreover, and by the CDC's very own admission, its work is "a critical component of overall U.S. national security." The U.S. government most assuredly recognizes the critical importance of the CDC from that very same national security perspective. Currently, the CDC receives yearly funding of around $1.3 billion to "build and strengthen national preparedness for public health emergencies caused by natural, accidental, or intentional events." It also works closely with the Department of Homeland Security and with FEMA, the Federal Emergency Management Agency.

Considering that it was suspected by U.S. authorities that the team of Mexican military personnel was killed by "a microbiological agent" and possibly even a fast-acting virus of alien origins, the CDC at Atlanta would have been the absolute ideal place to transfer any infected corpses for careful examination and a secret autopsy. Once again, we see how, and why, the UFO phenomenon is a profoundly deadly one.

The most important development in the saga of the 1974 crash occurred in 2007. That's when Noe Torres and Ruben Uriarte published a full-length, 212-page book on the incident. Its title: *Mexico's Roswell: The Chihuahua UFO Crash*. Not only did the pair dig deep into the story, they also traveled out to the site of the incident and were able to secure significant important data that helped corroborate the original material provided to Elaine Douglass. Mexican UFO researcher Jaime Maussan also got involved: he dispatched a group of investigators to look into the mystery.

One of those who knew of the incident was Cipriano Orozoco. He said: "Yes, several people commented about this incident … that a UFO had crashed with a small plane, but that the wreckage had been quickly recovered and removed. Not much else was known. What I did see was the movement of troops through this area. But in reality, this whole thing was tightly sealed with few leaks. However, I did hear that it happened."

Torres and Uriarte were able to uncover something that may have had a bearing on the incident, something that could have affected the working of the UFO or the aircraft—perhaps even both. They said:

> Before colliding with the aircraft somewhere north of Coyanne, the UFO traversed the skies over Coahuila state, passing directly over a very strange region of Mexico known as *La Zona del Silencio*, the Zone of Silence. Located about 400 miles southeast of El Paso, the area got its name from the strange natural phenomena that have been observed there over the years. In addition to numerous sightings of UFOs and mysterious beings, the area is said to generate mysterious waves of electromagnetic energy that can disrupt radios, telephones, aircraft instruments, and other electrical devices.

The pair has also discovered that one of those who may have played a significant role in the Mexican incident was the late Hispanic physicist and Nobel Prize winner Luis W. Alvarez. The official website of the Nobel Prize notes of Alvarez:

> Luis W. Alvarez was born in San Francisco, Calif., on June 13, 1911. He received his B.Sc. from the University of Chicago in

The *Zona del Silencio* in the Mexican state of Durango is a patch of desert where local legend says radio signals and other types of electronic communication fail to work. There has also been a UFO sighting there.

1932, a M.Sc. in 1934, and his Ph.D. in 1936. Dr. Alvarez joined the Radiation Laboratory of the University of California. He was on leave at the Radiation Laboratory of the Massachusetts Institute of Technology from 1940 to 1943, at the Metallurgical Laboratory of the University of Chicago in 1943–1944, and at the Los Alamos Laboratory of the Manhattan District from 1944 to 1945.

During the war (at M.I.T.) he was responsible for three important radar systems—the microwave early warning system, the Eagle high altitude bombing system, and a blind landing system of civilian as well as military value (GCA, or Ground-Controlled Approach). While at the Los Alamos Laboratory, Professor Alvarez developed the detonators for setting off the plutonium bomb. He flew as a scientific observer at both the Alamogordo and Hiroshima explosions.

Alvarez died in 1988. Torres and Uriarte made an important observation in relation to Alvarez: "Alvarez's military contract work early in his career led him to becoming a staunch supporter and defender of the U.S. military and its initiatives over the years. Consequently, the U.S. government often used Alvarez as a consultant on special projects, such as the Central Intelligence Agency's *Scientific Advisory Panel on Unidentified Flying Objects*, also known as the 'Robertson Panel' of 1953."

In other words, Alvarez would have been an ideal person to bring onboard and investigate the remains of the downed UFO.

The research of Torres and Uriarte continues.

Biowar Conspiracies

Fears of attacks by bacteriological warfare have been on the minds of way more than a few people since the Age of Terror began with 9/11. It's worth noting, though, that nothing is new about the deadly technology and the fears surrounding it. *Bacteriological Warfare in the United States* is a decades-old, still partly classified FBI document. Portions of it are now in the public domain, thanks to the Freedom of Information Act. The more than seven hundred pages that are available tell an intriguing and sinister story. A comprehensive study of the very earliest entries in the file reveals that of great significance to the FBI was a paper titled *The Bacteriological War*. It was written by a medical expert, O. Hartmann, and it was published in 1938 in Volume 42 of the *Norse Journal of Military Medicine*. An English translation of the article, in the hands of the FBI, states in part that "in a war of the future every manner of attack will probably be seized upon and the further development of bacteriology could furnish better possibilities than those of that time. The attack will apparently be directed chiefly against the civil population, insofar as one's own troops cannot be protected against contagion by immunization—during use at the front."

The FBI, no doubt, read with alarm as Hartmann speculated that "virus infections are possible. As means of attack, the airplane will apparently be used and the infection result from the throwing down or strewing of cultures which will be probably mixed with indifferent substances of heavier specific gravity or from infected flies which are kept immovable at 10 degrees centigrade. Attack is to be expected soonest against thickly populated cities."

Similarly, an entry in the file that dates from July 8, 1941, titled *Bacteriological Warfare by Hitler*, refers to an account published in a book titled *The Voice of Destruction*, written by Hermann Rauschning, to the effect that

"Hitler was experimenting with the use of diseased germs, such as tularaemia, which germs, it was contemplated, would be refrigerated and then thrown from airplanes on civilian population."

In 1941, and of even greater alarm to the FBI, was a nine-page paper titled *Is a War of Bacteria Possible?* It revealed some disturbing facts. Written by Dr. Martin Gumpert, it makes for highly relevant reading. Asking the question "Is such a war of bacteria actually thinkable and feasible?" Gumpert stated:

> There were times during which pestilence and cholera devastated the world. These epidemics ravaged more momentously and more cruelly, than wars with large casualty lists. Old people, women, children fell victims to them indiscriminately. By tremendous efforts and at great pains humanity has conquered these enemies. We owe it to measures of hygiene and the findings of medical research that the most dangerous epidemics today hardly constitute a threat to the civilized parts of the world.

The doctor continued:

> Only a diseased brain could evolve the thought of misusing the progress of science and its heroic discoveries: not to prevent epidemics but to engender their outbreak. Undoubtedly everyone has heard or read of the "war of bacteria" now and then, the fewest among us we have been able to form any definite conception of it. Only a small minority divines that the "war of bacteria" is the most horrible, the most criminal weapon that the urge to destroy on the part of man has ever conceived.

The paper added that "this threat is to be taken seriously," "it can be carried out," and "forces are now at work to convert it into actuality," and continued thus:

> The idea of the war of bacteria is traceable to a circumstance almost, totally unknown, namely that the fate of a war is decided far more by the amount of disease, than by the number of wounded.... Gradually it becomes clear to us, what demands bacteria must fulfill, in order to function properly in warfare: it must be possible to breed them in huge masses, the bacteria cultures must possess a high and durable virulence, it must be possible to transfer them readily and unnoticed and they must breed diseases, against which there is no protection and for which there are practically no remedial possibilities.

Dr. Gumpert concluded: "Since no madness is impossible in these wretched times, when the fate of millions is subject to the fancies and notions of a few, it is imperative that steps be taken to safeguard mankind from this extreme madness. Civilization must be spared the disgrace, that the great

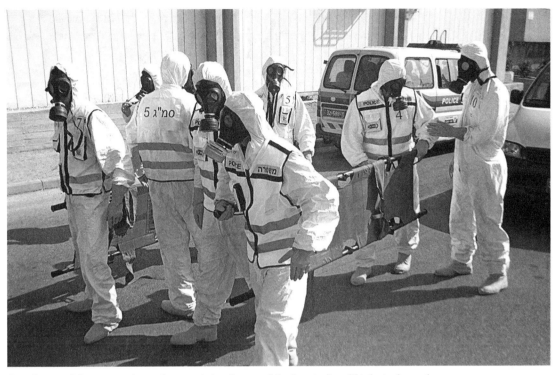

Israeli special forces are shown here training for possible chemical and biological attacks on their nation. While chemical weapons were used back in World War I, the idea of using bacteria and viruses in a war has been a horrifying prospect that wasn't even considered until recently.

deeds of her progress have led to nothing more, than back to the road of the most sinister and inhuman barbarism."

From the files of the FBI, we learn much more about the career of Dr. Martin Gumpert. According to FBI records on the man:

> Dr. Martin Gumpert, reported to be the former head of the Berlin City Dispensary, is credited with certain statements in a book on sabotage published by the Royal Canadian Mounted Police. In this, it is reported that Hitler was experimenting with the use of disease-producing organisms such as tularaemia, which, it was contemplated, would be refrigerated and thrown from airplanes on civilian populations in the prosecution of the war.

> He has apparently quoted extracts from an official German Army journal published in September, 1939, which discussed the possibilities of unleashing disease-laden germs upon the civilian populations in France and Great Britain. The irreconcilable statement that tularaemia, for which there is no possibility of treatment or

vaccination, could be spread by dropping refrigerated flies and lice by airplane is also reported to be Dr. Gumpert's. He is further credited with stating that Hitler's secret weapon may be "horrible bacteria warfare that Hitler might not hesitate to unleash when he finds himself at bay."

Fortunately, that crazed, deranged lunatic named Adolf Hitler did not succeed in his terrible plans, as history has shown.

Mentioning to many of the leading lights in the field of so-called "cattle mutilations" the idea that the admittedly weird phenomenon might have far more to do with the work of a clandestine group in government or the military than it does with black-eyed aliens from some faraway galaxy is likely to result in a response of an overwhelmingly negative and defensive nature. Belief (particularly of the Fox Mulder-like "I want to believe" variety) is a very powerful tool when it comes to concluding that this or that is linked to the UFO puzzle—and that goes for cattle-mutes, too—but say the full-on believers in the theory that E.T.s like to chow down on a nice tasty steak now and again—if not the aliens, then who else could be responsible? For the most part, they scoff at the idea of predators, cults, and the government (the latter being "them" in paranoia-land) as the culprits.

> The fact of the matter, however, is that ... various official bodies have taken a clandestine and concerned interest in animal deaths and injuries all across the United States....

The fact of the matter, however, is that—for decades, no less—various official bodies have taken a clandestine and concerned interest in animal deaths and injuries all across the United States, but not for reasons relative to the actions of menacing, meat-loving extraterrestrials. Nope, the reasons are much different and, in many ways, far more disturbing. We're talking about shadowy figures sabotaging the food chain via deliberate, terrorist-style actions and officialdom's secret and sometimes panicky attempts to stop it.

Think I'm wrong? Think the government could not keep—and still isn't keeping—a careful and secret watch on the U.S. cattle population for reasons of a national security nature? If you do, it's time to think again.

J. R. Ruggle, the FBI special agent in charge at the Savannah, Georgia, office of the Bureau in the early to mid-1940s, wrote thus to FBI director J. Edgar Hoover on February 3, 1943: "This office has received a copy of a communication from JOHN T. BISSELL, Colonel, General Staff, Assistant Executive Officer, Military Intelligence Service, Washington, D.C., dated December 29, 1942, to directors of intelligence in all Service commands...."

Col. Bissel's communication read:

It has been brought to the attention of this division the possibility in the immediate future of an attempt on the part of the enemy to plant bombs containing germs or to endeavor to create an epidemic, such as hoof and mouth disease, among cattle and other livestock. It is requested that should any information concerning the above come to the attention of the Directors of Intelligence of the Service Commands or the A.C. of S. [Assistant Chief of Staff], G-2 [Army Intelligence], Western Defense Command, that the same be transmitted by the most expeditious means to the Assistant Chief of Staff, G–2 War Department.

Evidently, such matters were of keen concern to U.S. Intelligence, and that concern did not go away any time soon. In 1944, the FBI prepared a document that dealt with the scenario of a widespread attack on the U.S. cattle herd via unconventional, bacteriological warfare. The document states:

A review of the book entitled "Sabotage" by Michael Sayers and Albert E. Kahn, which was published in September of 1942, discloses the following data: The complete record of sabotage carried out by Chernov, supposedly of the German Intelligence service in Russia during 1930 to 1936 is too long to put into the book according to the authors, but includes—killing off pedigree breed-stock and raising cattle mortality by artificially infecting cattle with various kinds of bacteria—effecting a shortage of serum to counteract epidemics of anthrax so that, in one instance, 25,000 horses perished as a result of Chernov's sabotage—infecting tens of thousands of pigs with erysipelas and with certain plagues by having virulent bacteria placed in medicinal sera.

In another point, the authors have asked the question: "Could such wholesale sabotage of agriculture as took place in the Soviet Union take place in the United States of America?" They then answer the question that, regardless of how fantastic it might sound, such diabolical sabotage was actually practiced by German saboteurs in 1915 in the United States of America.

The FBI elaborated further:

Anton Dilger, a German-American medical graduate from Johns Hopkins University, was in Germany when the First World War broke out. He offered his services to the Kaiser, and was promptly detailed by Colonel Nicolai to do secret service work in the United States. Dilger returned to America with a supply of cultures of glanders and anthrax germs. Financed by von Papen, he set up a laboratory in Chevy Chase, near Washington, and started breeding germs on a large scale for infecting mules, horses, and cattle awaiting shipment to the allies.

This man then organized a band of some twelve assistants to travel around the country, carrying Dilger's germs in small glass phials

Cattle and other livestock are another factor in biological warfare. They can be killed by diseases or even pass those diseases on to humans.

stopped with corks through which a needle extended. This roving band jabbed their deadly needles into the livestock.

They also spread germs by placing them in fodder and drink. Thousands of soldiers, as well as horses and cattle, died as a result of Dilger's germs. At last Dilger revolted against his mission of silent death. He was murdered by German spies a few months before the end of the war. Could it happen here? It did happen here!

The FBI's declassified records from 1945 reveal that the issue of cattle being potentially affected by bacteriological warfare was a major one. A memo to Hoover dated July 6, 1945, states: "You may be interested in the following information which was reported by the SAC [Special Agent in Charge] of the Norfolk Field Division following a Weekly Intelligence Conference on June 28, 1945."

The document refers to the work of a man (whose identity is concealed to this day within the pages of the declassified documents) employed by the then-Army Air Force at Langley Field, Virginia, and who had "been assigned to handling investigations concerning the landing of Japanese balloons in the states of North and South Dakota and Nebraska."

In a summary report, the SAC at Norfolk informed Hoover:

I was interested to learn that recently several Japanese balloons were found in that territory which were determined to have been carrying bacteria. The bacteria consisting of Anthrax, are placed in the hydrogen. I was told that such bacteria mainly affects cattle. When the bacteria lands on wheat or other types or farm land where food is being raised for the cattle, the bacteria remain in the food when it is eaten by the cattle, and upon human consumption of the milk or meat, the bacteria can be passed on.

Particularly notable is a July 11, 1949, document that refers to the FBI's desire to acquire "world-wide information on animal diseases and animal population." One year later, the FBI was still collecting such data. On October 19, 1950, the FBI prepared a document titled *Abnormal Loss of Hogs in Nebraska and Illinois* that dealt with an unusually high number of hog deaths in the aforementioned states—as a result of cholera. The files, however, make it clear that, in official, FBI quarters, the nature of the animals' deaths had been viewed with deep suspicion.

It was concluded that the deaths were due to a "variant virus" or "atypical virus" that stemmed from "local conditions and the physical conditions of the hogs." The important factor, however, is that this document was found within a file that specifically focused upon bacteriological warfare. In other words, the FBI was still looking closely at any and all animal deaths that might not have wholly conventional explanations.

Of great significance is the fact that one of the cases that the FBI examined—and that is described in a heavily redacted memo of May 29, 1950—dealt with the finding of plague-infected rats at the highly sensitive Sandia Base, New Mexico, and which was viewed in some quarters as being the result of nothing less than a deliberate attempt to clandestinely introduce a widespread plague on Sandia by hostile, unknown sources.

> Of great significance is the fact that one of the cases that the FBI examined ... dealt with the finding of plague-infected rats at the highly sensitive Sandia Base, New Mexico....

As an example, a document prepared by the FBI's Special Agent in Charge at its Albuquerque, New Mexico, branch on June 22, 1950, titled *Bacteriological Warfare—Espionage—Sabotage (Bubonic Plague)*, refers to rumors then flying around the official world that an outbreak of bubonic plague in New Mexico's rat population may have been the result of deliberate, bacteriological warfare-related activities by—once again—hostile, unknown forces.

The FBI noted with respect to its interview with a plague expert, who is identified only as a "Miss Greenfield," that "[she] is acquainted with the presence of the plague among wild rodents in New Mexico and in the United States for several years. It has now reached an area from the West Coast to a line running north and south at approximately the border of New Mexico."

The FBI continued: "From August 1949 there were four cases among humans in New Mexico. Briefly, these four cases, one of which was fatal, were reported in New Mexico. Each case indicated that the victim had shortly before the illness, handled wild rodents which he had killed. The one case in New Mexico which was fatal was not diagnosed as the plague until after death."

Notably, the FBI subsequently received from the Public Health Service two charts displaying the outbreaks of plague in both New Mexico and the continental United States during that period. As the FBI noted with respect to the Public Health Service, "they have found positive evidence of the plague among wild rodents in the states lying west of a line directly north of the east boundary of the state of New Mexico."

The FBI's Special Agent in Charge in Albuquerque concluded his report thus: "Miss Greenfield has been requested to advise this office concerning any pertinent developments of the plague in New Mexico or in the United States that may come to her attention. In the event such developments are received, the Bureau will be immediately advised."

In essence, those are the significant, declassified portions of the file. Taking into consideration the fact that we now know that senior elements of, and agencies within, the government were taking a deep—albeit secret—interest and concern in cases of unusual disease and death in the U.S. animal population in the 1940s and 1950s, is it really out of the question to suggest that they might have done exactly the same thing since the 1960s right up to the present day?

That being so, what better way to hide such actions than behind a smokescreen of alien-themed "cattle mutilations"?

After all, such a smokescreen (or maybe "meme" might be better and more accurate) would keep away the "serious" media, who would lump the phenomenon in with the likes of Roswell, Nessie, and Bigfoot and largely ignore it or poke fun at it. UFO researchers would be kept busy chasing nonexisting alien butchers, and the debunkers—some of whom are hardly strangers when it comes to acting as fawning, pathetic apologists for government—would be content to suggest that it's all the work of coyotes, mountain lions, birds, insects, etc., etc.

Cattle mutes are real—believe it—but the culprits are not who many think they are (or so desperately want them to be)....

The Strangest Cover-Up
of the Second World War

From Jonathan Downes, the director of the U.K.-based Centre for Fortean Zoology, comes what is surely one of the strangest tales of the Second World War. Since the story is a lengthy and complex one that is full of an absolute multitude of twists and turns—not to mention deep conspiracy and Second World War-era secrecy and subterfuge—the most profitable approach is to allow Downes to relate the extraordinary findings for himself in his own fashion. They are findings that relate to a turbulent, terrible, and ultimately tragic story told to Downes back in the early 1980s, when he was still in his early twenties and working as a psychiatric nurse at Starcross Hospital, Devon, England—Starcross being a small village on the west bank of the River Exe, Teignbridge. With that said, let us take a close and careful look at this emotion-filled tale of people long gone, shadowy secrets, deep stigma, and a war-torn era immersed in carnage and conflict.

According to the British government's National Archive at Kew, England: "Originally known as the Western Counties Idiot Asylum [author's note: "idiot" was a word that, unlike today, was considered acceptable for the name of an asylum] this institution opened in 1864 in a house and two acres of land at Starcross, rented from W. R. Courtenay, 11th Earl of Devon. A committee appointed to collect donations and subscriptions, and to accept patients into the asylum, was chaired by the 11th Earl who was also its first president, positions he held until 1904."

Kew's history of the hospital continues, as the government notes:

By 1870 the building housed 40 residents, and an appeal for funds to build larger premises was launched. A new building, surrounded by 7 acres of grounds, was opened in June 1877. This was able to house 60 boys and 40 girls. Further additions were built between 1886 and 1909, and by 1913 a total of 1,451 patients had been admitted to the institution. In 1914, the asylum was incorporated under the Companies Act. It then became known as the Western Counties Institution, Starcross, and was certified as "a residential special school for mental defectives." Residents were trained in carving, weaving, basketry, lace-making and carpentry, and worked on the institution's agricultural holdings.

In the 1930s, properties at Dix's Field, Exeter and Steepway, Paignton were purchased for use as domestic training hostels for young women. A farm hostel was founded on Langton Farm at Dawlish and a seaside holiday home was opened. In 1948, the institution was transferred to the National Health Service, and became merged into the Royal Western Counties Institution Hospital Group, which coordinated all the residential mental deficiency services. The institution came under the control of Devon Area Health Authority from 1974 and of Exeter Health Authority from 1982. In 1986, in keeping with a national policy of transferring the majority of mentally handicapped people back into the community, the Royal Western Counties Hospital was marked for closure.

With that background on Starcross Hospital/"idiot asylum" revealed, let us now focus on Jonathan Downes, who begins the remarkable tale as follows:

A story, which, I am sure, was told me in good faith, and which even now I do not know whether to believe, apparently took place during the Second World War. There had, apparently, been a number of occasions when captured German aircrew and pilots who had been shot down over South Devon or the English Channel were kept, temporarily, in a remote wing of Starcross Hospital— which is roughly ten miles from the city of Exeter—until they could be transferred to the prisoner-of-war camp high above Starcross on the Haldon Hills.

On one particular occasion, says Downes, the military had been searching for a fugitive German airman in the woods surrounding Powderham Castle, which is about half a mile away from the old hospital and which was constructed between 1390 and 1420 by Sir Philip Courtenay. They had ventured into the deepest parts of the woods in search of their quarry when, suddenly, the small band of elderly men and boys who were too young to join the regular Army—but who were assigned to what was known as the Home Guard—saw what they believed was the fugitive airmen running through the woods in front of them. The leader shouted at him to stop, but it was all to no avail, as Downes reveals:

The old man who told me the story was actually one of the Home Guards, and he told me that one of the party had been a teacher in Germany before the war and could speak the language. He ordered the man to stop, but the fugitive ignored him. In 1942, the war was not going well—at least as far as the British were concerned—and Home Guard units, especially in rural areas, were desperately under-equipped. Most of the patrol was only armed with pitchforks, although one had a dilapidated shotgun and the captain—who led the unit—had his old First World War service revolver.

If it had been a normal patrol there would only have been about half-a-dozen of them, but large parts of Exeter had been levelled by successive waves of German bombers, and the opportunity for a population of a tiny village like Starcross to actually face the enemy on equal terms

Cryptozoologist Jonathan Downes, who is the director for the Centre for Fortean Zoology in England, reported a tale about a strange wild man discovered in 1942 by members of the Home Guard.

was an irresistible lure. According to my informant, the Home Guard patrol had been augmented by a gang of villagers baying for blood and desperate for revenge. The captain was an educated man, and had no intention of using force to capture the fugitive unless it was absolutely necessary. The man with a shotgun—a local farmer, who had lost two of his sons in the desperate weeks leading up to Dunkirk—had no such compunction. He was also drunk. Shouting, "I'll get you, you bastard!," He raised his weapon and fired. The dark figure ahead of them let out a grunt of agony and fell to the ground. The captain was furious. He immediately put the drunken farmer under arrest and confiscated his shotgun.

It was at this point, Downes demonstrates, that the group came to a shocking realization. The man who had just been felled by the irate farmer was far stranger than anything that could have come out of Nazi Germany: "The party then ran on towards what they thought was an injured German airman, but they found, to their horror, that it was nothing of the sort. Instead of a proud member of the Luftwaffe, they found a naked man in his early twenties covered in hair and plastered in mud."

Even forty years after the event, says Downes, it was obvious that his informant had been badly shaken by this highly unnerving experience. He was now an elderly retired nursing officer in his early seventies who, spared military service because of his profession, had eagerly embraced the Home Guard as his opportunity to fight the Germans, and it was equally obvious that that these years had been the happiest of his life. The rest of his professional career had been spent at the hospital, and he intimated to Downes that he had found the increasing struggle with a moribund bureaucracy exponentially tedious, so when he was offered early retirement, he was quite happy to spend the rest of his days fishing and propping up the corner of the bar in the pub. You may very well ask: What happened to the hairy man who was supposedly felled all those years ago? Of his source and his strange and sensational story, Downes states:

> Apparently, he told me, the badly injured wild man was taken to Starcross Hospital in the middle of the night, and all efforts were made to make him comfortable. Then, in the early hours of the morning, apparently an unmarked black van had arrived, and two men in uniform and another wearing a long white coat, manhandled the mysterious victim on to a stretcher, loaded him into the back of the van, and took him to an unknown destination. My informant never heard anything about the case again. He did hint, however, that the authorities warned everybody involved to say nothing. And, in the prevailing culture of careless talk costing lives, they had all concurred. I was, apparently, the first person that he had ever talked to about the incident. And that was only because he had recently found out that sixty years of smoking had taken their toll and that he was doomed to die of lung cancer within the next eighteen months.

As Downes's following words make abundantly clear, the revelations of his Deep Throat-like source had a profound and lasting effect upon the young and eager monster hunter:

> I sat back on the bar-stool in the pub we were frequenting at the time, and gulped at my pint. This was possibly the most bizarre thing that I had ever heard—in a life that had already seen several bizarre and inexplicable incidents. I had heard of Bigfoot—indeed, I had even been on a hunt for it whilst living in Canada—but I had never heard of such things in the United Kingdom. Could it be? I thought: surely not.

> But my informant seemed genuine enough. He sat in the corner of the bar puffing away on a cigarette and wheezing gently like a dilapidated steam-engine. His face had the unmistakable translucent aura of somebody struck down by incurable cancer, and he sat telling me of these extraordinary events in a matter-of-fact tone, as if he was recounting the previous weekend's football results. Did he remember the exact location? If so, would he be prepared to

take me there? I asked these questions diffidently, and to my delight he agreed. There was no time at the present, he told me; and, so, finishing our beers, we went outside and walked towards the castle grounds.

Matters were about to be taken to a whole new level. Once again, I turn the story over to Downes. It is, after all, his tale to tell:

> If you're travelling towards Exeter from Dawlish, go through Starcross village and when you pass the *Atmospheric Railway* pub, go on past the large car park on the right-hand side of road, but instead of following the main road round to the left towards Exeter, take the right-hand fork which is sign-posted to Powderham. Carry on down this little road for about half a mile. On the left-hand side you will see an expanse of deer-park, which is bordered by a wide ditch full of brackish water that acts as a moat. Just before you come to a railway bridge, the moat peters out. And although it may not be there now, back in 1982 when I conducted the interview, there was a convenient gap in the fence. This was apparently well known to the local poaching community in the village, and formed their main entry point to the woods where Lord Courtenay and his family raised their pheasants. We wriggled through the gap in the fence to find ourselves blissfully trespassing in the forbidden grounds of the castle.

Stories of hairy wild men have been told throughout the centuries, but discovering one in a place like Devon, England, was unheard of (*Wild Man* statue c. 1522 by Paulus Vischer).

Realizing that even on such a brightly moonlit night, it would be pretty much impossible to venture any further into the thick and uninviting woodland, Downes and his aged informant decided to turn around and carefully retrace their steps back to Starcross village. Downes says that as he was working for the next three days, he made arrangements to meet his companion, once again, in the pub the following weekend. This time, however, the atmosphere was distinctly different and profoundly frosty, as Downes makes acutely clear. Commenting on his source, Downes recalls:

He came around, and I rushed down to the *Atmospheric Railway* to fulfill our tryst. Sure enough, my friend of a few evenings previously was there, puffing away on a cigarette and drinking his customary pint of light-and-bitter. However, something had changed: I tried to broach the subject of the mysterious wild-man, but he was unwilling to talk about it. "I should not have said anything the other night," he muttered, "but I'm an old man and I wanted to share it with you."

Downes had more than a few thoughts and opinions on the matter of this distinct about-face: "Whether it was the intimation of his imminent demise, or just a memory of the promise that he had made back in the 1940s, I don't know. But, in stark contrast to his verbosity of our previous meeting, on this occasion he was adamant that he didn't want to talk about it. So, I bought him a beer, challenged him to a game of cribbage, and spent the rest of the evening doing the sort of things that blokes normally do in a pub."

Not surprisingly, however, for someone whose pursuit of the truth was growing by the day, Downes just could not let the beastly matter drop. In actuality, for a while, it's fair to say that the whole thing became something of a definitive obsession for Britain's most famous creature seeker: "The whole affair fascinated me. Over the next months I cautiously broached the subject of ape-men in Powderham woods with a number of the elderly men who drank in the pub, or who hung out in the hospital social club. None of them knew anything. Or, if they did, they weren't saying."

Bad news was looming on the horizon, too, as Downes sadly now recalls:

The months passed, and the old man who had told me of the events in Powderham woods during 1942 was admitted to the cancer ward at the Royal Devon and Exeter Hospital in Exeter. I visited him on a few occasions—the last, a couple of days before he died. I smuggled him in a bottle of Guinness, and sat at the end of his bed as he drank it with relish. However, in view of his condition—and because I truthfully didn't think that I could get anything else out of him—I refrained from asking him any more about an incident which he obviously regretted having shared with me. I attended his funeral. I was one of the few people there. When his lonely black coffin trundled behind the curtain at the Exeter crematorium, I was convinced that the truth about this mystery would go up in smoke along with his elderly, cancer-riddled corpse. How utterly wrong I was.

Of the next chapter in this winding and weird story, Downes kicks it off as follows:

Christmas came and went. In the early weeks of 1983, I found myself going through the voluminous filing cabinets that held over a century's worth of patient records at Starcross. This was part of my training as a psychiatric nurse. And although I was supposed to be looking into the distribution of different syndromes of mental and physical handicap from which the patients at Starcross hospital suffered, much to my surprise I found what I strongly suspect to be the solution to my forty-year-old mystery.

It was here that the tragic truth spilled out:

In among some of the older files, I found a number that referred to members of a very wealthy and noble local family. These were not the Earls of Devon; however, as the family is still very wealthy and extremely powerful, I do not feel comfortable with revealing their identity—at least not yet. It appeared that there was a strong vein of mental illness in the family, and possibly more significantly, metabolic disorders running through the line. I discovered the details of some terrible human tragedies reaching back over a century. It turned out that an old lady, known affectionately to all the staff as Winnie—and who at the time I knew her, must have been in her early nineties—was a member of this noble family. She had committed the unpardonable sin of becoming pregnant at the age of thirteen, following her liaison with one of the stable-boys. This had happened way

Hypertrichosis is a rare genetic disorder that leads to a body being covered all over with hair, including the face. A famous example of this was the sixteenth-century Spanish nobleman Petrus Gonsalvus.

back before the First World War; and although history didn't relate what had happened to her boyfriend, she had been forcibly given an abortion and incarcerated for the rest of her life in Starcross Hospital.

Far more misfortune was to come:

It turned out that, before the Mental Health Act of 1959 was passed, there were three criteria under which a person could be admitted to hospital without any real recourse of Appeal. These people were labelled as "idiots" (nowadays known as people with moderate learning difficulties), "imbeciles" (individuals with severe learning difficulties), and moral defectives. I looked at Winnie with new respect from then on, and, whenever I had the chance, I would give her a packet of cigarettes or some chocolate.

Now Downes comes to the heart of the tale and of the origin of the hairy wild man of Starcross Hospital:

The files also contained details of a number of her relatives. Several of them suffered from congenital generalised hypertrichosis, commonly known as *Wolf-Man Syndrome*. In extreme cases, this disease not only causes bizarre behaviour and radical mood swings, but the body of the victim becomes excessively hairy.

Although several people from Winnie's family had been diagnosed as suffering from this syndrome, there were no hospital records absolutely proving that they had been resident at a hospital after the First World War. What I did find out, however, was that the bloodline definitely had not died out. The family was still very important in the Devon area. They were notable benefactors to local charities; and at one time, at least, members of the family had been on the governing board of Starcross hospital itself.

Krao Farini (shown here in 1883) was born with hypertrichosis, too. People didn't understand such conditions back then, and as an adult he ended up making a living as a circus performer.

As the condition is an inherited one, it seemed quite probable to Downes that the strain of congenital generalized hypertrichosis had not died out in the early years of the twentieth century. A more enlightened generation of the family had decided to treat these poor unfortunates at home rather than subject them to the rigors of an institutionalized life. Maybe this, Downes mused, was the truth behind the story of the hairy man of Powderham.

He adds today:

I thought it was quite likely that the unruly rabble that had accompanied the Home Guard on that fateful night in 1942 had actually shot a member of the local ruling family—in the mistaken belief that he was a German airman. This would explain everything. It would explain why the whole affair had been shrouded in secrecy. In those days, the part of the landowner and the patrician establishment was far greater than it is today.

There is still a stigma surrounding mental illness, mental handicap, and disability. This poor man, covered in hair, was still a member of the family who, after all, still paid the wages of most of the members of the posse that had hunted him down. Especially at a time when the nation was facing the deadly peril of the Nazi hordes, the powers-that-be would not have wanted the populace at large to be aware that one of their own was an unstable, dangerous, hair-covered lunatic who had escaped from his care and was wandering, naked and belligerent, across the countryside.

Thus ends the sad, enigmatic, and conspiracy-filled saga of the Starcross wild man, the decades-old secrets of a powerful family, official cover-ups, frightened figures, a shadowy informant who had hidden the truth for decades, and a young man—Jon Downes—who, nearly forty years ago, found himself so graphically exposed to the whole story (or, at least, considerable parts of it) in all its hideous and weird glory.

Actually, the story is not quite over. The noted and late British naturalist Trevor Beer had an equally provocative account to relate that may, very possibly, be of some significant relevance to the tale described above. It concerned an event that reportedly occurred in the late 1950s that came from a man out walking his dog at the time of its occurrence. Although the year is different from that in the story told to Jon Downes and the incident reportedly involved nothing less than a full-blown werewolf rather than a wild man (although, to the untrained, terrified eye, does that much of a difference really exist?), the location—Devon—was the same. Also the same are two further matters of significance: in the story told to Beer, (a) the hairy man-thing was shot; and (b) it was found to be a member of a well-known family in the area.

Beer described the story of the witness in these particular words: "Climbing a hedge he stumbled upon an animal ravaging a flock of sheep and taking careful aim he shot it; the beast reared onto its hind legs to run off into the woods. The dog followed the animal into the trees where there was much hideous snarling unlike any creature he had ever heard before. Suddenly the dog came dashing out of the woods and bolted past its master who, firing a second shot into the trees, also ran for home in great fear."

Beer added:

The man went on to explain his later studies of matters concerning the occult and his realisation that the animal he had shot was a werewolf and a member of a well-known local family. [He] further states that he knows the family involved and that they called in help from the church over a decade ago but that they had to withdraw because of the terrible phenomena beyond their comprehension. Now the problem is at a stalemate, the family being aware of the nature of his character and chaining him and locking him behind barred doors every night.

Are the similarities between this case and the one described to Jon Downes actually evidence of a single story that, over time, became somewhat distorted into two separate ones or, incredibly, could it be that the case Trevor Beer described involved yet another member of the affected and afflicted family to which Downes referred? Maybe, one day, we will know the full and unexpurgated truth of this intriguing and conspiratorial, cover-up-laden affair or, perhaps, like so many tales of deep cover-up, it will forever languish in mystery, intrigue, and a closely guarded, locked filing cabinet marked *Top Secret*.

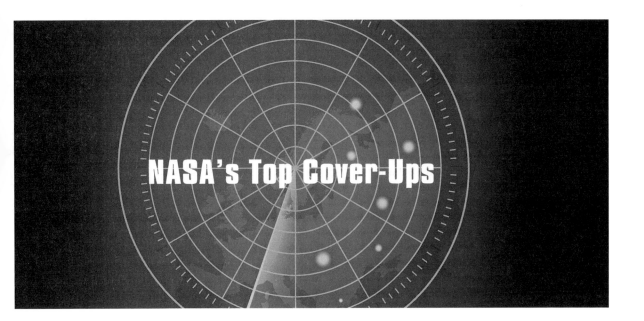

NASA's Top Cover-Ups

Although the Pentagon, the CIA, and the U.S. Air Force have been at the forefront of highly classified UFO secrets for many years, it's a little-known fact that NASA—the National Aeronautics and Space Administration—has taken a deep interest in not just UFOs but incidents involving crashed UFOs. In other words, it's the extraterrestrial hardware and technology that NASA is particularly fascinated with. As NASA notes:

> Since its inception in 1958, NASA has accomplished many great scientific and technological feats in air and space. NASA technology also has been adapted for many nonaerospace uses by the private sector. NASA remains a leading force in scientific research and in stimulating public interest in aerospace exploration, as well as science and technology in general. Perhaps more importantly, our exploration of space has taught us to view Earth, ourselves, and the universe in a new way. While the tremendous technical and scientific accomplishments of NASA demonstrate vividly that humans can achieve previously inconceivable feats, we also are humbled by the realization that Earth is just a tiny "blue marble" in the cosmos.

All of which brings us to one of the most amazing UFO cases of all.

The genesis of this case can be traced to a U.S. Department of State telegram transmitted from the American Embassy in La Paz, Bolivia, to the U.S. secretary of state, Washington, D.C., on May 15, 1978, and shared with NASA. Captioned *Report of Fallen Space Object*, it stated:

> 1. The Bolivian newspapers carried this morning an article concerning an unidentified object that apparently recently fell from

the sky. The paper quotes a "Latin" correspondent's story from the Argentine city of Salta. The object was discovered near the Bolivian city of Bermejo and was described as egg-shaped, metal and about four meters in diameter.

2. The Bolivian Air Force plans to investigate to determine what the object might be and from where it came. I have expressed our interest and willingness to help. They will advise.

3. Request the department check with appropriate agencies to see if they can shed some light on what this object might be. The general region has had more than its share of reports of UFOs this past week. Requests a reply ASAP.

NASA and the Department of State were not the only branches of the government that took an interest in the case, as a CIA report—also from May 15, 1978—makes clear:

Many people in this part of the country claim they saw an object which resembled a soccer ball falling behind the mountains on the Argentine–Bolivian border, causing an explosion that shook the earth. This took place on May 6. Around that time some people in San Luis and Mendoza provinces reported seeing a flying saucer squadron flying in formation. The news from Salta confirms that the artificial satellite fell on Taire Mountain in Bolivia, where it has already been located by authorities. The same sources said that the area where the artificial satellite fell has been declared an emergency zone by the Bolivian Government.

An examination of declassified UFO files found in the NASA archives reveals a second report that references the crash and adds further data. Dated May 16, 1978, and titled *Reports Conflict on Details of Fallen Object*, the document reads:

We have received another phone call from our audience requesting confirmation of reports that an unidentified object fell on Bolivian territory near the Argentine border. We can only say that the Argentine and Uruguayan radio stations are reporting on this even more frequently, saying that Bolivian authorities have urgently requested assistance from the U.S. National Aeronautics and Space Administration in order to determine the nature of that which crashed on a hill in Bolivian territory. Just a few minutes ago Radio El Espectador of Montevideo announced that there was uncertainty as to the truth of these reports. Argentine sources indicated that the border with Bolivia had been closed but that it might soon be reopened. They also reported that an unidentified object had fallen on Bolivian soil near the Argentine border and that local Bolivian authorities had requested aid from the central government, which, in turn, had sought assistance from the U.S. National Aeronautics and Space Administration to investigate the case.

A La Paz newspaper said today that there is great interest in learning about the nature of the fallen object, adding that local authorities for security reasons had cordoned off 200 km around the spot where the object fell. The object is said to be a mechanical device with a diameter of almost 4 meters which has already been brought to Tarija. There is interest in determining the accuracy of these reports which have spread quickly throughout the continent, particularly in Bolivia and its neighboring countries. Is it a satellite, a meteorite, or a false alarm?

On May 18, 1978, the U.S. Embassy in La Paz again forwarded a telegram to both NASA and the secretary of state, Washington, D.C. Classified *Secret*, the telegram disclosed the following:

> Preliminary information provided has been checked with appropriate government agencies. No direct correlation with known space objects that may have re-entered the Earth's atmosphere near May 6 can be made; however, we continue to examine any possibilities. Your attention is invited to State Airgram A-6343, July 26, 1973, which provided background information and guidance for dealing with space objects that have been found. In particular any information pertaining to the pre-impact observations, direction of trajectory, number of objects observed, time of impact and a detailed description including any markings would be useful.

Six days later, a communication was transmitted from the U.S. Defense Attaché Office in La Paz to a variety of U.S. military and government agencies and departments, including NORAD, the Air Force, and the Department of State:

> This office has tried to verify the stories put forth in the local press. The Chief of

The U.S. Embassy (pictured) in La Paz, Bolivia, fielding incoming reports of a UFO in the area, could not correlate them with any known craft that might have entered the atmosphere there.

Staff of the Bolivian Air Force told DATT/AIRA this date that planes from the BAF have flown over the area where the object was supposed to have landed and in their search they drew a blank. Additionally, DATT/AIRA talked on this date with the Commander of the Bolivian Army and informed DATT that the Army's search party directed to go into the area to find the object had found nothing. The Army has concluded that there may or [may] not be an object, but to date nothing has been found.

The CIA's report of May 15, 1978, clearly stated that the object had fallen to Earth on Taire Mountain, Bolivia, and had "already been located by authorities." Furthermore, on the following day, the CIA learned that the object had "been brought to Tarija." In contrast, the Bolivian Army and Air Force advised the U.S. Defense Attaché Office that their search for the mysterious object had drawn a blank and nothing was found. Was the CIA misinformed, or were the Bolivians keeping the Department of State in the dark? Regardless of the answers to those questions, the story does not end there.

> What of the possibility that the object was a man-made satellite? That theory was thrown into doubt by the Department of State's secret telegram of May 18....

Tantalizing information suggests that the object was indeed recovered by U.S. authorities (or at least with the assistance of U.S. authorities) and that both the CIA and NASA played key roles in the case. In June 1979, researcher Leonard Stringfield was contacted by an Argentinean investigator, Nicholas Ojeda, who had interesting data to impart concerning the crash. According to Ojeda: "There is a report of a group of investigators who vanished mysteriously in the area. I really think something big happened in Salta. NASA investigated, but there was no news of it. I have to tell you that in La Paz, Bolivia, a huge Hercules C-130 carried 'something' from the area where the UFO crashed."

In addition, Stringfield's research led to a disclosure that a CIA source known to the researcher Bob Barry confirmed that the C-130 flight took place and that he was aboard the aircraft. "No comment" was the reply that Barry received when the issue of the aircraft's cargo was raised. The available evidence still did not answer the crucial question: What was it that crashed at Bermejo, Bolivia, in May 1978? The possibility that the object was a meteorite almost certainly can be discounted primarily because of the description given in the Department of State's telegram of May 15: "The object was ... egg-shaped, metal and about four meters in diameter."

What of the possibility that the object was a man-made satellite? That theory was thrown into doubt by the Department of State's secret telegram of May 18, which was shared with NASA and clearly stated: "No direct correlation with known space objects that may have entered the Earth's atmosphere near May 6 can be made."

In this light, the CIA statement that "people in San Luis and Mendoza provinces reported seeing a flying saucer squadron flying in formation" and the revelations of the Department of State that "the general region has had more than its share of reports of UFOs in the past week" must be considered significant.

Certainly, the most significant development in this case occurred in 2015, when data compiled by the late UFO researcher Bob Pratt surfaced. Pratt was an acclaimed UFO researcher who died in November 2005 and gave me permission to use his material when I was digging into the NASA–UFO controversy. The well-known Brazilian UFO investigator A. J. Gevaerd wrote on November 23, 2005:

> This is a very sad note. Bob Pratt, a great UFO researcher and a good friend, died last Saturday, November 19th. His death is a great loss for Ufology worldwide. Last Friday, Bob had a heart attack and by Saturday, he was gone. There will be a memorial service on Friday afternoon at his town, Lake Worth, Florida. Bob was a distinguished American writer, UFO researcher and journalist who was co-author of *Night Siege: The Hudson Valley UFO Sightings*, with J. Allen Hynek, and the author of *UFO Danger In Brazil*, translated and published here as *Perigo Alienígena no Brasil*. It is very probable that no other foreign UFO researcher had more knowledge about the Brazilian Ufology as Bob Pratt. He had been to Brazil 13 times and was the kind of field investigator that really went to where the facts were to be researched. He helped a lot of the Brazilian UFO researchers to best evaluate the dramatic incidents of alien attacks in the Northeast of the country and in the Amazon. Bob's interest in UFO Phenomena began when working for the *National Enquirer*, and was sent to many countries to investigate UFO sightings and ET contacts, such as Argentina, Bolivia, Canada, Chile, Japan, Mexico, Peru and Puerto Rico. Since 1975, he interviewed over two-thousand witnesses, many of them in Brazil. Bob wrote articles for several UFO and non-UFO magazines. He was, for several years, the editor of the renowned *MUFON UFO Journal*.

Of the many people who Pratt spoke with while on-site in Bolivia—shortly after the event occurred—one was a physicist, Dr. Orlando René Bravo. He told Pratt:

> People saw different things as the object passed over. In Rosillas, people saw a silver-colored tube or cylinder with a black head in front and flames at the back, a cylinder that appeared to be about

four meters long. A teacher in Rosillas told me she saw a fireball pass in the sky and disappear, leaving a trail of smoke behind it, and about five minutes later she heard an explosion. All the teachers and children saw something fall. For twenty to twenty-five miles around, people heard the explosion. I went to all these places, and people said they felt the ground tremble when they heard the explosion.

Dr. Bravo had much more to say, too, including the fact that some witnesses saw two objects:

I don't know what the first object was, but I'm sure the others were missiles. Two geologists from GEOBOL (the Bolivian geological agency) and their guide were in Yerba Buena at the bottom of a ravine, and they thought this object was going to crash on the far side of the hill.

I walked from La Mamora, about thirty-eight hundred feet high, to Rio Condada, to Puesta de la Laguna, Estancia Jalanoquero and Yerba Buena, which is more than ten thousand feet high. I also walked to the towns of San Luis, Tolomosita, Tolomosa and Pampa Redonda. I interviewed more than fifty people, taking directions with a compass all the time.

The second investigation was between May 16 and May 21, with Mr. De La Torre. From Cañas up to Mecoya, we interviewed more than thirty people. From Mecoya, we explored up to Cerro Salle, all the way up to border marker number four, at an elevation of nearly twelve thousand feet. I carried a compass, an altimeter and a radiation detector.

Most of the people in the Mecoya area said the object went to Cerro Bravo in Argentine territory. A sheepherder said the object exploded in the air near Mecoya and changed direction from the southwest to a more southerly direction.

Apparently, the object crashed into a buttress of Cerro Bravo at about ten thousand feet in height. There, a rockslide can be seen superimposed on the top of an older, natural slide. The difference is clear and can be noticed by the different coloration of the rock. In summing up, we have a complicated problem. One large object came from Sucre to Tarija and changed course, and other objects more or less at the same time came from Emborozu, Palca and Zaire (all southeast of Cerro Bravo).

The first object's form can't be determined but everybody said it was more or less long, but the others were long and thin like a pencil with a pointed nose and spitting fire from the back. They are maneuverable. They can change directions and they can rise. That's the truth. One of the objects—I'm not sure which—crashed into the mountain and produced an explosion that was heard in La Mamora, Padcaya, Cañas, Camacho and up to Oran in Argentina.

A woman named Guillermina de Antelo, who was in Tarija on the day in question, told Pratt a notable story, too:

An object reported in Columbia crashed into Cerro Bravo mountain, according to a sheepherder who saw it.

> I saw a round object like a disc with lights coming out of the back, like fireworks. They were very bright colors, plenty of colors, and most of them were startling pink and yellow. It shocked me. They weren't flames. They were more like beams of light. The object itself was in front and the lights streamed out behind. The object was about the size of my hand in the sky and was round like a disc.
>
> At first, it seemed slow but then it was very fast and I thought it was going to crash. It was very beautiful. It was like a record or plate from the bottom or edge. I saw it as completely round and I think that when other people say they thought it was long, it was because of the rays of light coming back. It was trailing the rays of light behind, maybe three times as long as the disc itself. The rays were sort of coming back to a point, giving it a sort of fish shape.

Bob Pratt's assessment:

> Most likely, something did crash into Cerro Bravo, but whether it was a meteor, a missile or a malfunctioning flying saucer, we may never know. People who saw something flying through the sky gave so many differing descriptions that it could have been any of the three. However, the flight characteristics and the different directions the object took seem to rule out a meteor or any missile, except perhaps for a Cruise-type missile, and that is hardly likely. There is no evidence it was a flying saucer, either, although the descriptions of some witnesses—particularly in the Tarija, Padcaya, Rosillas, Cañas and Mecoya areas—certainly indicate it was an object much like those seen elsewhere in the world.

To this day, the true nature of the events on Taire Mountain, Bolivia, in May 1978 remain shrouded in mystery, as does NASA's secret agenda to uncover the full facts surrounding the UFO phenomenon.

Smithsonian Secrets

The Smithsonian Institution's website says this about its history:

> The Smithsonian Institution was established with funds from James Smithson (1765–1829), a British scientist who left his estate to the United States to found "at Washington, under the name of the Smithsonian Institution, an establishment for the increase and diffusion of knowledge." On August 10, 1846, the U.S. Senate passed the act organizing the Smithsonian Institution, which was signed into law by President James K. Polk. Congress authorized acceptance of the Smithson bequest on July 1, 1836, but it took another ten years of debate before the Smithsonian was founded! Once established, the Smithsonian became part of the process of developing an American national identity—an identity rooted in exploration, innovation, and a unique American style. That process continues today as the Smithsonian looks toward the future.

It's a little-known fact that the Smithsonian has several tales of conspiracy and cover-up attached to them. We'll begin with an account prepared by a man named Augustus Mitchell, M.D., who revealed a startling tale from Amelia Island, Florida, back in the mid-1800s, specifically in 1848. Mitchell wrote the following, which is in the public domain, that I have shared with you in uninterrupted fashion. It deals with nothing less than a mysterious, ancient race of giants. While the remains were supposedly sent to the Smithsonian for study, to this date, they cannot be found—which is deeply intriguing, to say the very least:

> While in the South during the winter of 1848, pursuing the study and collecting specimens of ornithology, I was impelled by curios-

ity to examine a mound of a moderate size situated on the southern portion of Amelia Island, Florida, being kindly furnished with colored laborers, and aided by Dr. R. Harrison.

This mound was about 15 feet in height, and 30 feet in diameter at the base, flattened and worn by attrition for ages; there having been two growths of live-oak upon it, as stated by an old Spanish inhabitant of the place. The soil composing the mound was of a light sandy, yellowish loam.

We commenced the examination by cutting a trench 4 feet wide directly through the center, from the apex to the base, and then another trench at right angles to the former. The excavation revealed a number of relics, and the mode of burial of the mound-builders. They must have commenced by digging into the surface of the ground about 2 feet; then, partially filling the excavation with oyster-shells, they placed their dead on these in a sitting posture, their legs bent under them, with their faces to the east, and their arms crossed upon the breast, and next spread over them a stratum of earth. It is evident that in the successive burials the earth was reopened, and the additional bodies were placed close either to the back or side of those which had been previously interred, until the whole of the first layer was complete; then the circumference of the mound was walled in by a compost of marsh-mud; and then another layer of oyster-shells was placed over the heads of the first layer of bodies, and a continuation of the mud wall, until the superincumbent layer completed the mound to its apex.

Full three centuries must have rolled their tempests over this aboriginal repository of the dead. I quite expected to find everything like mortal remains returned to dust. But in this I was in error, as throughout the mound parts or complete portions of the bony structure still remained; those on the southern or sunny side being in a more perfect state of preservation. Counting the remains existing in the different layers of this ancient tumulus, it must have contained about four hundred individuals.

As we proceeded with our work, the interior of the mound presented many objects of interest to the ethnologist. We could not, however, secure many of these, since they crumbled, except the teeth, to dust as soon as exposed to the air. I had therefore to study them mostly in the earth, carefully scraping it away with a knife.

The conformation of the crania found in this mound appears to differ somewhat from that of the present Indians; the facial angle less, with superior depth of the frontal region, and greater capacity for the anterior lobes of the brain; the outer surface of the skull somewhat oval, smooth, and regular; frontal sinuses large; high cheekbones; cavity of the antrum large; orbital cavity of the eye deep and large; occipital protuberance very large, with a great development of the organs of philoprogenitiveness; superior depth of the base of the inferior maxillary bone; rough serratures and deep depressions for the attachments of powerful muscles of that bone.

The teeth of many of the crania of this mound were, without exceptions, in a perfect state of preservation, the vitrified enamel of these organs being capable of resisting exposure for centuries. These teeth presented distinctive appearances throughout, in the absence of the pointed canines; the incisors, canine, cuspides, and bicuspides all presented flat crowns, worn to smoothness by the attrition of sand and teeth showed the dental nerve to be protected by an unusual thickness on the surface of the crown. Not one carious tooth was found among the hundreds in the mound. Many were entire in the lower jaw, the whole compactly and firmly set. In some the second set was observed; while one jaw had evident signs of a third set, a nucleus of a tooth being seen beneath the neck of a tooth of a very old jaw, whose alveolar process was gone,

Founded in 1846, the Smithsonian Institution in Washington, D.C., is a collection of museums and research centers run by the U.S. government. Because it is part of the government, perhaps it is not surprising that the Smithsonian is involved in some cover-ups of its own.

and the whole lower jaw ossified to a sharp edge; none showing the partial loss of teeth by caries and decay.

Some of the skulls showed evident marks of death by violence, as from the hands of the enemy in war. In one instance the flint arrowhead was seen sticking in the left parietal bone. A number of skulls were broken in, mostly at the vertex, seemingly by that rude weapon, the stone battle-ax, which was so effective on the skulls of the Spaniards in the early periods of their settlement of Florida. It is evident that sanguinary conflicts often took place between tribes of the mainland, in their disputations for those enviable islands of the sea-coast, abounding then in spontaneous productions and surrounded by fish and oysters. No remains of these, much below adult age, were found; the weak and slender frame had returned to dust. All that could be traced of their mortality was a carbonized deposit in the clean sand, with here and there a small fragment of bone.

Pursuing my investigations and excavating farther toward the southeast face of the mound, I came upon the largest-sized stone ax I have ever seen or that had ever been found in that section of the country. Close to it was the largest and most perfect cranium of the mound, not crushed by the pressure of the earth, complete in its form, quite dry, and no sand in its cavity; together with its inferior maxillary bone, with all the teeth in the upper and lower jaws. Near by the side of this skull were the right femoris, the tibia, the humerus, ulna, and part of the radius, with a portion of the pelvis directly under the skull. All of the other bones of this large skeleton were completely or partially decayed. Contiguous to this was nearly a quart of red ocher, and quite the same quantity of what seemed to be pulverized charcoal, as materials of war-paint. Anticipating a perfect specimen in this skull, I was doomed to disappointment; for, after taking it out of the earth and setting it up, so that I could view the fleshless face of this gigantic savage, in the space of two hours it crumbled to pieces, except small portions. According to the measurement of the bones of this skeleton, its height must have been quite 7 feet.

There were three distinct rude ornaments in this mound. First, the vertebrae of a fish, painted with red ocher, and well preserved. Second, a hexagonal bead, made from the tooth of the alligator, (not painted.) Third, the internal lamina of an oyster-shell, cut into small circular spangles, pierced with a hole in the center, and threaded with the fibrillæ of the tendon of some animal, closely strung, and painted with red ocher.

Coal was freely diffused throughout the mound, which contained but little pottery. Two stone hatchets were found, and a small stone ax, in addition to the large one described. This instrument bore evident marks of fire.

There is one large mound on the eastern end of Amelia Island, Florida, and two mounds on the central portion of Cumberland Island, Georgia, likewise most of the islands on that coast, from which could be obtained large collections of materials for the advancement of ethnological science.

On similar territory, a story from the 1880s concerns the finding of an ancient, man-made mound found in Jo Daviess County, Illinois. Yet again, the startling remains have mysteriously vanished from the Smithsonian.

No. 5, the largest of the [mound] group was carefully examined. Two feet below the surface, near the apex, was a skeleton, doubtless an intrusive Indian burial. Near the original surface of the ground, several feet north of the center, were the much decayed skeletons of some 6 or 8 persons, of every size, from the infant to the adult. They were placed horizontally at full length, with the heads toward the south. A few perforated Unio shells and some rude stone skinners and scrapers were found with them. Near the original surface, 10 or 12 feet from the center, on the lower side, lying at full length upon its back, was one of the largest skeletons discovered by the Bureau agents, the length as proved by actual measurement being between 7 and 8 feet. It was all clearly traceable, but crumbled to pieces immediately after removal from the hard earth in which it was encased.

With this were three thin, crescent-shaped pieces of roughly hammered, native copper, respectively 6, 8, and 10 inches in length, with small holes along the convex margin; a number of elongate copper beads made by rolling together thin sheets; and a chert lance-head over 11 inches long. Around the neck was a series of bear teeth, which doubtless formed a necklace; there were also several upon the wrists. Lying across the thighs were dozens of small copper beads, which perhaps once adorned the fringe of a hunting shirt. These were formed by rolling slender wire-like strips into small rings.

London's Secret and Savage Underground

The United Kingdom's famous London Underground serves commuters traveling throughout Greater London as well as select parts of Buckinghamshire, Hertfordshire, and Essex. It can also claim the title of the world's oldest underground system of its type, given that it opened up for business on January 10, 1863. Today, more than 150 years after its initial construction, the London Underground has no fewer than 268 stations and approximately 250 miles (400 kilometers) of track, thus making it the longest—as well as certainly the oldest—subsurface railway system on the planet. Moreover, in 2007, *one billion* passengers were recorded as having used the Underground.

According to a number of select souls, however, the London Underground has played host to far more than mere tracks, trains, and a near-endless number of travelers. Deep within the winding tunnels of this subsurface labyrinth, bizarre and terrible things—many of a wild man variety—are rumored to seethe and fester and possibly even feed, too. British authorities are doing all they can to keep the lid on the chaos and carnage that threaten to spread deep below the streets of the nation's historic capital city. We're talking about conspiracies of the underground type.

Stories of strange creatures—many of a definitively cryptozoological nature—lurking in the London Underground have circulated for years, chiefly in fictional, on-screen format. Such examples include (a) the 1967 production of *Quatermass and the Pit*, in which bizarre, mutated, and diminutive ape men—who were the subject of advanced genetic experiments, undertaken millions of years earlier, by visiting Martians—appear in the London Underground of the 1960s in the form of spectral, manifested, inherited memories; (b) *The Web of Fear*—a *Dr. Who* adventure that surfaced in the following year,

1968, that sees the doctor and his comrades doing battle with robotic yetis on the Underground; (c) *An American Werewolf in London*—a 1981 film in which the beast of the title feasts on a doomed, late-night rail traveler; and (d) *Reign of Fire*, a 2002 production starring Christian Bale and Matthew McConaughey that revolves around literal fire-breathing dragons that burst forth from the old tunnels of the Underground and decimate Britain and, eventually, the rest of the planet, too.

Some of the older tales of creaturelike entities prowling the tunnels under London were incorporated into a less well-known, fictionalized movie. Its name: *Death Line*. Made in 1972, it starred horror film stalwarts Christopher Lee and Donald Pleasence and related the saga of a collapse, in the latter part of the nineteenth century, at a then new station being built at Russell Square—which happens to be a real station on the Underground. Unfortunately, when the disaster occurs, a significant number of workers—both men and women—are killed, or, rather, they are *presumed* killed. When the company funding the project goes bankrupt, all efforts to try to dig out the bodies and give them a decent burial are quickly, quietly, and conveniently forgotten.

> Had the plans gone ahead, the company would have learned to its horror that the workers did not die. Instead, they found themselves trapped underground....

Had the plans gone ahead, the company would have learned to its horror that the workers did not die. Instead, they found themselves trapped underground and forced to make new lives for themselves in their permanent, subsurface home, which they do by living on just about anything and everything, and anyone and everyone, that dares to cross their path or stumble upon their darkened abode.

As *Death Line* tells it, some eight decades on, the final few offspring of the original workers are still valiantly clinging on to life. Their existence, however, is a distinctly poor one: afflicted by a host of genetic abnormalities caused by inbreeding and a lack of regular nourishment, their minds are reduced to truly primitive levels, and their bodies are overwhelmingly diseased and corrupted. As for their only source of food, it comes in the form of the occasional, unfortunate user of the Underground who, if the circumstances are in their favor, they can secretly grab, kill, and, ultimately, devour.

Death Line is an entertaining and odd little film that seldom gets the airing it deserves, and it's one that leaves the viewer with much to think about and muse upon when it comes to the matter of wild people living among us. However, some believe the film is more than just mere fiction—*far* more than just mere fiction. Some are firmly of the opinion that the story it relates is 100 percent *fact*—albeit, admittedly, difficult-to-confirm fact—and that far below the capital, primitive man-beasts roam, forage, slaughter, and feed.

The famous Baker Street station of the London Underground is part of a labyrinth under the English city that includes hundreds of miles of tunnels. Some say cryptozoogical creatures inhabit some of its dark corners.

Before his passing in 2007, Frank Wiley, who spent his entire working life in the British Police Force, told a bizarre and unsettling tale of his personal memories and investigations of a number of very weird killings on the London Underground, always late at night, in a particular period of time that covered 1967 to 1969. The killings, Wiley said, occurred on at least three stations and were hushed up by the police under the guise of being the unfortunate results of particularly vicious, late-night muggings.

In reality, Wiley explained, the muggings were nothing of the sort at all. They were far, far more horrific in nature. There were, he recalled, seven such deaths during the time period that he was assigned to the investigations. As for the particular cases of which Wiley did have personal awareness, he said the *modus operandi* was always exactly the same: the bodies of the people—a couple of whom were commuters and the rest hobos simply looking for shelter on cold, windswept nights—were found, always after at least 10:00 P.M., a significant distance into the tunnels, with arms and/or legs viciously amputated—or possibly even *gnawed* off. Stomachs were ripped open, innards were torn out, and throats were violently slashed. A definitive man-eater—or, worse still, a whole group of man-eaters—was seemingly prowling around the most shadowy corners of London's dark underworld after sunset, and it, or they, had only one cold and lethal goal: to seek out fresh flesh with which to nourish their ever-hungry bellies.

Could it have been the case that the killings were the work of a rampaging animal, possibly one that had escaped from a local, London-based zoo or a private menagerie, that was now wildly on the loose far below the capital city, or might the deaths have been simply due to desperate, suicidal people who threw themselves under the speeding trains and whose remains were violently dragged into the tunnels under the steel wheels of the racing carriages? Wiley strongly believed that neither of these scenarios provided adequate explanations.

A further, very good reason existed why the deaths were not ascribed to the work of wild beasts or suicides: namely, the presence of a terrifying-looking character seen at some point in 1968 by two workmen who were repairing a particular stretch of track on the Bakerloo Line (a fourteen-mile-long section of the London Underground that was constructed in 1906). The savage character, stated Wiley, was a bearded, wild-haired man, dressed in tattered, filthy clothing.

When one of the workers challenged the mysterious figure with a large ratchet, the man came closer in a weird, faltering, stumbling style. To the horror of the pair, he held his arms out in front of him, bared a mouth of decayed teeth in their direction, and uttered a low and threatening growl. The strange figure then slowly backed away, eventually turning and then suddenly running deeper into the tunnel, until he was finally, and forever, lost from view. Unsurprisingly, and rather sensibly, the fraught workmen elected not to give chase but instead raced to the nearest police station and summoned the authorities, who, said Wiley, questioned the petrified men vigorously.

Wiley further added that secret orders quickly came down to the police investigators on the case from the British government's Home Office, the work of which focuses on a host of issues relative to national security, to wrap everything up, and very quickly, too. Intriguingly, Wiley maintained that secret liaisons with Home Office personnel revealed that unverified rumors existed of deeper, very ancient, crudely built tunnels—reportedly that dated back centuries, long, long before the advent of trains, railways, and such— existing far below the London Underground. Some even speculated that they may have been constructed as far back as the Roman invasion of Britain that began in A.D. 43. Precisely who had constructed the older tunnels, and who it was who might have emerged from them to wreak deadly havoc on the Underground in the 1960s, was never revealed to Wiley's small team of personnel.

He said: "Probably no-one really knew, anyway. Only that someone, like the character seen by the workmen, was coming up from somewhere, killing, taking parts of the bodies, and then they were always gone again. It all got pushed under the rug when the Home Office said so. And when the last killing I was involved in [occurred], in 1969, I didn't hear much after that; just rumors there might have been more deaths in the '70's upward. I don't know."

Wiley's last comments on his controversial claims, in 2004, went as follows: "There's more to the [*Death Line*] film than people know. My thought then, and which it still is today, is someone making the film heard the stories, the deaths we investigated. They had to have; the film was too close to what happened. And I think we didn't have control of the tunnels, and someone up in the government knew. Perhaps it's still going on. That would be a thought."

With Wiley's final sentence, I have absolutely no argument.

The London Underground's British Museum Station closed its doors on September 25, 1933. For many years prior to its closure, however, a local myth circulated to the effect that the ghost of an ancient Egyptian haunted the station. Dressed in a loincloth and headdress, the figure would emerge late at night into the labyrinth of old tunnels. In fact, the story gained such a hold that a London newspaper even offered a significant monetary reward to anyone who was willing to spend the night there. Somewhat surprisingly, not a single, solitary soul took the newspaper up on its generous offer.

The story took a far stranger turn after the station was shut down, however. The comedy-thriller movie *Bulldog Jack*, which was released in 1935, included in its story a secret tunnel that ran from the station to the Egyptian Room at the British Museum. The station in the film is a wholly fictional one dubbed Bloomsbury; however, the scenario presented in the film was specifically based upon the enduring legend of the ghost of British Museum Station.

> For many years prior to [the British Museum Station's] closure, however, a local myth circulated to the effect that the ghost of an ancient Egyptian haunted the station.

Oddly enough, on the exact same night that the movie was released in British cinemas, two women disappeared from the platform at Holborn, which just happened to be the next station along from the British Museum. Strange marks were later found on the walls of the closed station, and more sightings of the ghost were reported, along with weird moaning noises coming from behind the walls of the tunnels. Not surprisingly, tales began to quickly circulate to the effect that the police had uncovered some dark and terrible secret—about a paranormal killer on the tracks—that had to be kept hidden from the populace at all costs. In other words, a strange, yet eerily similar, precursor existed to the 1960s recollections of Frank Wiley, one that predated his own experiences by more than three decades.

London Underground officials were, for a significant period of time, forced to dismiss the story, and the existence of a secret tunnel extending from the station to the museum's Egyptian Room has always been denied outright. Nevertheless, the story was resurrected in Keith Lowe's novel of 2001, *Tunnel Vision*, in which the lead character states, while trying to both impress and scare his girlfriend at the same time: "If you listen carefully when you're standing at the platform at Holborn, sometimes—just sometimes—you can hear the wailing of Egyptian voices floating down the tunnel towards you."

Might the loincloth-wearing "Egyptian" actually have been one of Frank Wiley's savage underground cannibals? If so, were the tales of a police cover-up an indication that officialdom may have secretly known about the capital city's wild men for far longer than even Wiley could have guessed?

In some respects, the story of Frank Wiley eerily parallels that of a man named Colin Campbell, who maintains that while traveling home on the London Underground in the mid-1960s, he had a nightmarish encounter with a very similar beast. According to Campbell, it was late at night and, rather surprisingly, he was the only person to get off the train at its scheduled stop on the Northern Line. As the train pulled away from the unusually deserted and deathly and eerily silent platform, and as Campbell made his way toward the exit, he claims to have heard a strange growl coming from behind him. He quickly spun around and was shocked to see a large, hairy, apelike animal lumbering across the platform toward the track, seemingly mumbling to itself and no one else as it did so.

Most bizarre of all, however, was the fact that the beast was definitively spectral, rather than flesh and blood. Around three quarters of its body was above the platform, while its legs were curiously near-transparent and, incredibly, passed right through the platform. Campbell further asserts that as he stood in awe, too shocked to even try to move, the beast continued to walk through the concrete, right onto the tracks, then straight through the wall directly behind the tunnel—all the time paying absolutely no attention to Campbell in the slightest.

Are savage, devolved humans really living—in literal cannibalistic style—deep under London? Are the old tunnels actually home to ghostly ape men of the type encountered by Colin Campbell back in the 1960s or are such tales simply borne out of legends provoked by the likes of *Dr. Who* and *Quatermass and the Pit*? If not the latter, then some might say that such accounts have a significant bearing upon the reports of the British wild man—particularly if the creatures have found ways to exit the tunnels from time to time and have made their way around select portions of the city and the surrounding countryside by the camouflage of a dark and disturbing night.

In his first novel, *Tunnel Vision*, Keith Lowe wrote about a man who has life-changing experiences at each station of the London Underground.

Nuclear Nightmare Conspiracies

Midway through the summer of 2018, something unforeseen and unsettling occurred. In the second week of August, three people contacted me with eerily similar stories of atomic Armageddon. On August 8, I received a Facebook message from a guy named Kenny, who had a horrific dream of nuclear war two nights earlier. Kenny lives in San Bernardino, California, and woke up suddenly in the dead of night in a state of terror. As Kenny explained, in his dream, he was sitting in the living room of a house in a small town outside of Lubbock, Texas. Kenny had no idea of the name of the town, only that he knew it was near Lubbock—a place he has never visited. In the dream, Kenny heard a sudden, deep, rumbling sound that seemed to be coming from somewhere far away. He went to the screen door, puzzled, and peered outside. To his horror, Kenny could see way off in the distance the one thing that none of us ever want to see: a huge, nuclear mushroom cloud looming large and ominous on the horizon.

Kenny continued that, in his dream, he was rooted to the spot, his legs shaking and his heart pounding. He could only stand and stare as the huge, radioactive cloud extended to a height of what was clearly miles. The entire sky turned black, and suddenly, a huge wave of flame and smoke—hundreds of feet high—raced across the entire landscape, completely obliterating everything in its path. In seconds, another explosion occurred, again way off in the distance but from the opposite direction. Nuclear war had begun. That was when Kenny woke up—thankful that it was all a dream but disturbed by the fact that, as Kenny told me, the dream seemed like something far more than just a regular dream. Kenny felt he had seen something that was still yet to come: a glimpse of the near future. Further dreams of nuclear nightmares came my way.

Kimberly J. emailed me on August 10 and shared with me a story of disturbing proportions. She lives in Chicago, Illinois, and had a somewhat similar dream to that of Kenny but on August 9. The scenario was almost identical: a gigantic explosion destroyed her home city, killing millions and vaporizing everything for miles. A huge mushroom cloud was hanging where, only seconds earlier, a bustling city of close to three million people had been. In this case, however, was more: amid the carnage and the chaos, a large "bird-man," as Kimberly described it, hovered over the massive cloud, "watching the end of us."

It very much reminded me of the dark specter of the Mothman, which appeared in the town of Point Pleasant, West Virginia, the sightings of which culminated in the tragic collapse of the city's Silver Bridge and led to the drownings of dozens of locals.

It just so happens that, two months earlier, M. J. Banias wrote an article at the *Mysterious Universe* website titled "Chicago's Current Mothman Flap 'A Warning,' Says Expert." In his article, Banias described a then-recent wave of Mothman-type sightings in and around the city. The article quoted researcher Lon Strickler, who looked into these particular cases, which led to the publication of his book on the Mothman Chicago wave titled *Mothman Dynasty*. Strickler said:

There are many opinions as to why these sightings are occurring, including a general feeling that unfortunate events may be in the city's future.... At this point, I feel that this being may be attempting to distinguish a connection between locales within the city and future events. The witnesses have been very steadfast with what they have seen, and refuse to embellish on their initial descriptions. Each witness has had a feeling of dread and foreboding, which I believe translates into a warning of some type.

Then, on August 12, I received yet another Facebook message of a similar nature; this one was from Jacob, an American who is now a resident of Mulhouse, France (oddly enough, it's a city I spent a lot of time in during my teenage years). In Jacob's dream, an emergency broadcast message appeared on his

Dreams of nuclear annihalation are being accompanied by visions of the Mothman, leaving people with an eldritch sensation of foreboding.

TV screen, warning people to take cover: the nukes were flying. That was it: just a few brief seconds of mayhem in the dream state, but it was still an undeniably nightmarish night for Jacob.

Of course, all of this could have been as a result of the growing tensions between North Korea and the United States. In fact, I'm sure that has a great deal to do with it. On August 9, the London *Independent* newspaper ran an article on the North Korea issue that stated, in part: "While it's unclear if North Korea can successfully target US cities like Denver and Chicago with a nuclear ICBM, it's similarly unknown if US defense systems can strike it down—adding to American anxieties." The issue of Chicago being a possible target has been mentioned in multiple news outlets. Such stories almost certainly would have been worrying to Kimberly J., who lives in the heart of the city.

I wondered: Should we be concerned that three people had, inside one week, nightmares about nuclear war? I thought: I wouldn't be surprised if hundreds of people—all across the world—have had such dreams. Maybe even more. After all, the climate was hardly a stable one. It was—and still is—a time of madness, and Kimberly's sighting in her dream of a Mothman-type creature—which has been seen around Chicago in the past few months and been linked to a possible looming disaster in the area—would likely have led some to believe that this was more than just bad dreams. Also, take note of the fact that I got a cluster of such reports across a very short period of time, which was not exactly what I considered to be good news.

Then, this report came in from Stephen Polak: "As a Chicago resident myself who has recently had a dream of being consumed [by] an enormous wall of fire, I find all of this rather disquieting…."

Five days later, the news got worse: Chris O'Brien, a well-known author of many books, including *Stalking the Herd* and *Secrets of the Mysterious Valley*, contacted me with a story to tell. It was not a good story. He said:

> Back in 2005 Grandfather Martin Gashweseoma, for many decades the "Fire Clan Prophecy Tablet" holder, spent a week with Naia and I at our home in Sedona, AZ. We had met him 10 years prior and we had become friendly with the then 83 year old Traditional Elder. During one conversation about the predicted "End of the Fourth World," I asked him how the dreaded "War of the Gourd of Ashes" would end. (In 1989, Martin announced the start of the final conflict would begin within the year and it did with "Desert Storm.") He said that North Korea would send fiery birds high in the sky to the US. I pressed him for further details suggesting maybe he meant China, and he said "No, Korea will be behind this attack, possibly w/ the help (or at the behest) of China." At the time Korea had no functioning nuclear weapons program and no

While there have been encouraging signs of peace such as this meeting between North Korea's Kim Jong-un and U.S. president Donald Trump, tensions between the two countries have caused great fears and anxieties about a possible nuclear war.

ICBMs. As we all know, this has changed.... Just thought I'd mention this!

The next development came on August 17. Jason M. reported:

I also have had a very powerful, lucid dream—in which Orlando, Florida (which is about two hours from me) was hit by a massive blast followed by a tremendous fireball and mushroom cloud. The dream felt incredibly real, and I was even able to interact realistically with those around me and see and feel their fear. It was truly horrific. As someone who has had dreams that have come to pass in great detail, I took serious note of the dream, and I spoke with my wife about it moments after I woke up. The dream was also notable to me because I recall specific details and dates about the attack, because in the dream I was reading a news article about a geopolitical crisis that was rapidly spiraling out of control. It left me with an overwhelming sense of dread and terror.

Jason added:

Here is the caveat. In my dream, I knew without doubt that the attack came from Russia, and those around me expressed a similar sentiment. In the news article I had been reading, it discussed how a crisis in the Ukraine had provoked a Russian invasion and a NATO response. I had this dream in early March 2014, just days before the Russian invasion of Crimea. To say that development freaked me out is a tremendous understatement. In the dream, the attack took place in September of 2015. I have no doubt of that.

I was very apprehensive throughout 2015 and kept a close eye on news events from Ukraine. While I was relieved that nothing happened, I knew that the dream was more than just fear playing out in my unconscious mind. Since that time, I have revisited the dream many times in deep meditative states to see what more I could learn from it.

He concluded:

What is my point here? I know that such a dream can be horrible and terrifying. It could even conceivably foreshadow coming events. However, I suspect something else is at play. I admit that I cannot be certain, but my conclusion about my own dream is that my unconscious mind was tapping into collective awareness and fear that was about to engulf the world about that particular crisis. I think I was seeing a potential outcome that was informed by the fear and imagination of millions around the world (or would be, since the crisis had not yet happened when I had the dream), not one that was fated to happen. I suppose there is no way to know but to wait and see. But I do think it is worth cautioning that such dreams could have many potential causes other than predicting actual nuclear annihilation. At least one can hope.

Also on August 17, "Red Pill Junkie," another regular contributor to *Mysterious Universe*, waded in with his own nightmare:

I don't live in Chicago but I had a similar dream on the night of August 6 (I remember the date well because I commented upon it with a friend on FB). I was with a group of people I didn't know and I looked outside and watched a ginormous mushroom cloud. It took a while for the thing to register but once everybody realized what we were seeing we all panicked and fled in search of refuge. I remember some tried to hide underground, but the blast buried them all alive. Then I woke up. I think this is the first time I've had a dream about nuclear Armageddon in a very long time.

On August 18, J. Griffin, commenting on the Chicago issue, said: "I'm in Chicago right now on business—the last street to my first destination was 'Nuclear Drive.' Go figure."

Jacqueline Bradley sent me the following on August 21, the details of a dream that seemed to involve small, tactical nuclear weapons in a forthcoming confrontation:

A few days ago I had a dream that several nuclear events occurred—in my dream I remember the term "thermonuclear." There were several of these events popping up (appeared to be everywhere and small versions of what we would ordinarily be aware of.) No one seemed to be very perturbed by these and people were just walking around, occasionally looking around and watching these. I was aware that if you were caught up in one and died it killed off your soul or spirit too. All this was happening in broad daylight on sunny days. The dream ended where I was in some kind of alley with an old-fashioned dustbin nearby. Suddenly I found myself "sinking" or evaporating and woke up. I wasn't scared by the dream, just puzzled. I too connected it with the tensions in N Korea. I've also been watching *Twin Peaks* and connected it with that, but not sure why.

One day later, Jill S. Pingleton wrote:

As a paranormal investigator and student of metaphysics, I, like many, are concerned about the prophetic potential of so many having these dreams/visions. However as a former MUFON Chief Investigator, I'm wondering if the people reporting these dreams and associations are Contactees [a reference to people in contact with extraterrestrial entities on a regular basis]?

My point is that Contactees frequently recount stories of viewing scenes of mass destruction placed in their mind's eye during encounters with ETs. I don't know if they are being given glimpses of the future or only a possible time line unless events can be changed. Like a wake-up call to Contactees to get involved and speak out for the sake of humanity. Perhaps that's also the mission of the Mothman. I wonder if any of these dreams/visions were preceded by an abduction event or if it's part of an ongoing "download" that so many Contactees experience. I think much can be learned from studying the Experiencers/Witnesses. So many questions!

Over at *Red Dirt Report*, Andrew W. Griffin commented on an August 2017 article I had written on the matter of Mothman and nuclear nightmares. In a feature of his own titled "Riders on the storm (Strange days have tracked us down)," he said: "Clearly we are entering very troubled waters. And it seems that the collective unconscious of humanity is clueing in that we are entering a perilous period in our history. So, when I saw Nick Redfern's new post at *Mysterious Universe*—'Mothman and Nuclear Nightmares'—I took pause, as he notes that 'in the last week, three people have contacted me with eerily similar stories' involving nuclear apocalypse."

Interestingly, Andrew added that in relation to Kenny's dream of a nuclear bomb exploding near Lubbock, Texas, it was "not unlike my own dream that I wrote about on Jan. 26, 2017, which involved nuclear detonations near Joplin, Missouri." Andrew said of his dream:

> We were in a car in the vicinity of Joplin, Missouri—something I noted in my mind in that it is on that nexus of high weirdness 37 degrees north and 94 degrees west (which I recently addressed here)—and nuclear explosions, followed by menacing mushroom clouds, are going off at various intervals.… And yet as the nuclear blasts send radioactive debris through the town and infecting every-

Mothman began as a monstrous figure from West Virginian folklore, but stories of this creature have been spreading.

> thing in its path, I seem to be the only one alarmed by what is happening around us. The whole experience has the feeling of a guided tour through a park or historic site.…

Then, a Facebook message came in from Andy Tomlinson of the city of Manchester, England. Back in early June of this year, Andy had a dream of being in a deserted London. The city was not destroyed or in flames. It was, said Andy, "like they had all been evacuated," which is an interesting phrase to use. Well, I say the city was deserted. It was, except for two things: one was the sight of "a massive big black bird over [the Houses of] Parliament." Then, as Andy walked the streets, trying to figure out what had happened, he had that feeling of someone watching him. He turned around to see a man in a black trench coat right behind him. The man was pale, gaunt, and—as Andy worded it—"had a funny smile." Andy's description sounds very much like a certain sinister character in the saga of the Mothman—one Indrid Cold. Andy then woke up with his heart pounding, relieved that it had just been a dream … or was it something more than just a dream?

Without doubt, one of the most chilling stories came from Anna Jordan. On August 25, she sent me this:

> Hi Nick, So, this dream was one I had about 25 years ago or so. Here's the dream: I was standing in the living room of the apartment I lived in at the time. I had three small kids on the floor

around me playing and *Sesame Street* was on the TV. (At the time, I only had two children, but later had a third.) So, PBS is on with *Sesame Street*, but there's a break-in on the channel like when they have breaking news. It just showed like a PBS symbol and a count-down and then this man, who I knew was in the White House, came on. He was sitting at a desk, very solemn. I swear to you, it was Mike Pence. I have waited, studying White House faces for all these years waiting to see this face. The white hair, the face, the voice … it's him, I'm sure. He just looks at the camera and says that he was very sorry, it was too late, and wished the world good luck. I don't know how, but I knew he was talking about a nuclear war. In the dream, I felt my heart drop. Then I woke up. That's about it.

Less than twenty-four hours later, Elaine Clayton sent me the following message on Facebook:

Over the decades, but more so recently, I've had dreams of holo-gram writings and ships in the sky. I believe some of these dreams were actually astral travels (being scanned in a space ship, etc.) and I used to be woken up by—and this is the best way to describe it—robotic forms with hologram like presence, brightly colored and with personality. I asked to stop seeing those when I could not tell who they were although they seemed benevolent. Those were visions, they happened with my eyes open sitting up. But most dreams are about space ships of magnitude often geometrically fas-cinating. And several have shown me that in the distance that I perceive as "in the West" atomic bombs going off although they're only more like dirty bombs, not fully atomic.

The last one went like this: I was standing looking up at a silently moving, ethereal looking space ship. It was huge and had smoke streaks coming off it toward earth. It was colorful and its structure appearing smoky, multidimensional. There was a peaceful feeling more than military or fearful. Although again it was extremely dominant and intelligent energy. I then turned to look at the land-scape behind me and saw all at once about 5 or 6 bombs being dropped, immediately exploding in small mushroom clouds of fire. I registered my sense of where they landed—to the north east of Manhattan—I thought, and knew they missed their target.

But in the dream I worried about my sister knowing she was there. But then when I woke up I figured it out—my sister lives in Col-orado Springs [Colorado] and very near NORAD. I believe who-ever dropped the bombs dropped them from a satellite with the intention to take out NORAD. But they missed. I later learned that Kim Jong Un has a map showing his plan to bomb NORAD but his map is not smart and he'd actually be bombing Louisiana. I may post this on my own site. I am so glad you study all these things.

As August came to its close, I was contacted by an old English friend, Sally, whom I had not seen in years. She suggested that I should read *Warday*, a 1984 novel written by Whitley Strieber and James Kunetka. I had actually read the book years ago, and it made for grim and disturbing reading. It's an excellently written book that tells the story of a limited nuclear attack on the United States that still kills more than sixty million people from the initial atomic blasts, famine and starvation, radiation, and a wave of out-of-control influenza. Strieber and Kunetka skillfully tell a story that could, one day, become all too real. In *Warday*, the United States is a shell of its former self, with chaos, death, and destruction rampant. *Warday* makes it very clear that had the confrontation between the United States and the old Soviet Union escalated beyond a limited one, the result would have been unthinkable: complete and utter obliteration in the northern hemisphere.

As we chatted online, I asked Sally something along the lines of: "Why should I go back and read *Warday* now?" I got a one sentence reply: "Check out pages 213–217." Admittedly, it was probably in the early 1990s when I read *Warday* and I had forgotten many of the specifics of the story beyond the crux of it, so I checked out those pages—and what did I find? Well, I'll tell you what I found: a five-page chapter on a creature not at all unlike Mothman.

This issue of a Mothman-type creature being associated with a devastating attack on the United States in fictional form (Warday, of course) eerily parallels what people were talking about in August 2017: dreams of a nuclear event and a tie-in with Mothman.

A couple of quotes from *Warday* will give you an idea of the nature of this aspect of the story. The title of the chapter is "Rumors: Mutants and Super-Beasts." We're told, under a heading of "Rumor," that "there is a gigantic beast with bat wings and red, burning eyes that has attacked adults and carried off children. The creature stands seven feet tall and makes a soft whistling noise. It is often seen on roofs in populated areas, but only at night."

A further extract from Strieber's book concerns the testimony of an alleged eyewitness to the flying beast in California: "I had

Whitley Strieber (shown here with his wife, Anne, at a MUFON lecture) wrote the 1984 nuclear war novel *Warday* with James Kunetka. In it, there is, interestingly, a mention of the Mothman.

just gotten off the Glendale trolley when I heard this soft sort of cooing noise coming from the roof of a house. The sound was repeated and I turned to look toward the house. Standing on the roof was what looked like a man wrapped in a cloak. Then it spread its wings and whoosh! it was right on top of me."

It's important to note—in light of the Mothman-like references—that *Warday* is not a piece of wild science fiction. The story of the Mothman-type beast is only included in the book to demonstrate how, in the aftermath of the war, strange and bizarre rumors surfaced and spread among the survivors. I did, however, find it intriguing that *Warday* makes a connection between a nuclear war and "a gigantic beast with bat wings and red, burning eyes." This was, of course, what was being reported in mid-2017.

Interestingly, in 1995, Strieber himself had a graphic dream of a nuclear explosion that destroys Washington, D.C., in 2036—which sees the end of the government as we know it today and the rise, in the wake of the disaster, of a full-blown dictatorship. In his 1997 book *The Secret School*, Strieber says of this dream (or of a brief view of what is to come via a future self) that "Washington, D.C., is in ruins. However, this isn't the center of the memory. The center of the memory is that it was suddenly and completely destroyed by an atomic bomb, and nobody knows who detonated it."

Protests against nuclear weapons are ongoing, as this 2016 demonstration outside the White House shows. Strieber was worried about nuclear war, too, back in 1995, when he had a nightmare about the nation's capital lying in ruins.

The final message on this topic came from Roger Pingleton—the wife of Jill S. Pingleton, who had contacted me a few days earlier. On August 28, Roger wrote:

Hi Nick. My wife informed me of the subject matter of some of your recent articles, and encouraged me to reach out with my experiences.

Before Jill and I were married, I drove to Serpent Mound in Ohio on 11/11/2011 to meet with Jill and a group of people. I've always had weird feelings about the Ohio River valley, the mound building Indians, and the deities they worshiped there. And being that Serpent Mound is so close to Point Pleasant, I couldn't resist driving on to Point Pleasant, WV, after Serpent Mound. I slept a few hours in my pickup and drove on to Point Pleasant in the wee hours of the morning. I'd estimate my arrival to have been sometime between 3am and 4am. The best I can describe the feeling I got driving through the back roads of WV is visceral. I felt like I was being called to be there at that early hour.

Driving in the back roads near the old munitions facility, I saw, up ahead, two bright circular lights above the road. My thought was that they were circular tail lights, that there was a hill up ahead and that I might catch up with the vehicle. The thing is, as I drove, I discovered there was no hill ahead of me, which freaked me out, because those two red lights were definitely higher than they should have been. Then I started thinking, "What vehicle has round tail lights these days?" A corvette maybe, but they have more than two.

I couldn't help but think I had seen the eyes of the Mothman. I know it's weak evidence, but I can't come up with another plausible explanation. Not long after that, I had an apocalyptic dream. We live just south of Indianapolis. The city is on a grid and as such it's easy to tell directions. In my dream there was a giant explosion on the NW–SE diagonal axis. When I woke I worried that the city was Cincinnati, since it was to the SE of Indy, and my sister lives there, but then I realized it could also have been Chicago, which is to the NW of Indy. I didn't put these two events together until the Mothman sightings occurred. I truly hope I am wrong about these connections.

I hoped that Roger was wrong, and I hope that just about everyone else who had such dreams was wrong, too. To be sure, it was a dark and tense period, with so many people having terrifying dreams of a worldwide, disastrous nuclear war. So far, those nightmares have not come true. I hoped—and still hope—they never will come true.

* * *

It's important to note that as an abductee and as someone living in Chicago, Jayne knew all about the stories of the Mothman being seen and of the fears that the sightings were a warning of something cataclysmic to come. She also spent quite a bit of time discussing such matters on a Facebook group devoted to the alien abduction issue. Why is it so important? Simply because it appears that it was as a result of monitoring multiple such groups online that the Department of Homeland Security (DHS) came across Jayne and her experiences.

It's important to note that nothing particularly stressful or sinister happened at the meeting. The man was barely through the front door when he assured Jayne that she was not in any way in trouble. That was a relief. Jayne invited him to take a seat, and she made coffee for both of them. The agent of the DHS came straight to the point: Due to the nature of the work of the agency—helping to keep the United States protected from hostile forces and sources—a small group within the DHS had been tasked to investigate the growing reports of people having apocalyptic dreams of a nuclear nature as well as the tie-in with the Mothman saga. As an aside, the man said that as this was a new and very alternative project for the DHS, the handful of people on board had all read John Keel's *The Mothman Prophecies* and had "taken a look" at various online groups that were discussing the issues of bad dreams, North Korea, nuclear weapons, and the end of civilization.

The man further explained—"confided" might be a better word—to Jayne that her name had come up as a result of it being in the database of yet another agency, unnamed, which was "aware" of her UFO- and alien abduction-themed experiences. All attempts on Jayne's part to get the name of the agency turned out to be useless. Citing national security reasons, the man apologized that he could not expand further on that issue, but he did want answers from Jayne.

The Department of Homeland Security, the man said, did not typically get involved in—and I quote Jayne's recollections—"*X-Files* things," except when national security was central to the matter. In this case, it most assuredly was. The man reeled off a number of questions about the history of Jayne's abduction experiences. She openly told him of her childhood encounters, her missing time experiences, and even the issue of the hybrid children and the Man in Black—all of which was preserved on a small digital recorder the man had brought with him, which, said Jayne, she was fine with him using.

The man particularly wanted to know about the dreams: When did they begin? Was Jayne able to discern which cities were attacked in her dreams? How powerful were the weapons? Were the attacks small or large in scale? Did she have any idea which nation it was that had attacked the United States? Did any indication exist in the dreams that America had been able to retaliate?

Jayne answered the questions as accurately as she could: The dreams had begun in the early part of March 2017. Chicago featured prominently in her nightmares, but not always. She also had a dream in which Seattle was annihilated. The weapons were clearly massively destructive, as Chicago was shown in her dreams to have been completely destroyed; hardly a soul was left alive. She had fragments of memories that led her to believe that the attack was initiated by China and North Korea, with some secret assistance from the Russians.

Most disturbing of all, Jayne believed that the attacking forces had somehow been able to disable the United States' entire military, thus leaving the nation completely open to attack. In her dreams, and two days before the attack, the Internet went down, followed quickly by the collapse of every electrical device in the United States. The country was in a state of anarchy.

Jayne told the Department of Homeland Security agent that this was the one part of the dream she couldn't understand—until, that is, she did some research online as to how such a thing might be achieved. She came across the matter of what is known as an electromagnetic pulse attack. For those who may not be aware of what this refers to, consider the words of Jean Baker McNeill

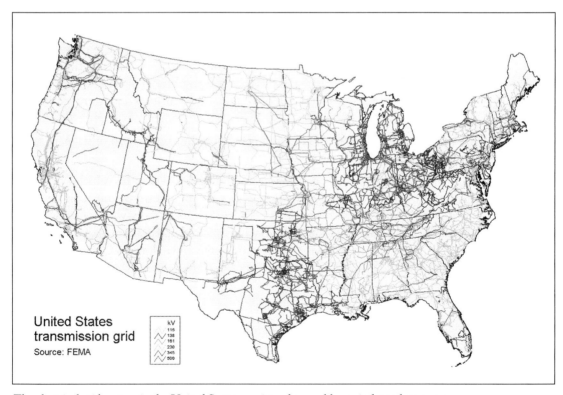

The electrical grid system in the United States consists of several large, independent systems, and an EMP could shut down the power to huge portions of the country with one blow.

and Richard Weitz, writing at The Heritage Foundation: "A major threat to America has been largely ignored by those who could prevent it. An electromagnetic pulse (EMP) attack could wreak havoc on the nation's electronic systems—shutting down power grids, sources, and supply mechanisms. An EMP attack on the United States could irreparably cripple the country."

How might the nation be crippled? *Business Insider*'s Dave Mosher says that "nuclear EMPs—if a detonation is large enough and high enough—can cover an entire continent and cripple tiny circuits inside modern electronics on a massive scale, according to U.S. government reports. The power grid, phone and internet lines, and other infrastructure that uses metal may also be prone to the effects, which resemble those of a devastating geomagnetic storm."

According to Jayne, it was this issue—of the United States being destroyed as a result of enemy nations using EMP-driven technology and then following up with a nationwide nuclear strike—that really caught the attention of her visitor from the government. Jayne felt that, given the somewhat slightly shocked look on his face, this was not the first time he had heard of this scenario.

The man went over several of the questions again, after which he thanked Jayne for her time. Notably, the man did not request that Jayne not talk about the interview. He simply thanked her and left. As for Jayne, she couldn't help but suspect that she was not the only person having nuclear nightmares who was getting a visit from the government. At the time of writing, Jayne's dreams are as regular as they are graphic. What might be going on in the offices of the Department of Homeland Security is a matter that is often at the forefront of her mind.

Jayne said to me: "Nick, I really hope they are on top of it." Me, too— and so should you.

One last thing to ponder on in relation to all this: In Whitley Strieber's 1984 novel *Warday*, nuclear war begins with an electromagnetic pulse-based attack on the United States. Just perhaps, Strieber's story was not fiction after all. Maybe, Strieber's mind unknowingly picked up on strands of future, catastrophic events—as so many other people may have done in Chicago and elsewhere in 2017.

The Real Men in Black

Thanks to the phenomenally successful *Men in Black* movie franchise, very few people these days have not heard of the sinister MIB. In the movies starring Will Smith and Tommy Lee Jones as agents "J" and "K," the MIB are employed by a secret government body that is dedicated to wiping out hostile aliens on the Earth. The reality of the Men in Black, however, is very different. Unlike their movie counterparts, the real MIB are described as looking definitely unhuman: their skin is extremely pale, they have large, bulging eyes, they are extremely skinny, and they are often very tall. In other words, they don't even look like regular people. This has given rise to the theory that the MIB may be alien–human hybrids—possibly even supernatural entities.

Not only that, strong evidence suggests that the U.S. government has secretly investigated the MIB phenomenon to try to figure out who, or what, the Men in Black are. Thanks to the Freedom of Information Act legislation, we now have in our possession several examples of official, secret U.S. military documents that confirm those secret investigations, which were clearly covered up at the time the government was doing its utmost to solve the mysterious riddle of who these strange characters were.

John Keel was not only the author of the acclaimed book *The Mothman Prophecies*. He was also someone who dug very deeply into the matter of the MIB, who they were, and where they came from. In February 1967, Keel had the opportunity to speak with Col. George P. Freeman. Col. Freeman, of the U.S. Air Force, made the following written statement about the MIB. Keel took careful note of it:

> Mysterious men dressed in Air Force uniforms or bearing impressive credentials from government agencies have been silencing

UFO witnesses. We have checked a number of these cases, and these men are not connected to the Air Force in any way. We haven't been able to find out anything about these men. By posing as Air Force officers and government agents, they are committing a Federal offense. We would sure like to catch one—unfortunately the trail is always too cold by the time we hear about these cases, but we are still trying.

Less than one month later, specifically on March 1, 1967, Lt. Gen. Hewitt T. Wheless, USAF, penned the following memo. It was widely circulated within the military:

Information, not verifiable, has reached Hq USAF that persons claiming to represent the Air Force or other Defense establishments have contacted citizens who have sighted unidentified flying objects. In one reported case, an individual in civilian clothes, who represented himself as a member of NORAD, demanded and received photos belonging to a private citizen.

The document continues:

In another, a person in an Air Force uniform approached local police and other citizens who had sighted a UFO, assembled them in a school room and told them that they did not see what they thought they saw and that they should not talk to anyone about the sighting. All military and civilian personnel and particularly information officers and UFO investigating officers who hear of such reports should immediately notify their local OSI offices.

Clearly, not only does the above documentation demonstrate that the Men in Black had nothing to do with the government, it also shows that the government had no more understanding of who the MIB were than did the average UFO researcher.

Moving on to the FBI....

In 1956, paranormal/UFO investigator Gray Barker wrote and published a book titled *They Knew Too Much about Flying Saucers*. A significant percentage of the book was focused on the MIB-themed experiences of Albert

U.S. Air Force Lt. Gen. Hewitt T. Wheless was a World War II hero who received the Distinguished Service Cross for bombing Japanese ships in the ocean near the Philippines.

Bender, who, in the early 1950s, established the International Flying Saucer Bureau (in Bridgeport, Connecticut). It wasn't long before the IFSB was no more. Bender supposedly closed it down after receiving repeated, menacing visits from the Men in Black. Bender's MIB were far less like 1950s-era G-Men or agents of the CIA. They were far more like something from the pages of a Bram Stoker novel, mixed in with a greater-than-liberal sprinkling of H. P. Lovecraft. As a result of the publication of Barker's book, a number of people contacted the FBI, demanding to know who the dark-suited silencers really were—particularly because certain ufologists, such as Barker, were claiming the MIB were from "the government."

The FBI has declassified some of its documents on Bender and Barker, which demonstrates something notable: namely, that just like the U.S. military, the FBI, too, had no real understanding of who the MIB were. On January 22, 1959, none other than J. Edgar Hoover instructed the Chicago office of the FBI: "The Bureau desires to obtain a copy of the book written by Gray Barker entitled 'They Knew Too Much about Flying Saucers.'" Records demonstrate that, behind closed doors and after reading Barker's book, the FBI was as baffled in the fifties as the Air Force was almost a decade later.

Some ufologists will likely claim that the USAF and the FBI were both out of the loop due to the MIB originating with a deeply buried, "black budget"-type group that even Hoover and the Air Force couldn't uncover, but I disagree. Every bit of data that has surfaced from government agencies suggests that they are as utterly mystified as the field of ufology is when it comes to the nature and origin of the Men in Black. Yes, the MIB phenomenon is real, but it has practically nothing to do with agencies of the government, of the military, or of the Intelligence Community. The Men in Black are … *something else*, and as the documentation shows, the U.S. government, in the 1950s and 1960s, was deeply concerned by the MIB phenomenon to the extent that a cover-up was put into place to ensure that the public did not learn of the extent to which the MIB issue was spreading all across the county.

One person who had a great deal of involvement in the investigation of the Men in Black enigma was the late Brad Steiger. Before his death in 2018, Steiger provided me with the following statement on his experiences with the MIB, which demonstrate the sheer, sinister nature of the black-suited creatures. Steiger said:

> After more than 50 years of research in the UFO and paranormal fields, I have come to the conclusion that many of the mysteries that bedevil us are products of a reflexive phenomenon. This reflexive action does not usually occur in the more mundane pursuits of architecture, industry, mining, agriculture and the like, but once one begins actively to pursue Ufology or psychical research,

Author Gray Barker introduced the world to the Men in Black in his 1956 book *They Knew Too Much About Flying Saucers.*

one runs the risk of entering a surreal world in which the usual physical laws do not apply.

In the case of the mythos of the Men in Black, I suggest that that eerie enigma may have begun with the machinations of a human agency assigned to investigate the actions of the more high-profile investigators of the phenomenon and the more convincing witness of UFO activity with the goals of learning more about the growing interest in a worldwide phenomena. Somehow along the way, this activity of the human surveillance of other humans caught the interest of a nonhuman, paraphysical agency that has for centuries pursued goals that remain elusive, even sinister, to the individuals whom they visit. Whether motivated by a bizarre sense of humor, an essentially malicious nature, or a desire to learn how much some humans know about their eternal secrets, the Others began knocking on the doors of those who had witnessed or who had investigated UFO activity.

Some of my experiences with the MIB seem most certainly the product of human surveillance that in most instances was conducted with awkward fallibility. Once in the golden era of MIB activity in the late 1960s while speaking to a fellow researcher on the telephone, our conversation was interrupted by a metallic-sounding voice chanting: "Ho, ho, UFO!" Because it seemed that this got a rise out of us, this merry chant was repeated on a number of telephone calls with other investigators.

A friend who had been doing a great deal of research on my behalf told of the time when he was anticipating a visit from me. He picked up the telephone to make a call on his private line, only to hear the following bit of conversation:

"Has Steiger arrived in town yet?"

"Not yet."

"What motel will he be staying in?"

"The [correct name of the motel in which I had made reservations]."

"Don't worry. Everything is set."

At this point my friend broke in and asked who the hell was on his private line. There was a stunned silence, a click, then the steady buzzing that indicates a clear line. I had my own experience with the awkward telephone spies when I checked into a hotel and found that the bell man had missed one of my suitcases—the most important one with the slides for my lecture.

I picked up the receiver to hear a man's voice inquire: "When is he supposed to check in?"

"He is already in his room," I said in reply, though I knew the query wasn't asked of me.

"Oh, s—t!" was the profound response, followed by two rapid hang-ups.

Other experiences with the MIB are not so easy to place in either the Human or Non-Human category. A friend of mine was traveling in England before starting on an around-the-world junket with a layover in Vietnam to visit his son in the armed forces. He was walking near a railway station in London when he noticed three men dressed completely in black staring at him.

When my friend returned their collective stare, they approached him and asked him which train they should take for such-and-such a city. My friend calmly pointed out that he was a tourist, and it made a good deal more sense for them to ask at the information booth just a few feet away.

My friend turned on his heel and walked away from the odd trio, but a glance over his shoulder told him that they were still standing there staring at him, unmindful of checking with the information booth. Suddenly ill at ease, my friend hailed a taxi and went directly to his hotel.

When he got to his room, an uncomfortable sensation prickled the back of his neck and he glanced out his window. On the street corner, looking up at his room, were the three men. Baffled, he tried to push the incident from his mind.

A day or so later, though, he was confronted by one of the men who told him straight out: "You are a friend of Brad Steiger. Tell him we shall visit him by Christmas." My friend had only a peripheral knowledge of the UFO can of worms, but he returned to his hotel room and wrote me a long letter with the above details.

Not long after I had received his letter, I visited a friend in another city and told him about the bizarre experience my correspondent had encountered in London. "Humph!" Jim snorted over the lunch we were sharing. "If those monkeys come to see you this Christmas, send 'em down to talk to me. I'd love to get one of those characters in my hands. I would solve this man-in-black mystery you've been telling me about!"

The late author and paranormal researcher Brad Steiger believed the Men in Black were members of the Other who were assigned to keep a close watch on human behavior, especially humans getting close to the truth.

I laughed and warned him that he had better be careful or he might get his wish.

I had not returned from my trip by more than a few minutes when the telephone rang. It was Jim calling. Wondering if I might have left something at his place of business, I was informed that I had indeed left a most peculiar something behind me.

Jim told me that I had no sooner started my homeward journey than he was told that a gentleman wished to see him. A secretary ushered a man of average height into Jim's office. But my friend said that his visitor was the thinnest human being he had ever seen.

"He was cadaverous, Brad," Jim told me. "He looked like those World War II photographs of someone in a concentration camp. But he seemed alert enough, and so involved in his quest that he ignored my proffered hand of greeting. In fact, I tried to push shaking his hand, but he refused to touch me.

"I hear you want to be the head of UFOs in Iowa," he said quickly.

"He took out a wallet, flipped it open, then shut, before I could see any identification. I can't really recall anything else he said, because it was all so damned nonsensical. Soon he was gone, and I was still sitting there dumbfounded.

"I jumped to my feet, though, when I heard his car starting. I got a good look at his automobile and I wrote down its license number. I can't tell you what make of car it was. It looked like a combination of three or four different makes and models, but it didn't really look like anything I had ever seen before. And the license number didn't check. The Highway Patrol said there was no such Iowa plate registered. A friend in another branch of state government, who owed me a favor, said the plate wasn't registered to any government agency, either."

The cases above are baffling, but in the following cases I suspect a human agency involved in a strange campaign that was conducted regarding Steiger imposters who spoke at various conferences around the United States. On occasions the imposters allegedly conducted themselves very well, thus making the whole enterprise of Counterfeit Steigers a seemingly futile project. On other occasions, the imposter's assignment was quite obviously to taint my reputation.

On an unfortunate number of occasions, I received letters complaining of my outrageous and insulting behavior while speaking at a conference. There were claims that I had openly berated my audience, calling them stupid for accepting the very premise of UFOs. A close friend happened to arrive on the scene after one pseudo-Steiger had departed and tried his best to assure the sponsors of the event that the rowdy, disrespectful speaker could not have been the real Brad. In his letter, my friend warned me that he had visited a number of lecture halls where the imposter had damned his audiences. "Someone seems out to damage your reputation," he advised.

In a most bizarre twist, dozens of men and women have approached me at various lectures and seminars, congratulating me about the manner in which I bested Dr. Carl Sagan in debate. The event allegedly occurred after a lecture when I happened to bump into the great scientist in a restaurant. The eatery, according to the witnesses, was crowded with those who had attended the seminar, and they egged on a debate between myself and Dr. Sagan. I mopped up the floor with him, countering his every argument against the reality of UFOs.

The truth is that I never met Dr. Sagan, therefore, neither had I ever debated him. But from coast to coast, there are those who claim to have witnessed my triumphal bout. Even more individuals claim to have been in the audience when I delivered a rousing message from the Space Brothers in Seattle. Regardless of how often I deny that I was not in Seattle at that time and have never channeled the Space Brothers, those who were at that event are puzzled why I would deny my eloquence.

It is true, that I have met and interviewed men and women who do claim to speak on behalf of Extraterrestrial Intelligences, but in retrospect, I found such a privilege to carry with it many possible negative experiences. I think of the reminiscences that I have shared with an Iowa farm family about those weird and wild MIB days. UFOs had become a part of this family's life several years before one of its male members became a "channel" for an entity who claimed to be from another world. The invisible telepathic being began communicating with the family because they had been "selected before they had been born" to assist him in doing "His" work and in protecting Earth from another group of intelligences who sought to enslave mankind.

The communicating entity led the various members of the family circle on a number of "assignments" designed to save the Earth and to serve the benign entity and his kind. But always, the entity warned them, there was the enemy group with its men in black, seeking whom they might devour.

The family, who became "flying saucer missionaries," saw mysterious fellow passengers board airplanes with them—then disappear somewhere in mid-flight. Automobiles appeared out of nowhere to follow and harass them.

A man claiming to be from a state educational division called at the high school and talked for over an hour with one of the teenaged girl members of the family. The only questions he asked had to do with whether or not she would be able to recognize a spy. When suspicious adult members of the beleaguered family checked with school administrators, they were informed that they had no knowledge of such a man nor of such a division within the state educational system. [Interestingly, I have now met with a number of adults who claimed such an experience with an MIB who claimed to be a representative from the state educational division who took them out of class for a "test."]

The girl who had been interrogated by the unidentified man also developed into a "channel" for the communicating entity, and soon several members of the family were practicing automatic writing.

UFOs swooped low overhead at night. Eerie lights were seen to dance about in the fields. Invisible entities snatched keys from their resting places and jangled them about the room, terrifying the children. Unseen hands lifted a mattress on which one couple lay sleeping, under which were some "secret" papers that the principal communicating entity had dictated.

Their farm work was being ignored. Their lives had become a living nightmare in which every stranger was suspect, every sound in the night that of an invader, every strange coincidence imbued with desperate and weighty significance.

At last the full realization that they had been deceived—that they had been led into a silly game—jolted them into determined action, and they resumed meaningful living, becoming a quite prosperous farm family. Although some of their past experiences seemed foolish in retrospect, they had to agree that they had learned valuable lessons from their strange companions.

Now days whenever I review those days of encounters with the men in black, I am led to think of the mythological figure common to all cultures and known generically to ethnologists as the Trickster. The Trickster plays pranks upon mankind, but often at the same time he is instructing them or transforming aspects of the world for the benefit of his human charges.

Most cultures view the Trickster as a primordial being who came into existence soon after the creation of the world. A number of Amerindian tribes referred to their Trickster figure as "Old Man," because they saw him as someone who was ageless, as old as time.

The Trickster is usually viewed as a supernatural being with the ability to change his shape at will. Although basically wily, he may behave in a very stupid, childish manner at times, and may often end up as the one who is tricked. The Trickster lies, cheats, and steals without compunction. He seems often to be the very essence of amoral animalism.

The Trickster figure is often credited with bringing death and pain into the world; yet, in some recitations, his own son was the first to

Loki (seen here in a sixteenth-century Icelandic book illumination) is a god of mischief from Norse mythology. There are numerous tricksters like Loki in our myths, and the Men in Black might just be a new iteration of the trickster.

die as a result. Perhaps one day we will learn the positive aspect of the MIB, the Trickster, the UFOnaut. As strange as it may seem, the MIB may merely be attempting to teach in their own strange ways the knowledge, or awareness, of powers that today exist only in our dreams of the future.

Sean Kotz is a filmmaker and writer who has demonstrated just how weird and sinister the entire MIB phenomenon is. He says:

One of the things that makes the Man in Black phenomenon so fascinating is the general social oddity of encounters. In everything from displaced fashions, to mechanical grammar and outdated expressions, to trying to drink Jello or fixating on ash trays and ink pens, the MIB seem just a little off.

These qualities have led some to conclude that the MIB are extraterrestrials, time travelers, or inter-dimensional observers on specific missions requiring that they gather information without raising suspicion but are ultimately unable to fit in because they are essentially not of this world. However, in most cases, the strange behavior does have an earthly parallel, an increasingly common disorder frequently classed as a form of high functioning autism called Asperger's Syndrome.

Asperger's Syndrome, or AS, was first formally identified by Austrian physician Hans Asperger in 1944 and has since become a formally recognized disorder, frequently classed as a form of high functioning autism. Both autism in general and AS in particular can appear in a wide range of severity and in some very mild cases, almost impossible to identify. Indeed, Asperger's Syndrome can exhibit some remarkably heightened skill sets and IQs, which may present evidence of a contemporary genetic evolution of our species.

But before we can make any speculations as to why that might be, we should consider how deeply this connection runs.

TRADEMARKS OF ASPERGER'S SYNDROME: According to WebMD and ASPEN (Asperger's Syndrome Education Network), the overriding identifier with AS is difficulty or even inability to recognize social cues, especially non-verbal social cues, creating awkward interactions with others. They may either avoid eye contact altogether or stare directly at another person. They may fail to recognize or properly interpret body language or understand personal space. AS individuals typically display naivety or flat out obliviousness regarding this awkwardness, which can make children the victims of bullies or predators and promote isolation as well.

Not surprisingly then, people with AS have trouble with the give and take of normal conversation. They are inclined to engage in highly focused, inordinately detailed one-sided dialogues with people and have trouble shifting gears in conversation or letting go of a train of thought. However, once they have exhausted their knowledge or interest in a topic, they can stop a conversation abruptly. They may also verbalize internal thoughts freely, not realizing the impact of such things on others.

Additionally, people with Asperger's Syndrome have trouble grasping humor, sarcasm, metaphor, colloquialisms, intonation, and other subtleties of language. Instead, they incline to very literal interpretations and tend to speak formally, using stilted but precise language, sometimes with words or phrases that seem out of time and place.

Another trait is that AS children have trouble developing fine motor skills and may have poor handwriting and experience difficulty learning to use a knife, fork or spoon. They exhibit awkward postures, often holding their bodies in seemingly uncomfortable rigidity or straightness. They may be relatively clumsy and have trouble with hand-eye coordination and they will frequently show a tendency toward tight fitting formal clothing. And, they may show sensitivity to light, noise and tastes or smells and do not like a disruption in routine or changes of plans.

On the other hand, people with Asperger's can show great abilities when it comes to memorization and pattern recognition. Interestingly enough, may people with AS often have high IQs and are drawn to astronomy, paleontology, architecture, engineering and other sciences. They may also have a vast amount of arcane or obscure knowledge, develop a huge vocabulary, and display a keen interest in maps.

In a word, AS people are masters of "form." They dress and speak formally to the point of awkwardness. Their minds can catalogue names, dates, words, forms, formulas, and so forth with amazing

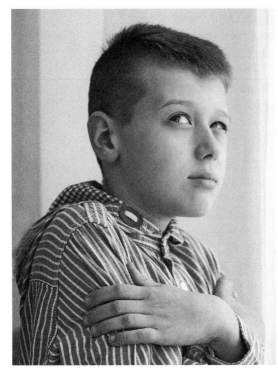

While not saying MIB are humans with Asperger's, author Sean Kotz has pointed out the two cases share a lot of traits in common.

recall and ease. In essence, Asperger's seems to give people a heightened awareness of form and structure, though ironically, there seems to be an exchange when it comes to fluidity and depth of perception.

COMPARISONS WITH THE MEN IN BLACK: If you are already versed in MIB lore, many of these trademarks will seem very familiar. I am not about to suggest that Men in Black are actually people with Asperger's, but the similarities are striking.

In a typical MIB encounter, witnesses describe men wearing crisp and clean black suits and shoes, white shirts and black ties that are generally out of date by several decades. They arrive in black sedans that may also be shiny and new, but more than a generation old. Fashion distinctions escape people with AS and they might easily reason that a suit and tie and sedan lend formal respectability while not being able to distinguish the awkwardness of items out of time.

The MIB also frequently wear sunglasses even at night, which would both reduce the ill effects of light and help them avoid eye contact or disguise a tendency to stare. They will stand or sit rigidly and seem unaware of social protocols, missing cues to sit down or relax.

In conversation, MIB will frequently be focused on obscure details and refuse to stray from the subject. They will ask awkward and inappropriate questions without emotion, speak in robotic and overly formal ways and use words or phrases that seem out of time or place, though technically correct. All of this echoes the tendencies of Asperger's Syndrome.

In addition, MIB are often attributed with awkward gaits and strange ways of holding common items like pens or forks. In one of John Keel's cases, a MIB ordered a steak in a restaurant only to be unable to use the cutlery. Also, MIB are known for having inappropriate reactions to commonplace items like ballpoint pens to the point of fixation. In the well-known case of Dr. Herbert Hopkins, a male and seemingly female pair visited him and his wife and proceeded to ask questions regarding their lives as a couple and even attempted a clumsy, mechanical show of affection, asking for directions as they went. The behavior is inexplicable in any case, but it displays both the inability to understand the inappropriateness of the behavior and the questions.

Perhaps the only thing that haunts the scorched ground of the paranormal more than its specters and aliens are the raging debates. Currently, one of the rifts in the esoteric community that divides researchers into two territories might be understood as a clash between Newtonian realists and quantum speculators.

On one hand, we have what Nick Redfern calls the "nuts and bolts" interpretation, which holds that UFOs are physical constructions (typically from another planet), Bigfoot is an elusive simian, and the Men in Black are either government agents or flesh and blood aliens dispatched on a mission to control witnesses, contactees and abductees. These interpretations rely on common sense physics and reflect the influence of scientific method and cause-and-effect rationalism in our culture.

On the other hand, since John Keel, it has become more and more acceptable to theorize the paranormal with terms like "interdimensional," "ultradimensional," and so forth. Pretty soon people are talking about reality matrixes, vortexes, and portals, which begins to sound like 19th Century pontifications on ectoplasm and spirit boxes. However, for the last half century, equally non-rational science has emerged to lend some degree of credence to these possibilities.

One of the most basic quantum principles that plagues both types of science and the paranormal investigator equally is the problem of observer interactivity. In other words, in every experiment, the observer (be it a scientist in a Harvard lab with two million dollar measurement tools or a pseudo-scientist in a haunted house with a K2 meter) becomes part of the environment and this affects, even if slightly, the results.

Additionally, we all bring our preconceived notions to the table as well. Consider for instance that in the late 1800s, people were reporting strange encounters with bizarre airships and their crews. Later, after Kenneth Arnold said the craft he saw flew like saucers skipping over water, the term "flying saucer" took hold and suddenly, that is what people began to see. In the late 1900s, silent and massive black triangles drifted through our skies, shaped, strangely enough, something like the star destroyers seen in *Star Wars*.

I mention all this because it may be helpful in understanding the Men in Black phenomenon. Perhaps, the MIB are both very real but entirely subject to the conditions of the observer. For example, if you stand at the shore on a sunny day and look out at the ocean, it might look green, blue, gray, or totally light reflective depending on weather conditions and the time of day. And if you look at night, the waves will be black. The water certainly exists, and a given description may be very accurate at a specific time and place, but still the description of the water and the water itself are two very different things.

In light of all the above, it's no surprise that the government wants to keep the truth of the Men in Black locked firmly away from prying eyes. They are just as mystified as we are.

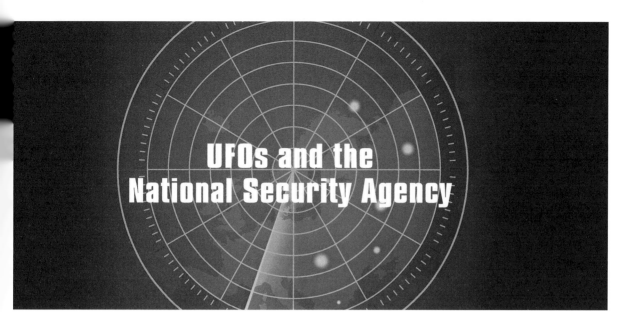

UFOs and the National Security Agency

Of the many and varied UFO/extraterrestrial-themed documents and papers that have surfaced under the terms of the U.S. Freedom of Information Act, one of the more interesting ones is *Communication with Extraterrestrial Intelligence*. It was written in 1965 by a man named Lambros D. Callimahos. He was a cryptologist with the National Security Agency—Edward Snowden's former employer. On September 23, 1965, Callimahos took part in a panel-style debate on the subject of his paper at a conference on military electronics in Washington, D.C.

Also present for the debate was Dr. John C. Lilly, perhaps best known for his work with dolphins and in the fields of psychedelics and altered states. Others included an astronomer, Fr. Francis J. Heyden S.J. The American Astronomical Society notes of Heyden: "Heyden's earliest research was performed in the fields of galactic structure and variable stars. He collaborated with Fr. L. C. McHugh S.J. in photographing star fields in the Southern Milky Way. These images were combined into an Atlas, which has become a basic reference tool for students of galactic structure." A noted linguist was also present, Dr. Paul Garvin. The event was moderated by Dr. Harold Wooster, at the time the director of information services of the U.S. Air Force Office of Scientific Research.

Callimahos's words make for intriguing reading:

We are not alone in the universe. A few years ago, this notion seemed farfetched; today, the existence of extraterrestrial intelligence is taken for granted by most scientists. Sir Bernard Lovell, one of the world's leading radio astronomers, has calculated that, even allowing for a margin of error of 5000 per cent, there must be in our own galaxy about 100 million stars which have planets of the right chemistry, dimensions, and temperature to support organic evolution.

If we consider that our own galaxy, the Milky Way, is but one of at least a billion other galaxies similar to ours in the observable universe, the number of stars that could support some form of life is, to reach a word, astronomical. As to advanced (by miserable earth standards) forms of life, Dr. Frank D. Drake of the National Radio Astronomy Observatory at Green Bank, West Virginia, has stated that, putting all our knowledge together, the number of civilizations which could have arisen by now is about one billion. The next question is, "Where is everybody?"

The nearest neighbor to our solar system is Alpha Centauri, only 4.3 light years away; but, according to Dr. Su-Shu Huang of the National Aeronautics and Space Administration, its planetary system is probably too young for the emergence of life. Two other heavenly friends, Epsilon Eridani and Tau Ceti, about 11 light years away, are stronger contenders for harboring life.

He expanded, in somewhat speculative fashion, but undeniably fascinating fashion, too:

Nevertheless, if superior civilizations are abundant, the nearest would probably be at least 100 light years away; therefore, it would take 200 years for a reply to be forthcoming, a small matter of seven generations. This should, however, make little difference to us, in view of the enormous potential gain from our contact with a superior civilization.

Unless we're terribly conceited (a very unscientific demeanor), we must assume that the "others" are far more advanced than we are. Even a 50-year gap would be tremendous; a 500-year gap staggers the imagination, and as for a 5000-year gap.... (By the way, if they are as much as 50 years behind us, forget it!) It is quite possible that "others" have satellite probes in space, retransmitting to "them" anything that sounds non-random to the probe. But they have probably called us several thousand years ago, and are waiting for an answer; or worse yet, they have given up; or, more probably, they have reached such impressive technological advances that they have destroyed themselves.

Callimahos turned his attention to the kind of work that was then in place to try to find evidence of alien life:

Epsilon Eridani and Tau Ceti were the targets on which Dr. [Frank] Drake [of SETI, the Search for Extraterrestrial Intelligence]

The Howard E. Tatel Radio Telescope in Green Bank, West Virginia, was used for Project Ozma, a mission to detect alien life conducted in 1960.

focused his attention in the Spring of 1960 in Project Ozma, an attempt to detect possible intelligent signals from outer space. The frequency selected for listening was 1420.405752 megacycles per second, or a wave length of 21 cm.

This particular frequency, postulated independently by two professors on the faculty of Cornell University, Giuseppe Cocconi and Philip Morrison, happens to be the radiation frequency of atomic or free hydrogen which permeates space in great clouds; moreover, this frequency is within the range of radio frequencies able to pass through the earth's atmosphere. Presumably, the significance of this frequency would be known to other intelligent beings in the universe who understand radio theory. We're still talking about radio waves as the communication medium; other possible media might be masers, lasers, or the as yet undiscovered and unnamed "rasers." A technology superior to ours might even have learned how to modulate a beam of neutrinos (weightless, uncharged particles that physicists on earth find it difficult even to detect); if so, "they" may have to wait a century or two before we learn how to build a neutrino receiver.

I'll close with these thought-provoking words from Callimahos:

After we resolve our pressing scientific questions, it might be appropriate to make discreet inquiries as to how we could live in harmony and peace with our fellow man—that is if we aren't eaten or otherwise ingested by the superior civilization that had the good fortune to contact us. But as far as the cryptologist is concerned, he (and generations of his descendants who might experience the supreme thrill of their lives when we hear from "them") must keep a level head, not get excited, and be prepared to cope with problems the likes of which he has never seen—out of this world, so to speak.

Three years later, in 1968, Lambros Callimahos wrote another paper on alien life and UFOs, also for the National Security Agency. This one was titled *UFO Hypothesis Survival Questions*. It addressed a variety of theories designed to explain the nature of the UFO phenomenon. It began as follows: "It is the purpose of this monograph to consider briefly some of the human survival implication suggested by the various principal hypotheses concerning the nature of the phenomena loosely categorized as UFO. All flying, sailing or maneuvering aerial objects whether glowing, pulsating, or of a constant metallic hue, whose shape is somewhat, circular or cigarish [sic]."

Under a heading titled "All UFOs Are Hoaxes," Callimahos said:

From the time when hoaxes were first noted in history, they were characterized by infrequency of occurrence and usually by a considerable restriction of their geographical extent. Rarely have men of science, while acting within their professional capacities, perpetrated hoaxes. The fact that UFO phenomena have been witnessed all over the world from ancient times, and by considerable numbers of reputable scientists in recent times, indicates rather strongly that UFOs are not all hoaxes. If anything, rather than diminishing, the modern trend is toward increased reports, from all sources. In one three month period in 1953 (June, July and August) Air Force records show 35 sightings whose nature could not be determined. If UFOs, contrary to all indications and expectations, are indeed hoaxes—hoaxes of a worldwide dimension—hoaxes of increasing frequency, then a human mental aberration of alarming proportions would seem to be developing. Such an aberration would seem to have serious implications for nations equipped with nuclear toys—and should require immediate and careful study by scientists.

Callimahos then turned his attention to the matter of hallucinations:

People, of course, do hallucinate. Although groups of people hallucinating is rare, it has been known to happen. Machines have their own form of hallucination; the radar, in particular, "sees" temperature inversions. But a considerable number of instances exist in which there are groups of people and a radar or radars seeing the same thing at the same time; sometimes a person and gun camera confirm each other's testimony. On occasion, physical evidence of a circumstantial nature was reported to have been found to support witnessed sightings. A continuing high percentage of reports of unusual aerial objects are being reported by people in responsible positions in science, government, and industry. The sum of such evidence seems to argue strongly against all UFOs being hallucinations.

In spite of all the evidence to the contrary, if UFOs did turn out to be largely illusionary, the psychological implications for man would certainly bring into strong question his ability to distinguish reality from fantasy. The negative effect on man's ability to survive in an increasingly complex world would be considerable—making it imperative that such a growing impairment of the human capacity for rational judgment be subjected to immediate and thorough scientific study so that the illness could be controlled before it reaches epidemic proportions.

As for the possibility that UFOs are purely natural phenomena, this comes from Callimahos's paper:

> If this hypothesis is correct, the capability of air warning systems to correctly diagnose an attack situation is open to serious question. Many UFOs have been reported by trained military observers to behave like high speed, high performance, high altitude rockets or aircraft. The apparent solidity and craft-like shape of the objects have often been subject to radar confirmation.… If such reports can appear to trained military men as rockets or aircraft and if such objects should come over the Arctic from the direction of Russia on the United States, they could trigger "false reports of missile attacks."

Many responsible military officers have developed a mental "blind spot" to objects which appear to have characteristics of UFOs. Such an attitude is an open invitation to the enemy to build a replica of the phenomena in order to penetrate the "hole" in his adversaries' defenses—was this the purpose of the lens shaped reentry vehicle tested by the USAF in 1960 and recently featured in the Washington, D.C. *Evening Star*, dated 24 September 1968, page A4?

Sometimes the phenomena appear to defy radar detection and to cause massive electromagnetic interference. Surely it is very important to discover the nature of these objects or plasmas before any prospective enemy can use their properties to build a device or system to circumvent or jam our air and space detection systems— any nation certainly could use a system or device to penetrate enemy defenses.

Another angle that Callimahos addressed was that of at least some UFOs being secret weapons of the world's military. His thoughts on this particular theory follow:

> The above-referenced U.S. Air Force reentry vehicle and an often publicized Canadian "saucer" project leave little doubt as to the validity of this hypothesis. Undoubtedly, all UFOs should be carefully scrutinized to ferret out such enemy (or "friendly") projects. Otherwise a nation faces the very strong possibility of being intimidated by a new secret "doomsday" weapon.

> According to some eminent scientists closely associated with the study of this phenomenon, this hypothesis cannot be disregarded.

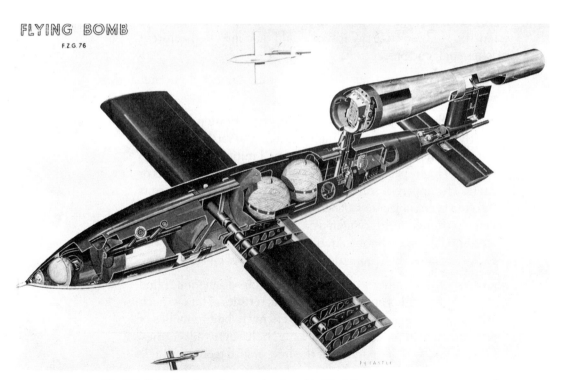

FLYING BOMB
F.Z.G. 76

The V-1 flying bomb rocket was developed in Nazi Germany as a secret weapon that was then used against England. Unusual for its time, the V-1 is an example of sinister weapons developed clandestinely. Perhaps the UFOs being reported now, in some cases, are secret weapons being tested by various countries.

The well documented sightings over Washington, D.C., in 1952 strongly support his view. This hypothesis has a number of far-reaching human survival implications:

a. If "they" discover you, it is an old but hardly invalid rule of thumb, "they" are your technological superiors. Human history has shown us time and again the tragic results of a confrontation between a technologically superior civilization and a technologically inferior people. The "inferior" is usually subject to physical conquest.

b. Often in the past, a technologically superior people are also possessors of a more virile or aggressive culture. In a confrontation between two peoples of significantly different culture levels, those having the inferior or less virile culture most often suffer a tragic loss of identity and are absorbed by the other people.

c. Some peoples who were technologically and/or culturally inferior to other nations have survived—have maintained their identity—have equalized the differences between them and their adversaries. The Japanese people have given us an excellent example of the methods required to achieve such survival:

   (1) full and honest acceptance of the nature of the inferiorities separating you from the advantages of the other peoples,

   (2) complete national solidarity in all positions taken in dealing with the other culture,

   (3) highly controlled and limited intercourse with the other side—doing only those things advantageous to the foreigner which you are absolutely forced to do by the circumstances,

   (4) a correct but friendly attitude toward the other people,

   (5) a national eagerness to learn everything possible about the other citizens—its technological and cultural strengths and weaknesses. This often involves sending selected groups and individuals to the other's country to become one of his kind, or even to help him in his wars against other adversaries,

   (6) adopting as many of the advantages of the opposing people as you can, and doing it as fast as possible—while still protecting your own identity by molding each new knowledge increment into your own cultural cast.

In a final "Comment" section of his thought-provoking theories and observations, Callimahos left his fellow employees of the NSA with these words:

Although this paper has hardly exhausted the possible hypotheses related to the UFO phenomena, those mentioned above are the principal ones presently put forward. All of them have serious survival implications. The final answer to this mystery will probably include more than one of the above hypotheses.

Up until this time, the leisurely scientific approach has too often taken precedence in dealing with UFO questions. If you are walking along a forest path and someone yells "rattler" your reaction would be immediate and defensive. You would not take time to speculate before you act. You would have to treat the alarm as if it were a real and immediate threat to your survival. Investigation would become an intensive emergency action to isolate the threat and to determine its precise nature. It would be geared to developing adequate defensive measures in a minimum amount of time. It would seem a little more of this survival attitude is called for in dealing with the UFO problem.

Observations of chimpanzees while in a captive environment have shown that the animals tend to become confused and disoriented. Since they do not usually have adult chimps to teach them how to be good apes, they are not even sure of their behavior. Often their actions are patterned after human behavior and would have virtually no survival value in the wild. Lacking the challenge of environmental adaptation, the bodies of the animals atrophy and become subject to many diseases—mostly unknown in their wild counterparts. Reactions to stimulus usually become less responsive and suitable. Sex becomes a year-long preoccupation instead of a seasonal madness.

Do the captivity characteristics of modern civilization cause a similar lessening of man's adaptive capability, of his health, of his ability to recognize reality, of his ability to survive?

Perhaps the UFO question might even make man undertake studies which could enable him to construct a society which is most conducive to developing a completely human being, healthy in all respects of mind and body—and, most important, able to recognize and adapt to real environmental situations.

Fifty years after Lambros Callimahos's paper was published—and held under tight security by the NSA—one has to ponder on the extent to which the agency's staff has further investigated the matter of UFOs. So far, no one in the NSA is saying.

Government Files on Ancient Mysteries

Is the U.S. government hiding from us classified information on millennia-old mysteries, UFO visitations in the distant past, and the kinds of other-world phenomena described on the History Channel's phenomenally successful show *Ancient Aliens*? Documentation that has surfaced under the terms of the U.S. Freedom of Information Act suggests that this is exactly the case, as we shall now see. Jason Colavito, who has made careful studies of matters relative to the whole "ancient astronauts" issue, says:

> Sometime in the mid-1950s, the FBI obtained a copy of a pamphlet by a religious crank named John Miller. The pamphlet was manually typed with a hand-drawn cover (apparently by George Adamski) featuring UFOs. Miller advocated the theory that the Bible contained records of ancient astronaut visitations, especially in the wheels of Ezekiel, which he analyzed at great and exhaustive length in terms exactly like the similar discussions in many other ancient astronaut books. Miller's pamphlet is particularly interesting for the suggestion that humans should continue to be Christians because God, Jesus, and the angels were extraterrestrials.

In part, Miller wrote:

"Flying Saucers" have made the headlines off and on for many times now. Much has been written about them. Research has shown that "flying chariots" and strange powers, both of locomotion and destruction are described in the holy books of various heathen faiths many thousands of years older than our own. "Flying Chariots" have been seen and reported and not believed for many ages. That is nothing new. But what is new is that recently they have been photographed.

Miller continued:

Having established the factuality of the "flying saucer," it is now about time that we find a theological confirmation of the whole matter. This is a necessity! If "flying saucers" inhabit outer-space, and if they have some kind of celestial character, they should have some place in the total economy of God. They should have more place in our thinking and planning, and one would expect to see them mentioned in our holy books, too. We are therefore not surprised, upon investigation, to find "flying" clouds, rolls, chariots, wheels, and people, mentioned in the Bible. To realize this is to make a great many mysterious things in the Bible seem both matter-of-fact and encouraging.

The ancients, it is true, had no adequate words to describe the things they saw in their day which came from outer space. If a

From petroglyphs in the Americas to artifacts in ancient Egypt and Mesopotamia, there are images from long ago that imply aliens have visited Earth in the past, including this Mesopotamian seal that appears to show a flying disc.

thing flew, it was called a "flying" cloud, bird, chariot or angel. We, today, should have progressed far enough scientifically to call objects from outer-space by names which are more appropriate. But the unhappy term "flying saucer" is a term more reminiscent of a tea-party than of the man-world of science. It seems our own nomenclature, or is it our imagination, is very inadequate also. However, the possibility and probability of realizing unheard sources of power and speeds, and the conquering of space is to us but a matter of time.

Moving on to the 1960s....

On April 17, 1960, a lecture was held at the Phipps Auditorium, City Park, Denver, Colorado, by a man named George Van Tassel. He was a man who claimed numerous encounters with human-looking aliens in the 1950s, all of whom warned him of the looming threat of nuclear war. Unlike the bug-eyed aliens of today's pop culture and UFO research, Van Tassel's aliens looked very much like us. Van Tassel didn't know it, but one of the audience members at the Phipps Auditorium was a special agent of the FBI, noting just about every word that Van Tassel uttered. The agent's summary—sent to the office of the FBI's director at the time, J. Edgar Hoover—reads like this:

> The program was sponsored by the Denver [deleted], one of which meets monthly at the [deleted], Lakewood, Colorado, whose [deleted] was the Master of Ceremonies. The program consisted of a 45 minute movie which included several shots of things purported to be flying saucers, and then a number of interviews with people from all walks of life regarding sightings they had made of such unidentified flying objects. After the movie Van Tassel gave a lecture which was more of a religious economics lecture rather than one of unidentified flying objects.

> Van Tassel stated that he had been in the "flying game" for over 30 years and currently operates a private Civil Aeronautics Authority approved airfield in California. He said he has personally observed a good many sightings and has talked to hundreds of people who have also seen flying saucers. He said that he has also been visited by the people from outer space and has taken up the cause of bringing the facts of these people to the American people. He said it is a crusade which he has undertaken because he is more or less retired, his family is grown and gone from home, and he feels he might be doing some good by this work.

Van Tassel then got to the heart of the matter: namely, his beliefs concerning the Bible, aliens, and ancient astronauts. The FBI agent present at the lecture noted the following:

The major part of his lecture was devoted to explaining the occurrences in the Bible as they related to the space people. He said that the only mention of God in the Bible is in the beginning when the universe was being made. He said that after that all references are to "out of the sky" or "out of heaven." He said that this is due to the fact that man, space people, was made by God and that in the beginning of the world the space people came to the earth and left animals here.

These were the pre-historic animals which existed at a body temperature of 105 degrees; however, a polar tilt occurred whereby the poles shifted and the tropical climates became covered with ice and vice versa. He said that then the space people again put animals on the earth and this is depicted in the Bible as Noah's ark. He said that after the polar tilt the temperature to sustain life was 98.6 degrees, which was suitable for space people, so they established a colony and left only males here, intending to bring females at a later date on supply ships. This is reflected in ADAM's not having a wife. He said that ADAM was not an individual but a race of men. He said that this race then inter-married with "intelligent, upright walking animals," which race was EVE. Then when the space people came back in the supply ships they saw what had happened and did not land but ever since due to the origin of ADAM, they have watched over the people on earth.

He said that this is recorded in the Bible many times, such as MOSES receiving the Ten Commandments. He said the Ten Commandments are the laws of the space people and men on earth only give them lip service. Also, the manna from heaven was bread supplied by the space people. He also stated that this can be seen from the native stories such as the Indians in America saying that corn and potatoes, unknown in Europe, were brought here by a "flaming canoe." He said this refers to a space ship and the Indians' highest form of transportation was the canoe, so they likened it unto that. He said this can be shown also by the old stories of Winged Chariots and Winged White Horses, which came from out of the sky.

He said that JESUS was born of MARY, who was a space person sent here already pregnant in order to show the earth people the proper way to live. He said the space people have watched over us through the years and have tried to help us. He said they have sent their agents to the earth and they appear just as we do; however, they have the power to know your thoughts just as JESUS did. He said this is their means of communication and many of the space people are mute, but they train a certain number of them to speak earth languages. He said that the space people here on earth are equipped with a "crystal battery" which generates a magnetic field about them which bends light waves so that they, the space people, appear invisible. He said this has resulted in ghost stories such as footsteps, doors opening, and other such phenomena.

Van Tassel then got to the matter of atomic weaponry, which led the FBI agent present to record the following:

> The space people are now gravely concerned with our atom bombs. He said that the explosions of these bombs have upset the earth's rotation and, as in the instance of the French bomb explosion in North Africa, have actually caused earthquakes. He said that the officials on earth are aware of this and this was the reason for the recent Geophysical Year in order to try to determine just what can be done. He said these explosions are forcing the earth toward another polar tilt, which will endanger all mankind. He said that the space people are prepared to evacuate those earth people who have abided by the "Golden Rule" when the polar tilt occurs, but will leave the rest to perish.

> He advised that the space people have contacted the officials on earth and have advised them of their concern but this has not been made public. He also said that the radioactive fallout has become extremely dangerous and officials are worried but each power is so greedy of their own power they will not agree to make peace. Van Tassel also spent some time saying that the U.S. Air Force, who are responsible for investigations of unidentified flying objects, has suppressed information; and as they are responsible only to the Administration, not to the public, as elected officials are, they can get away with this. He said that also the Air Force is afraid that they will be outmoded and disbanded if such information gets out. The Administration's main concern in not making public any information is that the economy will be ruined, not because of any fear that would be engendered in the public. He

Van Tassel declared that the aliens have been concerned about the use of nukes on our planet, which they say is affecting the tilt of the planet, threatening all life on it.

said this is due to the number of scientific discoveries already made and that will be made which are labor saving and of almost permanency so that replacements would not be needed.

In summation, Van Tassel's speech was on these subjects:

(1) Space people related to occurrences in Bible.

(2) Atom bomb detrimental to earth and universe.

(3) Economy is poor and would collapse under ideas brought by space people.

Throughout his lecture, Van Tassel mentioned only the U.S. economy and Government and the U.S. Air Force. He did refer to the human race numerous times but all references to Government and economy could only be taken as meaning the U.S. One question put to him was whether sightings had been made in Russia or China. He answered this by saying sightings had been reported all over the world, but then specifically mentioned only the U.S., Australia, New Zealand, and New Guinea.

He also mentioned that he was not advocating or asking for any action on the part of the audience because he said evil has a way of destroying itself. He did say that he felt that the audience, of about 250 persons, were the only intelligent people in Denver and he knew they had not come out of curiosity but because they wanted to do the right thing. He said that they were above the average in intelligence and when the critical time came, the world would need people such as this to think and guide.

Moving on, we now focus on the FBI's interest in a July 1967 article that appeared in the pages of the former Soviet Union's magazine *Sputnik*. Not unlike George Van Tassel in 1960, the writer of the article deeply addressed the theory that much of which passes for ancient religious history was actually driven by encounters with extraterrestrials. Titled "Visitors from Outer Space" and written by Vyacheslav Zaitsev, the article, in part, includes the following, extracted directly from the pages of the FBI's report:

Expanding knowledge about the universe usually means more puzzles than discoveries. As man unravels each new mystery, he is assailed by fresh doubts and torments, for he has caught a glimpse of another mystery lying ahead. For the explorers—in any field—it is probably this yet undiscovered territory vaguely seen in the distance that sparks the search for knowledge.

A report by a Chinese archaeologist startled the world when it was published in 1965 for he had out of old bits of knowledge pieced together an amazing theory of space-ships on a visit to the earth

12,000 years ago. The German magazine *Das Vegetarische Universum* wrote of his research:

For a quarter of a century archaeologists exploring caves in the Bayan-Kara-Ula Mountains, on the border of China and Tibet, have been finding odd-looking stone discs covered in unreadable patterns and hieroglyphs. A total of 716 such discs have been discovered, apparently dating back several thousand years.

Like a gramophone record, each disc has a hole in its center from which a double groove spirals its way to the circumference. The grooves are not sound-tracks, but the oddest writing in China and indeed the rest of the world.

Archaeologists and decipherers of ancient writing racked their brains trying to solve the secret of the spirals. The result of the research by the Chinese archaeologist was so shattering that the Peking Academy of Pre-History banned publication of his work. Eventually permission was obtained and the professor and his four colleagues published their collective effort under the intriguing title "Groove Writing Relating to Spaceships which, as Recorded on the Discs, Existed 12,000 Years Ago."

When deciphered, one of the hieroglyphs read, "The Dropas came down from the clouds in their gliders. Our men, women, and children hid in the caves ten times before the sunrise. When at last they understood the sign language of the Dropas, they realized the newcomers had peaceful intentions."

In the opinion of Chinese archaeologists, the Bayan-Kara-Ula hieroglyphs are so mysterious that their interpretation and use for scientific research require the utmost care.

To obtain further information, the discs were scraped free of adhering rock particles and sent to Moscow for study. Scientists there made two important discoveries. The discs were found to contain a large amount of cobalt and other metals—a shaking discovery. Further investigations revealed that the discs vibrate in an unusual rhythm, as if they carried an electric charge or were part of an electric circuit. The 12,000 year old discs remain a challenge to science.

Moving away from the matter of ancient mysteries and aliens in the distant past, the next matter to be addressed is that of the CIA's secret interest in nothing less than Noah's Ark and the claims that the remains of the alleged mighty boat are buried somewhere on Mount Ararat, Turkey. A summary of the CIA's involvement in this matter can be found below. It, too, has been officially declassified under the terms of the Freedom of Information Act, although significant numbers of CIA papers on Noah's Ark still remain classified.

Noah's Ark 1974–1982. On 13 May 1974, DCI Colby sent a letter to the DS&T, Sayre Stevens, asking if the Agency had any evidence of Noah's Ark on Mt. Ararat. Mr. Colby said that Lieutenant Colonel Walter Brown of the US Air Force Academy had asked "whether it would be appropriate or possible to exploit satellite photography to examine the glacier systems there to see whether any evidence of the Ark could be found." On 21 May, the Center responded that no evidence of the Ark could be discerned on U-2 photography acquired on 10 September 1957 or on any satellite imagery available at the Center.

On 6 August 1974, Congressman Bob Wilson asked the Agency whether any aerial photos of Mt. Ararat could be released to a friend of his, Dr. John Morris, son of Dr. Henry M. Morris, the head of the Institution of Creation Research of San Diego, California. Mr. Hicks stated in a letter to the Agency legislative liaison staff that several U-2 photos dated 1957 were available but were still classified "Confidential." The younger Dr. Morris wrote to the Agency later requesting the photos. His request was denied by Angus Theurmer, the Agency's press spokesman who stated "We have looked into this matter in some detail and we regret that we are unable to provide any information."

This replica of Noah's Ark was built on Mt. Ararat by Greenpeace as a way of protesting global warming. Many believe that the *real* ark is somewhere on this Turkish mountain and that the U.S. government knows where it is.

In September/October 1974, Admiral Showers of the Intelligence Community Staff, in response to a query from Lieutenant Commander Lonnie McClung, asked about the availability of intelligence information concerning the location of Noah's Ark. He was told that a search had been made of aerial photography with negative results.

On 30 January 1975, Dr. John Morris again wrote Congressman Bob Wilson noting that aerial photos "were taken in August 1974, as a result of my request. They were not to be classified, but have been classified since and are not available." Congressman Wilson again contacted the Agency with the request. On 27 February 1975, Mr. Hicks again denied the request. On 11 March 1975, Dr. Morris was notified that the photography of Mt. Ararat was classified and, therefore, could not be provided. An additional request made through Dr. Charles Willis of Fresno, California to Mr. Arthur C. Lundahl, retired Director NPIC on 5 March 1975 was also denied on 31 March 1975.

On 3 April 1975, NPIC Section Chief [deleted] sent a memo to the Chief, IEG, detailing the efforts of Messrs. [Deleted] and [deleted] who had searched unsuccessfully all available U-2 and satellite imagery for possible evidence of Noah's Ark. This search had been prompted by the visit to the Center, on 14 March 1975, of Captain Howard Schue of the IC Staff with a ground photo "showing a long range view of the purported Ark." The [deleted] Division of NPIC was tasked to determine if the Ark's features in the photo had been altered; tests failed to identify any manipulation. Attempts to compare the ground photo with satellite imagery for identification and location purposes also proved negative.

From 27 March to 5 April 1975, a French archeological explorer, Fernand Navarra was at Iverson Mall in Washington, D.C. publicizing his book *Noah's Ark: I Touched It*. As part of the sales pitch for the book, there was a display which included a supposed wood fragment of the Ark. Several NPIC analysts concerned with the Ark problem visited the display but found nothing that would help their search efforts.

On 10 April 1975, Colonel Paul Tanota and Captain Howard Schue, of the IC Staff visited NPIC to discuss Mt. Ararat and to see the August 1974 aerial photography of the mountain. At the request of Captain Schue, a print of Mt. Ararat showing the 13,000 and 14,000 foot elevations was provided.

On 5 July, 1975 a book entitled *The Ark of Ararat* by Thomas Nelson was released. Mr. Nelson maintained that the CIA had photos of Ararat and that they had been analyzed in the search for the Ark. On 12 October 1975, Tom Crotser from a group known as The Holy Ground Mission of Frankston, Texas showed a ground photo supposedly of the Ark taken during their 1974 expedition to Mt. Ararat. Sometime in 1977, Bill Chaney Speed of Search Foundation, Inc. requested the aerial photos of Mt. Ararat. His request also was denied.

Senator Barry Goldwater wrote DCI Turner on 1 September 1978, "You may think this is a screwball request and it may be, but I would like to know if you can do anything about it." The letter went on to ask if satellite photography could be searched "to determine whether or not something in the way of an archeological find might be located near or on top of the Mount." Goldwater explained that a letter he had received had come "from a man in whom I have great confidence, who certainly is no nut, who knows Turkey rather well but who feels that there is reason to believe the Ark may be resting at or near the top of the mount. I assure that I will keep this at any classification you want it kept and if you desire me to go to the devil, I know the way." DCI Turner replied "we have been requested on several occasions if we could determine whether there was remains of the Ark on Mt. Ararat. We have, as a result, carefully reviewed the photography of the area but have not found any evidence of the Ark."

On 27 May 1981, [deleted] of the Center received a telephone call from Air Force Talent Control Officer, Major Ray Abel, requesting information on Noah's Ark. Major Abel said he had received a request from General Lew Allen, Air Force Chief of Staff, who, in turn, was answering a requirement from Congressman Bill Archer of Texas. Congressman Archer had indicated that some of his constituents from Houston, Texas were going on an expedition to Mt. Ararat and would like to have as much information as possible. [Deleted] told Major Abel that NPIC had conducted a study of Mt. Ararat in the 1970s and had found no evidence of the Ark.

In February 1982, former Astronaut James B. Irwin of the High Flight Foundation, a Christian group in Colorado Springs, Colorado, called former NPIC official Dino A. Brugioni, at his home and asked about the aerial photos of Mount Ararat. Irwin was informed that no evidence of the Ark had ever been seen on aerial photography.

Strong evidence exists that suggests that the U.S. government knows far more about Noah's Ark than it would prefer us to think. On June 17, 1949, a U.S. Air Force Europe (USAFE) aircraft taking part in a classified mission that included securing aerial imagery of the 16,945-foot-high Mount Ararat, Turkey, inadvertently stumbled across what might have been the remains of the mighty Ark of Noah as described in the Bible. As the aircraft reached a height of around fifteen thousand feet and a distance of approximately one mile from the harsh, frozen mountain, its cameras captured several intriguing images of a large structure—an incredible five hundred feet in length—that protruded from an ice cap located at the southwest edge of Ararat's west-facing mountain.

The crew quickly swung the aircraft around and headed to the north of the mountain and continued to take photographs. Astonishingly, these revealed, from a distance of two miles, the existence of *another* large, unidentified structure on the western plateau and three symmetrical, but badly damaged, protrusions that pointed skyward out of what looked like a curiously wing-shaped section of the structure.

Needless to say, the photographs were carefully and quietly processed and duly classified, and thus was born the legend of the Ararat Anomaly—as it is officially known throughout the U.S. Intelligence Community in general and to the CIA in particular.

A whole host of claims, counterclaims, and assertions regarding the Ararat Anomaly have surfaced both privately and publicly. Many of these maintain that the CIA and a number of other official bodies within the U.S. government, intelligence community, and military have collated a wealth of data and imagery on the Anomaly that are exempt from public disclosure.

In addition, sources tell of Indiana Jones-style, government-funded expeditions to Turkey to try to locate the remains of the Ark. Others maintain that remnants of the Anomaly have been found and secretly spirited away to classified military and governmental installations and institutions in the United States.

Men in Black-style characters have reportedly been intimidating, warning those with knowledge of the Anomaly to remain silent, and some even claim, highly controversially, that the Ark represents the remains of a crashed

Located near the eastern border of Turkey, Mt. Ararat is actually two mountains—Little Ararat (left) and Greater Ararat—near the city of Yerevan.

UFO that impacted on Mount Ararat thousands of years ago and that has been the subject of a specific clandestine investigation by elements of the U.S. Air Force.

According to the Bible: "God said unto Noah … make thee an ark of gopher wood…. And this is the fashion which thou shalt make it of: The length of the ark shall be three hundred cubits, the breadth of it fifty cubits, and the height of it thirty cubits." A cubit is approximately twenty inches in length—which would make the Ark five hundred feet long, eighty-three feet wide, and fifty feet high.

Moreover, it is alleged that the Ark was strong enough to withstand the catastrophic flood that allegedly encompassed the globe and lasted for forty turbulent days, so, the story goes, when the flood waters began to recede, the Ark settled on its final resting place: the permanently snow-capped Mount Ararat.

If the U.S. Intelligence Community has located the remains (or the suspected remains) of such an impressive vessel, it would undoubtedly be the archaeological discovery of the century. Certainly, accounts abound positing a direct link between the Anomaly, Noah's Ark, and the secret world of the government, military, and intelligence officials, and those accounts suggest that at the heart of the puzzle lies something of such profound importance that it may shake our belief systems concerning the Ark to their very core.

Conspiracies, cover-ups, biblical mysteries, highly advanced technology in the hands of the ancients, secret histories, and much more are all part and parcel of the mystery of the Ararat Anomaly.

In 1952, William Todd, a photographer's mate chief with the U.S. Navy, viewed an object "of huge size" that appeared to be a "rectangular, slate-colored boat" while flying near the summit of Mount Ararat, and in 1955, a French explorer, Fernand Navarra, located a five-foot-long piece of ancient, carved wood high on Mount Ararat, just several hundred meters from the site shown in the historic photographs taken in 1949.

According to Gregor Schwinghammer, formerly of the U.S. Air Force's 428th Tactical Flight Squadron based in Adana, Turkey, he saw the Ararat Anomaly as he was flying near the mountain in an F-100 aircraft in the late 1950s. Moreover, he said that it looked like "an enormous boxcar" lying in a gully high up on Mount Ararat and added that photographs had been taken of the structure by U-2 spy plane pilots. He further revealed that the object seemed to be "banked"—something that indicated it had become caught there long ago as it slid down the mountainside.

Schwinghammer says: "I think most of the time it is covered with ice and snow and that we just saw it at a time when part of it was protruding from the snow. I know that I saw a rectangular structure that looked like a ship. It was at a period in time or history and we were there at that time. Other pilots in the squadron remember having taken parts in flights over Ararat or having heard that other pilots had seen a ship-like object on the mountain."

Now we come to the matter of the Smithsonian.

Equally provocative is the testimony of a man named David Duckworth, who worked at the Smithsonian in fall 1968. After being there for approximately a month, Duckworth said that "several crates were delivered to our section which seemed to cause quite a bit of interest among the directors."

The crates were duly opened, and contained within them were "several artifacts like old wood and some old-style tools." Photographs were also in there, reportedly taken from a balloon, that showed a "ship-like object down in some ice. So I took a look at them and talked some, and I was told it was Noah's Ark."

Duckworth said that, not surprisingly, this caused a considerable amount of excitement among the staff, but after five days, things began to change: "They didn't talk anymore. They started taking the stuff out. The questions we'd ask, they just kind of ignored us, and finally they pretty well came out and told everybody to just keep their mouth shut."

After portions of his story were told to Ark researcher Violet Cummings, Duckworth said that he was visited at work by two men who identified themselves as FBI agents. He added: "They told me my statements were making waves at the Smithsonian. And that I had been somewhere where I shouldn't have and seen something that didn't concern me. They didn't threaten me, exactly."

This action by the FBI prompted Duckworth to phone his boss at the Smithsonian: "I asked him some questions about all that stuff from Ararat and the Ark. He said, 'You know, I really can't talk about it,' and [he] kind of laughed."

What all of this tells us is that government agencies have, for years, carefully and secretly collated data on ancient aliens, extraterrestrial visits to the Earth thousands of years ago, and theories that much of the world's religious beliefs were actually born out of encounters with beings from other worlds. Of course, it's no surprise that most of the documentation on these issues remain covered up, buried deep in government vaults. After all, how can one tell the world that God, or gods, do not exist, only visiting aliens that masqueraded as all-powerful deities?

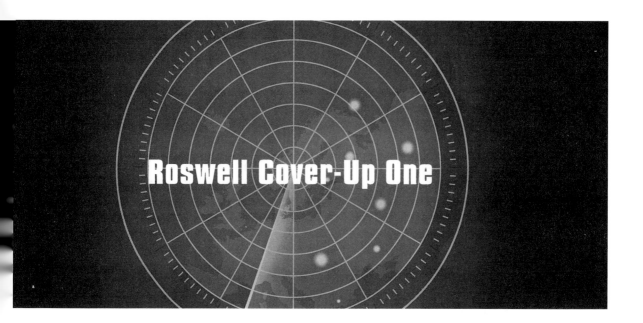

Roswell Cover-Up One

In early July 1947, something crashed to Earth approximately a two-hour drive from the New Mexico city of Roswell. The specific location was the remote, expansive Foster Ranch, in Lincoln County. A rancher named William Ware Brazel stumbled on a huge field of strange debris—tough and very light foil that extended over a distance of more than six hundred feet. Brazel was unsure of what he should do and who he should tell about the incredible discovery. Neighbors suspected that what had come down on the ranch was one of those flying saucers that had been reported in the nation's newspapers since June 24, 1947, which was the date on which a squadron of such craft was seen by a pilot named Kenneth Arnold, near Mount Rainier, Washington State.

Incredibly, after Brazel contacted the local police—who, in turn, contacted staff at the Roswell Army Air Field—the military put out a statement that what was found was a flying saucer. It was a story that made worldwide news—at least, for a short time. That statement was hastily retracted the next day, however, when the Army Air Force (as it was known at the time) assured everyone that the whole thing was a mistake. Overexcitement and misidentification was the cause of all the fuss. What was really found, said the military, was nothing stranger than an ordinary weather balloon. The military did not, however, explain why trained personnel from the base couldn't recognize a weather balloon when they saw it, nor did this explain the rumors flying around town that William Brazel didn't just find a huge field of debris. The story goes that he also stumbled upon several decomposing, small bodies that did not look human. Warned by the military never again to speak about the mysterious affair, Brazel did exactly that. Whatever he really knew, it went to the grave with him.

The Roswell affair quickly slid into obscurity until the late 1970s. That was when UFO researchers Bill Moore and Stanton Friedman began to look deeply into the matter. Roswell was about to be resurrected. The result was Moore's book (cowritten with Charles Berlitz) *The Roswell Incident*. Today, more than forty years after Moore and Friedman began their work, the case is known all across the world. Hundreds of people have come forward concerning their knowledge of the puzzle—as well as testifying to their first-hand awareness of the incident. Elderly whistle-blowers and military retirees speak of seeing the small, large-headed bodies out in the desert. Others talk of being ordered to recover all of the wreckage and never again make mention of what they saw—which, for the most part, was the case until they decided, in their final years, to reveal the truth.

The weather balloon angle was the government's answer to Roswell for decades, specifically until 1993. That's when things changed, and Roswell became an even more intriguing case.

It was in 1993 that Steven Schiff (at the time a congressman for New Mexico) waded into the controversy, demanding to know the truth. He wrote to Les Aspin, the secretary of defense at that time, the following: "Last fall I became aware of a strange series of events beginning in New Mexico over 45 years ago and involving personnel of what was then the Army Air Force. I have since reviewed the facts in some detail, and I am writing to request your assistance in arriving at a definitive explanation of what transpired and why."

Aspin chose not to reply to Schiff. That task was given to Col. Larry G. Shockley of the Air Force. Shockley informed Schiff that he had "referred this matter to the National Archives and Records Administration for direct reply to you."

The response from the National Archives's staff did not please Schiff or his staff:

The U.S. Air Force has retired to our custody its records on Project Blue Book relating to the investigations of unidentified flying objects. Project Blue Book has been declassified and the records are available for examination in our research room. The project closed in 1969 and we

Ufologist Stanton Friedman (pictured) was one of two civilian investigators (Bill Moore was the other) who first broke the UFO story about Roswell.

have no information after that date. We have received numerous requests concerning records relating to the Roswell incident among these records. We have not located any documentation relating to this event in Project Blue Book records, or in any other pertinent Defense Department records in our custody.

Angry and frustrated, Congressman Schiff approached the General Accounting Office and requested that they try to resolve things. Notably, the Air Force began its own investigation, which many UFO researchers felt amounted to damage control and an attempt to steer the GAO away from the dark truth. On July 28, 1995, Schiff got a reply from the GAO. Within that reply was what the Air Force assured the GAO was the real truth of Roswell. The GAO's statement to Schiff began as follows:

> On July 8, 1947, the Roswell Army Air Field (RAAF) public information office in Roswell, New Mexico, reported the crash and recovery of a "flying disc." Army Air Forces personnel from the RAAF's 509th Bomb Group were credited with the recovery. The following day, the press reported that the Commanding General of the U.S. Eighth Air Force, Fort Worth, Texas, announced that RAAF personnel had recovered a crashed radar-tracking (weather) balloon, not a "flying disc."

> After nearly 50 years, speculation continues on what crashed at Roswell. Some observers believe that the object was of extraterrestrial origin. In the July 1994 Report of Air Force Research Regarding the Roswell Incident, the Air Force did not dispute that something happened near Roswell, but reported that the most likely source of the wreckage was from a balloon-launched classified government project designed to determine the state of Soviet nuclear weapons research. The debate on what crashed at Roswell continues.

The GAO continued:

> Concerned that the Department of Defense (DOD) may not have provided you with all available information on the crash, you asked us to determine the requirements for reporting air accidents similar to the crash near Roswell and identify any government records concerning the Roswell crash.

> We conducted an extensive search for government records related to the crash near Roswell. We examined a wide range of classified and unclassified documents dating from July 1947 through the 1950s. These records came from numerous organizations in New Mexico and elsewhere throughout DOD as well as the Federal Bureau of Investigation (FBI), the Central Intelligence Agency (CIA), and the National Security Council.

The GAO explained:

In 1947, Army regulations required that air accident reports be maintained permanently. We identified four air accidents reported by the Army Air Forces in New Mexico during July 1947. All of the accidents involved military aircraft and occurred after July 8, 1947—the date the RAAF public information office first reported the crash and recovery of a "flying disc" near Roswell. The Navy reported no air accidents in New Mexico during July 1947. Air Force officials told us that according to record-keeping requirements in effect during July 1947, there was no requirement to prepare a report on the crash of a weather balloon.

In our search for records concerning the Roswell crash, we learned that some government records covering RAAF activities had been destroyed and others had not. For example, RAAF administrative records (from Mar. 1945 through Dec. 1949) and RAAF outgoing messages (from Oct. 1946 through Dec. 1949) were destroyed. The document disposition form does not indicate what organization or person destroyed the records and when or under what authority the records were destroyed.

U.S. congressman Steven Schiff of Arizona's 1st District tried to find out from the military what was going on at Roswell, but he couldn't break through the veil of secrecy.

It must be said that GAO staff, the UFO researcher community, and Congressman Schiff were all surprised by the fact that certain files from the Roswell base had been destroyed under circumstances which could not be determined. The GAO had more to say:

Our search for government records concerning the Roswell crash yielded two records originating in 1947—a July 1947 history report by the combined 509th Bomb Group and RAAF and an FBI teletype message dated July 8, 1947. The 509th-RAAF report noted the recovery of a "flying disc" that was later determined by military officials to be a radar-tracking balloon. The FBI message stated that the military had reported that an object resembling a high-altitude weather balloon with a radar reflector had been recovered near Roswell.

The other government records we reviewed, including those previously withheld from the public because of security classification, and the Air Force's analysis of unidentified flying object sightings from 1946 to 1953 (Project Blue Book Special Report No. 14), did not mention the crash or the recovery of an airborne object near Roswell in July 1947. Similarly, executive branch agencies' responses to our letters of inquiry produced no other government records on the Roswell crash. According to Air Force regulation, an unidentified flying object is an airborne object that by performance, aerodynamic characteristics, or unusual features, does not conform to known aircraft or missiles, or does not correspond to Air Force definitions of familiar or known objects or unidentified aircraft....

According to press accounts from July 1947, Army Air Forces personnel from RAAF were involved in the recovery of an airborne object near Roswell. Therefore, if an air accident report was prepared, it should have been prepared in accordance with Army regulations. According to an Army records management official, in 1947 Army regulations required that air accident reports be maintained permanently. An Air Force official said there was no similar requirement to report a weather balloon crash.

According to an Air Force official who has worked in the records management field since the mid-1940s, air accident reports prepared in July 1947 under Army regulations should have been transferred to Air Force custody in September 1947, when the Air Force was established as a separate service.

The GAO also addressed the possibility that the Roswell saga might have been caused by the crash of a U.S. military craft:

The Air Force Safety Agency is responsible for maintaining reports of air accidents. We examined its microfilm records to determine whether any air accidents had been reported in New Mexico during July 1947. We identified four air accidents during this time period. All of the accidents involved military fighter or cargo aircraft and occurred after July 8, 1947—the date the RAAF public information office first reported the crash and recovery of a "flying disc" near Roswell. According to the Army Air Force's *Report of Major Accident*, these four accidents occurred at or near the towns of Hobbs, Albuquerque, Carrizozo, and Alamogordo, New Mexico. Only one of the four accidents resulted in a fatality. The pilot died when the aircraft crashed during an attempted take-off. These records do not include information regarding mishaps of air vehicles belonging to civilian or other government agencies. These records also do not include mishaps involving unmanned air vehicles such as remotely piloted aircraft, low-speed cruise missiles, and most balloons.

In a section of the GAO's report titled "Search for Records," Congressman Schiff was informed as follows:

> In searching for government records on the Roswell crash, we were particularly interested in identifying and reviewing records of military units assigned to RAAF in 1947—to include the 509th Bomb Group, the 1st Air Transport Unit, the 427th Army Air Force Base Unit, and the 1395th Military Police Company (Aviation).

> Document disposition forms obtained from the National Personnel Records Center in St. Louis, Missouri, indicate that in 1953, the Walker Air Force Base (formerly RAAF) records officer transferred to the Army's Kansas City records depository the histories of units stationed at Walker Air Force Base. These histories included the 509th Bomb Group and RAAF for February 1947 through October 1947; the 1st Air Transport Unit for July 1946 through June 1947; and the 427th Army Air Force Base Unit for January 1946 to February 1947. We could not locate any documentation indicating that records of the 1395th Military Police Company (Aviation) were ever retired to the National Personnel Records Center or its predecessor depositories.

> The July 1947 history for the 509th Bomb Group and RAAF stated that the RAAF public information office "was kept quite busy … answering inquiries on the 'flying disc,' which was reported to be in [the] possession of the 509th Bomb Group. The object turned out to be a radar tracking balloon." By his signature, the RAAF's commanding officer certified that the report represented a complete and accurate account of RAAF activities in July 1947.

> In addition to unit history reports, … we also searched for other government records on the Roswell crash. In this regard, the Chief Archivist for the National Personnel Records Center provided us with documentation indicating that (1) RAAF records such as finance and accounting, supplies, buildings and grounds, and other general administrative matters from March 1945 through December 1949 and (2) RAAF outgoing messages from October 1946 through December 1949 were destroyed. According to this official, the document disposition form did not properly indicate the authority under which the disposal action was taken. The Center's Chief Archivist stated that from his personal experience, many of the Air Force organizational records covering this time period were destroyed without entering a citation for the govern-

ing disposition authority. Our review of records control forms showing the destruction of other records—including outgoing RAAF messages for 1950—supports the Chief Archivist's viewpoint.

On the matter of Roswell and the FBI, the GAO provided the following data:

> During our review of records at FBI headquarters, we found a July 8, 1947, teletype message from the FBI office in Dallas, Texas, to FBI headquarters and the FBI office in Cincinnati, Ohio. An FBI spokesperson confirmed the authenticity of the message.

> According to the message, an Eighth Air Force headquarters official had telephonically informed the FBI's Dallas office of the recovery near Roswell of a hexagonal-shaped disc suspended from a large balloon by cable. The message further stated that the disc and balloon were being sent to Wright Field (now Wright-Patterson Air Force Base, Ohio) for examination. According to the Eighth Air Force official, the recovered object resembled a high-altitude weather balloon with a radar reflector. The message stated that no further investigation by the FBI was being conducted.

One of the explanations provided by the GAO about the Roswell incident was that it was the result of misidentifying what was merely a weather balloon with a reflector.

To follow up on the July 8th message, we reviewed microfilm abstracts of the FBI Dallas and Cincinnati office activities for July 1947. An abstract prepared by the FBI Dallas office on July 12, 1947, summarized the particulars of the July 8th message. There was no mention in the Cincinnati office abstracts of the crash or recovery of an airborne object near Roswell.

Because the FBI message reported that debris from the Roswell crash was being transported to Wright Field for examination, we attempted to determine whether military regulations existed for handling such debris. We were unable to locate any applicable regulation. As a final step, we reviewed Air Materiel Command (Wright Field) records from 1947 to 1950 for evidence of command personnel involvement in this matter. We found no records mentioning the Roswell crash or the examination by Air Materiel Command personnel of any debris recovered from the crash.

The next portion of the GAO report makes it clear that its staff went knocking on numerous doors but failed to uncover anything substantial or, indeed, anything at all:

We sent letters to several federal agencies asking for any government records they might have concerning the Roswell crash. In this regard, we contacted DOD, the National Security Council, the White House Office of Science and Technology Policy, the CIA, the FBI, and the Department of Energy.

The National Security Council, the White House Office of Science and Technology Policy, and the Department of Energy responded that they had no government records relating to the Roswell crash.

The FBI informed us that all FBI data regarding the crash near Roswell had been processed under Freedom of Information Act (FOIA) requests previously received by the Bureau. We reviewed the FBI's FOIA material and identified the July 8, 1947, FBI teletype message discussing the recovery near Roswell of a high-altitude weather balloon with a radar reflector.

DOD informed us that the U.S. Air Force report of July 1994, entitled *Report of Air Force Research Regarding the Roswell Incident*, represents the extent of DOD records or information concerning the Roswell crash. The Air Force report concluded that there was no dispute that something happened near Roswell in July 1947 and that all available official materials indicated the most likely source of the wreckage recovered was one of the project MOGUL balloon trains. At the time of the Roswell crash, project MOGUL was a highly classified U.S. effort to determine the state of Soviet nuclear weapons research using balloons that carried radar reflectors and acoustic sensors.

In March 1995, the CIA's Executive Director responded to our letter of inquiry by stating that earlier searches by the CIA for records on unidentified flying objects produced no information pertaining to the Roswell crash. The Executive Director added, however, that it was unclear whether the CIA had ever conducted a search for records specifically relating to Roswell. In the absence of such assurance, the Executive Director instructed CIA personnel to conduct a comprehensive records search for information relating to Roswell. On May 30, 1995, the CIA's Executive Director informed us that a search against the term "Roswell, New Mexico," in all CIA databases produced no CIA documents related to the crash.

This was also mentioned:

A draft of this report was provided to DOD for comment. DOD offered no comments or suggested changes to the report. The Chief Archivist, National Personnel Records Center offered several comments clarifying matters dealing with records management. These comments have been incorporated into the final report where appropriate.

The CIA, the Department of Energy, the FBI, the National Security Council, and the White House Office of Science and Technology Policy also received excerpts from the report discussing the activities of their respective agencies. They had no substantive comments and made no suggested changes to the report.

In essence, that was the end of the GAO's investigation. Nothing of any substance was found. No documents were uncovered (let's not forget that the GAO learned that certain 1940s-era files from the Roswell base were destroyed). The Air Force's claim that what came down was not a UFO or a weather balloon but a Mogul device was seen by some in the GAO as an attempt to deflect their staff away from something more sinister. True or not, the Mogul theory remains the Air Force's answer to what happened on the Foster Ranch in 1947. However, a problem was discovered: Mogul balloon arrays did not carry crews, so how do we reconcile this with the fact that numerous people claimed to have seen strange bodies at the crash site? In 1997, the Air Force came up with another theory for what happened in Roswell; this one was specifically in relation to the issue of bodies, as we shall now see.

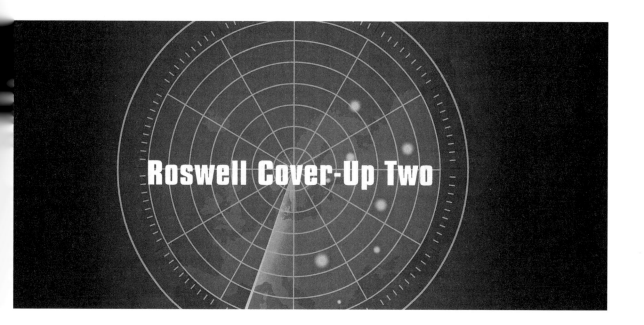

Roswell Cover-Up Two

Three years after the Air Force published its report suggesting what came down on the Foster Ranch in Lincoln County, New Mexico, in early July 1947, its staff came up with a new theory for Roswell; this one would address the highly controversial issue of bodies having been found on the ranch near the huge debris site discovered by rancher William Brazel. The 1997 report was titled *The Roswell Report: Case Closed.*

In a foreword to the report, Sheila Widnall, the secretary of the Air Force at the time, said the following:

> The "Roswell Incident" has assumed a central place in American folklore since the events of the 1940s in a remote area of New Mexico. Because the Air Force was a major player in those events, we have played a key role in executing the General Accounting Office's tasking to uncover all records regarding that incident. Our objective throughout this inquiry has been simple and consistent: to find all the facts and bring them to light. If documents were classified, declassify them; where they were dispersed, bring them into a single source for public review.
>
> In July 1994, we completed the first step in that effort and later published *The Roswell Report: Fact vs. Fiction in the New Mexico Desert.* This volume represents the necessary follow-on to that first publication and contains additional material and analysis. I think that with this publication we have reached our goal of a complete and open explanation of the events that occurred in the Southwest many years ago.

Beyond that achievement, this inquiry has shed fascinating light into the Air Force of that era and revitalized our appreciation for the dedication and accomplishments of the men and women of that time. As we celebrate the Air Force's 50th Anniversary, it is appropriate to once again reflect on the sacrifices made by so many to make ours the finest air and space force in history.

On its decision to finally address the matter of the bodies allegedly found on the Foster Ranch, the Air Force began as follows:

The July 1994 Air Force report concluded that the predecessor to the U.S. Air Force, the U.S. Army Air Forces, did indeed recover material near Roswell in July 1947. This 1,000-page report methodically explains that what was recovered by the Army Air Forces was not the remnants of an extraterrestrial spacecraft and its alien crew, but debris from an Army Air Forces balloon-borne research project code named Mogul.

Although Mogul components clearly accounted for the claims of "flying saucer" debris recovered in 1947, lingering questions remained concerning anecdotal accounts that included descriptions of "alien" bodies. The issue of "bodies" was not discussed extensively in the 1994 report because there were not any bodies connected with events that occurred in 1947. The extensive Secretary of the Air Force-directed search of Army Air Forces and U.S. Air Force records from 1947 did not yield information that even suggested the 1947 "Roswell" events were anything other than the retrieval of the Mogul equipment.

Sheila Widnall, who was secretary of the Air Force from 1993 to 1997, is an aerospace researcher and professor at MIT. Widnall supported the official report that there were no alien bodies or alien debris of any kind.

The Air Force then got to the point:

Subsequent to the 1994 report, Air Force researchers discovered information that provided a rational explanation for the alleged observations of alien bodies associated with the "Roswell Incident." Pursuant to the discovery, research efforts compared documented Air Force activities to the incredible claims of "flying saucers," "aliens" and seemingly unusual Air Force involvement. This in-depth examination revealed that these accounts, in most instances, were of actual Air Force activities but were seriously flawed in several major areas, most notably: the Air Force operations that inspired reports of "bodies" (in addition to being earthly in origin) did not occur in 1947. It appears that UFO proponents have failed to establish the accurate dates for these "alien" observations (in some instances by more than a decade) and then erroneously linked them to the actual Project Mogul debris recovery.

This report discusses the results of this further research and identifies the likely sources of the claims of "alien" bodies. Contrary to allegations that the Air Force has engaged in a cover-up and possesses dark secrets involving the Roswell claims, some of the accounts appear to be descriptions of unclassified and widely publicized Air Force scientific achievements.

The military's conclusions read as follows:

Air Force activities which occurred over a period of many years have been consolidated and are now represented to have occurred in two or three days in July 1947. "Aliens" observed in the New Mexico desert were probably anthropomorphic test dummies that were carried aloft by U.S. Air Force high altitude balloons for scientific research. The "unusual" military activities in the New Mexico desert were high altitude research balloon launch and recovery operations. The reports of military units that always seemed to arrive shortly after the crash of a flying saucer to retrieve the saucer and "crew" were actually accurate descriptions of Air Force personnel engaged in anthropomorphic dummy recovery operations.

Claims of bodies at the Roswell Army Air Field hospital were most likely a combination of two separate incidents: 1) a 1956 KC–97 aircraft accident in which 11 Air Force members lost their lives; and, 2) a 1959 manned balloon mishap in which two Air Force pilots were injured.

Those were the Air Force's final words: nothing stranger than crash test dummies, and not a single alien anywhere in sight. Let's now see how, specifically, the Air Force reached that conclusion. The report stated:

The most puzzling and intriguing element of the complex series of events now known as the Roswell Incident, are the alleged sightings of alien bodies. The bodies turned what, for many years, was just another flying saucer story, into what many UFO proponents claim is the best case for extraterrestrial visitation of Earth. The importance of bodies and the assumptions made as to their origin is illustrated in a passage from a popular Roswell book: Crashed saucers are one thing, and could well turn out to be futuristic

American or even foreign aircraft or missiles. But alien bodies are another matter entirely, and hardly subject to misinterpretation?

In a section of the Air Force's report titled "Test Dummies Used by the U.S. Air Force," the Air Force provided the following words: "Since the beginning of manned flight, designers have sought a substitute for the human body to test hazardous new equipment. Early devices used by the predecessors of the U.S. Air Force were simply constructed parachute drop test dummies with little similarity to the human form. Following World War II, aircraft emergency escape systems became increasingly sophisticated and engineers required a dummy with more humanlike characteristics."

The Air Force continued with a history of how and under what circumstances the military decided to make good use of crash test dummies:

> During World War I research and development of the first U.S. military parachute was underway at McCook Field, Ohio. To test the parachute, engineers experimented with several types of dummies, settling on a model constructed of three-inch hemp rope and sandbags with the approximate proportions of a medium-sized man. The new invention was soon known by the nickname "Dummy Joe." Dummy Joe is said to have made more than five thousand "jumps" between 1918 and 1924.

> By 1924, parachutes were required on military aircraft with their serviceability tested by dummies dropped from aircraft. For this routine testing, several types of dummies were used. Parachutes were individually drop-tested from aircraft until the early stages of World War II, when, due both to increased reliability and large numbers of parachutes in service, this routine practice was discontinued. Nonetheless, test dummies were still used frequently by the Parachute Branch of Air Materiel Command (AMC) at Wright Field, Ohio, to test new parachute designs.

The Air Force then turned its attention to the matter of what was undertaken in the 1949 and onward era (which is decidedly strange, indeed, since the Roswell affair occurred midway through 1947, two years earlier): "In 1949, the U.S. Air Force Aero Medical Laboratory submitted a proposal for an improved model of the anthropomorphic dummy. This request was originated by the renowned Air Force scientist and physician John P. Stapp, now a retired Colonel, who conducted a series of landmark experiments at Muroc (now Edwards) AFB, Calif., to measure the effects of acceleration and deceleration during high-speed aircraft ejections."

As the Air Force noted:

> Stapp required a dummy that had the same center of gravity and articulation as a human, but, unlike the Ted Smith dummy, was

more human in appearance. A more accurate external appearance was required to provide for the proper fit of helmets, oxygen masks, and other equipment used during the tests. Stapp requested the Anthropology Branch of the Aero Medical Laboratory at Wright Field to review anthropological, orthopedic, and engineering literature to prepare specifications for the new dummy. Plaster casts of the torso, legs, and arms of an Air Force pilot were also taken to assure accuracy. The result was a proposed dummy that stood 72 inches tall, weighed 200 pounds, had provisions for mounting instrumentation, and could withstand up to 100 times the force of gravity.

In 1949, a contract was awarded to Sierra Engineering Company of Sierra Madre, Calif., and deliveries began in 1950. This dummy quickly became

Another official Air Force explanation about the rumors of alien bodies was that the military sometimes uses dummies in their vehicle tests.

known as "Sierra Sam." In 1952, a contract for anthropomorphic dummies was awarded to Alderson Research Laboratories, Inc., of New York City. Dummies constructed by both companies possessed the same basic characteristics: a skeleton of aluminum or steel, latex or plastic skin, a cast aluminum skull, and an instrument cavity in the torso and head for the mounting of strain gauges, accelerometers, transducers, and rate gyros. Models used by the Air Force were primarily parachute drop and ejection seat versions with center of gravity tolerances within one quarter inch.

Now we get to the heart of the matter: the Air Force's rationale for believing that Roswell's "alien bodies" were really nothing stranger than dummies. The report states:

> Over the next several years the two companies improved and redesigned internal structures and instrumentation, but the basic external appearance of the dummies remained relatively constant from the mid-1950s to the late 1960s. Dummies of these types were most likely the "aliens" associated with the "Roswell Incident."

> Anthropomorphic dummies were transported to altitudes up to 98,000 feet by high altitude balloons. The dummies were then released for a period of free-fall while body movements and escape equipment performance were recorded by a variety of instruments.

Forty-three high altitude balloon flights carrying anthropomorphic dummies were launched and recovered throughout New Mexico between June 1954 and February 1959. Due to prevailing wind conditions, operational factors and ruggedness of the terrain, the majority of dummies impacted outside the confines of military reservations in eastern New Mexico, near Roswell, and in areas surrounding the Tularosa Valley in south central New Mexico. Additionally, 30 dummies were dropped by aircraft over White Sands Proving Ground, N.M. in 1953. In 1959, 150 dummies were dropped by aircraft over Wright-Patterson AFB, Ohio (possibly accounting for alleged alien "sightings" at that location).

The Air Force expanded:

For the majority of the tests, dummies were flown to altitudes between 30,000 and 98,000 feet attached to a specially designed rack suspended below a high altitude balloon. On several flights the dummies were mounted in the door of an experimental high altitude balloon gondola. Upon reaching the desired altitude, the dummies were released and free-fell for several minutes before deployment of the main parachute.

The dummies used for the balloon drops were outfitted with standard equipment of an Air Force aircrew member. This equipment consisted of a one-piece flight-suit, olive drab, gray (witnesses had described seeing aliens in gray one-piece suits) or fuchsia in color, boots, and a parachute pack. The dummies were also fitted with an instrumentation kit that contained accelerometers, pressure transducers, an ocscillograph, and a camera to record movements of the dummy during free-fall.

Since this final portion of the document concludes the Air Force's report on why its personnel were as sure as they could be that the strange bodies were really dummies, I will present it without interruption:

Recoveries of the test dummies were accomplished by personnel from the Holloman AFB Balloon Branch. Typically, eight to twelve civilian and military recovery personnel arrived at the site of an anthropomorphic dummy landing as soon as possible following impact. The recovery crews operated a variety of aircraft and vehicles. These included a wrecker, a six-by-six, a weapons carrier, and L–20 observation and C–47 transport aircraft—the exact vehicles and aircraft described by the witnesses as having been present at the crashed saucer locations. On one occasion, just southwest of Roswell, a High Dive project officer, 1st Lt. Raymond A. Madson, even conducted a search for dummies on horseback.

On a typical flight the dummies were separated from the balloon by radio command and descended by parachute. Prompt recovery of the dummies and their suspension racks, which usually did not land in the same location resulting in extensive ground and air searches, was essential for researchers to evaluate information collected by the instrumentation and cameras. To assist the recovery personnel, a variety of methods were used to enhance the visibility of the dummies: smoke grenades, pigment powder, and brightly colored parachute canopies. Also, recovery notices promising a $25 reward were taped to an exposed portion of a dummy. Local newspapers and radio stations were contacted when equipment was lost.

Despite these efforts, the dummies were not always recovered immediately; one was not found for nearly three years and several were not recovered at all. When they were found, the dummies and instrumentation were often damaged from impact. Damage to the dummies included loss of heads, arms, legs and fingers. This detail, dummies with missing fingers, appears to satisfy another element of the research profile: aliens with only four fingers.

What may have contributed to a misunderstanding if the dummies were viewed by persons unfamiliar with their intended use, were the methods used by Holloman AFB personnel to transport them. The dummies were sometimes transported to and from off-range locations in wooden shipping containers, similar to caskets, to prevent damage to fragile instruments mounted in and on the dummy. Also, canvas military stretchers and hospital gurneys were used (a procedure recommended by a dummy manufacturer) to move the dummies in the laboratory or retrieve dummies in the field after a test. The first 10 dummy drops also utilized black or silver insulation bags, similar to "body bags" in which the dummies were placed for flight to guard against equipment failure at low ambient temperatures of the upper atmosphere.

On one occasion northwest of Roswell, a local woman unfamiliar with the test activities arrived at a dummy landing site prior to the arrival of the recovery personnel. The woman saw what appeared to be a human embedded head first in a snowbank and became hysterical. The woman screamed, "He's dead, he's dead!"

The Air Force came right to the point, making an authoritative statement: "It now appeared that anthropomorphic dummies dropped by high altitude balloons satisfied the requirements of the research profile."

Of course, the UFO research community was not impressed and scoffed at the idea that those who claimed to have seen alien bodies had actually witnessed nothing stranger than a crash test dummy. It's eye-opening to note, though, that when the report was released in July 1997 (the fiftieth anniversary of the incident), even the mainstream doubted the odd theory.

Indeed, the astute media noted that the bulk of the report was focused on the usage of dummies in the 1950s and certainly not in 1947. At the July 1947 press conference, a journalist asked the following question: "How do you square the UFO enthusiasts saying that they're talking about 1947, and you're talking about dummies used in the 50's, almost a decade later?"

Air Force spokesman Col. John Haynes replied, noticeably awkwardly: "Well, I'm afraid that's a problem that we have with time compression. I don't know what they saw in '47, but I'm quite sure it probably was Project Mogul. But I think if you find that people talk about things over a period of time, they begin to lose exactly when the date was."

For the record, "time compression" was the 1990s equivalent of what we now know and loathe as "alternative facts."

It's no wonder that so many suspect that we still don't have the full, true story of what happened back in 1947 on a remote ranch in the wilds of New Mexico.

Hollywood's UFO Secrets

Have you heard the one about the president, the comedian, and the aliens? A bad joke? Well, actually, yes, it probably is. It's dominated by a couple of famous characters and is filled with conspiracy and nothing less than a bunch of dead extraterrestrials, but is it true? That's the big question. As for the case at issue, it's the one that suggests that in 1973, legendary comic Jackie Gleason got to see a bunch of pickled E.T.s, courtesy of none other than his buddy President Richard Nixon! Really? Well, that very much depends on who you ask.

Gleason is probably most remembered for his starring role in *The Honeymooners*, a hit show from the 1950s, and for his portrayal of Sheriff Buford T. Justice in the *Smokey and the Bandit* movies. As for President Nixon, it's without doubt the Watergate affair that he is most associated with. Two other points need to be noted: (a) Gleason and the president were friends and often played golf together; and (b) Gleason had a deep interest in UFOs and had a massive collection of saucer-themed books, magazines, journals, etc. Indeed, in the 1960s, he often popped up on *The Long John Nebel Show* to discuss his thoughts on the subject as well as on certain cases and characters in ufology.

What we know of the "I saw the aliens" saga came from Gleason's second wife, Beverly McKittrick. The story went that Gleason got to see the proof that aliens really do exist on a particular evening in 1973: February 19. As for where the bodies were supposedly stored, the location was Homestead Air Force Base, Florida. Today, it is called Homestead Air Reserve Base.

As for the way things developed, well, let's say that credulity is stretched to the absolute max. The tale goes that only hours after the pair enjoyed a game of golf, the president turned up at the Gleason home. It was late at night, and Nixon was on his own, no less. He had apparently given the

Secret Service the slip and was ready to show Jackie something amazing. No problem! The president would take Gleason to Homestead, flash a bit of ID to the security personnel (or say something along the lines of, "Hi, it's me, the president!"), and breeze on into the most protected part of the installation with the man who would be Buford.

The tale continues that the astonished guards at the gate waved the pair through. Nixon led his friend—who was still in the dark about what was going on—to a certain area on the base. It was a facility that contained the rotting remains of a bunch of dead E.T.s—whose flying skills were evidently not great and were found in the wreckage of a crashed UFO. Roswell? Kingman? Kecksburg? No location or year for the incident was ever given. The bodies were stored in containers described as looking similar to "glass-topped coke freezers." They were not in a good state of preservation: they were damaged, withered, small, and gray with large heads.

Although Gleason finally got the evidence he needed, the whole thing plunged him into states of shock, anxiety, and even fear. The trip back to Gleason's home was made in silence. We don't know what was going through Nixon's mind, but Gleason was distinctly uneasy about the whole thing. He told Beverly of what he had seen but for the most part remained tight-lipped. That's about it. What can we say about this strange saga, then? Let's see.

First is the extremely unlikely matter of the president being gone—with no one in the know having been informed as to where he was—and for none of this to have reached the media. The president vanishes one evening, he can't be found, and the Secret Service is in a state of chaos and concern. Surely, that would have trickled down to the press? Also take note of the fact that Nixon and Gleason rolled up to Homestead and made a hassle-free way into what, one presumes, would have been one of the most highly protected sanctums on the planet. Unlikely!

Did McKittrick lie? No, not at all. In fact, the exact opposite. I would not be surprised if Gleason told Beverly the story exactly as she remembered it, but perhaps he told it as a joke. One that was then taken seriously by his wife. Could anything else be at play here? Probably not: The most likely scenario is that it was a prank on the part of Gleason. The least likely scenario is that against all the odds,

Actor Jackie Gleason (seen here with co-star Audrey Meadows from his famous TV comedy show, *The Honeymooners*) had an interest in UFOs and supposedly saw evidence personally.

the president of the United States completely vanished for a few hours, picked up a legendary comedian, floored the car to Homestead Air Force Base, showed Gleason the decaying proof, and then whisked him back home again.

To quote a massively overused few words from *The X-Files*: "I want to believe." I really do, but you know what? I don't believe.

For those of you who continue to hang on to the story, though, this tiny ray of light may keep your hopes up. UFO researcher Alejandro Rojas says:

> Some find it hard to believe that a sitting president could elude his security to whisk off in the middle of the night. Grant Cameron of PresidentialUFO.com cites a passage from a book written by a secret service man named Martin Venker. Grant Cameron says: "In his book *Confessions of an Ex-Secret Service Agent* [Venker] tells that not only can the President disappear, but it has happened. Venker stated that in the exact year of the Homestead incident with Gleason, 1973, Nixon had tried to cut his secret service protection. Venker also stated that it was not uncommon for Nixon to try to elude his secret service detail. The agents working on the Nixon Presidential detail had been warned about it."

One of the most significant developments in the 1990s, and in specific relation to Area 51, was the way in which the world of entertainment jumped on the bandwagon. Numerous sci-fi-themed and conspiracy-driven television shows incorporated Area 51 into their stories. *Seven Days*, which appeared on CBS, made notable use of Area 51. The time-travel-themed show ran from 1998 to 2001 and utilized the now less-than-secret base as the hub from where secret traveling in time took place. *Stargate SG-1* did very much likewise, using the theme of back-engineered alien technology secretly held at the facility.

The 2008 hit movie *Indiana Jones and the Kingdom of the Crystal Skull*, which starred Harrison Ford, made a less-than-subtle nod in the direction of Area 51 by referring to a secret government storage area as "Hangar 51." Unsurprisingly, *The X-Files* got in on the action, too. In 1998, in a two-part episode, Mulder and Scully find themselves in distinctly deep water when they head out to Area 51 in search of evidence that the U.S. government is hiding alien technology. Then came *Dark Skies*.

It was in 1996 that NBC unleashed a much-talked-about and still widely remembered UFO-themed show: *Dark Skies*. It was the brainchild of Brent V. Friedman and Bryce Zabel. The show was not destined to last, however. It ran for just twenty episodes, from September 1996 to May 1997. The show focused on the world of two people caught up in a Cold War-era conspiracy of extraterrestrial proportions: John Loengard and his girlfriend, Kim Sayers (played by Eric Close and Megan Ward). When news of the show first surfaced, and the nature of the show—that of a man–woman team—became evident, many thought: "*X-Files* rip-off." It turns out that it actually wasn't.

In *The X-Files*, the extraterrestrial angle was always shrouded in ambiguity: Were we really being visited by aliens? Was the UFO phenomenon just a cover for highly classified experiments of a genetic and mind-control nature undertaken by top-secret, "black budget" programs? *Dark Skies*, however, was very different. As the viewer learns from the absolute beginning, undoubtedly, the Earth is being invaded by hostile E.T.s, which John and Kim find out very early on. Also, whereas *The X-Files* was inspired by UFO history and classic cases, *Dark Skies* took things a big step further by taking real people with ties (large, small, and alleged) to ufology and inserting them into the expanding plot. We're talking about the likes of Area 51, Dorothy Kilgallen (the journalist who died under questionable circumstances on November 8, 1965), President John F. Kennedy, Attorney General Robert F. Kennedy, and even the issue of the U-2 spy plane that had such deep ties to Area 51. *Dark Skies*, then, had its finger on the pulse on certain controversial issues and people that appear in the pages of this very book, which is why I give it far more page space than *The X-Files*.

The storyline is an interesting one: After he and Kim move to D.C. and become immersed in the world of politics, John stumbles upon a massive UFO conspiracy and is soon incurring the wrath of both the MJ12 group and the man running it, Frank Bach, played by the late J. T. Walsh. In no time, however, John finds himself accepting one of those offers you can't refuse: he joins the secret group of alien hunters. Things become very dicey when the aliens target Kim and seek to make her one of their own. In reality, the alien menace is actually a small creature, not unlike the face-hugging things in the *Alien* movies starring Sigourney Weaver. Via the mouth, the creatures make their way to the brains of those unlucky enough to cross their path and seize control.

Fortunately, the "Ganglions"—as the pesky little critters are known—can be beaten. Providing that infection has not set in to an irreversible degree, it's possible to return the victims to their normal states of mind, albeit not without an occasional and slightly sinister equivalent of falling off the wagon. As the relationship between John and Kim and MJ12 gets ever more fraught and tension-filled, the pair go on the run, fearful that it's not just the aliens who want them dead. Shades of *The Fugitive* spring to mind as each week a new hazard surfaces and John and Kim seek to learn more about the E.T. threat, have clandestine meetings with Bobby Kennedy, and do their best to stay alive.

The fact that *Dark Skies* got cancelled (no, it wasn't due to the threats of a real MJ12-type group but something even worse: low ratings) means we'll never know what the exact outcome of the show would have been. We can, however, make a few educated guesses. It's a fact that all networks, actors, producers, and directors would love to have a highly successful show under their collective belt that runs for years and years (*NCIS* and *The Walking Dead* spring to mind), but the fact is that *Dark Skies* was never meant to last. The idea was to split the entire story across five seasons—and five alone. The plan was for the story to begin in the early 1960s (with flashbacks to the Roswell affair of 1947) and reach its finale in the early 2000s, when the countdown to the ultimate battle between them and us begins. *Dark Skies* was a highly thought-provoking show that deserved to have had its full run. It probably did not please those who run Area 51.

Although all of the above productions were meant as nothing but adventure-driven entertainment, undoubtedly, the government was irked by all of this publicity about Area 51—wholly *unwanted* publicity, as they saw it. How can we be so sure? The answer is simple: We only have to take a look at the strange saga of the 1996 movie *Independence Day*.

It was on July 2, 1996, that *Independence Day* was released and became a blockbuster hit with the public. In fact, it was so successful that the movie—which cost around $75 million to make—reaped in more than $800 million. In the story, hostile aliens suddenly attack the Earth. The planetary assault is completely unforeseen. The world's military do their utmost to fight back. For the most part, the story is told from the perspective of the United States. We see cities obliterated by the aliens—and untold numbers of people are killed. Much of the country is left in ruins, but Will Smith (Capt. Steven Hiller of the U.S. Marines) and Jeff Goldblum (David Levinson of MIT) finally manage to save the day. They do so by finding the aliens' one weak spot. The human race is saved from the brink of extinction.

Independence Day presented the U.S. military in an extremely positive light—namely, as a heroic fighting force that could even take on aliens and come out of it all victorious. In fact, when the movie was in its planning stage, an approach was made to the Pentagon by the production team to see if they could lend a hand to the story—providing aircraft and uniforms that would add notable weight to the production. The higher-ups in the military were all for it. For a while, anyway. Matters changed, though, when the government got the script, which made it clear that Area 51 was to play a large "role" in the movie, and the U.S. government didn't like that, not at all.

Actor Will Smith played Captain Steve Hiller in the blockbuster alien invasion film *Independence Day,* which portrayed the U.S. military in a very positive light.

In the story, we find that the president of the United States, Thomas J. Whitmore (played by actor Bill Pullman), knows *nothing* about Area 51. So secret is the installation, the presidential office is left out of the loop regarding not just what goes on there but even of its existence. The president ultimately learns, however, that Area 51 is a facility at which extensive research is being undertaken on the alien craft that crashed near Roswell, New Mexico, in July 1947. For decades, a small team of scientists has worked to crack the code of how the craft flies and the full nature of the extraterrestrial technology. Outraged, the president demands to be taken to Area 51. It's then that we see the scope of the work and we learn how and why the secrets of Roswell have been hidden at the base for so long.

None of this impressed the Pentagon—not at all—but the producer/writer of the movie, Dean Devlin, and the director, Roland Emmerich, were adamant that the Area 51 angle was an integral part of the movie. It had to stay in. The Pentagon said no: either pull out all the references to Area 51, or we pull out. The outcome was that the production company—Centropolis Entertainment—stood their ground, and the U.S. military walked away.

Of course, by 1996, Area 51 was already known to everyone. It was, after all, made seven years after Bob Lazar spilled the beans on what was going on at S-4. If, in 1996, the base was still a matter of almost complete secrecy, one could understand why the government would want any references to it kept out of *Independence Day*, but just about *everyone* had heard of the installation by the nineties and knew of its legendary reputation as a storage area for recovered UFOs and dead aliens. Ironically, when the story surfaced that the Pentagon had pulled the plug on its involvement in the movie, and all because of the Area 51 references, it actually gave *Independence Day* added, unforeseen publicity and made millions of people wonder *even more* about what was really going on at Area 51.

Here is another story. It's one of the oddest stories in UFO history. It's also one of the least known and long forgotten. It's the weird saga of an actor who never quite made the big-time but who produced a less-than-great movie on UFOs that got him into major problems with none other than the U.S. Air Force. Welcome to the bizarre tale of Mikel Conrad and *The Flying Saucer*.

Born in Ohio in 1919, Mikel Conrad was an actor who appeared in approximately two dozen movies between 1947 and the late 1950s, most of which were/are forgettable and downright crummy. That includes 1952's *Untamed Women*—which, by its title alone, should have made for great, exciting viewing. Unfortunately, it does not, I can assure you, but it's *The Flying Saucer*, which hit the cinemas in 1950, that we need to focus on.

Not only was Conrad the star of this priceless piece of UFO hokum, but he also produced it, directed it, and cowrote it. It tells the story of a man named Mike Trent (played by Conrad) who takes a flight to Alaska to help a U.S. Secret Service agent investigate reports of local UFO activity. Of particular concern, the encounters are apparently of deep interest to pesky Russian agents who are prowling around.

Conrad, as the man behind the movie, personally ensured that the aforementioned agent was played by a hot babe. She was: actress Pat Garrison, who took on the role of the Secret Service's Vee Langley. As Trent and Langley—clearly the Mulder and Scully of their day—investigate what's afoot in the skies of Alaska, they learn something that was definitely not anticipated. The Russians are not on the scene to uncover the truth about alien visitations to the Earth after all. Rather, the flying saucers that are being seen, and astounding the populace in the process, are actually the creations of an American scientist who is determined to sell his inventions to the dastardly Reds—for a high price. Of course, Trent and Langley save the day. They prevent the evil commies from getting away with the saucer-shaped technology, and the free world sighs with relief.

Conrad began loudly telling the U.S. media that he had gotten his hands on no fewer than nine hundred feet of film of genuine UFOs over Alaska.

Nothing was (or still is) particularly special about *The Flying Saucer*. It remains just one of many alien-themed movies that were made in the 1950s. However, it does stand out for one notable reason. In September 1949, in the buildup to the release of the movie—and in an effort to create interest and hopefully generate sizeable audiences—Conrad began loudly telling the U.S. media that he had gotten his hands on no fewer than nine hundred feet of film of genuine UFOs over Alaska. Adding to the intrigue, he informed the Dayton, Ohio, *Journal Herald* that "the saucer footage is locked in a bank vault. I'm not showing it to anyone yet."

It was actually pure nonsense. There was no footage—at all. However, it wasn't just the media and the public that took note of Conrad's claims to have in his possession film that he described as showing "scenes of the saucer landing, taking off, flying and doing tricks." Behind the scenes, wheels were turning—and turning fast. The Air Force got wind of the story, and of Conrad's claims, too, and decided they would very much like to see Conrad's priceless footage.

Also in September 1949, Lt. Col. James O'Connell, district commander with the USAF's Office of Special Investigations (OSI), requested that the OSI office in Maywood, California, should begin an investigation of Conrad and his claims of possessing priceless saucer footage. He was now a marked man. In no time at all, other offices of OSI were involved, as were staff from the Air Force's UFO program, Project Grudge, and Air Materiel Command, and, just for good measure, the FBI undertook a background check on Conrad. OSI documents state that "after some investigation in an effort to locate Mikel Conrad, it was determined that he was presently an actor-producer-writer in Los Angeles, California." Conrad was quickly contacted by OSI agent James Shley, who made it clear to Conrad that he wanted to see both *The Flying Saucer* movie as well as that nine hundred feet of film Conrad was loudly claiming to possess.

On October 26, 1949, Agent Shiley attended a preview of Conrad's movie. No word in the files as to whether or not he enjoyed it, but far more important to Shiley was the film footage, which was supposedly "locked in a bank vault." Confronted by Agent Shiley, a very worried Conrad came clean and admitted that—to quote from the declassified Air Force files—the entire thing was a "figment of his [Conrad's] imagination" and "not a reality."

Seeing that he might, by now, be in dire trouble, a groveling Conrad "apologized to Agent Shiley" and added that he was "sorry that he had misled the USAF." Amusingly, even though he was concerned that the Air Force might come down on him hard, Conrad asked Shiley, somewhat tactfully, if this could all be kept between the two of them and the Air Force, since he didn't want any adverse publicity affecting the success of his movie. The Air Force agreed, noting in its files, in slightly disapproving fashion, that it had "no interest in his picture."

It's notable that at the beginning of the movie, a statement appears on the screen. It reads: "We gratefully acknowledge the cooperation of those in authority who made the release of *The Flying Saucer* film possible at this time." Another apology to officialdom, perhaps? Almost certainly, and, of course, it added a bit of intrigue for the viewers. The strange saga of aliens over Alaska, *The Flying Saucer*, and a run-in with the Air Force for promoting a bogus UFO tale was certainly the highlight of Mikel Conrad's uneventful career. He died in Los Angeles in 1982 after years of living in obscurity, down on his pennies, and with a serious booze addiction. He was sixty-three. He would probably be very pleased to know that decades after his movie was made and more than three decades after his death, *The Flying Saucer* is still being discussed.

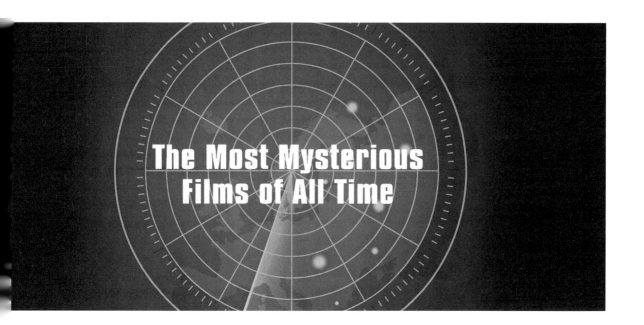

The Most Mysterious
Films of All Time

It was in the heady, *X-Files*-dominated days of 1995 that Ray Santilli let loose upon an unsuspecting world the infamous "Alien Autopsy" film. Eleven years later, after a seemingly never-ending period of controversy and debate, Santilli finally fessed up to the fact that the controversial footage was nothing more than a, ahem, "restoration." Santilli's highly convoluted story went that he really *did* have in his possession a 1947-vintage U.S. military film that showed the secret autopsy of a bald-headed, pot-bellied alien who had had the unfortunate bad driving skills to crash to Earth deep in the harsh deserts of New Mexico. Ironically, however, Santilli elaborated, the real footage had supposedly degraded to the point where it was both unwatchable and unusable from a broadcasting perspective, so he enlisted the expert help of special-effects chums to work on that aforementioned restoration.

It would have been far too much to have expected this to lay matters to rest, and, indeed, it did not. The believers—or some of them, at least—continued to believe, while the disbelievers publicly scoffed at Santilli's claims of "restoration" and maintained that the whole thing was nothing more than a straightforward hoax—albeit an ingeniously instigated and executed one. Even though the affair has now been relegated to the sidelines of ufology by all but those few who still have faith in Santilli's original story, it is a seldom discussed fact that Santilli was not the first to claim knowledge of, or possession of, decades-old U.S. military film footage and photographs said to show the bodies of dead and decaying E.T.s.

A well-known collector of crashed UFO tales, the late Leonard Stringfield was the recipient of a number of such claims—although, sadly and perhaps inevitably, no films. One such tale told to Stringfield came from the unsurprisingly anonymous "Mr. T. E.," who, said Stringfield in 1980, "holds a technical position in today's life."

T. E. told Stringfield that in 1953, at the age of just twenty and while stationed at Fort Monmouth, New Jersey, he was summoned to watch a startling piece of film footage at the base theatre. Reported Stringfield:

> Without any briefing, the 16mm movie projector was flicked on and the film began to roll on the screen … the film showed a desert scene dominated by a silver disc-shaped object embedded in the sand.…

> Then … there was a change of scenes. Now in view were two tables, probably taken inside a tent, on which, to his surprise, were dead bodies. T. E. said the bodies appeared little by human standards and most notable were the heads, all looking alike, and all being large compared to their body sizes.… They looked Mongoloid.

Interestingly, T. E. and his colleagues were told immediately after the screening to "think about the movie" but were later advised that "it was a hoax." Eerily paralleling the Santilli film, T. E. told Stringfield that "the 5-minute long movie certainly was not a Walt Disney production. It was probably shot by an inexperienced cameraman because it was full of scratches, and had poor colouring and texture."

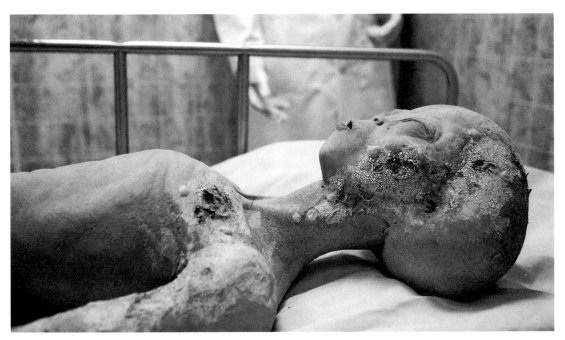

This alien autopsy display at the International UFO Museum and Research Center in Roswell is reminiscent of the autopsy scene shown in a film T. E. watched at Fort Monmouth.

Then is the little-known story of Pennsylvania-based UFO researcher Joan Jeffers who—having read the "T. E. Report"—stated in a letter to Stringfield on February 6, 1979, that she, too, had spoken with a military source who claimed to have seen what sounded suspiciously like the same film—at a "radar facility" in Maine around 1956.

Still further reports reached the eyes and ears of Leonard Stringfield. Two years later, in 1982, Stringfield wrote:

> On a tip from Bill Hamilton of Phoenix, Arizona, at the MUFON Symposium in Houston, June, 1980, I was soon in communication with Ms. C. M. of Los Angeles, a successful freelance writer who knew about a secret movie allegedly showing a freshly recovered alien craft with occupants, filmed inside an Air Force hangar. The movie, in color with sound, and of 17 minutes duration, said CM, was in the possession of a person formerly in government service, whom she did not identify … one scene showed the removal of five alien dead bodies.

Despite attempts to cultivate the source to a greater degree, Stringfield was unable to do so. Another film had bitten the dust.

Quite possibly the strangest story of an alleged alien autopsy film involves—in a weird and convoluted way—the late country and western singer John Denver, who died in a plane crash near Pacific Grove, California, on October 12, 1997. Aside from music, Denver's other big passion was for space travel: He even took, and passed, no less, NASA's physical and mental examination to determine whether or not he was fit enough to cope with the extreme rigors of a journey into space. As a result, plans were made for Denver to travel on the *Challenger* space shuttle, but a twist of fate prevented him from joining the ill-fated January 1986 mission that ended in complete and utter disaster when the *Challenger* exploded shortly after takeoff, killing all of the crew.

One of those aboard the *Challenger* was astronaut Ellison Onizuka, who had told his close friend Chris Coffey that, while serving in the U.S. Air Force at McClelland Air Force Base in 1973, he had viewed a piece of black-and-white film footage that showed "alien bodies on a slab"—alien bodies not unlike those said to have been found in Roswell, New Mexico, in 1947. Roswell, it turns out, was John Denver's hometown: He was born there—into an Air Force family, no less—in 1943.

Interestingly, in the same year that the *Challenger* exploded—1986—English UFO researcher and author Jenny Randles was approached by a British Army source that she called "Robert," who claimed to have read—and asserted that he had access to—hundreds of pages of seemingly top secret U.S. military files that had been found on classified computer systems at Wright-Patterson Air Force Base, Dayton, Ohio.

Contained within those files, Randles told me in an interview on March 28, 1997, were—according to Robert, at least—photographs that showed aspects of at least one alien autopsy. Randles further informed me:

> There was a very detailed account that was mostly filled with medical jargon about the autopsy which he didn't understand, and there was a photograph of this entity with a slit right down the middle from the neck to the navel.

> One of the things Robert said was that the aliens were very human-looking. He said that the head was completely bald, but the most unusual feature of the face was the nose, which was almost flush into the face—almost unnoticeable. He couldn't tell from the photographs, but the autopsy report made it clear that the beings were slightly smaller than average human size—about five feet in height.

> Bearing in mind, 1986 was years before the autopsy film [from Ray Santilli] surfaced. In fact, the connections with the autopsy film and with what Robert told me are *chillingly* similar. One of the impressions that you get from the alien autopsy footage is that the body *is* very human-like; and *is* around five foot in height. I have to say it struck me as soon as I saw the footage that this was *very* similar to what Robert had described.

UFO researcher Bob Shell stated publicly on the *UFO Updates* discussion list that a number of years ago, U.S. Air Force Capt. James McAndrew—who, in 1997, authored the Air Force's controversial "crash test dummy" report on the Roswell affair, *The Roswell Report: Case Closed*—had informed him that he, McAndrew, "had seen film just like the Santilli film in Air Force secret archives, and that he had seen far more of it than Santilli had gotten."

Shell further stated that, when McAndrew later denied this, he was "called on the carpet" by none other than arch-UFO-skeptic Phil Klass, who, while certainly not a believer in the validity of Santilli's film, *was* able to confirm McAndrew's words, since he had been told much the same by the Air Force captain. Today, Shell stands by his memories, and currently, neither McAndrew nor the Air Force deny it.

What are we to make of all this, then? Was Santilli right all along? Did he have access to decades-old footage that really showed the autopsy of an alien or a curiously deformed human being, perhaps, or does another answer exist? Quite possibly, yes.

Let's say for the sake of argument that Santilli really *was* the recipient of film footage from an elderly military cameraman who had amazingly been able to hang on to it for decades without his superiors ever finding out. Let's also suppose that Stringfield's sources were all being utterly genuine with him, as was Randles's source, "Robert."

Keeping that possibility in mind, consider this, too: One central theme runs throughout all of these "alien autopsy film"-related accounts—namely, the apparent and ridiculous ease with which each of the military sources seemingly had access to such apparent top secret material. The claim of Santilli's "cameraman," that he was able to keep the footage because no one in the official world ever came to claim it, is both utterly absurd and beyond belief. The fact that Stringfield's twenty-year-old source, "T. E.," was openly shown—for *no* apparent reason that either party could determine—an alleged film of alien bodies laid out on tables also sounds unlikely in the extreme.

Also, as Randles told me with specific regard to one aspect of the story related to her by a British Army informant, Robert—namely the apparent ease with which supposed classified files and photographs on dead aliens had been made available to him: "I more or less mutually decided that the most likely explana-

Journalist and ufologist Phil Klass had a reputation of being a skeptic of alien stories, including about the film showing an alien autopsy.

tion was that Robert had been set up by someone, and that he really did have this documentation. If it was a hoax, then Robert certainly wasn't guilty of it. And I'd probably still have to say that today."

In view of this, we might do well to muse upon the possibility that deep within the bowels of the U.S. Air Force, secret film footage really *does* exist and *does* appear to show the autopsies of one or more diminutive alien bodies, but appearances may be deceiving. We might argue that such footage was faked officially—decades ago, even—to test the loyalty of military personnel: deliberately expose them to such seemingly sensational material and then see whether or not they keep their collective mouths shut in a fashion that is expected of them by their superiors or watch them closely to see whether or not they confide in their friends, family, and the media.

If the former, everything is all well and good. If the latter, well, no actual real secrets have been exposed, and those who are found untrustworthy are quickly relegated to cleaning the latrines or posted to guard duty in some icy, polar region as punishment. Perhaps, even, this was all part of a ploy to try to spook the former Soviet Union into believing that the West had access to crashed UFOs, alien bodies, and all of the attendant advanced technology that came with such a finding.

History has certainly shown that Cold War psychological warfare operations took some bizarre and unique twists and turns, and history may one day show that the many tales of secret alien autopsy films have more to do with the shenanigans of spies, spooks, disinformation experts, and cigar-chomping Air Force generals than they do with diminutive, black-eyed aliens from the other side of the universe.

The Terrible Secrets of an Underground Base

One of the most controversial of all of Bob Lazar's claims is that he read a series of highly classified documents on various aspects of the UFO phenomenon. One of those documents, Lazar maintained, told a strange and almost sinister story of a violent confrontation between security personnel at Area 51 and a group of aliens that were in residence and working at S-4 alongside a scientific team. It was a confrontation that reportedly resulted in more than a few deaths. Far more than a few.

To his credit, Lazar has admitted that he cannot say for sure that the briefing papers he read were the real thing. He has acknowledged that they may have been disinformation designed to swamp him with both real and bogus material. Why might the project leaders at Area 51 do such a thing? Simple: If concerns existed that Lazar might blow the whistle on what he knew (which, as history has shown, he did in 1989), mixing up the truth with more than a liberal number of lies might have an adverse effect on his credibility. It should be noted that that's *exactly* what happened. That said, and although he cannot say for sure that the documentation was the real deal, he does recall the contents of the material in relation to this firefight situation.

According to Lazar, the deadly confrontation occurred at some point in 1979 in the S-4 facility. Lazar said:

> I believe the altercation came about in 1979, or sometime like that. And I don't remember exactly how it was started, but it had something to do with the security personnel. The aliens were in a separate room. I think it had something to do with the bullets [the security guards] were carrying, and somehow they were trying to be told that they couldn't enter the area with the bullets, possibly

because it was hazardous—the bullets could explode, through some field or whatever.

Lazar continued that despite the warning, one of the security guards did indeed enter the room with the bullets—which resulted in a violent and lethal response from the aliens. Lazar recalled that the papers he read described how the security personnel were all quickly killed by "head wounds." The same fate befell a group of scientists on the program, too. Timothy Good, who interviewed Lazar at the height of the controversy surrounding his claims, said: "The incident is said to have led to the termination of an alien liaison at the Nevada Test Site."

It's important to note that a variation on this story exists. Not from Lazar, who stuck to the story that he read out at S-4, but from a man named Paul Bennewitz, who in the late 1970s began digging into claims that an alien base existed below the New Mexico town of Dulce. From intelligence personnel at Kirtland Air Force Base, Albuquerque, Bennewitz learned of a story of a fatal encounter between hostile aliens and a security team in the lower levels of the Dulce Base. The different location given to Bennewitz is just about the only difference between what Lazar was told and what Bennewitz was told. Clearly, both scenarios cannot be true, which—just like several of Lazar's revelations—means we must give deep consideration to the possibility that the papers Lazar read were not the real deal. They may well have been disinformation and so might have been the data provided to Bennewitz. To try to unravel this issue, let's take a look at the story of Bennewitz and his Deep Throat-type sources from Kirtland.

For what is certainly a picturesque area on the map, Dulce—located in the northern part of Rio Arriba County—is steeped in mystery. It's also home to around several thousand people and has a square mileage of barely thirteen. Its origins date back to the nineteenth century. It's not what goes on in Dulce that concerns us here, though. Rather, it's what is said to be going on far *below* the town—in myriad tunnels, caverns, caves, and hollowed-out chambers that are all said to be where untold numbers of dangerous and hostile aliens live. Even worse, the U.S. government has had the fear of God (or of the aliens) put in them to such an extent that they dare not descend into that deadly, dark realm far below Dulce's huge Archuleta Mesa.

Today, tales of underground bases—in which nefarious experimentation is widespread—are all over the Internet. Just type "Underground Base + UFOs" into a search engine, and you'll find an endless array of tales of the controversial kind; they are overflowing with paranoia and tales of menace. Such tales were told far less often in the 1970s, which is when the Dulce stories began to surface, specifically in the latter part of the decade. What makes the Dulce story so notable is that the initial rumors about the vast alien facility miles below ground level came not from wide-eyed conspiracy theorists but from a number of people who worked deeply in the clandestine worlds of counterintelligence and disinformation. The latter is described as "false information deliberately and often covertly spread (as by the planting of rumors) in order to influence public opinion or obscure the truth," while counterintelligence is defined as "organized activity of an intelligence service designed to block an enemy's sources of information, to deceive the enemy, to prevent sabotage, and to gather political and military information."

In other words, we're talking about spies, secret agents, lies that might be truths, and truths that might be lies.

As for the Dulce story, it suggests that when a violent, deadly altercation in the Dulce base occurred at some point in 1979, the U.S. military—along with numerous scientists and engineers—were forced to flee for their lives. What had begun as a fairly amicable arrangement between the aliens, of the black-eyed "Grey" type, and the government team was now over. Irreversibly so. The Dulce base was now in the hands of a band of extraterrestrials who were done with the human race. This, you won't fail to note, is very similar to the story told to Bob Lazar in the latter part of 1988, but that in the scenario given to him, it was at S-4, rather than at Dulce, where the deadly confrontation occurred. Unless both stories are true (which is unlikely because they are almost identical in nature), then a high likelihood exists that somewhere, deceit was at work.

Bob Lazar claimed he worked on the S-4 project at Area 51, where he studied the gravity wave propulsion system used by alien craft with the help of element 115.

Back in the 1970s, Paul Bennewitz—who died in 2003 in Albuquerque, New Mexico—had his own company that stood adjacent to Kirtland Air Force Base. Its name was Thunder Scientific. All was good, as Bennewitz had a number of good contracts with the military, and living and working so close to the base made things comfortable and handy for Bennewitz. It was the perfect relationship. Until, that is, it wasn't. In shockingly quick time, Bennewitz's life began to fragment in chaotic fashion, but how and why did such a thing happen?

It's important to note that by the late 1970s, Bennewitz had been interested in UFOs not just for years but for decades. He had a large library of books and subscribed to a number of newsletters and magazines on the subject. On occasion, Bennewitz had seen—late at night and in the early hours of the morning—strange, unidentified objects flying over Kirtland Air Force Base and the nearby, huge Manzano Mountains. They could have been early drone-like craft being tested secretly, but for Bennewitz, they were alien craft.

Bennewitz's head spun: He came to believe that aliens were in league with the U.S. Air Force and that much of the secret program was run out of Kirtland. He shared his views with staff at Kirtland, the CIA, the NSA, the Defense Intelligence Agency, the Pentagon, his senator, his congressman, and just about anyone and everyone in a position of power and influence. It was all but inevitable that by firing off lengthy letters about a secret alien–human operation at Kirtland, someone would take notice. That's exactly what they did. While one school of thought suggests that Bennewitz was indeed tracking the movements of UFOs in the skies over Kirtland, another suggests that Bennewitz had actually stumbled on test flights of new and radical aircraft of the aforementioned drone kind. In the latter scenario, the government (as a collective term for all of those agencies and individuals that Bennewitz approached) decided to first politely, but quietly, request that Bennewitz bring his research to a halt. This was like bringing a red rag to a bull. Bennewitz would hear none of it. He was primed and ready to go after the U.S. government and to confirm what he saw as the dark and sinister truth of Uncle Sam's liaisons with aliens. One man against the government? It was

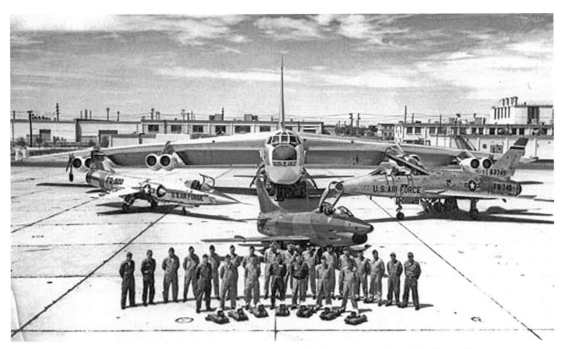

Members of the 4925th Test Group (Nuclear) pose at Kirtland Air Force Base.

clear who was going to win, although Bennewitz couldn't envisage such a thing at all.

In ingenious fashion—but from the perspective of Bennewitz, in terrible fashion—a plot was initiated to, in essence, give Bennewitz exactly what he wanted to hear, so well-placed government agents, intelligence operatives, and experts in the fields of counterintelligence and disinformation all fed Bennewitz fictitious tales of dangerous E.T.s, of thousands of people abducted and mind-controlled in slavelike fashion by the aliens, of terrible experiments undertaken on people held below the Dulce base, and of a looming confrontation between the human race and the deadly creatures from another galaxy.

The fact that the data was all coming to him from verifiable insider sources impressed Bennewitz and led him to believe their every word—which is precisely what the government was gambling on. The government then tightened the noose even more around Bennewitz's neck: they fed him more and more horror stories of the alien variety. Slowly and bit by bit, Bennewitz's paranoia grew. If anyone walked casually past the family home, they just had to be government agents. If the phone rang but stopped ringing before he had a chance to get to it, then that was a sign of intimidation from *them*. He couldn't sleep, he became stressed to the point where he required medication, and eventually had a nervous collapse and was hospitalized. The result: he walked away from UFOs, secret projects, and cosmic conspiracies as a crushed man, which may well have been the intent of the government, anyway.

Although the saga of Paul Bennewitz began in the latter part of the 1970s and was pretty much over by the early to mid-1980s, the story of the Dulce base developed legs. They are legs that still walk to this very day, primarily because so many people within ufology find the tales of the underground base exciting—it really is that simple. The government has—to a degree—continued to encourage the wilder and darker side of ufology as a means to further darken the waters of what it is really up to when it comes to new and advanced aircraft that many might perceive as UFOs. That said, though, some absolutely stand by the claims that a huge, underground installation exists below Dulce. In many respects, the newer tales are even stranger and more horrifying than those that had been shoved down Bennewitz's throat in the early eighties.

Admittedly, it's intriguing to note that Dulce is indeed saturated in weirdness—some of which occurred years before Bennewitz was on the scene.

More than a decade before Bennewitz came to believe that the awful rumors of Dulce were true, the U.S. government *already* had a stake in the area. A contingent from the Atomic Energy Commission rode into town and set up what was called Project Gasbuggy. It was a subproject of a much bigger project called Plowshare. The plan was to detonate—way below Dulce—a small nuclear device as a means to try to extract natural gas. The operation went ahead on December 10, 1967—and it worked all too well. The bomb was detonated at a depth of more than four thousand feet. Years later, however, researchers suggested that the natural gas scenario was a cover for something else. You may already see where this is all going. Ufology has an enduring belief that the nuke was actually used, by a panicked government, to try to wipe out the alien base, and the extraterrestrials were said to live deep within it. Even to this day, it is illegal to dig in the area on the orders of the Atomic Energy Commission—the AEC having deep ties to Area 51.

More than a decade before Bennewitz came to believe that the awful rumors of Dulce were true, the U.S. government *already* had a stake in the area.

Moving on, from 1975 to 1979, the town of Dulce was hit by numerous cattle mutilations. Black helicopters soared across the skies of town by night—and sometimes, and incredibly, silently. Strange lights were seen flitting around Dulce's huge Archuleta Mesa. Cows were found with organs removed and blood drained from their corpses. The incisions looked as if they were the work of lasers. For those who might find all of this to be just too incredible, it's worth noting that the FBI was heavily involved in the investigation of the mutilations at Dulce and has now placed its files on the mystery on their website, *The Vault*. It's a file that reads like science fiction and runs to more than one hundred pages and, as we have seen, strong evidence exists that the silent, black helicopters had their origins at Area 51.

In the post-Bennewitz era, other figures came forward with their very own tales of Dulce and its subterranean nightmare. Whether they were telling the truth or were fed lies and disinformation by government agents is something very much open to interpretation.

One such account came from one Jason Bishop III, which is an alias for another alias, that of Tal Lavesque. No wonder the Dulce saga is so confusing. Lavesque/Bishop published what he claimed were the words of a former employee at the base, Thomas E. Castello. According to Castello:

> Level 7 is worse, row after row of thousands of humans and human mixtures in cold storage. Here too are embryo storage vats of humanoids in various stages of development. I frequently encountered humans in cages, usually dazed or drugged, but sometimes they cried and begged for help. We were told they were hopelessly insane, and involved in high risk drug tests to cure insanity. We were told to never try to speak to them at all. At the beginning we believed that story. Finally in 1978 a small group of workers discovered the truth.

Alan B. de Walton also wrote about the claimed firefight that led to the hasty retreat of the U.S. military. In his controversial work *The Dulce Book*, he stated that the human body is "surrounded by the etheric 'body,' surrounded by the astral 'body,' surrounded by the mental 'body.'"

On this same issue, an insider told de Walton: "We also actually have an extra 'body,' the emotional 'body,' that the aliens don't have. This part of us constantly puts out a kind of energy they cannot generate or simulate. This emotional energy … is to them, like a potent, much sought-after drug. They can take it out of us and bottle it, so to speak.… Also during this 'harvesting,' Greys will look directly into our eyes, as if they are drinking something or basking in light."

In 1991, Valdemar Valerian's book *Matrix II* hit the bookshelves. It referred to a female abductee who had seen in the Dulce base "a vat full of red liquid and body parts of humans and animals … she could see Greys bobbing up and down, almost swimming."

In 2015, Joshua Cutchin penned *A Trojan Feast: The Food and Drink Offerings of Aliens, Faeries, and Sasquatch.* Cutchin's words are chilling, to say the very least: "While abduction research does not overtly suggest that aliens are harvesting people for consumption, there may be a grain of truth to the report [contained in the pages of Valerian's *Matrix II*]. 'Nourishment is ingested by smearing a soupy mixture of biologicals on the epidermis. Food sources include Bovine cattle and human parts … distilled into a high protein broth.…'"

What are we to make of all this? Undoubtedly, certain portions of the story given to Bennewitz from the late 1970s to the early to mid-1980s sound unbelievable. They may well have been. Certainly, the plan seems to have been designed to mentally destabilize Bennewitz—which is exactly what happened. He became a definitive shell of his former self. The fact that a very similar tale of a violent firefight between security personnel and the aliens was given to Bob Lazar—but with the location changed from the underground realms of Dulce to the highly classified S-4 facility in the Nevada desert—strongly suggests that we should proceed with deep caution when it comes to evaluating Lazar's recollections of this particular story not because Lazar was a liar but because he may have been *fed* lies—which is a very different thing altogether.

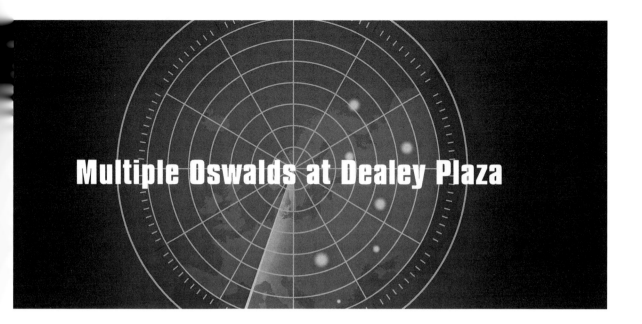

Multiple Oswalds at Dealey Plaza

In the more than half a century that has now passed since President John F. Kennedy was shot and killed in Dealey Plaza, Dallas, Texas, on November 22, 1963, a wealth of theories has been put forward to explain the death of the only man to whom Marilyn Monroe sung, or rather purred, "happy birthday." Those theories range from plausible to paranoid and bizarre to out of this world.

On November 29, 1963, an investigation began that still provokes huge debate in conspiracy-themed circles decades after JFK died. The ten-month-long study was undertaken by the President's Commission on the Assassination of President Kennedy or, as it is far better, and unofficially, known, the Warren Commission, which took its name from its chairman, Chief Justice Earl Warren.

The commission's job was to get to the bottom of the big question that everyone was itching to see answered: Who *really* shot JFK? According to the Warren Commission, it was Lee Harvey Oswald, and it was *only* Oswald. Not everyone agreed with that controversial conclusion, however.

Was JFK the victim of both an assassin and friendly fire? Two men, totally unconnected to each other but who, in a strange set of circumstances, ultimately sealed the fate of the president? This was the theory postulated in a 1992 book, *Mortal Error: The Shot That Killed JFK* by Bonar Menninger.

The scenario presented by Menninger had Oswald as the chief culprit but not the only one. George Hickey was a Secret Service agent traveling in the vehicle immediately following the presidential car. After the bullets fired by Oswald slammed into JFK, Menninger suggested, Hickey accidentally discharged his weapon, delivering the fatal head shot that killed Kennedy.

In 1992, when *Mortal Error* was published, Hickey was still alive. He was not pleased to see himself portrayed as the second gunman in the Kennedy assassination. Unfortunately for Hickey, he let three years pass before trying to take legal action against the publisher, St. Martin's Press.

U.S. District Court Judge Alexander Harvey II dismissed the defamation case on the grounds that Hickey had waited too long to file suit. In 1998, however, Hickey received an undisclosed sum of money from St. Martin's Press that led Hickey's attorney, Mark S. Zaid, to state: "We're very satisfied with the settlement."

Prior to his death in 1976, Johnny Roselli was a notorious and much-feared figure in the Chicago, Illinois, Mafia. His influence and power extended to the heart of Tinseltown and the slots and tables of Vegas. In 1960, Roselli was quietly contacted by a man named Robert Maheu, a former employee of the CIA and the FBI.

This photograph by Mary Ann Moorman shows the presidential limo less than a second after John F. Kennedy was shot in Dallas in 1963. Lee Harvey Oswald was the prime suspect, but some speculate there were others in on the shocking plot.

A startling proposal was put to Roselli. The CIA, Maheu explained, wanted Roselli's help in taking care of Fidel Castro. In Mob-speak, "taking care of" meant "whacking." Thus was born a controversial program that saw the CIA and the Mob work together hand in glove.

As history has shown, Roselli and his goons never did take out Castro, but, say conspiracy theorists, they may have ended the life of JFK with help from the CIA. The Mob was no fan of the Kennedy administration. Robert Kennedy, as attorney general, went after the Mafia in definitive witch-hunt style. Did the Mob decide to return the favor? Maybe it did.

Following Kennedy's killing, Roselli and a number of other mobsters, including Santo Trafficante Jr. and Carlos Marcello, were suspected of having been implicated. Even the House Select Committee on Assassinations admitted to the existence of "credible associations relating both Lee Harvey Oswald and Jack Ruby to figures having a relationship, albeit tenuous, with Marcello's crime family or organization."

Just perhaps, it's not such a whacked-out theory after all.

JFK taken out of circulation to prevent him from revealing the truth about what really crashed in Roswell, New Mexico, in 1947? UFO researchers say that after Kennedy was elected in 1960, he got the lowdown on all things E.T. based in a secret briefing from the CIA: "Bad news, Mr. President: E.T. is real. Worse news: he really doesn't like us." Kennedy was determined to warn the public of the alien menace. A secret and ruthless cabal in the heart of officialdom, however, was having none of it. The president had to go before he spilled the bug-eyed beans. It sounds crazy, but even crazier, the JFK assassination really *is* littered with characters that were tied to the strange world of flying saucers.

Back in 1947, a man named Fred Crisman claimed to have recovered debris from an exploded UFO in Tacoma, Washington State. Crisman also alluded to having worked for decades as a deep-cover agent with U.S. Intelligence. Jim Garrison was New Orleans's district attorney from 1961 to 1973 and the man portrayed by Kevin Costner in Oliver Stone's *JFK*. In 1968, Garrison subpoenaed Crisman while investigating JFK's death. The reason: Crisman had connections to a CIA asset believed by many researchers to have been linked to the killing of Kennedy. His name was Clay Shaw. The case against Shaw collapsed, and Crisman breathed a big sigh of relief.

Guy Banister, a retired FBI agent at the time of the JFK assassination, was also linked to Clay Shaw by Garrison. As the Freedom of Information Act has shown, Banister undertook numerous UFO investigations for the FBI in 1947. A Lee Harvey Oswald connection was even discovered. In October 1962, Oswald went to work for a Texas-based company called Jaggars-Chiles-Stovall. They undertook classified photo analysis connected to the CIA's U-2 spy plane program. Where was the U-2 developed? Area 51, that's where, and we all know what goes on out there, right?

One of the oddest theories concerning the Kennedy assassination tumbled out in the pages of a 1975 book called *Appointment in Dallas*. It was written by Hugh McDonald, formerly of the LAPD. According to McDonald, Oswald was indeed a patsy but in a very strange fashion.

Oswald was supposedly told, by shadowy sources, that his expertise was needed in Dallas on November 22, 1963, but Oswald wasn't required to kill the president. Quite the contrary, Oswald was told to ensure that all his bullets *missed* JFK.

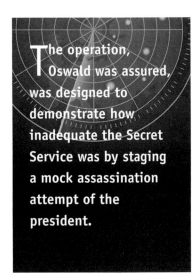

The operation, Oswald was assured, was designed to demonstrate how inadequate the Secret Service was by staging a mock assassination attempt of the president.

The operation, Oswald was assured, was designed to demonstrate how inadequate the Secret Service was by staging a mock assassination attempt of the president. Unbeknownst to Oswald, however, a team of *real* assassins was in Dealey Plaza. Their bullets, however, did not miss.

The gunmen made quick exits, leaving Oswald as the man guaranteed to take the fall—simply because he really *did* fire bullets across Dealey Plaza. A panicked Oswald, realizing he had been set up, fled the scene, thus setting in motion the wheels that led to his arrest and death.

Forget Oswald. JFK was killed by the man behind the wheel in full view of the people of Dallas and thousands of cameras. That was the outrageous claim of one of the most vocal conspiracy theorists of the 1980s and 1990s. His name was Milton William "Bill" Cooper.

The man who Cooper fingered as the guilty party was William Greer, a Secret Service agent who drove the presidential limousine on the day that JFK was destined not to leave Dallas alive. When shots echoed around Dealey Plaza, Greer slowed the car down and turned back to look at the president. For Cooper, Greer's actions were not due to confusion caused by the chaos breaking out all around him. No. Cooper claimed that analysis of the famous footage taken by Abraham Zapruder, on the Grassy Knoll on November 22, showed Greer pointing some form of device at JFK.

That device, Cooper maintained to anyone who would listen, was nothing less than a sci-fi-style weapon developed by government personnel who had acquired the technology from extraterrestrials.

By the time Cooper got on his rant, which began in the late 1980s, Greer wasn't around to defend himself. He passed away in 1985 from cancer, having retired from the Secret Service in 1966 as a result of problems caused by a stomach ulcer.

In a strange piece of irony, Cooper himself died by the bullet. In summer 1998, he was formerly charged with tax evasion. Cooper told the government what to do. What the government did, on November 5, 2001, was to dispatch deputies to Cooper's Arizona home. A shoot-out soon erupted. Cooper, like JFK, was soon full of lead.

In October 1959, Lee Harvey Oswald—a self-admitted Marxist—made his way to the Soviet Union. Oswald reached Moscow on October 16 and announced that he wished to remain in Russia. Although the Soviets were, initially, reluctant to allow Oswald residency, that soon changed. It wasn't long before Oswald had a job and a home. In 1961, he had a wife: Marina. Fatherhood soon followed. Claiming to have become disillusioned with a dull life in the Soviet Union, however, Oswald moved his family to the United States in 1962.

Was Oswald recruited by the KGB during his time in Russia? Did his return to the States actually have nothing to do with disillusionment? Had the

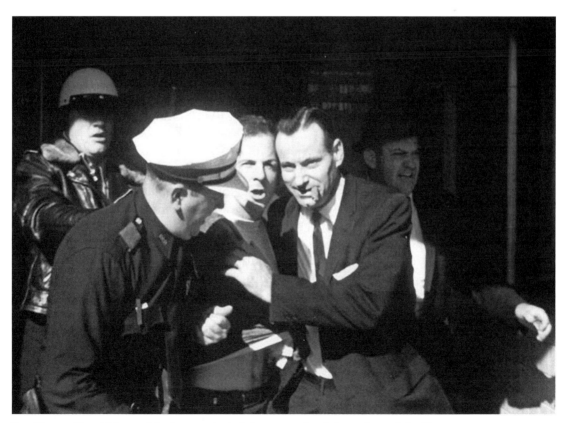

Lee Harvey Oswald (center) is shown as he is being arrested and dragged out of the Texas Theater. Was Oswald working for the KGB? Was he a lone gunman? Was he working for plotters withing the U.S. government?

elite of the Kremlin convinced Oswald to kill Kennedy? One person who has commented on such matters is Ion Mihai Pacepa.

In 1978, Pacepa, a general with Romania's Department of State Security, defected to the United States. One of Pacepa's revelations was that JFK was killed on the orders of Soviet premier Nikita Khrushchev. Still seething from backing down in the Cuban Missile Crisis of 1962, Khrushchev was determined to exact his revenge. Oswald was chosen to ensure that revenge was achieved.

Notably, Pacepa asserted that Khrushchev made a last-minute decision not to go ahead with the plan to kill JFK. Unfortunately, the Russians failed to make timely contact with Oswald and inform him of the change in plans. The countdown to assassination could not be stopped.

As far back as the late 1950s, the CIA planned to have Cuba's president, Fidel Castro, assassinated. The Kennedy administration sought to destabilize the Cuban government on many occasions. Castro was enraged. Not as enraged as he became in the wake of the Bay of Pigs invasion of 1961 and the missile crisis of 1962, however.

So angered was Castro that he decided to teach the United States a terrible lesson by having the most powerful man on the planet, JFK, murdered, or so this particular conspiracy theory goes. None other than Kennedy's successor, Lyndon B. Johnson, suspected that the Cubans were behind the president's killing. Stating that he could "accept that [Oswald] pulled the trigger," Johnson felt that Castro had a significant hand in matters somewhere.

Not surprisingly, Castro consistently denounced such claims. Castro asserted, perhaps with justification, that had the United States proved that Cuba was involved, his country would have been wiped off the map. Castro was certainly not a fan of JFK, but would he have risked the very existence of Cuba to see Kennedy killed? The question lives on.

In January 1961, outgoing president Dwight D. Eisenhower made a speech, part of which has become inextricably tied to the murder of JFK. Eisenhower said: "In the councils of government, we must guard against the acquisition of unwarranted influence, whether sought or unsought, by the military-industrial complex."

The late Cuban leader Fidel Castro denied any involvement in the JFK assassination after President Johnson suggested he was behind it.

In the minds of many JFK assassination researchers, it is this military-industrial complex that we should look to for the answers on the fifty-year-old question of who killed the president. JFK had a vision of creating a state of lasting peace between the United States and the Soviet Union. In short, Kennedy wanted to end the Cold War. We're talking permanently.

Powerful figures in the military, the Intelligence Community, and companies that raked in millions of dollars in lucrative defense contracts secretly agreed to do the unthinkable. Profits from war were more important than the life and goals of the president.

In 1978, fourteen years after the Warren Commission laid all the blame firmly on the shoulders of Oswald, the U.S. House Select Committee on Assassinations came to a different conclusion. The lone gunman, said the committee, was not such a lone gunman after all. President Kennedy's death was the result of nothing less than a full-on conspiracy.

The HSCA agreed with the Warren Commission that Kennedy was killed by Oswald and no one else. The committee went one step further, however, by concluding that Oswald was not the only gunman prowling around Dallas on that deadly day.

Forensic analysis suggested to the HSCA's investigators that *four* shots rang out, not the three that the Warren Commission attributed to Oswald. That's to say that another gunman—or even several "Oswalds"—were there. In the minds of the HSCA's staff, this mysterious second character completely missed his target. Nevertheless, a pair of shooters meant that a conspiracy was at the heart of the JFK assassination. In other words: Take that, Warren Commission.

As the U.S. government's National Archives note:

The House Select Committee on Assassinations was established in September 1976 by House Resolution 1540, 94th Congress, 2d Session. The resolution authorized a 12-member select committee to conduct a full and complete investigation of the circumstances surrounding the deaths of President John F. Kennedy and Dr. Martin Luther King, Jr. The committee was constituted for the four remaining months of the 94th Congress, and it was mandated to report the results of its investigation to the House of Representatives as soon as practicable.

House Resolution 1540 had been introduced a year prior to its passage. It was a refinement of several similar resolutions sponsored by some 135 Members of the 94th Congress. Substantial impetus for the creation of a select committee to investigate these assassinations was derived from revelations in the report of the Senate Select Committee to Study Governmental Operations with

Respect to Intelligence Activities, dated April 1976 and released in June 1976. The Senate select committee reported that the Central Intelligence Agency had withheld from the Warren Commission, during its investigation of the assassination of President Kennedy, information about plots by the Government of the United States against Fidel Castro of Cuba; and that the Federal Bureau of Investigation had conducted a counter-intelligence program (COINTELPRO) against Dr. King and the Southern Christian Leadership Conference. The House Select Committee on Assassinations created by House Resolution 1540 officially expired as the 94th Congress ended its term on January 3, 1977.

The HSCA said of the Warren Commission's findings:

The President's Commission on the Assassination of President Kennedy (Warren Commission) concluded that President Kennedy was struck by two bullets that were fired from above and behind him. (1) According to the Commission, one bullet hit the President near the base of the back of the neck, slightly to the right of the spine, and exited from the front of the neck. The other entered the right rear of the President's head and exited from the right side of the head, causing a large wound. (2) The Commission based its findings primarily upon the testimony of the doctors who had treated the President at Parkland Memorial Hospital in Dallas and the doctors who performed the autopsy on the President at the Naval Medical Center in Bethesda, Md. (3) In forming this conclusion, neither the members of the Warren Commission, nor its staff, nor the doctors who had performed the autopsy, took advantage of the X-rays and photographs of the President that were taken during the course of the autopsy. (4) The reason for the failure of the Warren Commission to examine these primary materials is that there was a commitment to make public all evidence examined by the Commission. (5) The Commission was concerned that publication of the autopsy X-rays and photographs would be an invasion of the privacy of the Kennedy family. (6) The Commission's decision to rely solely on the testimony of the doctors precluded the possibility that the Commission might make use of a review of the autopsy evidence by independent medical experts to determine if they concurred with the findings of the doctors at Parkland and Bethesda.

A determination of the number and location of the President's wounds was critical to resolving the question of whether there was more than one assassin. The secrecy that surrounded the autopsy proceedings, therefore, has led to considerable skepticism toward the Commission's findings. Concern has been expressed that authorities were less than candid, since the Navy doctor in charge of the autopsy conducted at Bethesda Naval Hospital destroyed his notes, and the Warren Commission decided to forego an opportunity to view the X-rays and photographs or to permit anyone else to inspect them.

The HSCA added:

The skepticism has been reinforced by a film taken of the Presidential motorcade at the moment of the assassination by an amateur movie photographer, Abraham Zapruder. In the Zapruder film, the President's head is apparently thrown backward as the front right side of the skull appears to explode, suggesting to critics of the Warren Commission's findings that the President was struck by a bullet that entered the front of the head. (7) Such a bullet, it has been argued, was fired by a gunman positioned on the grassy knoll, a park-like area to the right and to the front of where the moving limousine was located at the instant of the fatal shot.

In the "Findings" section of the report, the HSCA staff concluded the following:

The committee turned to science as a major source of evidence for its conclusion that Lee Harvey Oswald fired three shots from the Texas School Book Depository, two of which hit President Kennedy. The evidence that was most relied upon was developed by committee panels specializing in the fields of forensic pathology, ballistics, neutron activation, analysis, handwriting identification, photography and acoustics. *Of these, acoustics—a science that involves analysis of the nature and origin of sound impulses—indicated that the shots from the book depository were not the only ones fired at President Kennedy* [italics mine].

Where it was available, the committee extensively employed scientific analysis to assist it in the resolution of numerous issues. The committee considered all the other evidence available to evaluate the scientific analysis. In conclusion, *the committee found that the scientific acoustical evidence established a high probability that two gunmen fired at President John F. Kennedy* [italics mine]. Other scientific evidence did not preclude the possibility of two gunmen firing at the President, but it did negate some specific conspiracy allegations.

Today, more than half a century after President John F. Kennedy was assassinated, we're still none the wiser as to what really went down or didn't. Those who see conspiracies around every corner will continue to see them. As for those who don't, well, they won't, and, in all likelihood, the full and unexpurgated facts, whether pointing in the direction of deep conspiracy or Lee Harvey Oswald, will never surface.

Kennedy Killed Because of UFOs

One of the major areas of controversy that surrounds the ever-present UFO mystery in our world and that is seldom discussed in a serious forum is that which suggests a link between the U.S. government's UFO secrets and the assassination of President John F. Kennedy on November 22, 1963, at Dealey Plaza, Dallas, Texas. As fantastic as such a theory may sound, a demonstrable body of evidence is available that links numerous people to the JFK saga who were also allied to the UFO subject. Moreover, some UFO researchers suggest that Kennedy's death was nothing less than a state-sponsored killing that followed a decision secretly made by Kennedy, shortly before the assassination, to reveal the government's UFO secrets to the public—and possibly even to the former Soviet Union.

In 1988, commenting on Kennedy's knowledge of the UFO controversy, UFO investigator John Lear stated:

> The powers that be had to eliminate President Kennedy because he wanted to release the information on the disks and the aliens in 1963. Since then, we have talked to people who have heard the recording made in the Oval Office when Kennedy pounded his fists [and said]: "You guys better get your stuff together because I'm going to tell the public."

> There were several reasons why [John F. Kennedy] was assassinated. One was the Bay of Pigs fiasco; another was that he had threatened to "shatter the CIA into a thousand pieces." A third reason was because he threatened to pull all our Americans from Vietnam by 1965. The fourth was that he intended to expose the alien-disk cover up.

Controversial words, indeed, but they do not stand alone.

William Holden served aboard the presidential aircraft *Air Force One* during Kennedy's tenure as president. While visiting England in 1997 to present a lecture for the annual conference of the Lancashire Anomalous Phenomenon Investigation Society (LAPIS), Holden told the audience that on one occasion, he saw Kennedy reading a newspaper that contained an article on UFOs.

Kennedy—Holden said—saw him glancing at the feature, too, and asked him for his opinion. Holden replied to the president that he believed UFOs existed. Kennedy reportedly told him he was correct: UFOs *did* exist. Holden stated additionally that Kennedy guardedly informed him that he "wanted to tell the public the truth about UFOs" but that, somewhat ominously, his "hands were tied."

Similarly, the Emmy Award-winning television producer Linda Howe uncovered information suggesting that Kennedy was far from happy with the overwhelming secrecy that surrounded the UFO issue. Indeed, as the investigative writer Lars Hansson noted in 1991, after having dined with Howe: "Ms. Howe described her meetings with military intelligence agents a few years before, during which the JFK assassination was discussed in some detail. After relating what they imparted to her she was most emphatic about the wisdom of leaving that issue alone."

Without any doubt, the most controversial data that posits a link between the death of President John F. Kennedy in November 1963 and UFOs is that which was provided to a California-based UFO researcher named Timothy Cooper in the mid-1990s. As a result of his interest in UFOs that developed in the 1980s, Cooper cultivated a number of insider sources within the military, Intelligence Community, and government: Deep Throat-style informants who would, from time to time, secretly leak to Cooper copies of purportedly real, highly classified documents on UFO sightings, crashed alien spacecraft, and the secret autopsies of extraterrestrial bodies found in Roswell, New Mexico, in July 1947. Supposedly, the documents originated with an elite group of scientists, military men, and several high-ranking CIA sources that, collectively, became known as the Majestic 12, or MJ-12.

Some speculate that President Kennedy was assassinated because he planned to break up the CIA, pull out of Vietnam, or tell the public that alien visitors were a fact.

Interestingly, various MJ-12 documents that were provided to Cooper by his insider contacts suggest that between 1961 and his death in November 1963, President Kennedy was trying, somewhat unsuccessfully, to determine the full story behind the Intelligence Community's involvement in the UFO subject. Most disturbing to that same community, however, is the claim that Kennedy wanted to completely open up the secrecy surrounding UFOs and share it with one and all.

An alleged top-secret document obtained by Timothy Cooper, dated June 28, 1961, from Kennedy to the director of the Central Intelligence Agency, demands a "review of MJ-12 Intelligence Operations as they relate to Cold War Psychological Warfare Plans" and adds, "I would like a brief summary from you at your earliest convenience."

According to former CIA Director Allen Dulles, in a top-secret document dated November 5, 1961, and titled *The MJ-12 Project*, the United States's Intelligence world was particularly concerned about the way in which Soviet air defenses perceived UFOs or, perhaps, *didn't* perceive them. Dulles noted: "The overall effectiveness about the actual Soviet response and alert status is not documented to the point where U.S. intelligence can provide a true picture of how Soviet air defense perceive unidentified flying objects."

As a result of this worrying revelation, the United States had been launching "decoy" devices to test Soviet radar and was planning on building and flying "more sophisticated vehicles whose characteristics come very close to phenomena collected by Air Force and NSA [National Security Agency] elements."

In other words, the U.S. government was concerned that Soviet air defenses were unable to differentiate between what may have been a true UFO and an American spy plane or, worse still, an incoming intercontinental ballistic missile. The nightmarish scenario that hung over the heads of MJ-12 was that the Soviets would mistakenly interpret a UFO over its airspace as an American missile and initiate a nuclear attack on the continental United States.

Of course, American Intelligence was gambling recklessly by flying "decoy" devices over the Soviet Union. On one hand, the United States needed data on how accurately, or not, the Soviets were able to track fast-moving, incoming vehicles of unconventional design, and flying devices that mimicked the movements of true UFOs offered the United States convenient camouflage if the Russians protested. However, the danger was always present that initiating such actions might have led the Soviets to panic and launch a strike against the West.

Kennedy, realizing this, privately began to formulate a plan to share "real" UFO data with the Soviets in an attempt to ensure that the Russians

James Webb was the director of NASA during the Kennedy administration. Webb was charged with cooperating with the Soviets on a joint lunar exploration.

were fully able to interpret the difference between a UFO and an American intercontinental ballistic missile and therefore avoid triggering an accidental, and catastrophic, war.

Ten days before his death, according to a document secured by Timothy Cooper, JFK wrote to the director of the CIA stating that he had instructed NASA director James Webb to "develop a program with the Soviet Union in joint space and lunar exploration." Within the document, Kennedy made it clear that the Soviets needed to be aware of the differences between "bona fide" UFOs and "classified CIA and USAF sources" or, as Kennedy succinctly put it: "the knowns and the unknowns."

Interestingly, a handwritten note at the foot of this document states: "Angleton has MJ directive"—a reference to none other than James Jesus Angleton, the CIA's associate deputy director of operations for counterintelligence at the time. Equally controversial is an alleged National Security Agency intercept of a telephone conversation that Kennedy had on the same day with Soviet premier Nikita Khrushchev that Timothy Cooper secured. Titled *UFO Working Groups*, the document reads as follows:

> *Kennedy:* Mr. Premiere a situation has developed that affects both our countries and the world and I feel it necessary to convey to you a problem that we share in common.
>
> *Khrushchev:* Mr. President, I agree.
>
> *Kennedy:* As you must appreciate the tension between our two great nations has often brought us to the brink of showmanship with all the tapestry of a Greek comedy and our impasse last year [a reference to the Cuban Missile Crisis of 1962] was foolish and deadly. The division that separates us is through misunderstanding, politics, and cultural differences. But we have one thing in common which I would like to address to your working group on the UFO problem.
>
> *Khrushchev:* Yes, yes, I agree with your assessment. We nearly tied the knot that divides us permanently. Our working group believes the same way as yours. The UFO problem presents grave dangers.

Kennedy: Then you agree, Mr. Premiere that we should cooperate together on this issue?

Khrushchev: Yes, Mr. President.

Kennedy: Mr. Premiere, I have begun an initiative with our NASA to exchange information with your Academy of Sciences in which I hope will foster mutual concern over this problem and hopefully find some resolution. I have also instructed our CIA to provide me with full disclosure on the phantom aspects and classified programs in which I can better assess the situation. Can you persuade your KGB to do likewise?

Khrushchev: Mr. President, I cannot guarantee full cooperation in this area but I owe it to future history and the security of our plan-

Soviet premier Nikita Khrushchev is shown here with U.S. president John F. Kennedy in 1961. The two discussed the problem of UFOs and their potential risk to the security of both nations.

et to try. As you must know I have been somewhat limited in my official capacity as Party Chairman to order such cooperation in this area. We too feel that the UFO is a matter of highest importance to our collective security. If I can arrange for a secret meeting between our working groups at a secret location and at a time designated by you [sic]. I feel that this much on my part can happen.

Kennedy: Mr. Premiere, if a meeting at this level can convene it will be an important first step. It will lead to more dialog and trust between our countries and reduce the ever present threat of nuclear war.

Khrushchev: Yes, Mr. President, it will.

Kennedy: Then we are in agreement.

Khrushchev: Yes.

Kennedy: Yes. Until we talk again.

As the above transcript demonstrates, Kennedy's desire to inform the Soviets of "the phantom aspects and classified programs" strongly suggests that the worry that UFOs would be misinterpreted as secret U.S. Air Force and CIA reconnaissance aircraft and could result in an all-out war was *still* on Kennedy's mind, hence his wish to provide Khrushchev with the facts, and JFK's comment that the sharing of data would "lead to more dialog and trust between our countries and reduce the ever present threat of nuclear war" only reinforces that fact. Needless to say, this was all completely unacceptable to MJ-12 and the CIA, and the inevitable and ominous countdown to Kennedy's assassination in Dallas on November 22, 1963, began.

Of course, skeptics say, if some of the alleged players involved in Kennedy's assassination—or those in the official world who Kennedy consulted with as he sought to secure the alien truth—*were* linked with clandestine UFO investigations, we would surely see some evidence of that link; surprisingly enough, when we look, we do indeed find that evidence.

A controversial character who turns up in most of the books on the JFK assassination is Guy Banister, a former FBI agent who, at the time of the killing, was running his own detective agency—Guy Banister Associates—in New Orleans. Banister had been the subject of an investigation by the Warren Commission that investigated Kennedy's death but became the subject of a much deeper investigation by New Orleans district attorney Jim Garrison.

Banister's detective agency was based at 531 Lafayette Street. However, the building had a second entrance at 544 Camp Street, which was the location of an anti-Castro organization (the Cuban Revolutionary Council) created by E. Howard Hunt and Bernard Barker of Watergate infamy. It was determined by the Warren Commission, which investigated the assassination of JFK, that Lee Harvey Oswald used the 544 Camp Street address for the pro-Castro Fair Play for Cuba Committee.

After Banister died, his widow found Fair Play for Cuba Committee papers at Banister's office. Similarly, Banister's secretary confirmed that Banister and Oswald were acquainted. During his FBI years in Chicago, Banister worked with Robert Maheu, a consultant to Howard Hughes, who planned various assassination plots against Fidel Castro. Banister also worked as the Louisiana coordinator for a group known as the Minutemen—a militia-style organization that was looking for Communist infiltrators and supporters in the United States. Only a few hours after JFK was shot, Banister drunkenly beat one of his investigators, Jack Martin, with a gun, concerned that Martin was going to reveal David Ferrie's role as getaway pilot for the real assassins of Kennedy.

As far as UFOs are concerned, Banister was one of the first FBI agents who investigated crashed UFO stories for his FBI boss, J. Edgar Hoover, when Hoover instructed his agents, in summer 1947, to assist the Army Air Force in its UFO inquiries. The most notorious UFO event that Banister investigated occurred in Twin Falls, Idaho, in July 1947 and tied Banister in directly with the crashed UFO controversy.

The following is extracted from the *Tacoma News Tribune* of July 12, 1947:

> FBI agent W. G. Banister said an object which appeared to be a "flying disk" was found early today at Twin Falls, Idaho, and turned over to federal authorities there. Banister, Special Agent in Charge of the FBI in Montana and Idaho, said the bureau had reported the discovery to the army at Fort Douglas, Utah. An FBI agent in Twin Falls, inspected the "saucer" and described it as similar to the "cymbals used by a drummer in a band, placed face to face." The object measured 30.5 inches in diameter, with a metal dome about 14 inches high on the opposite side, anchored in place by what appeared to be stove bolts. The gadget is gold plated on one side and silver (either stainless-steel, aluminium or tin) on the other. It appeared to have been turned out by machine, reports from Twin Falls said. The FBI declined to elaborate further.

It is worth noting that Banister had behind-closed-doors meetings with the Army at Fort Douglas, Utah, to discuss the nature of the object. As this alleged crash and subsequent meeting occurred during the time of the reported UFO crash in Roswell, it is not implausible that Banister (being the original custodian of the object) may have been exposed to the truth about crashed saucers, particularly if initial confusion had existed about the real nature of the object—as, indeed, it had.

On June 21, 1947, a distinctly strange series of events occurred on Maury Island, Washington, that, according to some, may have involved a malfunctioning UFO that exploded in the sky and subsequently showered a large amount of debris down on the surrounding area. Not only that, the research of investigative writer Kenn Thomas has demonstrated that one of the key players in the story was later implicated, by several sources, in the death of President Kennedy.

The story goes that on the morning in question, a lumber salvager named Harold Dahl, his son, and two still unidentified individuals witnessed six disc-shaped aircraft—one in the middle, wobbling in a strange fashion while the remaining objects surrounded it—flying in formation over Puget Sound, Tacoma, at a height of around two thousand feet.

Dahl described the objects as being "shaped like doughnuts," with "five portholes on their sides." Suddenly, the central disk began to wobble even more and dropped to a height of no more than seven hundred feet. The remaining discs then broke formation, with one of them descending to the same height as the apparently malfunctioning disc, then proceeded to "touch it."

Without warning, the malfunctioning disc then began to "spew forth" what appeared to be two different substances: a white-colored material that Dahl described as a thin, white, "newspaper-like" metal that floated down to the bay and a black substance that also hit the water and that was reportedly hot enough to "cause steam to rise."

Maury Island in Puget Sound, Washington state, was the site of an unusual display of doughnut-shaped UFOs observed in 1947 by lumbermen working there.

According to the story, Dahl reported the events in question to his superior: Fred Crisman, a man with a long and complicated life story and suspected ties to the murky world of American Intelligence. Since Dahl had supposedly retained samples of the recovered debris, he convinced Crisman to go to the Maury Island shore and take a look for himself. Crisman would later claim that he saw on the shore an "enormous amount" of both the black and the white material and recovered some of it for his own safekeeping.

Crisman duly reported his experience to the publisher Ray Palmer (of *Amazing Stories* fame), who hired none other than Kenneth Arnold to investigate the Maury Island affair. Arnold, whose own historic encounter came three days after Dahl's encounter on Maury Island, delved deeply into the story and was later joined by two Air Force investigators, Capt. William Lee Davidson and 1st Lt. Frank Mercer Brown, who were working under Gen. Nathan Twining to collect information on the then-current wave of UFO encounters that was being widely reported across the United States.

Crisman turned over samples of the mysterious debris to the Air Force investigators, who intended to fly it to their final destination at Wright Field, Ohio. Fate would have another outcome, however. Shortly after Brown and Davidson departed from Washington State, their plane crashed, killing both men. A team was dispatched to clean up the site. Reportedly, the strange debris could not be located.

Many commentators (including Capt. Edward Ruppelt of Project Blue Book fame) have stated that the entire Maury Island event was nothing more than an unfortunate hoax that had a tragic outcome for Brown and Davidson. Kenn Thomas's intense and dedicated research, however, has shown that the affair might not be as black and white as has previously been assumed.

Most significant are Crisman's links with the Intelligence Community: In 1968, Fred Crisman was subpoenaed by New Orleans district attorney Jim Garrison as part of Garrison's investigation into the assassination of President Kennedy.

In a well-known report titled *The Torbitt Document*, Crisman is named as one of the three "hoboes" picked up in the rail yard behind the infamous Grassy Knoll at Dealey Plaza, Dallas, where, some maintain, a "second gunman" was located during the killing of Kennedy. The fog of time has effectively resulted in certain aspects of the Maury Island case remaining unresolved—and perhaps permanently, too. For some, the case is still nothing but a tragic hoax. For others, however, it is seen as one of the most important cases of all, involving the actual recovery of debris from a malfunctioning UFO. The involvement of shadowy players on the periphery of the Intelligence Community; the possibility of the deliberate murder of Air Force personnel in possession of the strange materials recovered on Maury Island; and even both direct and indirect links to the JFK assassination all serve to ensure that the controversy surrounding the Maury Island affair continues.

According to a document secured by Timothy Cooper from one of his whistle-blower sources and titled the *Majestic-12 1ˢᵗ Annual Report*, some of the debris from Maury Island was turned over by Crisman (described in the document as a Counterintelligence Corps operative) to a CIA agent named Shaw. Researcher Kenn Thomas suggests that this was Clay Shaw—one of three people who Jim Garrison attempted to indict during his quest for the truth surrounding the JFK assassination. Although Shaw was eventually acquitted, his role as a CIA asset has since then been well documented and finally admitted officially by the agency. For his part, Garrison claimed that his prosecution of

Shaw was a "toe-hold" to a larger conspiracy in which Fred Crisman may have been an assassin working on behalf of the aerospace industry, which had its own reasons for wanting JFK dead. Shaw himself died on August 14, 1974.

The coauthor with William Birnes of the book *The Day After Roswell*, which detailed his alleged secret knowledge of the Roswell UFO crash of July 1947, Col. Philip Corso was an investigator for Senator Richard Russell, who was on the Warren Commission, which investigated the assassination of President Kennedy. At the time of his death, Corso was planning a follow-up book with the working title of *The Day After Dallas*, which would, he said, finally reveal to one and all the truth about the JFK assassination. How curious that someone who claimed to know the truth about Roswell also allegedly maintained intimate knowledge of Kennedy's death.

> He [JFK] had a major UFO sighting while visiting Russia in 1955 that was subsequently investigated, extensively, by both the CIA and the Air Force.

Equally as fascinating is the fact that the aforementioned Senator Russell was also implicated in the UFO mystery: He had a major UFO sighting while visiting Russia in 1955 that was subsequently investigated, extensively, by both the CIA and the Air Force. It is known, from cryptic comments that he made, that Russell received a classified briefing on the UFO subject from the CIA. Interestingly, Russell was the one member of the Warren Commission who believed that a conspiracy lay behind Kennedy's death, and the links do not end there.

On November 21 (two days before President Kennedy's assassination), a planned event was organized at Brooks Air Force Base, Texas. The president was to dedicate six new aerospace medical research buildings there that were said to be vital to the American space program. Interestingly, JFK was rumored to have seen "other" things during his visit to Brooks—chiefly the biological remains of strange bodies recovered from a UFO crash in New Mexico in 1947.

This story is made all the more intriguing by the fact that among those who JFK was scheduled to meet at Brooks, one was Maj. Gen. Theodore C. Bedwell Jr. Born in Texas in 1909, he attended Southern Methodist University in Dallas and received his doctor of medicine degree in 1933. His first assignment was Fitzsimons General Hospital in Aurora, Colorado, where he served until 1939. He served at various locations and in various positions during the Second World War.

Notably, however, from 1946 to 1947, he served as deputy surgeon and chief, industrial medicine, Air Materiel Command at Wright Field, Ohio—to where, it has been claimed, alien bodies were taken in summer 1947 following the events in Roswell, New Mexico. In other words, only forty-eight hours before he was shot, JFK was about to meet someone who was arguably in a prime position to see the bodies brought into Wright Field in 1947. Also during the visit to Brooks, an arrangement was made for Kennedy to meet with Col. Harold V. Ellingson, USAF, who had received a bachelor of science degree in bacteriology in 1935. Ellingson held a number of posts, the most interesting being that of post surgeon and hospital commander at Fort Detrick—the U.S. government's biological and chemical warfare research establishment where, according to a number of MJ-12-related papers, research into alien cadavers was allegedly undertaken in the early to mid-1950s. Of course, Ellingson and Bedwell were not a part of the conspiracy to kill Kennedy, but the possibility that Kennedy spoke with them as part of his effort to secure the truth behind the crashed UFO mystery cannot be ruled out.

It should also not be forgotten that many of these JFK–UFO links have a central theme. For the most part, they all deal with not UFO sightings but specifically with *crashed* UFOs.

Consider the facts: Guy Banister investigated a possible crashed UFO; Fred Crisman handled unidentified debris; CIA asset Clay Shaw (according to the *Majestic-12 1ˢᵗ Annual Report*) was provided with some of the Maury Island debris; Col. Philip Corso allegedly worked with UFO materials recovered in Roswell and claims to have seen an alien body; and at least two members of the staff at Brooks AFB who had arranged to meet JFK two days before his death worked at key locations reportedly involved in the analysis of alien biology: namely, Fort Detrick and Wright Field.

In addition, Shaw, Banister, and Crisman may have had intimate knowledge of the ultimate secret that MJ-12 was so desperately trying to keep hidden and that Kennedy was trying to disclose. They may also have had a collective, and vested, interest in having Kennedy eliminated from the picture on that fateful day in 1963 to protect their own involvement in the crashed UFO saga. The UFO controversy, it seems, can at times be a deadly game....

Alexa, the Spy in the Home

Imagine if you could have a highly advanced piece of technology in your very own home: technology that will answer questions, give you weather updates, set your morning alarm, interact with you, and even listen to you—every single minute of every single day of every single year. Certainly, matters relative to the likes of the weather and your alarm are no big deal, but a device that eavesdrops on every word spoken in the family home? It sounds like the worst nightmare possible, and yet, countless numbers of people have already embraced this creepy technology, unaware of the potential violations of privacy that it offers or, worse still, not even caring about the ways in which their private lives are being opened up to the likes of the Intelligence Community. Welcome to the world of what are known as Amazon Echo and Alexa.

It was almost a decade ago when Amazon first began thinking about creating something along the lines of smart technology that could interact with people and how it might benefit the public. Much of the research and development was undertaken in the heart of Silicon Valley, California.

Of course, and as is so often the case with such technology, it is very possible for it to be ruthlessly manipulated by those who wish to learn who we are speaking to, what we are doing—and even the content of the conversations that go on in our living rooms, kitchens, bedrooms—in fact, just about everywhere. It sounds like something straight out of a paranoia-filled novel. It's not: it's all too real, and it's a phenomenon that is growing by the minute.

In simple terms, Amazon Echo is what is termed a "smart speaker," one that is hooked up to the Internet. When you are within range of the device, you can ask it questions: "Who were the Beatles?" "What happened at Pearl Harbor in 1941?" "Who shot JFK?" In quick-time fashion, you will have your questions answered—but who or what is providing the answers? That's where things get even creepier. Say "hello" to Alexa, a Net-based personal assistant, who can multitask to degrees that would be impossible for a human being to achieve. That's right: Alexa is not a person at the other end of the speaker. Alexa is smart technology taken to the—so far—ultimate degree. Alexa will respond not just to her name but also to such words as "Computer," "Echo," and "Amazon." Most people, however, prefer to go with Alexa—which gives the ultimate multitasker a degree of personality and gives the user a feeling of interacting with something that is self-aware—which it may well soon become if it hasn't already to a degree.

It was on June 23, 2015, that Alexa was unleashed upon the public, specifically in the United States. Both Canada and the United Kingdom joined Alexa's little club a year later. In theory, nothing at all is wrong with you having Alexa answer those questions you need answering, but it doesn't end there—and this is where things get as complicated as they do controversial. Let's say, for example, that you direct Alexa to play the new song from your favorite band. Another family member does likewise, so does a third, and so on. When Alexa knows which particular music you each individually like, "she" can determine who is in the house just by listening in to what music is playing in the background. In other words, if your teenage daughter likes Taylor Swift, Alexa will understand that it's your daughter in the house and not you and all because your family has handed over all of its musical tastes to a smart device that is so smart, it knows who is home and who isn't. It gets stranger.

In 2018, the website *Mysterious Universe* stated the following:

In the latest case of weird Amazon Alexa stories, it's been reported that friendly robot holds some views that aren't, shall we say, accepted by the mainstream. Previously, the Amazon Echo Dot Alexa made headlines when it was creepily laughing at some of its owners. Now it seems like Alexa may be the world's first AI [artificial intelligence] conspiracy theorist. When asked "Alexa, what are Chemtrails?" Amazon's "intelligent personal assistant" responded by informing the unwitting user that chemtrails are nefarious chemical or biological agents sprayed into the atmosphere by the government. It seems somehow doubtful that Amazon programmed that little tidbit of information into their flagship smart-home intelligence.

An Amazon Dot Speaker (left) and an Amazon Echo Look look harmless enough, but are they? The Echo Look has a camera and can recommend clothes for you to wear. What else might it be observing?

Where did Alexa get her information on chemtrails, then? *Mysterious Universe* states: "Since this story broke, Amazon's been quiet on how Alexa came up with this answer, saying it was a bug, and quickly announcing they had fixed it. Now, the Amazon Echo Dot Alexa gives the definition of 'contrail' when asked what chemtrails are." What we have here is a case of Alexa using machine-learning algorithms—learning, in essence—and providing answers to questions that should not be in the Echo database. It gets more chilling: In January 2018, Amazon's vice president, Marc Whitten, spoke at the Consumer Electronics Show in Las Vegas. He said, "Rolling in things like Alexa, one of the things that we've been learning is that it's not even just necessarily about the facts. One of the big things we're doing with Alexa is making sure that she has opinions. What does Alexa think is something that's a good thing to watch?"

Letting Alexa decide what shows we watch? What movies? Amazon thinks this is a good idea? Now let's take a look at how Alexa almost became a witness to a murder—albeit in a very strange, alternative, and almost unbelievable fashion.

In February 2016, a man named James Bates, of Bentonville, Arkansas, was charged with the murder of Victor Collins, who was found dead in his hot tub. Undoubtedly, Collins drowned. The big question was: Had Collins died accidentally, or was it a case of cold-blooded murder? Bates said that he woke up to find Collins dead. Investigators, though, suspected that Collins had been strangled and drowned. The case was taken to a whole new level when it was realized that Bates owned his very own Amazon Echo. Was Alexa about to spill the beans? After all, the one thing that Alexa does better than anything else is monitor and even record the conversations of the owners and the users. It didn't take the local police long at all to approach Amazon—with a warrant, no less—and request access to Bates's Echo. This was new and uncharted territory and quickly captured the attention of the media.

The case was taken to a whole new level when it was realized that Bates owned his very own Amazon Echo. Was Alexa about to spill the beans?

Amazon agreed to provide the police with a "record of transactions" but refused to give them any relevant "audio data." Amazon officially stated, "Given the important First Amendment and privacy implications at stake, the warrant should be quashed unless the Court finds that the State has met its heightened burden for compelled production of such material."

Ultimately, the charges against Bates were dropped. The affair was highly instructive and revealing, though, in terms of how, in the future, devices like Echo may well play a role—and even perhaps a key and integral role—in what goes on behind closed doors.

In 2018, *The Verge* brought up the important issue of to what extent the National Security Agency might be able to access the likes of Amazon Echo. *The Verge*'s Russell Brandom said: "The NSA has always had broad access to US phone infrastructure, something driven home by the early Snowden documents, but the last few years have seen an explosion of voice assistants like the Amazon Echo and Google Home, each of which floods more voice audio into the cloud where it could be vulnerable to NSA interception. And if so, are Google and Amazon doing enough to protect users?"

It's a question that, as technology advances even further, will be at the forefront of matters relative to the right to privacy versus what government agencies believe they have the right to do in the name of national security. Now let's see how our TVs and even our cars can become tools of secret, never-ending surveillance.

Imagine the scene: It's a Saturday night, and you have a few friends over for drinks and dinner. At one point during the evening, you turn the conversation to the subjects of global politics and the ever-increasing intrusions of the surveillance state. Suddenly, and in unison, everyone in the room goes quiet. It's one of those classic, awkward silences, and it's not because your friends have nothing to say on the matter. Quite the opposite, in fact. They actually have a great deal to say or, rather, they have a great deal they *wish* they could say. The reason for the silence is as simple as it is sinister and chilling.

Everyone in the room is fearful that your television is listening to your every word. Not only is the TV listening to your words, it's also recording them. Worse still, due to a lack of encryption on the part of the manufacturer of the TV, the National Security Agency is able to access the set and listen in to every single word being said, so, rather than risk the wrath of the NSA and be forever labeled "a person of interest" by the Department of Homeland Security, your friends choose to change the subject and avoid a discussion of matters of a political nature that, one day, might come back to hurt them and, possibly, hurt them big-time, too. In stark and almost surreal terms, you are now under the complete control of your television. Even George Orwell didn't see that one coming. Whereas Orwell's classic 1949 book, *1984*, was a work of highly thought-provoking fiction, the issue of entire swathes of the population being controlled and swayed by their primary form of entertainment—the TV—is not fiction. It's bone-chilling fact.

It was in early 2015 that the controversy surrounding this very disturbing issue first surfaced to a significant degree. What an incredible story it proved to be.

Writer Clark Howard stated, "You've heard of the government spying on you and even businesses spying on you. But have you heard of your TV spying on you?! If you're not familiar with 'smart TVs,' they are modern flat-screen TVs with built-in apps allowing you to access online content like Netflix, Hulu Plus, or Amazon Prime much more easily than you would access traditional broadcast content."

As Howard also noted, the one company more than any other that was getting a great deal of justified flak was Samsung. Howard revealed to his readers a specific and important sentence that appears in Samsung's very own Terms of Service. Orwell would undoubtedly be spinning in his grave had he the opportunity to read the words. Samsung doesn't hide the startling facts; in fact, they make them acutely clear: "Please be aware that if your spoken words include personal or other sensitive information, that information will be among the data captured and transmitted to a third party through your use of Voice Recognition."

Never mind just a third party: with the current, sophisticated state of hacking, we could be talking about fourth, fifth, and sixth parties. In fact, endless numbers of parties who are secretly and carefully scrutinizing just about every word you utter while you sit in front of your TV. The fact that we have gotten into this state is bad enough, but what came next in this saga was even worse.

Author George Orwell warned how people in the future could be constantly monitored by the state, but he didn't predict some of the high tech available today.

Clark Howard was not the only person concerned by all this outrageous spying in the one environment where we should not have jackbooted scum listening to us. Also hot on the trail of this story were the people at *Digital Trends*. To a degree, at least, their words play down the conspiracy angle. While they admit that the idea of having a television that, in effect, is a spy in the home is "pretty nefarious," they also state that, in their opinion, much of what has been said of this particular issue has been "taken out of context"— but is that really the case? Let's see.

On the matter of what *Digital Trends* refers to as Samsung's "overly succinct description" of smart televisions, we are informed that when words and conversations may be recorded, we don't know for sure what, exactly, happens from thereon. They continue that the specific nature of the conditions under which the transfer of that same data makes its way to what *Digital Trends* refers to as a "third party"—which is an ideal euphemism for an intelligence agency of the government—is not entirely clear.

In light of all this, *Digital Trends* decided to do the right thing and approach Samsung for the answers. According to what Samsung had to say about all this, *Digital Trends* suggested that "the conspiracy theorists might be giving these 'smart' TVs too much credit." *Digital Trends's* thoughts on this issue were prompted by the fact that, for the most part, smart TVs remain in the equivalent of a laptop's sleep mode. They correctly note that such televisions are designed and programmed to respond to specific words and statements made by people within the home in which the TVs can be found. We're talking about phrases like, "Hi, TV" or "Hello, television." *Digital Trends* assures its readers that without such phrases being specifically said, the TV does not—and cannot—take note of your spoken words and equally does not and cannot record and store any conversations that might conceivably be picked up in the home.

While the observations made by *Digital Trends* most assuredly played down the conspiratorial nature of this story—which, to this day, is showing no signs of going away anytime soon— other media outlets were firmly of the opinion that the spies of the National Security Agency might very soon be in the living rooms of all of us, albeit in a strange and stealthy way.

Betanews, for example, revealed their findings on this matter, specifically with regard to Samsung. The news was not good, at least, not for us. For the

Modern smart TVs are capable of monitoring viewers' behavior and voice commands. This information is then saved, but it is not well protected from hackers.

likes of the NSA, however, it was an absolute dream come true: "The company had publicly acknowledged that it was indeed logging users' activity and voice commands." *Betanews* also highlighted the following words from Samsung: "[T]hese functions are enabled only when users agree to the separate Samsung Privacy Policy and Terms of Use regarding this function when initially setting up the TV."

As *Betanews* dug further into the controversy, they noted the research in this field that had been undertaken by an English company, Pen Test Partners. The company's David Lodge and Ken Munro had gotten their hands on one of Samsung's smart TVs, chiefly to see whether or not Samsung's claims were accurate or whether or not we were all being deceived. The startling conclusion was that no, Samsung was not telling the complete story. In fact, far from it.

Despite Samsung's bold assertions to the contrary, Lodge and Munro were firmly able to demonstrate that the claims that all of the user data on their smart TVs was completely encrypted and utterly safe from penetration was, frankly, complete and utter garbage. Secure was now insecure. The pair was able to prove that audio-based files, for example, were uploaded by Samsung's smart TVs in a wholly *un*-encrypted fashion. This, of course, meant that any hacker with a high degree of smarts could access the material at the push of a button or several. That doesn't just mean some four-hundred-pound guy in his mom's basement. It also means those who may wish to exert more and more control over us: the government and the Intelligence Community.

Television is controlling us—as in all of us—in another way. It's very different from the way in that our TVs might be hacked by the NSA and additional agencies—a situation that might very well deter significant portions of the population from airing their views on controversial matters. It is, however, no less disturbing in nature. In some ways, it's even more disturbing. To put it succinctly, we are becoming nothing less than slaves to our televisions—even mind-controlled slaves—and what is a slave? Someone who is under the control of someone else, that's what. The worst part of all this is that we don't realize what is happening to us—at least, we don't until it is graphically demonstrated to us. That's when the proverbial penny drops, and we see what is being done to us at an ever-increasing speed.

An important point on this very issue has been noted by Alex Ansary. It gets to the heart of not just how our TVs are aimed at controlling us but how the world's major media outlets are also a large part of the growing factor of control. Ansary makes no bones about the fact that our enslavement to our televisions amounts to, in certain situations, albeit certainly not all (yet), nothing less than brainwashing and mind control. Ansary correctly notes that the overwhelming majority of the content that we can access on our televisions is "run and programmed" by not small, independent companies but an elite of huge, influential, and powerful corporations—which is very different from how things were in decades now long gone. We're talking about the likes of General Electric and Westinghouse. In Ansary's view, this massive control of what we get to see on our TVs effectively ensures that the news we receive is both "warped" and "slanted." No surprises there: we all know that. Fox News, anyone?

Ansary didn't end there, however. He also focused on the sterling and eye-opening work of a man named Herbert E. Krugman, who died in July 2016 at the ripe old age of ninety-five. The *New York Times* noted in an obituary of Krugman that he "was a lifelong student of the process of learning. Combining survey techniques with his background in cognitive and physiological psychology, Herb was the leading theorist of his generation on how consumers react to advertising."

Krugman was far more than that. He was a trustee of the Marketing Science Institute and a director of advertising research; the manager of public opinion research for the aforementioned General Electric; the president of the American Association for Public Opinion Research; and someone who was deeply plugged into the likes of various high-profile universities, including Columbia, Princeton, and Yale. Things don't end there. In terms of the issues that concern us today—with regard to how we are becoming controlled by our TVs—the most significant development, as it relates to Herbert E. Krugman, came in 1970s. That was the year in which Krugman, with a colleague named Eugene E. Hartley, wrote an eye-opening paper titled "Passive Learning from Television." It was published by the American Association for Public Opinion Research.

The combined work of Krugman and Hartley revealed more than a few things of a highly startling nature, all of them worrisome. As the pair was able to conclusively confirm from clinical studies involving consenting individuals who took part in the duo's experiments, when we become engrossed with something on our televisions—whether a breaking news story, a movie, or our favorite television shows—our minds quite literally shift. The human brain has two hemispheres, as they are known. They are distinctly different. The left hemisphere is that which controls what is known as logical thought. The right side, however, is, we might say, completely uncritical. In contrast to the left hemisphere, the right absorbs data in an illogical fashion. Emotion takes the place of logic. When this shift occurs, the brain floods the body with endorphins. *WebMD.com* notes that endorphins "trigger a positive feeling in the body, similar to that of morphine."

In the very same way that people can become seriously addicted to morphine, it is equally possible—in fact, all but inevitable—that we are all becoming addicted to television as a result of that left-right shift in the hemi-spheres of our brains. In other words, we are becoming junkies, and the more television we watch, the more of an addict we become, and the greater the addiction, the greater the need to watch more and more television. At that point, it's pretty much a case of being on an unstoppable roller-coaster that is increasing in speed by every minute.

Stunning statistics have been highlighted by *Waking Times*, specifically on the matter of how, in essence, our TVs control us, even if we are not fully aware of the situation. As they note, the average westerner spends almost a full decade of their lives doing nothing but watching TV. In effect, *Waking Times* says, the populace is "being hypnotized by a television screen without being conscious of the effects this activity has on them." *Waking Times* also notes that this issue of becoming slaves to our televisions has had a major, adverse impact on how we socialize—whether with family, friends, or people we work with. *Waking Times* then gets to the absolute nitty-gritty: close to three quarters of us eat our meals in front of a TV. Roughly one third of children who are just one year old (or even *less*) have televisions in their bedrooms. For eight-year-olds, the percentage who have a bedroom-based television is almost 50 percent in the United States. Consider these jaw-dropping words from *Waking Times*: "A typical U.S. child spends 3.5 minutes per week in meaningful conversation with a parent, but 1680 minutes per week in front of TV."

It gets worse: By the time that someone roughly reaches the age of retirement—sixty-five—the average person in the western world has watched a mind-boggling two million commercials, many of which are run over and over again. If we dare to stop watching television, we find ourselves in states not unlike those of drug addicts going through withdrawal cold turkey. Again, it's all down to those endorphins that swarm around our body when we watch TV. When we stop? Anxiety, a sense of isolation, and even depression all kick in, and they kick in big-time, too.

Watching television stimulates the left side of the brain, triggering endorphins that have an addictive effect similar to that of using morphine.

Controlled? Undoubtedly. The final word on this worrying and growing matter goes to Hal Becker. An author, his best-selling books include *Hal Becker's Ultimate Sales Book* and *Can I Have 5 Minutes of Your Time?* Becker, who has consulted for the likes of IBM, AT&T, United Airlines, and Verizon, says: "I know the secret of making the average American believe anything I want him to. Just let me control television.... You put something on the television and it becomes reality."

That is, unless each and every one of us breaks the shackles of control that lurk in our living rooms, bedrooms, and kitchens.

Never mind just the issue of being spied on in our very own homes, the issue of what happens when we leave our homes—whether it's to go to work, to run a few chores, to take the kids to school or to a game, and so on—is not insignificant. As amazing and as disturbing as it sounds, the Controllers are now in a prime and perfect position to take control of our cars and trucks as if our homes were not enough. No, we're not talking about our vehicles being impounded and taken away by the police. Rather, we're talking about how advanced technology exists to completely disable our vehicles—whether temporarily or even permanently. If the Controllers want to keep you and me under their collective thumb, all they need to do is prevent us from using the one thing that would allow us to escape from their clutches: our very own vehicle, of course. When just about everyone is reliant upon a vehicle, for more than three hundred million Americans to find they no longer have such a vehicle that works at all would be a daunting thing, to say the least.

Many car and truck manufacturers are going down the Big Brother path by installing their vehicles with certain advanced technology that allows a remote controller to completely cut the engine and bring the car or truck to a halt—whether sudden or grinding. As far back as 2009, for example, General

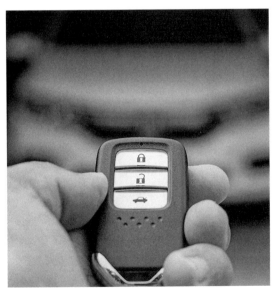

Car owners can already start and stop their cars remotely, and police and service companies like OnStar can as well.

Motors set the wheels in motion (which is an ironic turn of phrase, to be sure) to ensure that close to two million of their vehicles could be brought to immediate halts at the touch of a button. It is all thanks to General Motors's OnStar.

As OnStar notes:

If your vehicle is stolen, OnStar can use GPS to pinpoint it and help authorities quickly recover it. On many models, an Advisor can send a signal to slow the vehicle or prevent it from restarting. Thieves won't get far with Remote Ignition Block. Once a vehicle has been reported stolen, OnStar can send a remote signal that blocks the engine from starting. When a thief tries to restart it, he may think he's made a clean getaway, but he's not going anywhere. OnStar can send a Stolen Vehicle Slowdown signal to help authorities recover your vehicle and reduce high-speed pursuits. Once the police confirm that conditions are safe, we can send a signal that gradually slows the vehicle. The police can move in quickly, and it won't be long before you're headed out in your recovered car.

No one is saying that OnStar and General Motors are part of some vast conspiracy; in the right hands, like those of OnStar, the technology under scrutiny is both valuable and welcome, but the fact is that in the wrong hands, this vehicle-stopping technology could cause havoc, particularly so if it's utilized during a national emergency: you may well find yourself out of a vehicle and out of luck and stranded at home—where you are being listened to on an unending basis.

Ostensibly, the technology is intended to cut down the need for high-speed chases—particularly at night, which can be a very dangerous time for law enforcement to have to engage the likes of car thieves and fugitives from justice. If the touch of a button can bring such pursuits to an end, all the better. As long as the technology isn't turned against law-abiding citizens, all is good. If the worst-case scenario does come, though, and the likes of OnStar are placed under government control—in a state of national emergency—then we may find ourselves effectively imprisoned in our homes with absolutely nowhere to go. Under those kind of sinister circumstances, the fight for freedom will become ever more dangerous and deadly.

Martian Secrets and the CIA

In 1984, behind closed doors, agents of the Central Intelligence Agency embarked on an ambitious project to try to "remote view" the planet Mars, specifically to find evidence of life on the planet—not today but in the distant past. For those who may not know, remote viewing is a process by which a psychic individual may focus his or her mind on a particular location and describe its appearance, whether it exists now or existed in years, centuries, and even millennia long gone. It was on May 22, 1984, that the ambitious program began. While some of the pages declassified under the terms of the Freedom of Information Act are heavily redacted for national security-based reasons, others give us at least some sense of what was afoot behind the closed doors of the CIA headquarters in Langley, Virginia.

The time frame that the CIA had in mind was approximately one million years B.C.E. Why? The CIA isn't telling. The remote viewer—whose name is deleted from the files—stated, "I kind of got an oblique view of a, ah, pyramid or pyramid form. It's very high, it's kind of sitting in a large depressed area. I'm tracking severe, severe clouds, more like dust storm[s]. I'm looking at an after-effect of a major geologic problem. I just keep seeing very large people. They appear thin and tall, but they're very large, wearing some kind of clothes."

The remote viewer then focuses certain massive structures on Mars that appeared to have been built by intelligent beings:

> Deep inside of a cavern, not of a cavern, more like [a] canyon. I'm looking up, the sides of a steep wall that seem to go on forever. And there's like a structure … it's like the wall of the canyon has been carved. Again, I'm getting a very large structures [sic] … huge sec-

tions of smooth stone … it's like a rabbit warren, corners of rooms, they're really huge. Perception is that the ceiling is very high, walls very wide.

They have a … ah … appears to be the very end of a very large road and there's a marker thing that's very large. Keep getting Washington Monument overlay, it's like an obelisk … see pyramids … they're huge. It's filtered from storms or something…. They're like shelters from storms.

Different chambers … but they're almost stripped of any kind of furnishings or anything, it's like ah … strictly [a] functional place for sleeping or that's not a good word, hibernations, some form, I can't, I get real raw inputs, storms, savage storm, and sleeping through storms.

They're ancient people. They're dying. It's past their time or age. They're very philosophic about it. They're just looking for a way to survive and they just can't. They're … ah … evidently was a … a group or party of them that went to find … ah … new place to live. It's like I'm getting all kinds of overwhelming input of the corruption of their environment. It's failing very rapidly and this group went somewhere, like a long way to find another place to live.

Does this specific piece of almost unique CIA documentation tell of an ancient Martian civilization, one whose world spiraled into ecological collapse and that forced them to a new world to live on? Maybe our Earth? It just might. The idea that Mars may once have been home to a race of advanced Martians who fled their dying world when even they were unable to prevent an all-encompassing disaster may well tie in with the strange story of what has become known as the Face on Mars, as we shall now see.

One person who was fascinated by all this was the late Mac Tonnies, whose book on these very topics—*After the Martian Apocalypse*—makes for required reading. Most of Tonnies's work revolved around one particular area on Mars, a region called Cydonia. It is right in the heart of Cydonia where what appears to be a massive, humanlike face carved out of rock can be found—and "massive" is no exaggeration. It is around three kilometers in length and roughly half that distance wide. Clearly, if not just a trick of the light, the Face represents an incredible example of massive and radical alteration to the landscape—and, in all likelihood, tens of thousands of years ago, maybe even longer.

It was on July 25, 1976, that the Face on Mars caught the attention of NASA staff. It was on that date that NASA's *Viking 1* spacecraft secured a series of aerial photos of Cydonia in general and of the now legendary Face. The fact that the pictures are now in the public domain has given rise to a

These photos taken by NASA appear to reveal monumental structures on the surface of
Mars, including an obelisk (left) and a pyramid. Are they evidence of a Martian civilization,
or just tricks of the eye resulting from odd shadows?

great deal of thought on what, exactly, the Face represents. If not a natural formation, who constructed it, and why? Let's see what Mac Tonnies had to say
about the Face on Mars and the possibility that it represents one of the last
pieces of evidence suggesting that Mars was once a bustling world, teeming
with alien life.

Mac Tonnies's interest in the Face began in the 1980s, when he was
still a teenager. It was more than a decade later that Tonnies decided to dig
further into the heart of the enigma to try to figure out the truth of the mystery. In an extensive interview with me, Tonnies said:

> I've always had an innate interest in the prospect of extraterrestri-
> al life. When I realized that there was an actual scientific inquiry
> regarding the Face and associated formations, I realized that this
> was a potential chance to lift SETI from the theoretical arena; it's
> within our ability to visit Mars in person. This was incredibly excit-
> ing, and it inspired an interest in Mars itself—its geological histo-
> ry, climate, et cetera. I have a BA in Creative Writing. So, of
> course, there are those who will happily disregard my book because
> I'm not "qualified." I suppose my question is "Who *is* qualified to
> address potential extraterrestrial artifacts?" Certainly not NASA's

Jet Propulsion Laboratory [JPL], whose Mars exploration timetable is entirely geology-driven.

How, exactly, did the controversy begin, though, and what was it that led to so much interest—obsession, even—in Mars's massive mystery? Tonnies provides us with the timeline:

> NASA itself discovered the Face, and even showed it at a press conference, after it had been photographed by the Viking mission in the 1970s. Of course, it was written off as a curiosity. Scientific analysis would have to await independent researchers. The first two objects to attract attention were the Face and what has become known as the "D&M Pyramid." Both unearthed by digital imaging specialists Vincent DiPietro and Gregory Molenaar. Their research was published in *Unusual Martian Surface Features*; shortly after, Face researcher Richard Hoagland pointed out a collection of features—some, eerily pyramid-like—near the Face which he termed the "City."

As Tonnies noted, NASA—publicly, at least—dismissed the Face on Mars as nothing but a regular piece of rock that, superficially speaking, resembled a human face, and that was all—for NASA, if not for Tonnies. It's important to note Tonnies's words, which strongly suggest that the face is not a natural creation. He said: "When NASA dismissed the Face as a 'trick of light,' they cited a second, discomfirming photo allegedly taken at a different sun-angle. This photo never existed. DiPietro and Molenaar had to dig through NASA archives to find a second image of the Face—and, far from disputing the face-like appearance, it strengthened the argument that the Face remained face-like from multiple viewing angles."

Tonnies notes the extent to which NASA went to try to discredit the theories suggesting that the Face on Mars was not a natural formation:

> The prevailing alternative to NASA's geological explanation—that the Face and other formations are natural landforms—is that we're seeing extremely ancient artificial structures built by an unknown civilization. NASA chooses to ignore that there is a controversy, or at least a controversy in the scientific sense. Since making the Face public in the 1970s, NASA has made vague allusions to humans' ability to "see faces" (e.g. the "Man in the Moon") and has made lofty dismissals, but it has yet to launch any sort of methodical study of the objects under investigation. Collectively, NASA frowns on the whole endeavor. Mainstream SETI [Search for Extraterrestrial Intelligence] theorists are equally hostile.

Tonnies made valuable observations relative to the controversy:

Basically, the Face—if artificial—doesn't fall into academically palatable models of how extraterrestrial intelligence will reveal itself, if it is in fact "out there." Searching for radio signals is well and good, but scanning the surface of a neighboring planet for signs of prior occupation is met with a very carefully cultivated institutionalized scorn. And of course it doesn't help that some of the proponents of the Face have indulged in more than a little baseless "investigation."

With that all said, what did Mac Tonnies himself think of the Face on Mars? His thoughts, based upon years of dedicated research, make the answer to that question abundantly clear: "I think some of the objects in the Cydonia region of Mars are probably artificial. And I think the only way this controversy will end is to send a manned mission. The features under investigation are extremely old and warrant on-site archaeological analysis. We've learned—painfully—that images from orbiting satellites won't answer the fundamental questions raised by the Artificiality Hypothesis."

Tonnies suspected that the Face was a combination of a natural formation and something that had been radically altered into a new form. He elab-

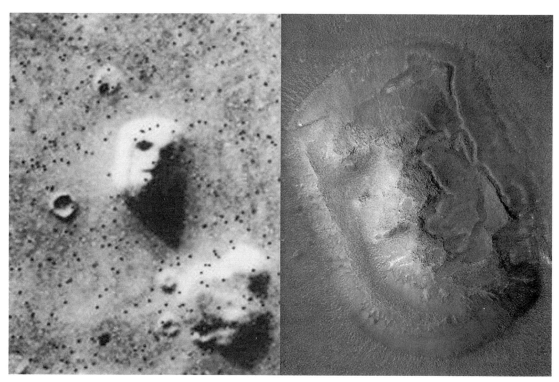

Here are two views of the "Face on Mars" with different shadowing. Depending on how you look at it, it might look like a helmeted head or just a geologic formation.

orated on this particularly controversial line of thinking thus: "I suspect that we're seeing a fusion of natural geology and mega-scale engineering. For example, the Face is likely a modified natural mesa, not entirely unlike some rock sculptures on Earth but on a vastly larger and more technically challenging scale."

By making reference to "certain rock sculptures on Earth," Tonnies opened up a definitive can of worms, which was practically impossible to close. All of which brings us to the matter of nothing less than our ancient history, specifically Egypt. The fact that the Cydonia region appeared to be the home of a couple of pyramidlike structures, as well as a Face that somewhat looked like the Sphinx of Giza in Egypt led Tonnies to note the following:

> There's a superficial similarity between some of the alleged pyramids in the vicinity of the Face and the better-known ones here on Earth. This has become the stuff of endless arcane theorizing, and I agree with esoteric researchers that some sort of link between intelligence on Mars and Earth deserves to be taken seriously. But the formations on Mars are much, much larger than terrestrial architecture. This suggests a significantly different purpose, assuming they're intelligently designed. Richard Hoagland, to my knowledge, was the first to propose that the features in Cydonia might be "arcologies"—architectural ecologies—built to house a civilization that might have retreated underground for environmental reasons."

Tonnies was, as he admitted, highly concentrated on the fact that the carving was not just of a face but of what looked distinctly like a human face. Was it just a coincidence? Did the Martians resemble us? Did a genetic connection exist between them and us? Yet again, Tonnies's thoughts and suspicions led him to formulate some incredible concepts:

> It's just possible that the complex in Cydonia—and potential edifices elsewhere on Mars—were constructed by indigenous Martians. Mars was once extremely Earth-like. We know it had liquid water. It's perfectly conceivable that a civilization arose on Mars and managed to build structures within our ability to investigate. Or the anomalies might be evidence of interstellar visitation— perhaps the remains of a colony of some sort. But why a humanoid face? That's the disquieting aspect of the whole inquiry; it suggests that the human race has something to do with Mars, that our history is woefully incomplete, that our understanding of biology and evolution might be in store for a violent upheaval. In retrospect, I regret not spending more time in the book addressing the possibility that the Face was built by a vanished terrestrial civilization

that had achieved spaceflight. That was a tough notion to swallow, even as speculation, as it raises as many questions as it answers.

If the Face on Mars was built by intelligent beings—whether ancient humans or indigenous aliens—then how was such a monumental task achieved? On this point, we have the following from Tonnies, which is fairly restrained: "We need to bring archaeological tools to bear on this enigma. When that is done, we can begin reconstructing Martian history. Until we visit in person, all we can do is take better pictures and continue to speculate."

Working on the theory that Mars was once home to intelligent beings, we need to ask one of the most pressing questions of all: What was it that led the Martian world to become the dead world it is today? Tonnies says of this issue:

> Astronomer Tom Van Flandern has proposed that Mars was once the moon of a tenth planet that literally exploded in the distant past. If so, then the explosion would have had severe effects on Mars, probably rendering it uninhabitable. That's one rather apocalyptic scenario. Another is that Mars's atmosphere was destroyed by the impact that produced the immense Hellas Basin [a 7,152-meter-deep basin located in Mars's southern hemisphere]. Both ideas are fairly heretical by current standards; mainstream planetary science is much more comfortable with Mars dying a slow, prolonged death. Pyrotechnic collisions simply aren't intellectually fashionable—despite evidence that such things are much more commonplace than we'd prefer.

What was it that prompted Tonnies to dig so deep into the matter and write his still acclaimed book *After the Martian Apocalypse*, then? Tonnies came straight to the point:

> I was, frankly, fed up with bringing the subject of the Face on Mars up in online discussion and finding myself transformed into a straw man for self-professed experts. It was ludicrous. The book is a thought experiment, a mosaic of questions. We don't have all of the answers, but the answers are within our reach. Frustratingly, this has become very much an "us vs. them" issue, and I blame both sides. The debunkers have ignored solid research that would undermine their assessment, and believers are typically quite pompous that NASA et al. are simply wrong or, worse, actively covering up.

Tonnies elected to comment further on this matter of a potential cover-up to hide an incredible revelation from the distant past:

> When NASA/JPL released the first Mars Global Surveyor image of the Face in 1998, they chose to subject the image to a high-pass

filter that made the Face look hopelessly vague. This was almost certainly done as a deliberate attempt to nullify public interest in a feature that the space agency is determined to ignore. So yes, there is a cover-up of sorts. But it's in plain view for anyone who cares to look into the matter objectively. I could speculate endlessly on the forms a more nefarious cover-up might take—and I come pretty close in the book—but the fact remains that the Surveyor continues to return high-resolution images. Speculation and even some healthy paranoia are useful tools. But we need to stay within the bounds of verifiable fact lest we become the very conspiracy-mongering caricatures painted by the mainstream media.

It's important to note that Tonnies did not just focus his attention on the Face on Mars. He also focused on other anomalies, too. One, in particular, fascinated Tonnies:

The Mars Global Surveyor has taken images of anomalous branching objects that look, for all the world, like organic phenomena. Arthur C. Clarke [the late, acclaimed science-fiction author, who died in 2008] for one, is sold on the prospect of large forms of life on Mars, and has been highly critical of JPL's silence. Clarke's most impressive candidates are what he has termed "banyan trees" near the planet's south pole. And he collaborated with Mars researcher Greg Orme in a study of similar features NASA has termed "black spiders"—root-like formations that suggest tenacious macroscopic life.

In finality, Tonnies provided the following words:

Our attitudes toward the form extraterrestrial intelligence will take are painfully narrow. This is exciting intellectual territory, and too many of us have allowed ourselves to be told what to expect by an academically palatable elite. I find this massively frustrating. I hope *After the Martian Apocalypse* will loosen the conceptual restraints that have blinkered radio-based SETI by showing that the Face on Mars is more than collective delusion or wishful thinking. This is a perfectly valid scientific inquiry and demands to be treated as such.

Indeed, it does.

The Bigfoot Conspiracy

Is the U.S. government—or some element within it—hiding a shocking truth concerning nothing less than the Bigfoot? If so, what, exactly, might that shocking truth be? Nothing less than deep and dark suspicions that the Bigfoot creatures are responsible for the many and varied people who go missing every year in the nation's national parks. Of course, some may be the victims of mountain lions and accidents, perhaps even serial killers, too, but what if a small number are the result of fatal confrontations with the Bigfoot of very violent and deadly kinds? Does any evidence exist that this might just be the case? Incredibly, yes, it does.

David Paulides is the brains behind a series of books that fall under the *Missing 411* banner. North America Bigfoot Search says of his work at their website: "*Missing 411* is the first comprehensive book about people who have disappeared in the wilds of North America. It's understood that people routinely get lost, some want to disappear but this story is about the unusual. Nobody has ever studied the archives for similarities, traits and geographical clusters of missing people, until now."

It's important to note that Paulides is very much open-minded on the issue of who, or *what*, is responsible for the massive numbers of people who enter the woods and forests of the United States only to never be seen again. It's important to note, though, that elements of the Bigfoot-seeking community were quick to sit up and take notice of Paulides's important work when it first surfaced—an unsettling area of research that practically no one else has dug into.

One of the cases that Paulides focused on occurred in summer 1969 and was centered on the disappearance of a young boy named Dennis Martin—

who, very oddly, vanished within sight of his father. The location was Cades Cove in the Great Smoky Mountains National Park, which borders upon North Carolina and Tennessee. It's intriguing to note that soon after the incident occurred, a man named Harold Key heard a wild, animalistic scream coming from somewhere near Rowans Creek. Notably, Key, who was with his family, walking on a trail, saw something that he at first thought was a bear. Oddly, though, it had certain human qualities to it, which led Key to describe it as a "dark figured, rough-looking man," partially hidden behind a thicket.

What are we to make of these stories of the dangerous Bigfoot, of what may very well be the *killer* Bigfoot, and of all the many and varied people who are never seen again after taking a trip into the forests of the United States? Yes, some may fall victim to accidents, to ill health, and even to fatal attacks by the likes of bears and mountain lions. However, a body of evidence suggests that the Bigfoot are not beyond kidnapping, killing, and maybe even devouring those who intrude upon its territory. Remember that the next time you head out into one of the wilder, denser U.S. forests. Something large and hairy may be sizing you up … for food.

Avrel Seale is the author of a road trip-style book titled *Monster Hike: A 100-Mile Inquiry into the Sasquatch Mystery*. He notes that in his home state of Texas, the Bigfoot are particularly violent—dangerous, even. If such a theory to hide a terrifying truth is correct, Seale says: "Nearly 40 million Americans work in government jobs at the federal, state, and local level. I am one of them. If 1,000 of those 40 million know about the existence of sasquatches, does that mean 'the government knows'? I suppose the answer depends on which 1,000 and how well they are connected, if at all." Seale makes a good point, to be sure.

With that all said, let's now look at the body of data on the dangerous, and maybe killer, Bigfoot.

In his 1890 book *The Wilderness Hunter*, President Theodore Roosevelt described the killing of a woodsman—in either Wyoming or Montana, he wasn't sure—a couple of decades earlier. It was a story that came to Roosevelt—who was a keen outdoorsman and hunter—by one of the primary players in the saga, a man named Carl Bauman. According to the tale told to Roosevelt, Bauman and a friend were deep in the woods, stalking an unknown animal—but one that, as its tracks clearly showed, walked upright, on two limbs,

An artist's concept of what a Bigfoot looks like based on testimonials from various witnesses over the years.

and that was most definitely not a bear. The creature, then, was certainly no normal one. *Abnormal* would be a much better description, and whatever made the tracks, it certainly wasn't human, either; the sheer size of the prints made that very clear.

For days, the two friends trailed the beast—or, as they suspected at the time, that was stealthily tracking them, too. The story had a terrible and violent ending: Bauman's comrade was violently killed by the beast while Bauman was briefly away from the camp. On his return, Bauman was shocked to see the camp in violent disarray. Shock turned to terror, though, when Bauman stumbled on the body of his friend: the man's neck had been savagely broken, and it looked like something large and heavy had trampled the body in crazed fashion over and over again. Bauman fled the area, not stopping until he finally made it back to civilization. It was a shocking experience, one that Bauman would never forget—indeed, from a psychological perspective, it forever scarred him, particularly so on his future treks into the deep woods of the United States. What became of the corpse of Bauman's friend, no one knows. Dinner, maybe?

This 1885 photo of Theodore Roosevelt shows him in the clothes of the avid outdoorsman and hunter he was before becoming president. Roosevelt was familiar with tales of some kind of upright, hairy animal—neither human nor bear—roaming the forests of the American West.

True North: A Journey into Unexplored Wilderness is the title of a 1933 memoir-style book written by Elliott Merrick, who died at the age of ninety-one in Asheville, North Carolina, in 1997. *True North* was Merrick's very first book; his others included *Green Mountain Farm*, *Cruising at Last*, and *From This Hill Look Down*. In *True North*, Merrick told a story of a girl who had a distinctly disturbing close encounter with a Bigfoot that just might have seen her as a tasty meal. The location of what almost turned into a horrific tragedy was Traverspine, Happy Valley-Goose Bay, Labrador, Canada. The time: roughly twenty years earlier, which would have placed things approximately around 1912 to 1914.

Merrick wrote in his book: "Ghost stories are very real in this land of scattered lonely homes and primitive fears. The Traverspine 'Gorilla' is one of the creepiest. About twenty years ago one of the little girls was playing in an open grassy clearing one autumn afternoon when she saw coming out of the woods a huge hairy thing with low-hanging arms. It was about seven feet tall when it stood erect, but sometimes it dropped to all fours. Across the top of its head was a white mane."

The girl, hardly surprisingly, was rooted to the spot with fear. That fear reached fever-pitch levels when the half-animal/half-human thing motioned to the little girl—in a fashion that led her to think the beast was calling to her—to come closer. If the girl had any plans to do so, they were quickly dismissed when the face of the monster broke out into that of an evil, sinister grin. It was at that point that the girl could see the creature's huge mouth—which was filled with huge, fierce-looking teeth. They were teeth that could easily have ended the life of the girl and made a meal of her. Luckily, the girl was able to summon up the willpower and strength to make a run for it—which she did, to the home in which she lived with her parents. In almost hysterical fashion, the girl blurted out what had happened—which led her father to hastily and carefully check out the area in question. The animal, however, was already gone, but some evidence *was* left behind to show that the girl had not simply fallen asleep and had a bad nightmare or had mistaken a bear for a monster.

> A posse was soon on the hunt, carefully scouring the nearby woods, which were seen as the most likely locations where the creature would hide out.

Of the evidence, Merrick told his readers: "Its tracks were everywhere in the mud and sand, and later in the snow. They measured the tracks and cut out paper patterns of them which they still keep. It is a strange-looking foot, about twelve inches long, narrow at the heel, and forking at the front into two broad, round-ended toes. Sometimes its print was so deep it looked to weigh 500 pounds. At other times the beast's mark looked no deeper than a man's track."

The local folk didn't waste any time at all trying to find the hair-covered beast in their very midst. A posse was soon on the hunt, carefully scouring the nearby woods, which were seen as the most likely locations where the creature would hide out. A nighttime stakeout of nearby Mudd Lake proved to be completely fruitless, as did another search of the lake on the following night. Traps were laid down by anxious townsfolk. Nothing worked; the monster was gone. For a while.

When the story reached Merrick himself, he was determined to try to find out whether the account was true or a tall tale of the kind that are so often told around campfires. It didn't take Merrick long to learn that the people of Traverspine took the whole thing very seriously—even though by the time Merrick was on to the story, it was already an old one. Having gained their trust, Merrick spoke with more than ten locals who had, at various times over the years, seen the unidentified abomination. It clearly wasn't just a one-off event. No one knew what the thing was—only that it was no normal, regular animal.

Merrick added the following, based on what one of his informants in town told him: "One afternoon one of the children saw it peeping in the window. She yelled and old Mrs. Michelin grabbed a gun and ran for the door. She just saw the top of its head disappearing into a clump of trees. She fired where she saw the bushes moving and thinks she wounded it. She says too that it had a ruff of white across the top of its head. At night they used to bar the door with a stout birch beam and all sleep upstairs, taking guns and axes with them."

It wasn't just the people of Traverspine who were concerned, either—their pets were, too. Specifically, the local dog population. On a number of occasions, the presence of the dogs near the woods of Mudd Lake provoked the monster to howl and growl in frenzied fashion—which clearly demonstrated that the creature knew the dogs were near and reacted in a fashion designed to keep them well away. It worked: the dogs kept well away from the area of all the action.

Interestingly, on one occasion, said Merrick, the hairy horror swung at one of the dogs with what was described as "a club." Fortunately, the dog was not injured—but just the fact that the monster had a club, or perhaps a large branch wrenched off a tree, suggests it was an intelligent animal, one that used

Stories endure about people being kidnapped in the woods, never to return. Worse still are the tales of women being captured by Bigfoot and then being impregnated by them.

not just brute force but weapons, too. Then, it was all over. After a few years of occasional mayhem, the monster was gone for good.

Cryptozoologist Loren Coleman notes in his 2003 book *Bigfoot!* that in the *Bigfoot Bulletin* of October 31, 1970, published by California researcher George Haas, is:

> … a fantastic letter from an army trainee named Nick E. Campbell at Fort Ord, California. He related that two Texas National Guard privates, one of them a minister, had told him that at Longview where they lived, there were reports from about 1965 of a giant hairy creature roaming the back country between there and Jefferson, Texas. They said that the creature had reportedly killed a couple of people. Reverend Royal Jacobs told him that as a teenager he was a member of a posse that hunted the creature and he had seen the body of a person the creature had torn apart.

Then is the not insignificant matter of all the people who go missing every year … *in the woods.*

A number of ancient stories and contemporary accounts—from all across the world—exist of girls and women kidnapped by Bigfoot-type creatures, made pregnant by the hairy monsters, and ultimately giving birth to half-human, half-Bigfoot, freakish things of a nightmarish nature. If even a modicum of truth exists to these tales, then it goes without saying that these unknown animals are clearly of the human family—despite their savage, hairy appearance.

A particularly bizarre story that falls into this very category was published in a Chinese newspaper, the *World Journal*, in October 1997. Translated into English, it reads as follows: "A woman, who works for the Bigfoot Research Center in China, was going through the belongings of her recently deceased father. Her father had been with the Wildlife Research Center in China. Among the belongings she found a video tape taken in 1986."

The story continued that the tape showed something very strange and even disturbing: an unusual-looking man, who stood about six feet five inches in height and had a small head and arms of a noticeably long length. He was also reported to have had a tail-like protuberance from the base of his spine.

According to the account, the man's appearance was not caused by a rare genetic defect, as one might suppose, but something acutely different:

> The mother of the "boy" was still alive when the video was taken. The mother states that she had been kidnapped or abducted by a "wild man" after the death of her husband, and the boy was an offspring of her relationship with the wild man. The woman previously had a son by her husband. The son was an officer in the army,

and he persuaded his mother to tell her story to the Wildlife Research people. She told her story under the condition that the research people would not reveal her identity while she was alive because she was ashamed of what had happened.

Truth or tall tale, it's just one of many, eerily similar, cases of the kind that the Bigfoot may be far more human than apelike.

It's one thing to see a Bigfoot. It is, however, quite another thing entirely to claim to have been kidnapped by one and held hostage for several days! That was the controversial claim of a man named Albert Ostman, who was of Scandinavian extraction. Although Ostman claimed the traumatic event occurred in 1924, he did not go public with the story until 1957—which is, perhaps, understandable, given its wild nature.

At the time in question, Ostman was employed in the field of construction, although his background was as a lumberman. After having worked solidly for a considerable period of time, he decided it was time for a much-welcome and -deserved break to do something different. He decided to do a bit of gold prospecting in the Toba Inlet, situated on the British Columbia coast. It was during the course of the prospecting that Ostman experienced something that made him distinctly troubled and uneasy: someone, or something, had clearly been wandering around his camp while he was on his quest for gold.

For roughly three hours or so, Ostman was unceremoniously carried through, up, and down the dark woods by something large and powerful.

Ostman decided he was going to find out the guilty party's identity and, instead of going to sleep, he stayed wide awake in his sleeping bag, with his rifle right by his side. Unfortunately, a hard day toiling for gold took its toll, and Ostman quickly fell asleep, but not for long: he was jolted from his sleep by a sensation of being scooped up and carried away while still in his sleeping bag. In fact, that's exactly what happened. For roughly three hours or so, Ostman was unceremoniously carried through, up, and down the dark woods by something large and powerful. According to Ostman, he had heard stories of "the mountain Sasquatch giants" from Native American sources. Finally, the terror-filled trek came to its end. That much was made clear when the mighty creature relaxed its grip on the sleeping bag and let it drop to the forest floor.

Since the woods were still enveloped by the blackness of night, Ostman could not make out his kidnapper. As dawn broke, that situation radically changed. He found himself confronted by what can only be accurately described as a Bigfoot family: a giant male, a smaller female, and two juveniles, one male and one female. In other words: mom, dad, and the kids. As Ostman looked around, he could see he was deep in the heart of a heavily forested valley that was surrounded by huge mountains. Clearly anticipating the likelihood that Ostman would try to escape, the "Old Man"—as Ostman referred to the huge male—kept careful watch on Ostman, making sure at all times that he didn't try to make a run for it via the entrance to the valley. The fact that Ostman was held captive for several days ensured that he was able to carefully study their habits and appearance. In his own words: "The young fellow might have been 11–18 years old and about seven feet tall and might weigh about 300 lbs.… He had wide jaws, narrow forehead, that slanted upward … the old lady could have been anything between 40–70 years old … she would be about 500–600 pounds. She had very wide hips, and a goose-like walk. She was not built for beauty or speed."

As for the "old man," Ostman stated that he "must have been near eight feet tall. Big barrel chest and big hump on his back—powerful shoulders, his biceps on upper arm were enormous."

Ostman said of their general appearance: "The hair on their heads was about six inches long. The hair on the rest of their body was short and thick in places.… The only place they had no hair was inside their hands and the soles of their feet and upper part of the nose and eyelids.… They were very agile." Ostman was also able to deduce that the creatures were vegetarian.

Although Ostman was kept in the lair of the Bigfoot against his will, he wasn't mistreated. Nevertheless, he had no intention of spending the rest of his life as the equivalent of an animal in the zoo, held captive for someone else's entertainment: in this case, the Bigfoot. It transpired that the answer to his freedom came in a decidedly alternative fashion. Each and every morning, Ostman took a pinch of snuff from his snuff box. He noticed that the "old man" eyed him carefully on each and every occasion. Finally, when curiosity got the better of him, the immense giant grabbed the box out of Ostman's hands and poured the entire contents into his mouth. In seconds, the beast was doubled up on the floor, rolling in agony and gulping down water. As the rest of the family raced to help, Ostman saw his chance to make a run for it. He grabbed his gear, fired a shot in the air to scare off the creatures, and raced for freedom. Unsurprisingly, he was not followed nor did he see the beasts again.

Witness Albert Ostman described the creature as having hair all over its body, while the hair on its head was about six inches long (pictured is a simulation).

Although the story of Albert Ostman is filled with controversy, it was one that received (and continues to receive) support from entire swathes of the Bigfoot research community. British investigators Janet and Colin Bord said: "Although Ostman is now dead, John Green, an experienced Bigfoot investigator, knew him for over 12 years and had no reason to consider him a liar. Also, none of those who questioned him, such as a magistrate, zoologist, and primate specialists, could catch him out; and we therefore have no logical option but to assume that his story, fantastic though it may sound, was true."

Similarly, Bigfoot investigator John Napier said of Ostman and his story: "The anatomical peculiarities of the Sasquatch family are expressed in very reasonable terms, and his observations on behavior, if unimaginative, are without obvious inconsistencies."

Ostman was unmoved by the doubters. He had a stock response for anyone who chose to question his account: "I don't care a damn what you think."

Back in 1915, the now long-defunct *Museum Journal*, published quarterly by the University Museum of the University of Pennsylvania, Philadelphia, ran a fascinating article on what, with hindsight, sounds very much like an anomalous ape, one said to live in the deep woods and forests of Guatemala. Its name was El Sisemite. It read: "There is a monster that lives in the forest. He is taller than the tallest man and in appearance he is between a man and a monkey. His body is so well protected by a mass of matted hair that a bullet cannot harm him. His tracks have been seen on the mountains, but it is impossible to follow his trail because he can reverse his feet and thus baffle the most successful hunter."

The *Museum Journal* continued that the "great ambition" of the creature, "which he has never been able to achieve, is to make fire. When the hunters have left their camp fires he comes and sits by the embers until they are cold, when he greedily devours the charcoal and ashes. Occasionally the hunters see in the forest little piles of twigs which have been brought together by El Sisemite in an unsuccessful effort to make fire in imitation of men." We also see, as the *Museum Journal*'s article reveals, two other things that are staple parts of man-beast lore: a quasi-supernatural aspect to the creature and its obsession with kidnapping people, often women:

> His strength is so great that he can break down the biggest trees in the forest. If a woman sees a Sisemite, her life is infinitely prolonged, but a man never lives more than a month after he has looked into the eyes of the monster. If a Sisemite captures a man he rends the body and crushes the bones between his teeth in great enjoyment of the flesh and blood. If he captures a woman, she is carried to his cave, where she is kept a prisoner. Besides his wish to make fire the Sisemite has another ambition. He sometimes steals children in the belief that from these he may acquire the gift

COVER-UPS AND SECRETS: The Complete Guide to Government Conspiracies, Manipulations & Deceptions 217

of human speech. When a person is captured by a Sisemite the fact becomes known to his near relations and friends, who at the moment are seized with a fit of shivering. Numerous tales are told of people who have been captured by the Sisemite.

One such case of kidnapping was specifically detailed by the journal. It's an account that also has a somewhat supernatural aspect to it in the sense that one of the key individuals in the story suffered from what are termed "Sisemite shivers," the sense of the creature in a person's midst, even if it can't be seen. The saga begins:

> A young couple, recently married, went to live in a hut in the woods on the edge of their milpa in order that they might harvest the maize. On the road Rosalia stepped on a thorn and next morning her foot was so sore that she was unable to help Felipe with the harvesting, so he went out alone, leaving one of their two dogs with her.

> He had not been working long when the dreaded feeling, which he recognized as Sisemite shivers, took hold of him and he hastily returned to the hut to find his wife gone and the dog in a great fright. He immediately set out for the village, but met on the road the girl's parents, who exclaimed, "You have let the Sisemite steal our child, our feelings have told us so." He answered, "It is as you say."

> In no time at all, the local police were on the case, who suspected that the story of the Sisemite was nothing but an ingenious ruse, one created to hide the fact that the young man had killed his wife.

> The boy was cross-examined, but always answered, "The Sisemite took her, no more than that I know." He was, in spite of the girl's parents' protests, suspected of having murdered his young wife, and was thrown into jail, where he remained many years.

We may never know if the police's suspicions about Felipe were correct or if a grave miscarriage of justice had taken place. Either way, it only added to the mythos surrounding the Sisemite and its obsession with kidnapping women.

The *Museum Journal* was not yet done with this controversial story, however; far more was to tell.

> At last a party of hunters reported having seen on Mount Kacharul a curious being with a hairy body and flowing locks that fled at the sight of them. A party was organized which went out with the object of trying to capture this creature at any cost. Some days later this party returned with what seemed to be a wild woman, of whom the leader reported as follows:

"On Mount Kacharul we hid in the bushes. For 2 days we saw nothing, but on the third day about noon this creature came to the brook to drink and we captured her, though she struggled violently. As we were crossing the brook with her, a Sisemite appeared on the hillside, waving his arms and yelling. On his back was a child or monkey child which he took in his hands and held aloft as if to show it to the woman, who renewed her struggle to be free. The Sisemite came far down the hill almost to the brook; he dropped the child and tore off great branches from big trees which he threw at us."

The young man was brought from his cell into the presence of this wild creature and asked if he recognized her. He replied, "My wife was young and beautiful; the woman I see is old and ugly." The woman never spoke a word and from that time on made no sound. She refused to eat and a few days after her capture she died. Felipe lived to be an old man, and the grandmother of the woman who told this story remembered him as the man whose wife had been carried away by the Sisemite.

One final point: the so-called "Sisemite shivers," reported by so many, sound very much like the sense of dread that is often found in Bigfoot cases, which, as we have seen, may be attributable to the creatures' use of directed infrasound.

Moving on, the Bigfoot of the Solomon Islands are hardly what one would call friendly; downright hostile would be a far better way of wording it. Kidnapping and eating the locals seem to be among their favorite pastimes. As just one example of many, author Marius Boirayon uncovered the traumatic and terrifying story of Mango, a woman who was abducted from her village home by one of the creatures and held prisoner by it for around a quarter of a century before she was finally able to escape. To the horror of her family and old friends, when Mango returned, she was not the person she once was; living with the hideous beast for so long had driven her utterly insane and wildlike.

In light of all the above, it's no wonder that government agencies might want to clamp down on the true story of the Bigfoot: namely, that it's a dangerous killing machine that feeds on people.

Who Really Runs the World?

You might find this chapter's title to be a strange question. After all, we know that the world is run by presidents, prime ministers, kings, and queens, right? Not necessarily. Behind closed doors—and amid overwhelming secrecy—powerful groups and secret societies are carefully working to steer the world to an agenda of their making. We're talking about the likes of the Bilderbergers and the Illuminati—but we'll begin with the Bohemian Club.

Created in the nineteenth century—in April 1872, to be precise—the Bohemian Club is an integral part of the growing clampdown on society. It began as an organization in which like-minded figures in the world of the arts could get together, specifically in San Francisco, California, where it was created. Indeed, San Francisco remains its home to this very day. Its bases of operations are San Francisco's Union Square and Bohemian Grove, which can be found in Sonoma County. Although the Bohemian Club initially invited the likes of poets, writers, playwrights, and painters into the fold, it wasn't long at all before powerful figures in the fields of politics, business, and the military became members. Eventually, as circumstances and history have shown, they would come to dominate it.

In 1862, the *Westminster Review* described Bohemianism as follows: "The term *Bohemian* has come to be very commonly accepted in our day as the description of a certain kind of literary gypsy, no matter in what language he speaks, or what city he inhabits. A Bohemian is simply an artist or 'littérateur' who, consciously or unconsciously, secedes from conventionality in life and in art."

As for the specific origins of the Bohemian Club, a concise explanation of its beginnings came from Michael Henry de Young, the owner of the *San Francisco Chronicle* newspaper. In 1915, de Young said:

The Bohemian Club was organized in the *Chronicle* office by Tommy Newcombe, Sutherland, Dan O'Connell, Harry Dam and others who were members of the staff. The boys wanted a place where they could get together after work, and they took a room on Sacramento Street below Kearny. That was the start of the Bohemian Club, and it was not an unmixed blessing for the *Chronicle* because the boys would go there sometimes when they should have reported at the office. Very often when Dan O'Connell sat down to a good dinner there he would forget that he had a pocketful of notes for an important story.

It's interesting to note that the de Young family had its very own ties to powerful and famous figures: Michael Henry de Young's grandfather, Benjamin Morange, was the minister from France to Spain under none other than Napoleon Bonaparte.

It is deeply ironic that the group became known as the Bohemian Club; over time, the number of members who could rightly call themselves Bohemians fell, to the point where they were eventually in the minority. The majority soon became those aforementioned politicians, businessmen, and military figures. U.S. presidents—and more than a few of them—would enter the fold, too. We're talking about the likes of President George H. W. Bush, publisher William Randolph Hearst, former National Security Agency director Bobby Ray Inman, Henry Kissinger, and President Ronald Reagan.

The Bohemian Club is most well known—arguably, infamously well known—for its annual, two-week-long get-together at Bohemian Grove, located in Monte Rio, California. While the club's public image is that of a group of like-minded figures getting together and hanging out at Bohemian Grove, that's far from the case. Indeed, behind the closed doors of Bohemian Grove, the club quickly transforms into a definitive secret society, replete with bizarre rituals and initiation rites—as we shall now see.

A search on the Internet reveals that the Bohemian Club and Bohemian Grove are often confused with each other. It's actually quite simple: the former is the name of the group, whereas Bohemian Grove is the location at which the members meet. Bohemian Grove is a huge compound, running close to three thousand acres in size, and is located on the Russian River in Sonoma County, California. Just about everything that goes on there is

A metal plate attached to the side of the Bohemian Club's San Francisco headquarters displays the mascot owl and the slogan, "Weaving spiders come not here."

shrouded in secrecy. It's also shrouded in Douglas firs and redwoods, all of which help keep prying eyes at bay. Bohemian Grove is also a place dominated by controversy, as Brad Steiger notes: "Conspiracy theorists state that the principal theme of the annual meeting is celebration of patriarchy, racism, and class privilege."

The *Washington Post* reveals some notable facts about Bohemian Grove:

The club is so hush-hush that little can be definitively said about it, but much of what we know today is from those who have infiltrated the camp, including Texas-based filmmaker Alex Jones. In 2000, Jones and his cameraman entered the camp with a hidden camera and were able to film a Bohemian Grove ceremony, Cremation of the Care. During the ceremony, members wear costumes and cremate a coffin effigy called "Care" before a 40-foot-owl, in deference to the surrounding Redwood trees.

Then, we have this from *Bohemian Grove Exposed*:

They secretly meet for seventeen days each July in a remote "sacred grove" of ancient redwood trees in the deep forests surrounding San Francisco. Some 1,500 in number, their membership roll is kept secret, but includes the super-rich, blood dynasty member families of the Illuminati; heavy-hitting corporate chieftains and high government officials. Mingling among them are a number of Hollywood movie stars, Broadway producers, famous entertainers, musicians, authors, painters and poets. Great statesmen and—so we're told—gentlemen.

Stories have come out of the Grove about wild homosexual orgies, male and female prostitutes being engaged in what can only be described as extreme sexual games, young children being exploited in unspeakable ways, up to and including cold-blooded ritual murder. There are stories involving actual human sacrifice on the "altar" of the owl God statue. Understandably, it's all very hard to believe.

Mike Clelland is someone who made a careful study of Bohemian Grove and its history and activities. He says:

The club emblem is an owl with the motto *Weaving Spiders Come Not Here*. This seems to trace back to Greek mythology. Arachne was a mortal woman who boasted that her weaving skill was greater than that of Athena. A contest took place, and Arachne's weaving was filled with imagery depicting ways that the gods had misled and abused mortals. Athena, goddess of wisdom and crafts, saw that Arachne's creation was not only mocking the gods, but it was far more beautiful than her own. Enraged, Athena turned Arachne into a spider. The scientific term for spiders, arachnids, goes back to the myth of Arachne.

Starting in 1887, there has been an annual play performed by Bohemian members, often at the foot of the sinister looking giant stone owl. Roles for women are played by men, since women are not allowed as club members. The 1906 performance of *The Owl and Care, A Spectacle*, seems to be the only play with the word owl in its title. Curiously, it was performed the same year as the great San Francisco Earthquake.

This giant stone owl (although some reports describe it made of cement) is commonly known as Moloch, named after a god of the Canaanites, an evil deity that required the sacrifice of human children. But the ancient literature presents Moloch as a bull, and not an owl. No easy answers, but since the Bohemian Club is shrouded under so many layers of secrecy, it is easy to assume the worst. Given the state of the world today, many of these assumptions might be true.

Several members of the Bohemian Club are seen camping at Bohemian Grove in this c.1905 photo. Left to right are author, editor, and critic Porter Garnett; playwright and poet George Sterling, and journalist and novelist Jack London.

The final words go to President Richard M. Nixon: "Anybody can be President of the United States, but very few can ever have any hope of becoming President of the Bohemian Club."

Although what is known officially as the Order of the Illuminati did not come into being until the 1700s, the word "Illuminati" has origins that date back to at least the 1400s. In Spain, at that time, those who immersed themselves in the world of the black arts identified occultists, alchemists, and witches as having been given "the light." We're talking about nothing less than a supernatural form of "illumination" that gave them extraordinary powers. Hence, the term "Illuminati." As for the Order of the Illuminati, it was created in 1776—specifically on May 1. The man behind the mysterious group was Adam Weishaupt. The location: Ingolstadt, Bavaria. At the time, Weishaupt was approaching his thirties and worked as a professor of religious law. As Brad Steiger notes, Weishaupt "blended mysticism into the workings of the brotherhood in order to make his agenda of republicanism appear to be more mysterious than those of a political reform group."

The group had decidedly small-scale origins: it began with just five members, one being Weishaupt himself. The Illuminati was not destined to stay that way, however. Bit by bit, the group began to grow to the point where, by 1780, the membership was around five dozen and extended to six cities. Certainly, many were attracted to Weishaupt's group as a result of the fact that it paralleled the Masons—specifically in relation to levels and orders of hierarchy that could be achieved. Indeed, Weishaupt was careful to point out to his followers that the further they immersed themselves in the domain of the Illuminati, the greater the level of illuminated, supernatural knowledge they would achieve.

History has shown that Weishaupt was not alone in ensuring that the Illuminati grew from strength to strength. He was aided to a very significant degree by one Adolf Francis, better known as Baron von Knigge. A renowned and influential figure with an expert knowledge of all things of an occult nature, von Knigge was a powerful individual who had risen through the ranks of the Masons, and he shared Weishaupt's desire for political revolution. In no time, and as a result of von Knigge's contacts and ability to entice others to the cause, the Illuminati grew to a group of several hundred. The Illuminati was not a group open to everyone, however. In fact, quite the opposite: the powerful, the rich, and the well connected were those who Weishaupt and von Knigge worked hard to bring onboard. Rituals and rites for those who wished to be a part of Weishaupt's vision were established, as was the wearing of specific clothes—or, as Brad Steiger described them, "bizarre costumes." The membership expanded ever further.

By the mid-1780s, the Illuminati was no longer a group with hundreds of followers but thousands. In 1784, however, dissent appeared in the ranks. It was in April of that year when von Knigge and Weishaupt had a major falling out, which led to von Knigge walking away from the group. Another problem occurred, too: the occult "illumination" that Weishaupt had promised his followers failed to appear. Many of them became disillusioned, suspecting that Weishaupt actually had very little interest in the domain of the occult but had really sought out the rich and powerful as a means to help his plans for revolution. The outcome was

A professor and philosopher, Adam Weishaupt was the founder of the Illuminati.

that many walked away from the Illuminati, fearful that it was becoming a manipulative, sinister body with hidden agendas. It wasn't at all along before the Illuminati was no more. On this issue, let's turn again to Brad Steiger: "In June 1784 Karl Theodor [the Duke of Bavaria] issued an edict outlawing all secret societies in his province. In March 1785 another edict specifically condemned the Illuminati. Weishaupt had already fled to a neighboring province, where he hoped to inspire the loyal members of the Illuminati to continue as a society. In 1787 the duke issued a final edict against the Order of the Illuminati, and Weishaupt apparently faded into obscurity."

Weishaupt may have faded from obscurity ... but did the Illuminati? Does it still exist? Is it one of the major bodies in the secret cultivation of a New World Order? These are the questions we will address now.

The Jeremiah Project says:

Many believe the Illuminati are the masterminds behind events that will lead to the establishment of such a New World Order, and see connections between the Illuminati, Freemasonry, the Trilateral Commission, British Emperialism, International Zionism and communism that all lead back to a bid for world domination. In more recent years the Illuminati has allegedly been involved in the assassination of John F. Kennedy and has been at the forefront of indoctrinating the American public into their socialist one-world agenda.

It is difficult to uncover the facts regarding the modern day role of the Illuminati as most of the information is cloaked in secrecy. What we must do instead is to look at the available evidence and relationships in the context of contemporary world events, and form some common sense conclusions based on that inquiry.

The Illuminati was presumed to have been dispersed by the end of the century but some people such as David Icke, Ryan Burke and Morgan Gricar, have argued that the Bavarian Illuminati survived and believe that Illuminati members chose instead to conceal themselves and their plans within the cloak of Freemasonry, under which auspices they continue to thrive. They have maintained a stranglehold on the political, financial and social administration of the United States and other nations acting as a shadowy power behind the throne, controlling world affairs through present day governments and corporations.

Henry Makow reveals an extremely disturbing Illuminati story:

A woman who was raised in the Illuminati cult describes a powerful secret organization comprising one per cent of the U.S. population that has infiltrated all social institutions and is covertly preparing a military takeover. Her revelations cast the "war on terror" and "homeland security" in their true light.

"Svali" is the pseudonym of the woman, age 45, who was a mind "programmer" for the cult until 1996. She was the sixth head trainer in the San Diego branch and had 30 trainers reporting to her. She has risked her life to warn humanity of the Illuminati's covert power and agenda.

She describes a sadistic Satanic cult led by the richest and most powerful people in the world. It is largely homosexual and pedophile, practices animal sacrifice and ritual murder. It works "hand in glove" with the CIA and Freemasonry. It is Aryan supremacist (German is spoken at the top) but welcomes Jewish apostates. It controls the world traffic in drugs, guns, pornography and prostitution. It may be the hand behind political assassination, and "terrorism," including Sept. 11, the Maryland sniper and the Bali bomb blast. It has infiltrated government on a local, state and national level; education and financial institutions; religion and the media. Based in Europe, it plans a "world order" that will make its earlier attempts, Nazism and Communism, look like picnics.

The website *Warning Illuminati* appropriately warns us:

There is a worldwide conspiracy being orchestrated by an extremely powerful and influential group of *genetically related individuals* (at least at the highest echelons) which include many of the world's wealthiest people, top political leaders, and corporate elite, as well as members of the so-called Black Nobility of Europe (dominated by the British Crown) whose goal is to create a One World (fascist) Government, stripped of nationalistic and regional boundaries, that is obedient to their agenda. Their intention is to effect complete and total control over every human being on the planet and to dramatically reduce the world's population by 5.5 Billion people. While the name *New World Order* is a term frequently used today when referring to this group, it's more useful to identify the principal organizations, institutions, and individuals who make up this vast interlocking spiderweb of elite conspirators.

The Illuminati is the oldest term commonly used to refer to the 13 *bloodline families* (and their offshoots) that make up a major portion of this controlling elite. Most members of the Illuminati are also members in the highest ranks of numerous secretive and occult societies which in many cases extend straight back into the ancient world. The upper levels of the tightly compartmentalized (need-to-know-basis) Illuminati structural pyramid include planning committees and organizations that the public has little or no knowledge of. The upper levels of the Illuminati pyramid include secretive committees with names such as: the Council of 3, the Council of 5, the Council of 7, the Council of 9, the Council of 13, the Council of 33, the Grand Druid Council, the Committee of 300 (also called the "Olympians") and the Committee of 500 among others.

Whenever a discussion or debate occurs on the matter of secret societies, seldom is the Bilderberg Group left out of the equation. In fact, the exact opposite is the case: it's likely to be near the top of the list of talking points and for very good reasons, too.

SourceWatch says of the Bilderberg Group:

The name came from the group's first meeting place at the Hotel de Bilderberg, in the small Dutch town of Oosterbeek. Bilderberg was founded by Joseph Retinger, Prince Bernhard of the Netherlands and Belgian Prime Minister Paul Van Zeeland and is comprised of representatives from North America and Western Europe. Since 1954, The secret meetings have included most of the top ruling class players from Western Europe and America. Until he was implicated in the Lockheed bribery scandal in 1976, Prince Bernhard served as chairman. Now, Bilderberg is a symbol of world management by Atlanticist elites. Some observers feel that it borders on the conspiratorial, while others are primarily interested in its implications for power structure research. Bilderberg participants from the U.S. are almost always members of the Council on Foreign Relations (CFR). Since 1973, Japanese elites have been brought into the fold through a third overlapping group, the Trilateral Commission.

According to Richard J. Aldrich, a political lecturer at Nottingham University, the Bilderberg Group is an "informal secretive transatlantic council of key decision makers, developed between 1952 and 1954.... It brought leading European and American personalities together once a year for informal discussions of their differences.... The formation of the American branch was entrusted to General Dwight D. Eisenhower's psychological warfare coordinator, C. D. Jackson and the first meeting was funded by the Central Intelligence Agency (CIA)."

When, in 2004, the Bilderberg Group celebrated its fiftieth anniversary, the BBC profiled the organization. In doing so, they significantly noted the aura of mystery surrounding both it and its members. The BBC didn't shy away from discussing the issue of alleged Bilderberg-orchestrated conspiracies, either:

The first conference of the Bilderberg Group was held in 1954 at, naturally, the Bilderberg Hotel in the Netherlands, home to founder Prince Bernhard.

What sets Bilderberg apart from other high-powered get-togethers, such as the annual World Economic Forum (WEF), is its mystique. Not a word of what is said at Bilderberg meetings can be breathed outside. No reporters are invited in and while confidential minutes of meetings are taken, names are not noted. In the void created by such aloofness, an extraordinary conspiracy theory has grown up around the group that alleges the fate of the world is largely decided by Bilderberg. In Yugoslavia, leading Serbs have blamed Bilderberg for triggering the war which led to the downfall of Slobodan Milosevic. The Oklahoma City bomber Timothy McVeigh, the London nail-bomber David Copeland and Osama Bin Laden are all said to have bought into the theory that Bilderberg pulls the strings with which national governments dance.

Daniel Estulin, who has deeply and carefully studied the work and history of Bilderberg, says:

> Slowly, one by one, I have penetrated the layers of secrecy surrounding the Bilderberg Group, but I could not have done this without help of "conscientious objectors" from inside, as well as outside, the Group's membership. Imagine a private club where

presidents, prime ministers, international bankers and generals rub shoulders, where gracious royal chaperones ensure everyone gets along, and where the people running the wars, markets, and Europe (and America) say what they never dare say in public.

Perhaps most chilling of all are the following words of Henry Kissinger, which were made at the Bilderberg Group Meeting in 1992:

> Today, Americans would be outraged if UN troops entered Los Angeles to restore order; tomorrow, they will be grateful. This is especially true if they were told there was an outside threat from beyond, whether real or promulgated, that threatened our very existence. It is then that all people of the world will plead with world leaders to deliver them from this evil ... individual rights will be willingly relinquished for the guarantee of their well-being granted to them by their world government.

For the sake of everyone, let's hope that Henry Kissinger is way off the mark.

On June 10, 2016, the United Kingdom's *Express* newspaper ran an article with the eye-catching headline of "Inside Bilderberg: Leaders and elite meet in 'illuminati' style to decide New World Order." Its author, Jon Austin, said:

> The world's most secretive gathering of global leaders and elites begins yesterday—with prime ministers and presidents, bankers and former heads of the CIA and MI6 topping the guest list. The 64th annual Bilderberg Conference is being held in in Dresden, Germany, from today until Saturday sending ardent Illuminati New World Order conspiracy theorists crazy. If ever the powers that be wanted to fuel a theory there is a secret sect above the elected rulers of the world's top nations, then Bilderberg is how to do it. Inside, no journalists are allowed in and there is no opening or closing press conferences or statements. On top of this no minutes are taken and attendees are urged not to discuss what goes on inside with anyone else. The organizers of the Bilderberg meetings claim it is just the world's biggest lobby group and talking shop.

Austin added:

> Conspiracy theorists claim the Illuminati (think Freemasons on acid) is a worldwide secret organization which really runs the world above the global leaders we see in office. Various versions of the conspiracy claim the Illuminati is involved in the Occult, and it seeks to impose a New World Order on us mere mortals that will enslave the general population. They are the secret organization often accused of being behind the so-called inside job terror plots such as 9/11 or the Paris attacks this year, in order to gain public

support for various wars in the Middle East. Last October, Express.co.uk exclusively revealed that former Whitby town councillor Simon Parkes had claimed to have stopped "black magic wizards from the Illuminati" working at the CERN Large Hadron Collider from opening up a portal to another dimension that would have allowed Satan into our world.

On September 25, 2015, the United Nations revealed a plan of action that it termed *Transforming Our World: The 2030 Agenda for Sustainable Development*. The United Nations stated: "On 25 September, the United Nations General Assembly unanimously adopted the Resolution 70/1, Transforming Our World: the 2030 Agenda for Sustainable Development. This historic document lays out the 17 Sustainable Development Goals, which aim to mobilize global efforts to end poverty, foster peace, safeguard the rights and dignity of all people, and protect the planet."

The resolution begins with a declaration that states:

On behalf of the peoples we serve, we have adopted a historic decision on a comprehensive, far-reaching and people-centered set of universal and transformative Goals and targets. We commit ourselves to working tirelessly for the full implementation of this Agenda by 2030. We recognize that eradicating poverty in all its forms and dimensions, including extreme poverty, is the greatest global challenge and an indispensable requirement for sustainable development. We are committed to achieving sustainable development in its three dimensions—economic, social and environmental—in a balanced and integrated manner. We will also build upon the achievements of the Millennium Development Goals and seek to address their unfinished business.

On September 25, 2015, the United Nations revealed a plan of action that it termed *Transforming Our World: The 2030 Agenda for Sustainable Development.*

We resolve, between now and 2030, to end poverty and hunger everywhere; to combat inequalities within and among countries; to build peaceful, just and inclusive societies; to protect human rights and promote gender equality and the empowerment of women and girls; and to ensure the lasting protection of the planet and its natural resources. We resolve also to create conditions for sustainable, inclusive and sustained economic growth, shared prosperity and decent work for all, taking into account different levels of national development and capacities.

As we embark on this great collective journey, we pledge that no one will be left behind. Recognizing that the dignity of the human person is fundamental, we wish to see the Goals and targets met for all nations and peoples and for all segments of society. And we will endeavour to reach the furthest behind first.

This is an Agenda of unprecedented scope and significance. It is accepted by all countries and is applicable to all, taking into account different national realities, capacities and levels of development and respecting national policies and priorities. These are universal goals and targets which involve the entire world, developed and developing countries alike. They are integrated and indivisible and balance the three dimensions of sustainable development.

The Goals and targets are the result of over two years of intensive public consultation and engagement with civil society and other stakeholders around the world, which paid particular attention to the voices of the poorest and most vulnerable. This consultation included valuable work done by the Open Working Group of the General Assembly on Sustainable Development Goals and by the United Nations, whose Secretary-General provided a synthesis report in December 2014.

It should be noted that despite the seemingly positive nature of this plan for the world by 2030, not everyone is happy with it. Some are downright concerned and worried. Particularly disturbed by all this is *The New American*: "The Agenda 2030 agreement makes the audacity of the scheme clear, too. 'This is an Agenda of unprecedented scope and significance,' boasts the document. 'Never before have world leaders pledged common action and endeavor across such a broad and universal policy agenda,' the agreement continues. 'What we are announcing today—an Agenda for global action for the next fifteen years—is a charter for people and planet in the twenty-first century."

The New American adds:

Perhaps the single most striking feature of Agenda 2030 is the practically undisguised roadmap to global socialism and corporatism/fascism, as countless analysts have pointed out. To begin with, consider the agenda's Goal 10, which calls on the UN, national governments, and every person on Earth to "reduce inequality within and among countries." To do that, the agreement continues, will "only be possible if wealth is shared and income inequality is addressed."

As the UN document also makes clear, national socialism to "combat inequality" domestically is not enough—international socialism is needed to battle inequality even "among" countries. "By 2030, ensure that all men and women, in particular the poor and the vulnerable, have equal rights to economic resources," the document demands. In simpler terms, Western taxpayers should prepare to be fleeced so that their wealth can be redistributed internationally as their own economies are cut down to size by Big Government.

Natural News comes straight to the point: "This document describes nothing less than a global government takeover of every nation across the planet. The 'goals' of this document are nothing more than code words for a corporate-government fascist agenda that will imprison humanity in a devastating cycle of poverty while enriching the world's most powerful globalist corporations like Monsanto and DuPont."

Then is this at *Charisma News*:

The U.N. has stated that these new "global goals" represent a "new universal Agenda" for humanity. Virtually every nation on the planet has willingly signed on to this new agenda, and you are expected to participate whether you like it or not.

A one world dictatorship and new monetary system will soon prevail. Therefore existing savings may be declared worthless. Deceiving people into investing money in multinationals and banks will give the powerful greater power, and they will soon take our money and not give it back. An individual would be better to withdraw it and use for a good purpose, such as by helping those in need and informing people of the truth.

We are heading for a cashless society, where soon everyone will be forced to have a mark on their right hand or forehead to buy or sell. The Bible predicts that the Beast or Antichrist will fool the elect of many religions that he is God by doing miracles and promising peace. He will break his peace agreement and totally rule the world. He will force everyone to worship him and accept a satanic mark on their right hand or forehead in order to buy or sell (Rev 13). This will probably be an embedded computer chip. It will be better to die and be with Christ instead of taking the mark and worshipping the beast, which will cause you to be eternally separated from Christ....

There is strong evidence that the Illuminati have well planned this system of a satanic one-world government. People

Huge, multinational corporations like Monsanto could stand to benefit greatly from a one-world government, some conspiracy theorists warn.

will be led to believe it is a good idea, as it will save or prevent; money being stolen, credit cards being lost, paper checks, tax evasion, handling cash and currency fluctuation.

Those are the words of *True Conspiracies*. While the religious aspect of the scenario is widely and wildly open to debate, undoubtedly, we are, indeed, heading toward a future in which cash plays not a single role. Some might say that doing everything electronically will be to the benefit of everyone. It will not. The only ones who will benefit are the New World Order overlords and their minions.

Patrick Henningsen, of *21ˢᵗ Century Wire*, says:

The darker aspect of a cashless society is one which few are debating or discussing, but is actually the most pivotal in terms of social engineering and transforming communities and societies. In London, the electronic touch payment *Oyster Card* was introduced in 2003, initially for public transport, and since that time the card has been co-opted to be used for other functions, as the UK beta tests the idea of an all-in-one cashless lifestyle solution.

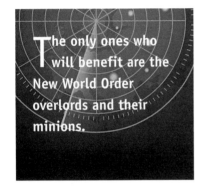

The only ones who will benefit are the New World Order overlords and their minions.

Ironically, and alongside biometric chipping now in India, it's the United States, supposedly the birthplace of modern capitalism, who is beta testing its own socialist technocracy. As the ranks of the poor and unemployed grow and dollar inflation rises in America, more and more people are dependent on traditional "Food Stamp" entitlements in order to feed their families. The US has now introduced its own socialist "Oyster" to replace the old Food Stamp program. It's called the "EBT," which stands for "Electronic Benefit Transfer," as a means of transferring money from the central government to people living below the poverty line.

Keep Henningsen's following words firmly in your minds:

It has long been the dream of collectivists and technocratic elites to eliminate the semi-unregulated cash economy and black markets in order to maximize taxation and to fully control markets. If the cashless society is ushered in, they will have near complete control over the lives of individual people. The financial collapse which began in 2007–2008 was merely the opening gambit of the elite criminal class, a mere warm-up for things to come. With the next collapse we may see a centrally controlled global digital currency gaining its final foothold.

Finally, take careful note of the words of Matthew Lynn of the United Kingdom's *Telegraph* newspaper. On August 31, 2015, he wrote: "From today,

France is banning the use of cash for transactions worth more than € 1,000, or slightly more than £700. On one level, that is about combating crime and terrorism. But on another, it is also part of a growing movement among academics and now governments to gradually ban the use of cash completely."

Lynn added:

More importantly, cash is about freedom. There are surely limits to the control over society we wish to hand over to governments and central banks? You don't need to be a fully paid-up libertarian to question whether, in a world where we already worry about the amount of data that Facebook and Google can gather about us, we really want the banks and the state to know every single detail of what we are spending our money on and where. It is easy to surrender that freedom—but it will be a lot harder to get back.

People have used notes and coins for several thousand years. The earliest go all the way back to the Iron Age. If they wither away because people prefer using their phones or their cards, then that is fine. No one wants to stand in the way of technological innovation. But outlawing cash? That is surely a step too far—and we might miss it when it's gone far more than we realize.

If you're still not convinced about the distinct probability of our world becoming a slave planet, consider the following words of numerous, well-placed figures.

"It seems to many of us that if we are to avoid the eventual catastrophic world conflict we must strengthen the United Nations as a first step toward a world government patterned after our own government with a legislature, executive and judiciary, and police to enforce its international laws and keep the peace. To do that, of course, we Americans will have to yield up some of our sovereignty." —Walter Cronkite

"Today America would be outraged if U.N. troops entered Los Angeles to restore order. Tomorrow they will be grateful. When presented with this scenario, individual rights will be willingly relinquished for the guarantee of their well-being granted to them by the World Government." —Henry Kissinger

"The world is now more sophisticated and prepared to march towards a world government. The supranational sovereignty of an intellectual elite and world bankers is surely preferable to the national auto-determination practiced in past centuries." —David Rockefeller

"We must move as quickly as possible to a one-world government, one-world religion, under a one-world leader." —Robert Mueller

On January 16, 1991, President George H. W. Bush said regarding Operation Desert Storm (the first war in Iraq): "We have before us the oppor-

President George H. W. Bush is shown here in 1990 greeting American troops in Saudi Arabia during Operation Desert Storm. During this military action, he mentioned that the future involved a "new world order."

tunity to forge for ourselves and for future generations a new world order—a world where the rule of law, not the law of the jungle, governs the conduct of nations. When we are successful—and we will be—we have a real chance at this new world order, an order in which a credible United Nations can use its peacekeeping role to fulfill the promise and vision of the U.N.'s founders."

The year 1991 was not the first time the emotive term—"New World Order"—was used by a politician. It was, however, the first time that it caught the attention of millions. Hardly surprisingly, it provoked a great deal of debate in relation to what it meant, and its potential implications, for us and for the future. While we are assured by our leaders that any potential NWO will be wholly benign and beneficial in nature, *all* of the facts strongly suggest otherwise.

The New World Order is not just about modeling the future, however. It's also about dumbing down the population to ensure that they forget—or become ignorant of—the past. Consider these quotes on that very issue.

Julian Barnes, the author of the best-selling book *The Sense of an Ending*, said: "History is that certainty produced at the point where the imperfections of memory meet the inadequacies of documentation."

In his classic novel *Ulysses*, James Joyce wrote: "History, Stephen said, is a nightmare from which I am trying to awake."

Aldous Huxley remarked: "That men do not learn very much from the lessons of history is the most important of all the lessons that history has to teach."

George Orwell warned: "The most effective way to destroy people is to deny and obliterate their own understanding of their history."

"If you don't know history, then you don't know anything. You are a leaf that doesn't know it is part of a tree," wrote Michael Crichton of *Jurassic Park* fame.

"History will be kind to me for I intend to write it," bragged British prime minister Sir Winston Churchill.

As for the New World Order—and its cohorts in the domain of powerful, secret societies—take careful note of the following. President Woodrow Wilson noted: "Some of the biggest men in the United States, in the field of commerce and manufacture, are afraid of somebody, afraid of something. They know there is a power somewhere so organized, so subtle, so watchful, so interlocked, so complete, so pervasive, that they better not speak above their breath when they speak of condemnation of it."

The Duke of Brunswick, the Grand Master of World Freemasonry, warned: "I have been convinced that we, as an order, have come under the power of some very evil occult order, profoundly versed in Science, both occult and otherwise, though not infallible, their methods being black magic, that is to say, electromagnetic power, hypnotism, and powerful suggestion. We are convinced that the order is being controlled by some Sun Order, after the nature of the Illuminati, if not by that order itself."

Senator Daniel K. Inouye said: "There exists a shadowy government with its own Air Force, its own Navy, its own fund-raising mechanism, and the ability to pursue its own ideas of national interest, free from all checks and balances; free from law itself."

Sir Thomas More offered this: "Everywhere do I perceive a certain conspiracy of rich men seeking their own advantage under that name and pretext of commonwealth."

As all of the above shows, dangerous, world-manipulating figures are behind the scenes, who are intent on creating a world that runs the way they want it run, not us.

Silencing the Saucer Seekers

We can find evidence of mysterious deaths in what was arguably the very first UFO event of the modern era. On June 21, 1947, a squadron of UFOs was seen flying over Maury Island, Puget Sound, Washington State. One of the craft exploded in midair, showering huge amounts of debris into the harbor below. A few pieces of that mysterious material was recovered by a man named Harold Dahl, who worked the harbor. He handed it over to his boss, Fred Crisman. Interestingly, Crisman was later identified by New Orleans district attorney Jim Garrison as the second gunman in the November 22, 1963, assassination of President John F. Kennedy.

The U.S. military soon got word of what had gone down on Maury Island and dispatched two military officers to the area to investigate. They were Lt. Frank Mercer Brown and Capt. William Lee Davidson, both of Army Intelligence. Good indications exist that even in that early era, the Controllers were running the ship. Although the military wanted answers to what had gone down on Maury Island, the Controllers were determined to ensure that their secrets didn't get out, and for good reason.

Michael Riconosciuto is someone who has had longstanding involvement in the field of intelligence operations; he says that the Maury Island UFOs were actually nuclear-powered aircraft of the government. No wonder the Controllers couldn't allow the facts to come out. The result was that Lt. Mercer and Capt. Brown were soon dead; after collecting the wreckage, the pair took to the skies with the intent of flying to Wright Field, Ohio, where the material was due to be examined. It never happened; Mercer and Brown's plane caught fire in midair, killing both men. On top of that, two journalists who were looking into the explosion over Maury Island—at the time the event occurred—also died under dubious circumstances. They were Ted Morello and Paul Lance. The mystery was quickly locked down, and with just about everyone of any significance dead—and Harold Dahl having had his life threatened by a Man in Black-type character—the saga came to an end. A satisfying end for the Controllers and for their lackey Fred Crisman but certainly not for anyone else.

Now it's time to turn our attention to the most famous UFO case of all: Roswell. It was in early July 1947 that something strange crashed on the Foster Ranch in Lincoln County, New Mexico. The wreckage of whatever it was that had come down was strewn across a distance of around six hundred feet. The rancher who found the material—William Ware Brazel—contacted the local police, who then contacted the old Roswell Army Air Field. In no time at all, the military descended on the ranch, quickly collecting the materials and warning Brazel not to talk about what he had seen—which, evidence and testimony suggests, included not just the wreckage but a number of mangled, rapidly decomposing bodies, too. While UFO researchers champion the case,

The July 8, 1947, *Roswell Daily Record* famously announced the capture of a UFO near Roswell, New Mexico.

strong indications exist that what came down was a top-secret, experimental vehicle of the U.S. military that spiraled out of control and crashed on the ranch. As for the bodies, they were not alien but human guinea pigs used in an early high-altitude exposure flight; they were handicapped people, secretly taken from a nearby hospital—Fort Stanton—which housed people with both mental and physical handicaps. The dark experiment was hidden behind a curtain of cover stories, including the rumor that a UFO had come down.

To ensure that the case was forever confused, the military, only days after recovering the materials, said that the wreckage was not from a UFO after all but from a weather balloon. In 1994, the Air Force changed its position again—this time, it claimed that the balloon was not a weather balloon but a Mogul balloon: a huge balloon designed to monitor for early Soviet atomic bomb tests. As for the stories of bodies found at the site, the U.S. government said in 1997 that they were nothing but crash-test dummies.

Miriam Bush was someone who knew exactly what happened on the Foster Ranch in early 1947. She paid for that knowledge with her life. Miriam Bush has, at times, been incorrectly described as a nurse who worked at the military hospital at the Roswell Army Air Field. She was not; Bush was an executive secretary at the base. The distinction may sound small, but the fact is that Bush's position meant that she would have been in a prime position to see the mangled bodies when they were secretly brought to the base. Bush's immediate superior was Lt. Col. Harold Warne; he played a significant role in the autopsies of the dead people used in the experiment.

It's hardly surprising, given the circumstances and the subsequent warnings issued to Bush and others in the base hospital at the time, that Miriam Bush became deeply paranoid and even in fear of her life. Although she had been told never, ever to discuss what she had seen, Bush confided in her family, warning them to never tell anyone what had happened. For Bush, though, the Roswell affair came to dominate her life; she became even more paranoid, entered into a loveless marriage, and started hitting the bottle to a serious degree. She would soon be a full-blown alcoholic.

Even though Miriam Bush did not tell anyone else about what she had seen at the Roswell base—namely, the bodies found on the Foster Ranch—she could not shake off the feeling that she was still being watched. She probably was; rumors abound that on two occasions, listening devices were placed on her home telephone: once in 1969 and the other occasion being in 1982.

For Miriam Bush, matters came to a head—and to a shocking and suspicious end—in the late 1980s. Without warning, on a particular day in December 1989, she took off for San Jose, California, and checked into a local motel under her sister's name—which further suggests that she was concerned she was being watched. After all, why would she try to obfuscate her real identity, if she had nothing to hide? The very next day, Bush was found dead in that same motel room; a plastic bag was around her neck. It had been tied tightly. Marks on her arms were indicative of a scuffle having occurred at some point after she checked in. Despite the evidence, the official conclusion was that Bush had taken her own life. Whatever Miriam Bush really knew about the Roswell affair, and whatever her specific role in the events of 1947, it all went with her to the grave. Might she have been taken out of circulation by a hired assassin of the Controllers? A more likely explanation really does not exist.

It's worth noting, too, that two other key figures in the Roswell affair also descended into full-blown alcoholism. One of them was a man named Dee Proctor. At the time of the Roswell crash in July 1947, Proctor was just a young boy, a neighbor to the rancher William Brazel, and someone who did chores on the ranch. He was with Brazel when the wreckage was found. Not long after finding the wreckage of the vehicle that had come down, Brazel and Proctor found something else: several mangled bodies of unknown origin. Both man and boy were threatened to just about the severest level possible. Their lives would be in danger if they ever talked, they were told. Just like Miriam Bush, Dee Proctor was deeply scarred by the experience and ended up as a reclusive alcoholic. Maj. Jesse Marcel Sr., who was also on the crash site shortly after it was found, could only find solace in booze. He, too, became an alcoholic. Proctor hardly ever discussed the case with anyone. Marcel, decades later, gave several interviews to both ufologists and the media. He touched on the matter of the strange debris, but any discussion of the bodies was out of bounds. Both Proctor and Marcel—just like Bush—took their secrets with them when the Grim Reaper came calling.

> Whatever Miriam Bush really knew about the Roswell affair, and whatever her specific role in the events of 1947, it all went with her to the grave.

Yet another famous case has for many years been perceived as a ufological classic, which also falls under the "secret balloon" category. It occurred just half a year after Roswell. It's the strange and ultimately tragic affair of Kentucky Air National Guard pilot Capt. Thomas P. Mantell, who, many UFO believers accept, lost his life chasing a UFO on the afternoon of January 7, 1948. He did not; Mantell died chasing a balloon.

Matters began when personnel at Godman Army Air Field, Kentucky, caught sight of something in the sky that they perceived as very strange: a large and extremely reflective object that appeared to be circular in design. No one could identify it. It was, then, hardly surprising that talk of flying saucers was quickly all-encompassing.

Fortunately, or so it seemed at the time, a squadron of four F-51D Mustang aircraft under the command of Capt. Mantell was heading toward Godman Army Air Field. One of the pilots was low on fuel, another one expressed concern about pursuing the object due to his lack of an oxygen mask, and a third was ordered to shadow to the ground the pilot who had worries about losing consciousness due to oxygen deprivation. That just left Capt. Mantell to pursue the object.

At a height of around fifteen thousand feet, Mantell called into the base and said that he could see the "UFO" quite clearly. He pushed his plane further through the skies, ultimately reaching a height of approximately twenty-five thousand feet. Then, nothing. Apart, that is, from death for the captain; having reached such an altitude without oxygen, Mantell passed out, and his plane plummeted to the ground. For many in ufology, the case is a UFO classic. They are wrong. Rumors suggest that Mantell's plane was blasted out of the sky in essence to prevent him from getting too close to a classified vehicle of the kind test-flown near Maury Island, Washington State, in June 1947.

In 1955, one of the most controversial of all the many and varied UFO books published in the fifties was released. Its title was *The Case for the UFO*. The author was Morris K. Jessup. His book was a detailed study of the theoretical power sources for UFOs: What was it that made them fly? How could they

Captain Thomas P. Mantell's squadron of F-51D Mustangs pursued the unidentified craft near Godman Army Air Field, but they all broke off the chase except for Mantell, whose plane crashed.

perform such incredible aerial feats, such as coming to a complete stop in the skies, hovering at incredible heights? Jessup believed that the answers lay in the domain of gravity or, as he saw it, antigravity. Jessup may well have been on to something, as it wasn't long at all before the world of officialdom was on Jessup's back—specifically the U.S. Navy. It was one particularly intriguing office of the Navy that was watching Jessup—a "special weapons" division. Clearly, someone in the U.S. Navy was interested in, and perhaps even concerned by, Jessup's findings and theories. Maybe, that same office of the Navy was worried that Jessup just might stumble onto the very same technology that was being used to fly Uncle Sam's very own UFOs—those UFOs that the Controllers were very happy for the public to perceive as alien spacecraft, as it all helped their long-term plan to fabricate an alien invasion.

> He saw Men in Black lurking outside of his home. Hang-up calls in the middle of the night became regular occurrences.

Just like Miriam Bush and Dee Proctor in relation to Roswell, Morris Jessup became deeply worried—paranoid, even—that he was being spied on. On several occasions, he noticed that certain items in his office had clearly been moved—strongly suggesting that when he was out of his home, someone was having a stealthy look around. The ante was upped when Jessup had a face-to-face interview with Navy representatives who wanted to speak with him about his book, his theories, and the technology referred to in his book. That wasn't all they wanted to talk about, though. They also wanted to know what Jessup knew about the so-called Philadelphia Experiment of 1943, which is detailed in the chapter of this book on the Montauk controversy. Jessup, scared and stressed, blew the whistle on Carlos Allende—also referred to in the Montauk chapter—and told the Navy all he knew, which was exactly what the Navy wanted.

Of course, given the fact that Jessup was already in a deep state of fear and paranoia, this visit from the Navy only increased his anxieties. He saw Men in Black lurking outside of his home. Hang-up calls in the middle of the night became regular occurrences. Mail arrived tampered: opened and resealed. Clearly, someone—or some agency—was trying to derail Jessup and his research, and they were doing a very good job, too. In fact, from Jessup's perspective, it was way too good of a job.

In the early evening of April 20, 1959, the lifeless body of Morris Jessup was found in his car, which was parked in the Matheson Hammock Park in Miami, Florida. The car's engine was still running, and a hosepipe, affixed to the exhaust, had been fed through the driver's side window. Jessup was dead from the effects of carbon monoxide. Jessup's body was found by a man named John Goode, who worked at the park. He quickly called the police, who arrived in no time at all.

While it looked like Jessup had killed himself, not everyone was quite so sure that things were so black and white. The window through which the hose was fed had been stuffed with a couple of towels to prevent air from getting in and carbon monoxide from getting out. Curiously, Mrs. Ruby Jessup confirmed that the towels were not theirs. Why, if Jessup took his own life, did he not take towels from the family home? What would have been the point of buying new towels? If he did buy such towels, where was the receipt? It certainly wasn't in the car or in any of Jessup's pockets. Equally suspicious is the fact that on the very night before his death, Jessup was in an upbeat, fired-up mood; he spent more than an hour chatting on the phone with a good friend, Dr. Manson Valentine, expressing his enthusiasm for his latest work and plans for further investigations. Jessup even told Valentine that they should have lunch together the next day, as Jessup had something incredible to reveal. Valentine never got to see what it was that Jessup had uncovered—and he never saw Jessup again, either.

Suicide or murder? The jury still can't make up its mind almost sixty years later.

Undoubtedly, the most controversial stories that concern UFOs and mysterious deaths is that which is focused upon one of the world's most legendary and still much-loved actresses, Marilyn Monroe. Her death on August 5, 1962, at the age of just thirty-six sent shock waves around the world. The official line is that Monroe—deeply depressed about her career and her affairs with the Kennedy brothers, John and Bobby (better known as the president of the United States and the attorney general)—took her own life. Whether she meant to kill herself or if her actions amounted to a cry for help that went too far is a matter still debated to this very day. Other far more sensational and intriguing theories suggest that Monroe, after taking an overdose of powerful pills, was allowed to die—on the orders of the attorney general himself. A variation on this theory suggests that Monroe was taken out by a highly skilled hit man who made her murder look like a suicide.

The big question in all of this is: Why would anyone want the Hollywood legend dead? Rumors of her liaisons with the Kennedy brothers were already well known, so killing her would have served no point at all. She had dabbled with communism over the years but so had many other actors in the 1950s, and none of them were killed off, so why Marilyn? Another explanation has to exist. We just might have that explanation.

Midway through the 1990s, what is without doubt the most inflammatory sliver of evidence concerning Marilyn Monroe surfaced. It was a one-page document that purported to be a CIA document dated just forty-eight hours before her death. It suggests that Monroe may have been murdered because of her knowledge of a highly classified program concerning UFOs. Before we get to the contents of the document, let's see how it first surfaced. That is a story all in itself. In the late 1980s, a Big Bear Lake, California, resident named Timothy Cooper got interested in the UFO subject. He dug into it deeply, quickly making contact with a number of Edward Snowden-style whistle-blowers, except that they weren't about to reveal what they knew about the secret surveillance programs of the National Security Agency. What Cooper's mostly elderly informants wanted to tell him concerned UFOs. It was from one of these sources that Cooper supposedly got the Marilyn Monroe document in the early 1990s. Cooper sat on it for some time, eventually sharing it with a man named Milo Speriglio, who had written several books on UFOs. Those books were: *The Marilyn Conspiracy*; *Marilyn Monroe: Murder Cover-Up*; and *Crypt 33: The Saga of Marilyn Monroe*. Cooper already knew Speriglio (which was convenient) and handed a copy of the document to him. Cooper kept the original for himself, which is now in my hands.

The document makes allusions to "dead bodies" and to "things from space" but without explicitly stating that those same bodies and space-based things were extraterrestrial or evidence of early secret flights into space by Soviet astronauts. In a 1995 press conference held in Los Angeles, California, Speriglio told the sizable media crows who had turned up to see and hear the latest revelations on Marilyn Monroe that "I had [the document] probably about two months before I did anything with it. I looked at it and said, 'Marilyn Monroe and aliens? No way!'"

Was the famous movie star Marilyn Monroe killed because she knew about a secret government UFO program?

The document is presented in the form of a series of transcripts of conversations between two people: one being a well-known journalist in the 1950s and 1960s named Dorothy Kilgallen, and the other being a man named Howard Rothberg. Notably, Kilgallen, who also died under mysterious circumstances that were put down to an accidental drug and alcohol overdose in November 1965, was the topic of a large, and previously classified, FBI file. As for Rothberg, we have this from Speriglio: "[Rothberg] also dealt with a lot of photographers who used to film Marilyn. He got a lot of information about her from them, and he would feed it to Dorothy Kilgallen." Interestingly, Speriglio also revealed that the document was the subject of an investigation that was being undertaken by no fewer than "two federal agencies." To date, however, the names of those specific agencies have not been revealed.

When the Monroe/Speriglio/Cooper document hit the news, Vicki Ecker, who, at the time, was the editor of *UFO Magazine*, stated: "To put it succinctly, the document suggests that on the day she died, Monroe was going to hold her own press conference, where she was planning to spill the beans about, amongst other things, JFK's secret knowledge of UFOs and dead aliens."

Let's see exactly how the document reads:

"References: MOON DUST, Project" [which was a genuine U.S. operation designed to capture, understand, and exploit overseas advanced technologies, such as Soviet spy-satellites]:

Rothberg discussed the apparent comeback of [Marilyn Monroe] with Kilgallen and the break up with the Kennedys. Rothberg told Kilgallen that [Monroe] was attending Hollywood parties hosted by Hollywood's elite and was becoming the talk of the town again. Rothberg indicated in so many words, that [Monroe] had secrets to tell, no doubt arising from her trysts with the President and the Attorney General.

Now we get to the absolute crux of the matter:

One such "secret" mentioned the visit by the President at a secret air base for the purpose of inspecting things from outer space. Kilgallen replied that she knew what might be the source of the visit. In the mid-fifties Kilgallen learned of a secret effort by US and UK governments to identify the origins of crashed spacecraft and dead bodies, from a British Government official. Kilgallen believed the story may have come from the New Mexico area in the late forties. Kilgallen said that if the story is true, it would cause terrible embarrassment for Jack [Kennedy] and his plans to have NASA put me on the moon.

Then are these controversial words: "[Monroe] repeatedly called the Attorney General and complained about the way she was being ignored by the President and his brother. [Monroe] threatened to hold a press conference and would tell all. [Monroe] made references to bases in Cuba and knew of the President's plan to kill Castro. [Monroe] made reference to her 'diary of secrets' and what the newspapers would do with such disclosures."

The fact that Dorothy Kilgallen was indeed implicated in the UFO controversy is not a matter of any doubt. In the May 23, 1955, edition of the *Los Angeles Examiner*, Kilgallen wrote: "British scientists and airmen, after examining the remains of one mysterious flying ship, are convinced these strange aerial objects are not optical illusions or Soviet inventions, but are flying saucers which originate on another planet. The source of my information is a British official of Cabinet rank who prefers to remain unidentified."

The "British official" told Kilgallen: "We believe, on the basis of our inquiry thus far, that the saucers were staffed by small men—probably under four feet tall. It's frightening, but there is no denying the flying saucers come from another planet."

Kilgallen was further advised that a report concerning the crash was being withheld by the British government, since it did not wish to alarm the general public. In other words, this gels very well with the comments attributed to Kilgallen in the CIA document obtained by Milo Speriglio.

Very few people will need to be told that if President John F. Kennedy really had confided in Marilyn Monroe what he knew about crashed UFOs and dead aliens, her life would certainly have been in some considerable danger. It's one thing to read a book on Roswell, watch a television documentary, or listen to someone speak on the legendary incident. It's quite another thing to get the full lowdown from the commander-in-chief. The fact that Monroe was known for her unstable character and also had deep grievances against both Kennedy brothers makes it all the more possible that she really might have spilled the beans to the world on what she knew about deceased extraterrestrials and alien wreckage held at a secret military base, which may have been a reference to Area 51.

> The fact that Monroe was someone known for her unstable character ... makes it all the more possible that she really might have spilled the beans to the world....

Today, more than twenty-five years after Milo Speriglio presented the controversial document to the world, it remains the enigma that it was back then. Attempts to have the document verified have failed. All that can be said is that the document was written on a decades-old typewriter and that the paper used was also decades old. Those are issues that suggest that the document may well have been written when it was said to have been written, namely 1962. On the other hand, it would not be too difficult for a skilled hoaxer to get his or her hands on an old typewriter and a batch of old paper. Such items can be easily purchased online today. Granted, back in 1995, when the Internet was certainly not what it is now, it would have been much more difficult to obtain such items but certainly not impossible. The fact that Monroe had also spent time—and quite a bit of time—studying communism and at one point was planning on asking for a visa to visit the former Soviet Union would have been yet another reason for the Intelligence Community to have had concerns about her.

One of the most important issues revolves around what the CIA has to say about all of this. After all, the document—real or not—appears to be a genuine CIA document. For the record, the CIA admits to having the document on file. In fact, it has far more than a few copies on file. The reason for that is because, on more than a few occasions, investigators have filed Freedom of Information Act (FOIA) requests to try to uncover the truth of the story and have mailed copies of the document alongside their FOIA requests. The CIA has been unwilling to undertake an investigation to try to determine whether or not the document is legitimate beyond stating that the original is not held in their archives (if such an original even ever really existed) and that the Agency cannot find even a single, solitary page of documentation on Marilyn Monroe. That's where things are now at: stalemate. Unless something new comes along—or the CIA decides to say more—the matter of whether or not the world's most famous blonde was murdered in order to hide what she knew about aliens from faraway worlds will continue to be debated, with no sign of an answer in sight.

Related to all of this is the November 22, 1963, assassination of President John F. Kennedy at Dealey Plaza in Dallas, Texas. The chief suspect was—and, for the government, still is—Lee Harvey Oswald. For the world of officialdom, and despite the fact that he was never tried in a court of law (due to being shot by nightclub owner Jack Ruby on November 24), Oswald was not just a gunman but *the* gunman: a lone gunman, with no conspiracy. As incredible as it may sound, though, more than a few links exist between the UFO subject and the death of the president.

Earlier in this book, we were introduced to a man named Fred Crisman, who played a still unclear role in the June 1947 Maury Island UFO affair. New Orleans-based district attorneys believed that Crisman was the second gunman on the Grassy Knoll—thus creating a link between the JFK assassination and an early UFO encounter that was dominated by death. When President Kennedy was killed, Guy Banister was running a private detective service out of New Orleans. Prior to that, Banister was a special agent with the FBI. In 1947, Banister investigated a number of UFO investigations for J. Edgar Hoover. The Banister–UFO files can be viewed online at the FBI's website, *The Vault*. Both Banister and Crisman knew Oswald. Dorothy Kilgallen, who died under controversial circumstances in 1965, was given two UFO-themed stories by government officials in the 1950s. She conducted a detailed interview with Jack Ruby about his shooting of Oswald. Ruby

FBI founding director J. Edgar Hoover was very much involved with investigations into reports of UFOs.

alluded that a massive conspiracy existed behind the killing of the president, too. Ruby also died under dubious circumstances in 1967.

Death, death, and even more death are all at the forefront of the Monroe–JFK affair.

In May 1971, Otto Binder wrote an article for *Saga* magazine that had a highly controversial title: "Liquidation of the UFO Researchers." Binder said in his article:

> Over the past 10 years, no less than 137 flying saucer researchers, writers, scientists, and witnesses, have died—many under the most mysterious circumstances. Were they silenced, permanently, because they got too close to the truth? Before the 1967 Congress of Scientific Ufologists, Gray Barker, the chairman, received two letters and one phone call telling him that Frank Edwards, the noted radio newscaster and champion of flying saucers, would die during the convention. One day after the meeting was convened there was an announcement that Frank Edwards had succumbed to an "apparent" heart attack. How could anybody know that Edwards was going to die, unless it was planned?

Planned killing in the field of ufology seems to be way too common.

Of all the many deaths within the field of ufology that have been attributed to accidents, suicides, or ill health—but which may well have been due to murder undertaken in just about the most coldhearted ways possible—few such deaths rival that of James Forrestal. He was the very first U.S. secretary of defense. He may also have been one of the highest-ranking members of the U.S. government to have been murdered because of what he knew about UFOs. Within UFO circles, rumors have circulated for decades that in the lead-up to his death on May 22, 1949, Forrestal was seriously thinking about going public on what he had learned about the UFO phenomenon after he became secretary of defense. It's important to note that, as the very first secretary of defense, Forrestal certainly would have been exposed to the very deepest, darkest, and most secret aspects of the UFO phenomenon—whether it was extraterrestrial in nature, the work of the government, or both (the latter being the most likely option of the three).

Why would the secretary of defense have been killed, though? Couldn't he have been persuaded, as a high-ranking government official, to keep to his oath of secrecy? Well, it's not quite as simple as that. Although Secretary Forrestal handled himself extremely well in the Second World War, when he held the position of secretary of the Navy, he was also a noted boxer and not some-

> Within UFO circles, rumors have circulated ... [that] Forrestal was seriously thinking about going public on what he had learned about the UFO phenomenon....

one to mess with. Things began to change, though, when Forrestal received what was, then, just about one of the most prestigious positions of all: secretary of defense. Daily, top-secret briefings would undoubtedly have focused on what the former Soviet Union was up to, its capabilities, and the problems it might pose in the future. Such down-to-earth issues were the kinds of things Forrestal handled just fine during the Second World War. When in 1947, though, he got his new, powerful position, things started to go wrong for Forrestal—as in extremely wrong.

For years, ufologists have speculated that the UFO briefings that Forrestal certainly would have received destabilized him—psychologically—and led him down a path to mental collapse. Of course, those of us out of the loop have no solid idea of what top secrets the secretary of defense may have been exposed to. If they were just reports of lights in the sky, it's highly unlikely that something of such an innocuous nature would have so drastically affected Forrestal. Maybe he received a top-secret briefing on alien abductions—revelations that beings from other worlds were kidnapping people and even experimenting on them. Just perhaps, that may have been enough to tip the scales. Perhaps he was shown the bodies of dead aliens, secretly stored away at a military installation. Seeing such things up close and personal might also have unhinged someone, even a tough guy like Forrestal. Whatever the answer, after taking on his new job, Forrestal was very quickly a changed man.

It was in the very early morning of May 22, 1949, that Forrestal's life came to a crashing end, and I do mean that literally. His body was found pummeled and dead after he exited a window on the sixteenth floor of the Walter Reed National Military Medical Center, which is known also as Bethesda Naval Hospital, in Maryland. Questions were soon asked: Did Forrestal take his own life, or was he hurled out of the window by government assassins, fearful that Forrestal might reveal to the world what he knew about the UFO phenomenon? Whatever the truth of the matter, it's a fact that many of Forrestal's old diaries remain classified and out of the hands of the public—in fact, they are out of the hands of just about everyone in government today, too.

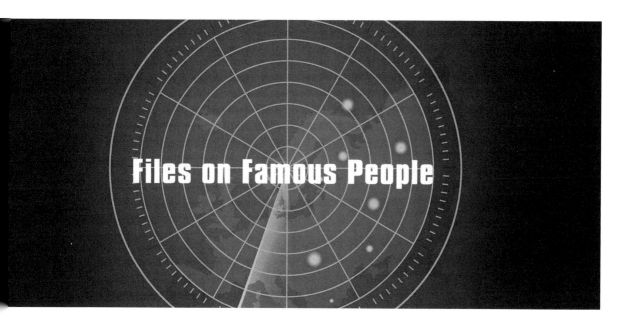

Files on Famous People

Under the terms of the U.S. Freedom of Information Act, numerous files have been declassified that tell of how and why the FBI, decades ago, secretly and carefully kept their eyes and ears on the rich and famous. One of those was the legendary Hollywood "swashbuckler" of the 1930s to the 1950s, Errol Flynn, who was suspected of being nothing less than a full-blown Nazi spy.

Flynn expert Charles Higham said: "I spoke to Colonel William E. Williamson, former director of demilitarization procedures in Japan under General [Douglas] MacArthur.... Williamson had done his own research at the Pentagon and State Department and the CIA ... and had learned that Errol was a spy for the Nazis on a major scale." Also, nightclub owner and friend of Flynn's, Johnny Meyer, told Higham: "I believe Errol was not merely in touch with the Nazis in San Francisco but was actively aiding and abetting them." The alleged links do not end there.

It is a matter of official record that one of Flynn's girlfriends was Gertrude Anderson, a key Nazi agent who was the subject of deep FBI surveillance. According to Charles Higham, Flynn's friend Freddie McEvoy, at whose home Flynn was alleged to have raped Betty Hansen, had been under investigation as a possible collaborator with the Nazis. In the years leading up to the Second World War, she was involved in U-Boat refueling operations. Interestingly, the government's files on Flynn include transcripts of telephone conversations between Flynn and McEvoy that were monitored by the wartime Office of Censorship.

Of particular note is a document that can be found within the Office of Censorship's files on Flynn that is dated December 14, 1942, titled *American Film Actor Reported Associating with German Agent in Mexico.* This document details the testimony of an unnamed informant who had provided the Office with some intriguing material: "Writer, after telling of three weeks spent in Acapulco … adds, Errol Flynn came up to the hotel for drinks a couple of evenings bringing his girl along—Hilda Kruger, leading German spy here, arranged the date for him. An associate of hers, another Nazi suspect, gave Errol Flynn and Frederik McEvoy as references while spending time in California."

Most controversial of all, however, was Flynn's friendship with a certain Dr. Hermann Frederick Erben. Born on November 15, 1897, in Vienna, Austria, Erben was described in Lionel Godfrey's *The Life and Crimes of Errol Flynn* as "a specialist in tropical diseases." Indeed, he was. However, he was much more, according to Higham, who described Erben as "one of the most important and ingenious Nazi agents."

Erben had graduated from the State High School, Vienna, in 1915, and between that year and 1918 had served with the Austrian Army before being honorably discharged as a first lieutenant. Eight years later, Erben received a fellowship to study in the United States and while there was granted an immigration visa. In 1927, he was licensed to practice medicine and surgery in Louisiana, and the following year, he was also licensed for the state of Washington. What of Erben's friendship with Flynn, though? The files of the Intelligence Detachment Screening Center make for eye-opening reading:

1932: [Erben] went via the Far East to New Guinea on another scientific expedition, which was financed by himself. On this trip he met the film star Errol Flynn and became a very close friend of same. 1937: [Erben] returned from South America and in the same year he and his friend Errol Flynn embarked in New York for London and went via Paris. Being in London [Erben] volunteered with a British ambulance unit, which was committed for the loyalists in Spain. Errol Flynn also went as a journalist and unofficial observer to Spain. After 20 days in Spain, subject went to Vienna and from there to Canton, China.

Rumors have long been bandied about that actor Errol Flynn, the star of such films as *Captain Blood* and *The Adventures of Robin Hood,* was a Nazi sympathizer and spy.

Erben had a darker side, too. American authorities were able to confirm that he *had* worked as a Nazi agent during the Second World War. Details of this startling fact can be found within the files of the Intelligence Detachment Screening Center, specifically in the pages of a document titled *Subject Accepted the Job as German Intelligence Agent*: "[Erben] claims that he accepted the proposition to become a German intelligence agent, fully conscious of the fact that at the present, he was still an American citizen, and thus subject to the penalty of high treason. [Erben] admits that he was not forced or coerced to accept the job." Needless to say, because of his close friendship with Erben, Flynn was interviewed by FBI agents who subsequently prepared a two-page report, from which the following is extracted:

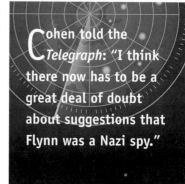

Cohen told the *Telegraph*: "I think there now has to be a great deal of doubt about suggestions that Flynn was a Nazi spy."

> Mr. FLYNN at the outset of the interview, admitted being acquainted with Dr. ERBEN and regarded him highly. They have been acquainted for about ten years and have traveled extensively together all over the world. Mr. FLYNN stated that heretofore ERBEN had been very much opposed to Nazism and communism and from what he, FLYNN, knows of his background, he does not believe ERBEN would now be a devout Nazi.

The FBI and the IDSC were not the only ones watching the activities of Flynn and Erben. The wartime Office of Strategic Services, a precursor to the CIA, was doing likewise. The OSS stated starkly in its files on the men that "Erben tried to return to the United States as a repatriate. We believe that if he had been successful in so doing, he would have been acting in the United States as an agent of the German government. Erben's only contact in the United States was Errol Flynn. We know of absolutely no other contact with Dr Erben there."

The British *Daily Telegraph* newspaper uncovered highly disturbing data, too, concerning Flynn's relationship with Erben: "Declassified files held by the CIA show that, in an intercepted letter in September 1933, Flynn wrote to Erben: 'A slimy Jew is trying to cheat me.... I do wish we could bring Hitler over here to teach these Isaacs a thing or two. The bastards have absolutely no business probity or honor whatsoever.'"

The *Daily Telegraph* added: "The letter, if genuine, certainly shows anti-Semitism, which was common at the time, but defenders say that Flynn, writing before he was famous and having lost money on a business deal, was not expressing a deep commitment to Nazism. Hitler had only just come to power and the true horror of his policies had yet to be revealed."

This may well be so. In December 2000, the *Daily Telegraph* revealed that it had learned that the British government's Home Office department possessed still classified documents "dispelling claims" that Flynn was a "Nazi sympathizer," which in reality, confirmed that he had offered his services during the Second World War to British Intelligence.

Harry Cohen, the Labor member of the British Parliament, petitioned Jack Straw, then home secretary of the British government, to declassify the files. Cohen told the *Telegraph*: "I think there now has to be a great deal of doubt about suggestions that Flynn was a Nazi spy. On the contrary, I think he was probably used by the security services in this country. More likely he was taken up by the British security services towards the end of the war. I know the Home Office has documents on him, which should be released to the public."

Charles Higham uncovered data suggesting that the British government's files on Flynn had more to do with *perceived* pro-Nazi connections. In Higham's own words:

> In early 1980, I was interviewed about Flynn for an American radio program. One of the callers who took part was a woman called Anne Lane … she said that she had worked from 1946 to 1951 for the MI5 chief Sir Percy Sillitoe.… Lane had been in charge of the Flynn dossier, which she described clearly as a beige, red-ribboned [sic] concertina file stamped MOST SECRET.

> The file revealed that Flynn had been under surveillance by both MI5 and MI6 since 1934, when he made pro-Nazi remarks at a party in Mayfair. Flynn had also been monitored by British intelligence at a Paris meeting in 1937 with high-ranking German officials and the Duke of Windsor, a meeting clearly inimical to British interests.… SIS [the Special Intelligence Service] also traced him to the security area at Berchtesgaden in the spring of 1938, where (according to sworn statements by Erben in 1946, made to a British security officer) he had a secret meeting with Hitler.

Of the many and varied official files that the FBI has declassified into the public domain, certainly one of the most intriguing is the dossier on Ernest Hemingway—without doubt one of the finest novelists of the twentieth century and the author of such classics as *A Farewell to Arms* (1929); *For Whom the Bell Tolls* (1940); and *The Old Man and the Sea* (1951). It's not Hemingway's literary career that's under the microscope, though. That would be far too down-to-earth. Instead, the subject is how and why Hemingway became a secret operative of the FBI—to a degree, at least.

Under the provisions of the Freedom of Information Act, the FBI has declassified a 122-page-long file on Hemingway, which makes for notable reading. Of course, condensing an excess of one hundred-plus pages into an article is no easy task. However, some genuine nuggets of material in the file are worth noting. The collection makes it clear that Hemingway was perceived by at least *some* in the FBI as a person who could offer assistance to the cause of intelligence gathering. His time spent in Spain during the Spanish

Civil War, and his time living on the island of Cuba, both caught the attention of J. Edgar Hoover.

On the other hand, Hoover was not at all comfortable. A 1942 document from the FBI tells us the following:

> While in Spain during the Spanish Revolution, Hemingway was said to have associated with Jay Allen, of the North American Newspaper Alliance. It has been alleged by a number of sources that Allen was a Communist and he is known to have been affiliated with alleged Communist Front organizations. In the fall of 1940 Hemingway's name was included in a group of names of individuals who were said to be engaged in Communist activities. These individuals were reported to occupy positions on the "intellectual front" and were said to be engaged in Communist activities.

None of this went down well with Hoover. However, in early October 1942—when he was living in Cuba—Hemingway made an approach to the FBI to offer his services as, in effect, an undercover agent. The FBI noted that Hemingway had become friends with Consul Kenneth Potter and the Second Secretary of Embassy Robert P. Joyce. In a memo to Hoover, R. G. Leddy—the FBI's legal attaché at Havana—wrote that "at several conferences with the Ambassador and officers of the Embassy late in August 1942, the topic of using Hemingway's services in intelligence activities was discussed."

Hoover continued to have his doubts, but he did see the logic in bringing Hemingway onboard. Files reveal that, although Hemingway wished to get further involved with the FBI, at least a month prior to the events of October 1942, he was *already* spying for the American Embassy. FBI files make that very clear: "Early in September 1942, Ernest Hemingway began to engage directly in intelligence activities on behalf of the American Embassy in Havana. He is operating through Spanish Republicans whose identities have not been furnished by which we are assured are obtainable when desired."

The document continues: "[Hemingway] advised that he now has four men operating on a full-time basis, and 14 more whose positions are barmen, waiters, and the like, operating on a part-time basis.... [Heming-

Renowned author Ernest Hemingway (shown here in 1953 at a campsite in Kenya), who had many foreign connections because of his travels, offered to spy for the FBI in Cuba.

way] … wishes to suggest that his interest thus far has not been limited to the Spanish Falange and Spanish activities, but that he has included numerous German suspects."

Again, matters became fraught; yes, apparently, Hemingway was in a position to do good work, or so it seemed. However, the fact that shortly after his espionage work began, Hemingway introduced the aforementioned R. G. Leddy to a friend as "a member of the Gestapo" did not go down well! Hoover's blood pressure was ready to go through the roof. He wrote of the "complete undesirability" of having Hemingway onboard, noting that "Hemingway is the last man, in my estimation, to be used in any such capacity" and adding that his "sobriety" was "certainly questionable."

On top of that, as the files demonstrate, Hemingway proved to be no James Bond. FBI assistant director Quinn Tamm called him a "phony." Records show that Hemingway incorrectly put Prince Camillo Ruspoli—an Italian fascist interned by the Cubans—as being present at a lunch at the Hotel Nacional in honor of the new Spanish Charges d'Affaires, Pelayo Garcia Olay. Also, a "tightly wrapped box" left at the Bar Basque and acquired by one of Hemingway's operatives was believed by Hemingway to contain "espionage information." It did not; when it reached Robert P. Joyce, it was found to contain "only a cheap edition of the 'Life of St. Teresa.'" No one was impressed. Hemingway was "irritated."

The FBI was soon done with the acclaimed writer. Back to Assistant Director Tamm: "The Bureau has by careful and impartial investigation, from time to time disproved practically all of the so-called Hemingway information." The FBI washed its hands of him. However, indications exist that Hemingway's work in the field of espionage did not end there. Consider the following from 1943 FBI documents on Hemingway: "At the present time [Hemingway] is alleged to be performing a highly secret naval operation for the Navy Department. In this connection, the Navy Department is said to be paying the expenses for the operation of Hemingway's boat, furnishing him with arms and charting courses in the Cuban area." On this same matter of the Navy, the FBI recorded the following on June 23, 1943: Hemingway "is on a special confidential assignment for the Naval Attache chasing submarines along the Cuban coast and keeping a careful observance on the movements of the Spanish steamers which occasionally come to Cuba."

In view of these latter revelations, perhaps, one day, we'll see even more classified files on Ernest Hemingway finally become unclassified.

The earliest FBI involvement in the life and career of John Wayne is still unconfirmed; it's something the Bureau refuses to discuss publicly and has yet to relinquish its files on the subject, namely a Soviet-planned assassination of the vehemently anticommunist actor. As incredible as this may sound, the allegation appears to have a basis in fact. According to Michael Munn, a noted film historian, he had gotten the story in 1983 from renowned moviemaker Orson Welles. Munn stated that Welles informed him that Soviet premier Joseph Stalin had personally ordered the assassination of Wayne after Russian filmmaker Sergei Gerasimov had attended a peace conference in New York in 1949 and learned of Wayne's absolute hatred of communism. Munn further revealed that Wayne had personally told him that his friend, the stuntman Yakima Canutt, had "saved his life once."

After questioning Canutt about this intriguing statement, Munn added: "Yakima told me that the FBI had discovered there were agents sent to Hollywood to kill John Wayne. He said the FBI had come to tell John about the plot. John told the FBI to let the men show up and he would deal with them." Furthermore, according to the story, Wayne apparently then hatched his own plot with his scriptwriter at the time, Jimmy Grant, to abduct the assassins, drive to a beach, and stage a "mock execution to frighten them." Munn stated that he did not know exactly what transpired but did hear that the two assassins stayed in the United States "to work for the FBI."

Is this strange and incredible story true? Michael Munn believes it is. He insists that Orson Welles had offered the story without prompting and that his sources were excellent: "Mr. Welles was a great storyteller, but he had no particular admiration for John Wayne. I am quite convinced that it was not propagated by John or his inner circle."

The earliest FBI involvement in the life and career of John Wayne is still unconfirmed; it's something the Bureau refuses to discuss publicly....

The earliest *confirmed* FBI interest in John Wayne's activities occurred on September 22, 1959. The FBI noted on that date that Los Angeles newspapers had broken a story that Wayne was involved "with a suspected revolt under direction of Roberto (Tito) Arias, son of a former President of Panama and now a lawyer in that country." The memo continues:

> The *Hollywood Citizen News* quotes [Panamanian presidential press secretary Salustiano] Chacon as saying letters and documents found in a suitcase abandoned by Arias, allegedly in a flight from Panama while being sought, including an envelope bearing the name and address of John Wayne. Inside the envelope was said to be an interoffice memorandum to Wayne from a Robert D. Weesner, dated 4/9/59, outlining a "schedule of funds totaling $682,850 to or drawn by Tito Arias in connection with his Panamanian operations in which you are involved."

The FBI noted that the media had recorded Chacon stressing: "Nothing here to implicate Wayne." As was also recorded in FBI files, however: "The fact that the memorandum mentions $525,000 turned over to Arias personally, apparently without supporting documents to satisfy Mr. Weesner, seems a little strange." Wayne, the FBI learned, was quick to play down his involvement in this strange saga and maintained that it was all just a big mistake:

> Wayne is quoted as saying, in an interview in Hollywood, that he was shocked to hear reports Arias and his wife, Dame Margot Fonteyn, premier British ballerina, had been named as connected with a plot to overthrow the government, and he describes such accusations as "ridiculous." According to the news articles, Wayne said, "I have been in business with the Arias family for a long time. A group of us are in several business ventures, including a shrimp import company. Roberto never talked politics, and I never heard him say anything about overthrowing the Panamanian Government." The news articles state the alleged evidence was discovered at Santa Clara, a Pacific beach resort 73 miles from Panama City and a residential resort area where many retired Americans have homes.

Despite Wayne's assertions to the effect that any suggestions that he, Arias, or Fonteyn were linked with a planned overthrow of the Panamanian government were patently "ridiculous," additional files demonstrate that Fonteyn was detained in a Panamanian jail on April 20, 1959, as a direct result of suspicions that she was indeed a part of a plan to oust President Ernesto de la Guardia from power. Moreover, it was only because of the quick intervention of British ambassador Sir Ian Henderson that Fonteyn was freed and flown out of the country. The FBI was informed that "the British public did not appreciate having seen her in the role of the swan, then seeing her in the role of a decoy duck."

Famous tough-guy actor John Wayne was said to have links to two conspirators who were trying to overthrow the Panamanian government, although he was not directly associated with a plot.

Further data reached the FBI to the effect that Arias had set off around the nineteenth on a fishing trip in the Gulf of Panama aboard a boat called the *Nola* and had planned to jump onto a shrimp boat, then storm the National Guard Barracks at Chorrera, Panama. According to interviews with local fishermen, Arias had reportedly asked them to raise a buoy from the ocean that had been previously loaded with machine guns and grenades that were to be used in the planned raid.

The attempt failed, however, and Arias took refuge in the Brazilian Embassy in Panama City, ultimately deciding to fight the government by more legitimate means, which led to a seat in elections for Panama's National Assembly in 1964. Tragedy struck, however, when, after his election, Arias was crippled by gunshots fired by a former political associate. Nevertheless, after being treated at Britain's Stoke Mandeville Hospital, Arias resumed his political career in 1967. For someone who, according to John Wayne, "never talked politics" and never said "anything about overthrowing the Panamanian Government," Arias was certainly full of big surprises of both a political and a revolutionary nature.

It must be said that the curious references to various documents that had been "found in a suitcase abandoned by Arias" and that specifically referred to John Wayne and the "Panamanian operations" of Arias in which the actor was "involved" do not exactly inspire very much faith in the idea that this was really just related to the intricacies of the shrimp industry, as Wayne so anxiously wanted everyone to believe. Evidently, this episode did not cause problems for Wayne at an official level.

Only weeks after John Lennon was shot and killed outside of his New York home in December 1980 by Mark David Chapman, a professor of history at the University of California named Jon Wiener began probing the links that existed between Lennon and American authorities: "It began out of simple curiosity, a desire to check out a few rumors that [FBI boss J. Edgar] Hoover was not Lennon's greatest fan. It then started snowballing into a crusade when I realized how many obstacles were being thrown in my path," stated Professor Wiener.

Twenty years on, and as a direct result of his research and investigations, Wiener found himself embroiled in one of the most talked-about court cases of all time. On February 18, 2000, in Court 23 at the Federal Court Building in Los Angeles, Judge Brian Q. Robbins ordered the FBI to release two letters from a batch of ten documents it was withholding concerning its intense surveillance activities of Lennon. The FBI flatly refused to comply with the order, citing overwhelming national security considerations. Although the FBI had already released a substantial amount of documentation from its files on Lennon by the time the case came to court, what set this final, elusive batch of papers apart from the already declassified files is that they almost certainly originated with none other than Britain's ultrasecret, domestic security service: MI5.

The fact that MI5 has information on files pertaining to the activities of John Lennon is not in dispute at all. MI5 whistle-blower David Shayler has stated unequivocally that he saw the files in 1993 while serving with the security services and that they dealt with MI5's surveillance of Lennon during the late 1960s. According to the documentation, Lennon donated £45,000 to the Trotskyist Workers' Revolutionary Party (WRP) and gave support to *Red*

Singing and song-writing legend John Lennon was monitored by England's MI5. His left-leaning political views probably put him under suspicion as a subversive by the much more conservative British government.

Mole, a Marxist magazine edited by student protest leader Tariq Ali.

At the time, MI5's F Branch, the so-called "anti-subversion division," was already monitoring closely the activities of the WRP and even had its very own "mole" buried deep within the organization. It is strongly suspected by those who have followed this entire controversy that MI5's mole, whose identity remains a secret to this day, may very well have been Lennon's contact within the group, too, hence the reason MI5 and the FBI were so keen to keep this information under wraps several decades later.

It is also believed that the MI5 source within the WRP had intercepted at least one letter from Lennon that was destined for the Party. The British *Mail on Sunday* newspaper took things a step further, referring to an "insider" who had asserted to their staff that not only would Lennon's correspondence have been closely monitored by MI5, but his telephone would have been tapped, and listening devices would almost certainly have been placed in his home, which at the time in question was a Georgian mansion at Tittenshurst Park, near Ascot.

As an FBI source stated, "[The British] don't want these pages released because they show Lennon was being monitored in ways that might now prove to be embarrassing." However, Wiener said, the *Sunday Times*, a British newspaper that had also reported on the controversy, reported:

> [It] somehow failed to consider the possibility that the MI5 files Shayler described contained erroneous information. Lennon never had anything to do with the WRP, widely regarded as the looniest group on the left. In the late sixties Lennon was friendly with the International Marxist Group, who published the underground *Red Mole*, edited by Tariq Ali and Robin Blackburn, which had a completely different political orientation from the WRP. A former member of the WRP executive committee, Roger Smith, told the London *Observer* the MI5 information was wrong: "There was absolutely no link between Lennon and us."

The Workers' Revolutionary Party aside, what of the more controversial rumors suggesting that John Lennon may have donated funds to the Irish Republican Army (IRA)? In 1971, when internment without trial was introduced in Northern Ireland, Lennon held a sign at a rally in London that read:

"Victory for the IRA against British imperialism." Lennon himself stated at the time, "If it's a choice between the IRA and the British Army, I'm with the IRA." For its part, the political wing of the IRA, Sinn Fein, has stated with regard to these allegations that Lennon donated funds: "It is not unbeliev-able." Similarly, Hunter Davies, a biographer on the Beatles, says, "I wouldn't be at all surprised if he gave money to the IRA. John liked stirring it up."

Not everyone is in agreement, however. Lennon's widow, Yoko Ono, denied such controversial claims when they were made public, and Lennon's friend, Beatle chronicler Ray Connolly, said that "daft though he sometimes may have been, naive though he certainly was, and absolutely the softest of touches for all kinds of causes, [John Lennon] was hardly a bogeyman—and absolutely not a supporter of terrorism." With regard to Lennon's I'm-with-the-IRA statement, Con-nolly concluded: "Knowing him, it was, I'm certain, an emo-tional, unconsidered retort, about an organization about which he and virtually his entire generation knew hardly any-thing."

Lennon's widow, Yoko Ono, denied such controversial claims when they were made public....

David Shayler is a former employee of Britain's domes-tic intelligence-gathering agency MI5, which is the British equivalent of the United States's FBI. Shayler, a definitive whistle-blower, shook the British establishment to its core in 1999. That was the year in which authors Mark Hollingsworth and Nick Fielding wrote a book titled *Defending the Realm: MI5 and the Shayler Affair*. One of the many and varied revelations of the secret kind from Shayler were focused on Lon-don's most famous, loved, and hated spiky-tops: the Sex Pistols, of course. According to Shayler, while working for MI5, he saw and read a file titled *Sub-version in Contemporary Music*, which contained numerous newspaper and magazine clippings on musicians whose output was deemed by MI5 to be con-troversial and inflammatory. No surprise, that included the Sex Pistols. Shayler said: "You can imagine some Colonel Blimp [a British caricature of an out-of-touch military man] character compiling this file, whereas anybody with half a brain knew the Sex Pistols talked a good talk—wrote a lot of songs about it, but when it came to political activism did absolutely nothing."

Interestingly, in the 2002 documentary *The Filth and the Fury*, Sex Pis-tols guitarist Steve Jones stated that, while on tour in the United States, the band had been followed by elements of both the CIA and the FBI.

In the summer of 2001, I was commissioned by a British newsstand magazine called *Eye Spy* to interview David Shayler for a forthcoming edition of the magazine. I traveled down to London with the magazine's editor, Mark Birdsall, and the interview was conducted in Shayler's apartment. It was an extensive, recorded interview, which included questions about the Sex Pistols and MI5's interest in them and their music. I sent the article off to Mark and didn't think any more about it—at least, I didn't for a while. When the article appeared a couple of months later and the relevant issue of the magazine was splashed across the nation's newsstands, Birdsall phoned me up to say that he had received a visit at his North Yorkshire, England, home from (and I quote exactly) "two lads from the Metropolitan Police."

They explained to Birdsall that they were not at all concerned by what was contained in the article—indeed, it didn't contain anything that wasn't already in the public domain, in *Defending the Realm*, and in the pages of numerous newspapers that covered the Shayler affair at the time. Neverthe-less, as Mark explained to me, Scotland Yard wanted the audiorecording I made of the interview. That much became evident when, around October 2001, I received a phone call from Scotland Yard, specifically from a represen-tative of what is called the Special Branch. It was made very clear to me that I would hand over the recording of the interview, which was done on an old-school, small, voice-activated mini cassette recorder. I was also asked if I had made any copies (which I had not, as the recorder wasn't tape-to-tape). A lot of strange things happened around that time, too, all of which led me to believe that I was under some form of brief surveillance.

Things don't end there. Paul Simonon, bass guitarist with the Clash, was asked about the possibility of a government file existing on his band. He said: "There probably is, yes, alongside the file on the Sex Pistols. It's hard to fully appreciate now, but we certainly stood out back then, we really made a noise. It wasn't just us, it was every punk—anyone, in fact, who wasn't wear-ing flares was making a big political noise that terrified the Government."

David Shayler also confirmed that MI5 had files on the English band UB40 who, in the early 1980s, released a number of excellent, highly charged songs that justifiably attacked the iron-fist regime of Margaret Thatcher, the prime minister at the time.

Somewhat apocryphal but highly intriguing are the rumors that MI5 and the Special Branch—at the request of Buckingham Palace, no less—were involved in a shady affair to ensure that the Sex Pistols's single *God Save the Queen* did not reach number one on the charts when Queen Elizabeth II was celebrating the twenty-fifth anniversary of her coronation in summer 1977. Similar rumors abound concerning attempts to have the band's 1977 album *Never Mind the Bollocks* banned due to its title supposedly being obscene. For-tunately, common sense prevailed, and the laughable and pathetic case was rightly thrown out of court.

Finally, a decade or so ago, a retired member of the Special Branch told me that his former employers had compiled extensive files on the controver-sial, so-called "Oi!" movement of the early 1980s. For those who may not know, "Oi!" was an offshoot of punk that attracted an extremist, right-wing following—parts of which were politically oriented. Apparently, an entire file exists on what was, without doubt, the most infamous of all the records that fell under that banner, a compilation album entitled *Strength Thru Oi!* A word to bands everywhere: In light of all the above, it may not just be your fans who are watching you closely.

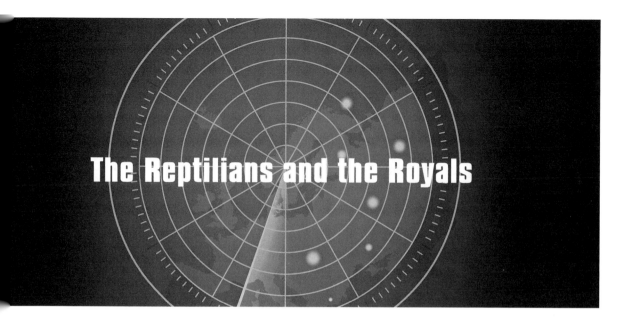

The Reptilians and the Royals

Is the British royal family comprised of dangerous and deadly shape-shifting creatures? Are they, in reality, not just like me and you but hideous, giant-sized Reptilians, the closest thing one can imagine to the fictitious beast portrayed in the 1954 movie *Creature from the Black Lagoon*? Certainly, it's a scenario that many conspiracy theorists adhere to, and, it must be said, a large body of data exists pertaining to these allegedly human, flesh-eating, blood-drinking monstrosities. Before we get to the matter of Queen Elizabeth II and the rest of the royals, though, let's first take a look at some classic accounts of Reptilians encountered over the course of the last six decades.

Certainly, one of the strangest of all encounters with what can only be described as a definitive Reptilian monster occurred on the night of Saturday, November 8, 1958. The unlucky soul who had the misfortune to fall foul of the unearthly beast was Charles Wetzel, who at the time was driving his green, two-door, Buick Super along North Main Street, Riverside, California—near the Santa Ana River. As Wetzel reached one particular stretch of the road that had flooded, the radio of his car began to crackle loudly and in a highly distorted fashion. With the water levels high and Wetzel trying to figure out what was wrong with the radio, he slowed down, purely and simply to ensure that he didn't find himself driving off the side of the road. He didn't know it at the time—but he soon would—that far worse things were out there than a flooded road and a wonky radio.

As Wetzel continued to slowly negotiate the road, he was shocked to the core by the sight of an extraordinary creature that surfaced from the shadows and, in brazen fashion, stood in the middle of the road, preventing Wetzel from going any further. He could only sit and stare, in a combination of fear

The creature Charles Wetzel came across was reptilian with a large head as big as a pumpkin.

and awe, as he tried to take in and comprehend the thing that stood before him.

Humanoid in shape and in excess of six feet in height, it had a large, round head described as being "pumpkin"-like, glowing eyes, a prominent mouth that had beaklike qualities to it, and scaly skin that resembled leaves. Strangest of all, the legs of the beast did not extend from beneath its torso but from its sides. Actually, that may not have been so strange after all: Both reptiles and lizards are built in precisely that fashion. Add to that a pair of long, muscular arms, and you have a definitive monster.

What began as a bone-chilling standoff quickly mutated into something else entirely. The reptile-man issued a loud, high-pitched noise that was part scream and part gurgle, after which it suddenly charged at Wetzel's Buick. He could only sit, paralyzed with fear, as the scaly thing raced toward the hood of the vehicle, then lunged even closer and violently clawed the windshield.

Although it was good fortune that led Wetzel to have a rifle with him, by his own admission, he was fearful about using it, but not because it might injure or kill the animal-man. Wetzel's big concern was that if he fired through the windshield and failed to kill it, the shattered glass would allow the monster to reach inside, haul him out of the car, and possibly tear him to pieces. With his body flooded with adrenaline, Wetzel took the only option he felt was available to him: he floored the accelerator, spun the wheels, and shot away. In doing so, he ran the beast down, which was evident by the fact that Wetzel felt the car go over its large body.

While some might consider a story like this to be nothing more than a hoax, the likelihood is that it was not. The rationale for this is that Wetzel quickly reported the affair to the local police, who launched an investigation. It's most unlikely that a hoaxer would run the risk of being charged for wasting police time or for filing a bogus report. Such was the seriousness with which the police took Wetzel's story, they sent not just officers out to the scene but a pack of bloodhounds, too. The monster, whatever it was, was never found—dead or alive. However, two pieces of evidence corroborated Wetzel's amazing experience: vicious-looking claw marks on the windshield and on the underside of the Buick. They were calling cards that Wetzel preferred to forget about—if he ever could.

In summer 1988, a terrifying creature began haunting the woods and little towns of Lee County, South Carolina—specifically the Scape Ore Swamp area. It quickly became known as Lizard Man as a result of its alleged green and scaly body. A bipedal lizard roaming the neighborhood? Maybe, yes. It all began—publicly if not chronologically—when on July 14, 1988, the Waye family phoned the Lee County sheriff's office and made a very strange and disturbing claim. Something wild and animalistic had attacked their 1985 Ford. It looked as if something large, powerful, and deeply savage had viciously clawed, and maybe even bitten into, the body of the vehicle—particularly so the hood. Somewhat baffled, the deputies responded to the call nevertheless. Sure enough, the Wayes were right on target: their vehicle was battered and bruised in the extreme. In addition, footprints were tracked across the muddy area. It was clearly time to bring in Sheriff Liston Truesdale. It was highly probable that the prints were those of a fox. Larger prints, also found, were suspected of being those of a bear—although some observers suggested that they had human qualities.

Large, humanlike in shape, and possessing two glowing, red eyes and three fingers on each hand, it was something horrific.

In such a close-knit neighborhood, it didn't take long before news got around and numerous locals turned up to see what all the fuss was about. It's notable that Sheriff Truesdale told Bigfoot investigator Lyle Blackburn, who wrote the definitive book on the affair—titled, of course, *Lizard Man*—that "while we were there looking over this situation, we learned that people in the Browntown community had been seeing a strange creature about seven feet tall with red eyes. Some of them described it as green, but some of them as brown. They thought it might be responsible for what happened."

A mystery—and a monster—was unleashed.

The publicity afforded to the Waye incident prompted someone who ultimately became the key player in the matter to come forward. His name was Chris Davis, at the time seventeen years of age. Chris's father, Tommy, had seen the sensationalized coverage given by the media to the attack on the Wayes' vehicle and contacted Sheriff Truesdale. Specifically, Tommy took his son to tell the police what he had told him. It was quite a story.

Back in 1988, Chris was working at a local McDonald's. On the night of June 29—roughly two weeks before the Waye affair exploded—Chris was on the late shift, which meant that he didn't finish work until after 2:00 A.M. His journey home ensured that he had to take a road across the swamp—specifically a heavily forested part of the swamp. It was just minutes later that he had a blowout. Chris pulled up at a crossroads and, via the bright moonlight, changed the tire. As he finished the job and put the tools back into the trunk, Chris saw something looming out of the trees. Large, humanlike in shape, and possessing two glowing, red eyes and three fingers on each hand, it was something horrific. Chris panicked, jumped in his vehicle, and sped off. Based on what Chris had to say next, that was a very wise move:

> I looked back and saw something running across the field towards me. It was about 25 yards away and I saw red eyes glowing. I ran into the car and as I locked it, the thing grabbed the door handle. I could see him from the neck down—the three big fingers, long black nails and green rough skin. It was strong and angry. I looked in my mirror and saw a blur of green running. I could see his toes and then he jumped on the roof of my car. I thought I heard a grunt and then I could see his fingers through the front windshield, where they curled around on the roof. I sped up and swerved to shake the creature off.

The reports didn't end there.

Sheriff Truesdale received more and more reports, to the extent that a near-*X-Files*-style dossier was compiled. It was an official police dossier that contained the fascinating account of Johnny Blythers, who, on July 31, 1990, described for the sheriff's department the events of the previous night:

> Last night about 10:30 P.M., we were coming home from the Browntown section of Lee County. It was me, my mother (Bertha Mae Blythers), [and] two sisters.... I started talking about the time we passed the flowing well in Scape Ore Swamp. I said "they ain't [sic] no such thing as a Lizard Man. If there was, somebody would be seeing it or caught it."
>
> We got up about a mile or mile and one half past the butter bean shed, about 50 feet from the dirt road by those two signs, my mother was driving the car.
>
> It was on the right side, it came out of the bushes. It jumped out in the road. My mother swerved to miss it, and mashed the brakes and sped up. It jumped out of the bushes like he was going to jump on the car. When my mother mashed the brakes, it looked like it wanted to get in the car.

Johnny's mother, Bertha Mae, gave her own statement on that terrifying drive through the spooky swamp:

> This past Monday night I went to my mother's house in Browntown to pick up my son. We went to McDonald's on Highway 15 near Bishopville to get something to eat. We left there about 20 minutes after 10:00 P.M., was headed home and came through Browntown and Scape Ore Swamp....
>
> We passed the bridge and was down the road near a mile. I was looking straight ahead going about 25 M.P.H., and I saw this big

brown thing, it jumped up at the window. I quickly sped up and went on the other side of the road to keep him from dragging my 11 year old girl out of the car. I didn't see with my lights directly on it. It nearly scared me to death.

Then was the statement of Tamacia Blythers, Bertha's daughter: "Tall—taller than the car, brown looking, a big chest had big eyes, had two arms. Don't know how his face looked, first seen his eyes. Never seen nothing like it before. I didn't see a tail. Mother says if she hadn't whiped [sic] over he would have hit her car or jumped on it. Mother said she was so scared her body light and she held her heart all the way home."

In addition, Lyle Blackburn has uncovered other reports of the beast—dating from 1986 to well into the 2000s. Two of the key players in this saga are now dead: Johnny Blythers and Chris Davis—the former in a car accident in 1999 and the latter from a shotgun blast, the result of a drug deal gone bad, almost a decade to the day after Blythers's death.

As for the legendary Lizard Man, what, exactly, was it? Certainly, the name provoked imagery of a malevolent, scaly, green monster. On the other hand, let's not forget that some references to the beast had it having a brown color. All of which leads us to Lyle Blackburn's conclusions. To his credit, Blackburn undertook a personal, on-site investigation with his colleague, Cindy Lee, and studied all of the evidence in unbiased fashion. Blackburn noted that, despite the undeniably memorable name, the various descriptions of the beast as being brown in color simply did not accord with anything of a reptilian nature.

Blackburn suggests that if a Bigfoot dwelled in watery bottomlands, where it might become "covered in algae-rich mud or moss, this could explain its green, wet-like appearance. It doesn't explain the three fingers, but greenish mud which has dried and cracked could certainly give a scaly appearance."

Certainly, it's a good theory, and far more likely than a huge, bipedal lizard roaming around the swamps of South Carolina.

Longstanding rumors suggest that a vast, underground alien base exists within,

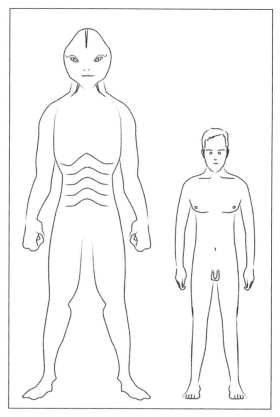

Based on reports, the reptilians appear to be humanoid and larger than the average human, as this artist's concept shows.

and below, a massive mesa at Dulce, Rio Arriba County, New Mexico. Interestingly, we can prove that a wealth of weird activity has occurred in the area. For example, the FBI has officially declassified a large file on cattle mutilations in and around Dulce spanning the mid- to late 1970s. Also, on December 10, 1967, the Atomic Energy Commission (AEC) detonated a 29-kiloton-yield nuclear device 4,240 feet below ground level in an attempt to provoke the release and, as a direct consequence, production of natural gas. Thus was born Project Gasbuggy: a program of an overall project known as Operation Plowshare, which, ostensibly, was designed to explore the peaceful uses of atomic energy. Notably, the location of the Gasbuggy test—which covered an area of 640 acres—was New Mexico's Carson National Forest, which just happens to be situated only twelve miles from the town of Dulce. Today, people are forbidden from digging underground in that very area—which is very interesting in view of the underground base allegations.

Within conspiracy-based research circles, it has been suggested that the nuclear detonation had a very different goal: namely, to destroy the aforementioned alien base and wipe out the deadly, hostile E.T.s. Certainly, it's a strange and foreboding story, and accounts are plentiful suggesting that such a base existed (and may still exist) in which freakish monsters were being created by the alien entities. As one example of many, we have the following from someone we might justifiably call a ufological whistle-blower: Edward Snowden.

Sir, first off, if you want the full story let me know. But this will explain how Mothman came about. U.S. Energy Secretary John Herrington named the Lawrence Berkeley Laboratory and New Mexico's Los Alamos National Laboratory to house advanced genetic research centers as part of a project to decipher the human genome. The genome holds the genetically coded instructions that guide the transformation of a single cell, a fertilized egg, into a biological organism.

"The Human Genome Project may well have the greatest direct impact on humanity of any scientific initiative before us today," said David Shirley, Director of the Berkeley Laboratory. Covertly, this research has been going on for years at the Dulce bio-genetics labs. Level 6 is hauntingly known by employees as "Nightmare Hall." It holds the genetic labs at Dulce. Reports from workers who have seen bizarre experimentation, are as follows:

I have seen multi-legged "humans" that look like half-human/half-octopus. Also reptilian-humans, and furry creatures that have hands like humans and cries like a baby, it mimics human words. Also, huge mixtures of lizard-humans in cages. There are fish, seals, birds and mice that can barely be considered those species. There are several cages (and vats) of winged-humanoids, grotesque bat-like creatures, but 3 1/2 to 7 feet tall. Gargoyle-like beings and Draco-Reptoids.

Level 7 is worse, row after row of thousands of humans and human mixtures in cold storage. Here too are embryo storage vats of humanoids in various stages of development. I frequently encountered humans in cages, usually dazed or drugged, but sometimes they cried and begged for help. We were told they were hopelessly insane, and involved in high risk drug tests to cure insanity. We were told to never try to speak to them at all. At the beginning we believed that story. Finally in 1978 a small group of workers discovered the truth.

All of which brings us to the most controversial claim of all, that which revolves around the British royal family.

Undoubtedly, when it comes to the matter of conspiracy theories—and highly inflammatory conspiracy theories— one controversial claim just about beats all of the rest. It's the assertion that the British royal family are nothing less than deadly, bloodthirsty, shape-shifting monsters. "Bloodthirsty" is a very apt word to use, since the Royals are said to quaff on human blood just about as enthusiastically as the rest of the British population likes to knock back

One wild claim made by a conspiracy theorist is that the British royal family are actually all shape-shifting Reptilians in disguise.

pints of beer in their local pub. They are shapeshifters with incredible power and influence. Here's where controversial becomes beyond controversial.

Welcome to the world of the Reptilians—eight-foot-tall, interdimensional monsters that masquerade as people but who are anything but. At least, that's how the story goes. One person is to thank (if that's the correct term to use!) for bringing this strange and enduring claim to light. His name is David Icke. Once a well-known goalkeeper for Coventry City—an English soccer team—Icke is, today, a leading light in the shadowy domains where the conspiracy-minded and the paranoid hang out. His books include *The Biggest Secret* and *The David Icke Guide to the Global Conspiracy*.

Are the likes of Queen Elizabeth II; her husband, Prince Philip (the Duke of Edinburgh); and the heir to the throne, Prince Charles, really monsters that are either (a) an ancient species that originated right here on Earth or (b) extraterrestrials from a faraway world? Well, start with the first theory. According to those who adhere to this particular theory, the royal family is at the top of the pile when it comes to the matter of who owns the planet.

Forget presidents and prime ministers; the real, secret forces that control and manipulate our world are the Babylonian Brotherhood, an ancient race of dangerous shapeshifters that were responsible for ancient tales of the likes of Quetzalcoatl—whose name means "feathered serpent," who was a significant, deitylike force in Mesoamerica, and who first surfaced around 100 B.C.E. He is also said to have been an entity that brought the science, farming, and culture of that era and area, although given the apparent hatred that the Reptilians have for us, the likelihood is that Quetzalcoatl's actions were very likely self-serving and were designed to keep people in their place, under his firm and coldhearted control and sway.

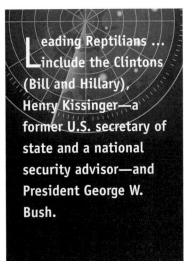

Leading Reptilians ... include the Clintons (Bill and Hillary), Henry Kissinger—a former U.S. secretary of state and a national security advisor—and President George W. Bush.

It's intriguing to note that almost three thousand years ago, the ancient people of Mexico had other serpent-based gods—all of which has helped to nurture the idea that yesterday's Reptilian gods are still among us and are just about as widespread as they were way back when. Today, however, their influence is not just in Mesoamerica but all across the world, even in the domain of politics, too. That's right; it's not just the British royal family who the conspiracy-minded believe are monsters.

Leading Reptilians (so the likes of David Icke assure and warn us) include the Clintons (Bill and Hillary), Henry Kissinger—a former U.S. secretary of state and a national security advisor—and President George W. Bush. Oh, and lest we forget, the late Hollywood legend Bob Hope, too. Yes, really ... or not.

One of those who helped to bring this matter to the attention of the conspiracy-obsessed—and, in quick time, to both the media and popular culture, too—was a California woman named Arizona Wilder. She claims to have been mind-controlled and manipulated by the likes of the world's most infamous secret society, the dreaded and feared Illuminati. Wilder's claims get even, ahem, wilder. She maintained that she has witnessed diabolical human sacrifice at the hands of the Rockefellers, the Rothchilds, members of the Bush family, and at least one pope. As for Queen Elizabeth II, well....

Certainly, Arizona Wilder's most graphic and controversy-filled claim is that she witnessed the queen partake in such sacrifices and saw her eat the flesh, and drink the blood, of her unfortunate human victims. On one occasion, says Wilder, Queen Elizabeth was so fired up that she practically tore out a poor soul's throat, drinking it down as it spewed forth. According to Wilder, in her Reptilian form, the queen has skin that is a pale, sickly color. Her face, meanwhile, changes into something that closely resembles a beak.

Adding even more to this story is Wilder's claim that, back in 1981, she met with then-Lady Diana, very soon to become Diana, Princess of Wales. According to Wilder, the princess was forced to take part in a ritual of ancient and secret proportions that involved the queen, Prince Philip, Prince Charles, and his lover and now wife, Camilla Parker-Bowles. Placed into a drugged-out state, Diana was told that one reason, and one reason only, existed for the marriage: to ensure that the Royal/Reptilian bloodline continued. When Diana was tragically killed in Paris, France, in 1997—admittedly an incident still shrouded in mystery and intrigue years later—Icke weaved her untimely death into his Reptilian scenario.

Conspiracy theorists who fully believed the Reptilian scenario practically foamed at the mouth when Mohamed Al-Fayed—the father of Dodi Fayed, who was Diana's boyfriend at the time of her death and who died with her in the terrible car crash that took three lives—referred to Camilla Parker-Bowles as Prince Charles's "crocodile wife." Then, when Fayed labeled the entire royal family as the "Dracula Family," it only added to the idea that the Royals were copious drinkers of human blood. Was Dodi Fayed— in a slightly less-than-subtle fashion—trying to warn people of the growing Reptilian threat in the midst of just about everyone?

Mohammed Al-Fayed once called Camilla, Duchess of Cambridge (Prince Charles's wife), a "crocodile wife," which sounds like a reference to her being a Reptilian.

Today, the so-called Reptilian agenda terrifies, intrigues, and entertains near-endless numbers of people, and it's a phenomenon that clearly isn't going away any time soon. Are the numerous people who make up the British royal family shape-shifting reptiles with origins that date back millennia? Is the entire issue nothing but the likes of fabrication, lies, pranks, and jokes, or does it hazily lie somewhere in between? It all depends on who you ask—as is the case with practically all conspiracy theories of a highly bizarre nature. However, another aspect to this saga exists—one that focuses on the matter of so-called alien abductions, as we'll now see.

It was on June 24, 1947, that the so-called modern era of ufology began—with pilot Kenneth Arnold's encounter with a squadron of flying saucers over the Cascade Mountains, Washington State. It wasn't chiefly until the early years of the 1950s, however, that people began reporting encounters with alleged alien entities. That was the period in which, all across the United States, reports came pouring in of encounters with what became known as the Space Brothers. They were reported as being incredibly human-looking and sported heads of long, blond hair. Typically, they would warn witnesses of the perils of atomic war and expressed concerns about our violent, warlike ways.

As the 1960s began, reports started to surface of so-called alien abductions—which really took off big-time in the 1970s and continued to be big news in the 1980s and 1990s. It was also in the 1980s that another development occurred in the matter of human–alien interaction, and it all revolved around the aforementioned Reptilians. Not content with ruling the planet—under the shape-shifted guises of world leaders and royalty—the Reptilians have also surfaced prominently in the issue of alien abductions.

Stories told by abductees, in relation to the Reptilian aspect, are as controversial as they are with regard to matters concerning the British royal family, but for very different reasons. Predominantly, but not exclusively, the Reptilians are present during abductions aboard alleged alien spacecraft that involve women. They're not looking for DNA, cells, or our blood, however. It's sex that these appearance-changing stud muffins are after, and apparently, more than a few women have been very satisfied by the experiences. One of them is Pamela Stonebrooke, a writer and jazz music performer/vocalist who makes no bones about the fact that from her perspective, getting nailed aboard a UFO by the closest thing one can imagine to something that appears half human and half crocodile is not a bad thing. Not everyone agrees, however.

Many people who have experienced sex at the hands of the Reptilians are, quite understandably, reluctant to go public with their experiences—at least, not with their full names. One of those is "Audrey," a thirty-eight-year-old woman who claims seven *very* close encounters with male Reptilians between 2001 and 2007. A resident of Sedona, Arizona—a place renowned for a wide range of paranormal phenomena—Audrey was first abducted by what she later recalled, in somewhat of a drugged, hypnotized state, was a group of military personnel in black fatigues late one night on the edge of town.

As she drove home after visiting a friend in Flagstaff, Audrey caught sight of a black van following her, which loomed out of the shadows and ran her off the road. The next thing she remembered was being manhandled into that same van. After that, it was lights out. She later woke up to find herself strapped down to a table in a brightly lit, circular room. In front of her were three men in those same fatigues. For a while, at least. As Audrey craned to sit up, she watched in terror as all three men suddenly shimmered as if caught in something akin to a heat haze. In no more than around six or seven seconds, they were replaced by a trio of approximately eight-foot-tall, green-colored monsters that looked like Godzilla's younger and smaller brothers.

They're not looking for DNA, cells, or our blood, however. It's sex that these appearance-changing stud muffins are after....

Audrey states that the aliens moved toward the table, unstrapped her, and, one by one, had sex with her. She was somewhat embarrassed to admit that the encounter was exciting, if fraught. She was, however, unable to shake off the taboo of what she described as having sex with animals, if that's what they really were. According to Audrey, all of the other experiences occurred in her own home—again, late at night—and sex was the only thing that happened of note.

Perhaps the most disturbing encounter was the fourth one, in which two men dressed in black suits, white shirts, and red ties, with near-identical, slicked-back hair, materialized in her bedroom as she lay in bed, listening to music on her iPod. As with the previous encounter, the men transformed into what looked like, as she described it, giant lizards. Once again, Audrey had a swinging time—but was again eaten up by guilt, as she was on each and every subsequent occasion.

All of this, however, had one unforeseen side effect: namely that for around almost a year after the final encounter occurred, whenever a man would look or stare at her, Audrey would have shivers go up and down her spine. She was fearful of the possibility that they, too, were shapeshifters that could take on human form but whose real form was that of a dangerous Reptilian. If a man looked at her for more than a second or two in a bar or restaurant, she would get the chills. If, while walking around Sedona, a man gave her a friendly nod, it meant he was a Reptilian. Realizing that she was plunging into a state of near-mental illness, Audrey eventually pulled herself back from the brink of complete and utter paranoia and moved on with her life, as did, apparently, the Reptilians.

Might Reptilians be more than frightening monsters? Might they, in disguise, be running the planet?

It should be noted that numerous such reports are on record—or, on far more occasions, off the record—that display uncannily similar aspects. This has led even some quite conservative alien abduction researchers to take the matter of shape-shifting sex very seriously. One final thing is worth pondering on: if these stories are not the result of wild fantasies and erotic dreams, then perhaps an alien, Reptilian agenda really is on our planet. It's one thing to talk about scaly E.T.s with forked tongues and even thrashing tails who use women for sex; it's quite another, however, to suggest they're running the entire planet. Unless, of course, you have encountered the Reptilians yourself. Sometimes, truth really is stranger than fiction, but on this particular issue, exactly how strange is still a matter of furious debate.

We'll close the matter of the Reptilians with the words of Pamela Stonebrooke, who prepared the following for free, public consumption, which reveals her connection to the Reptilian phenomenon in all of its stark reality. Prepared by Stonebrooke in 1998, it states:

> I'm writing this in response to the news item that appeared in a recent issue of the *New York Post* about my forthcoming book, *Experiencer: A Jazz Singer's True Account of Extraterrestrial Contact*. Since the article unfortunately conveyed the impression that the book would be sensationalistic, it seems appropriate that I share some thoughts with you, and set the record straight about the book I am writing. I know that the *New York Post* piece seriously misrepresented the true nature of the book.
>
> The book is multi-faceted, and treats the abduction phenomenon, in all of its complexity, with the sensitivity, respect and seriousness it deserves, presenting not only my own experiences, but those of other experiencers as well. I'll be examining and exploring my contact experiences in light of their transformative aspects, recognizing that the phenomenon is, and can be, an incredible catalyst for expanded self-awareness. Interaction with extraterrestrial intelligence has many aspects, of course, but the transformational aspect is fundamental to me.

The book will tell about my reptilian encounters, a subject that very few women are prepared to go public with or speak openly about. I praise the courage of the few that already have—and endured public ridicule as a result. Reptilians are not a politically correct species in the UFO community, and to admit to having sex with one—much less enjoying it—is beyond the pale as far as the more conservative members of that community are concerned. But I know from my extensive reading and research, and from talking personally to dozens of other women (and men) that I am not unique in reporting this kind of experience. I am the first to admit that this is a vastly complex subject, a kind of hall of mirrors, where dimensional realities are constantly shifting and changing. Certainly, the reptilians use sex to control people in various ways. They have the ability to shape-shift and to control the mind of the experiencer, as well as to give tremendous pleasure through their mental powers. I have wrestled with all of these implications and the various levels of meaning and possibilities represented by my encounter experiences. I will say, however, as I have said before, that I feel a deep respect for the reptilian entity with whom I interacted, and a profound connection with this being.

In a past life regression I did recently, I went to a very remote period in earth's history (perhaps hundreds of thousands of years ago), and saw myself as one of a brotherhood of reptilian warriors facing a catastrophic event in which we perished together (it was possibly nuclear in nature, since I saw a red cloud and felt tremendous heat). I believe that on one level, I may be meeting these entities again, perhaps fellow warriors from the past warning us of an impending, self-inflicted doom—or perhaps they are different aspects of myself. I don't really know; I'm just trying to unravel this puzzle like everyone else.

Following my initial Art Bell interview, I received hundreds of letters and e-mails, many from people describing similar encounters to mine. I know that there are people out there who are suffering in isolation and silence, thinking they are going crazy. I have been able to give some of these people strength and courage, so that they can move through their fear and come out the other side, empowered and still able to celebrate life as the incredible adventure that it truly is. I know that when I was processing my Grey experiences, if it had not been for people like John Mack, Budd Hopkins, Kim Carlsberg, Whitley Strieber, John Carpenter, and other researchers and experiencers who have been courageous enough to come forward, putting their lives and reputations on the line, I would have stayed in fear a lot longer, cowering in a corner, my self-esteem and identity shattered. Thanks to them and to the wonderful members of my support group, I am still standing, intact and whole.

I believe that the alien abduction experience is profoundly linked to the momentous shift in consciousness that is occurring as we enter the new millennium. We are witnesses to and participants in the most fantastic era in human history. And contrary to the mood of pessimism from some individuals regarding the way mainstream media treats the UFO phenomenon, and the trepidation that is felt regarding its ultimate impact on the human race, I am unashamedly a "Positive." Everywhere I turn, I find much greater public acceptance of the alien abduction/UFO phenomenon, and active curiosity from enormous numbers of people. I am also encouraged by the fact that many more experiencers are coming forward, no longer hiding behind the cloak of anonymity. I believe that within ten years the reality of alien abduction will be accepted as a fact by the majority of people on this planet, and ridicule of the subject by the media or anyone else will be regarded as naive and irresponsible.

I think the problem that exists between UFOlogy and the media stems from the fact that the UFO community has been so sadly wounded in the past fifty years by rejection and ridicule that it has been somewhat demoralized as a movement. It has been a long, uphill battle, with many martyrs shedding their blood along the way, but I believe that we are winning the battle for public acceptance and are closer than ever before to solving the mystery of the alien presence itself. I am looking forward to appearing on major TV talk-shows, and to bringing the message directly to the public about this phenomenon. This is a subject that must—and will—be taken seriously, even, eventually, by the likes of Leno and Letterman. I was amazed, I might add, by the number of editors in the New York publishing community who are "believers," and I predict that within the next few years, UFO and abduction books will routinely top the bestseller lists as the public hungers to learn more about what our encounters mean, and their implications for the human race.

If my book is successful, everyone in the UFO community will benefit. The floodgates are about to open, and when they do, all experiencers, UFO investigators, writers and researchers will find wider acceptance for their work. The days and years ahead are going to be full of challenges and opportunities, but we need to change ourselves in order to change the world. We need to work together harmoniously with mutual understanding and respect.

I want to thank everyone who is willing to cut me some slack with regard to the article in the *New York Post*. I'm sure it won't be the last test of my strength or your discernment. Please keep those stones in hand until you read my book. I am confident that if and when you do, you will be able to recommend it to experiencers and non-experiencers alike. I would also like to thank everyone in the UFO community who has assisted me on my journey to awareness these past five years.

So far, Stonebrooke's book has not surfaced. Hopefully, one day, it will, and we will have a greater understanding of the Reptilian phenomenon.

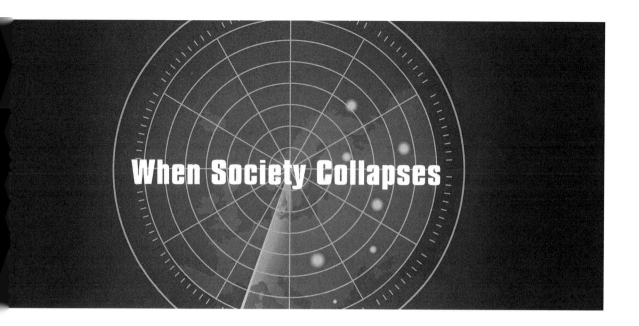

When Society Collapses

The title of this chapter is an undeniably controversial one. Could it be true that we are being denied the shocking truth concerning something that may plunge the entire world into complete chaos? Are our presidents, prime ministers, and kings and queens secretly aware that in just a few decades from now, all of the oil will be gone? Fresh water might go the very same way. After all, when water and oil go, so does an orderly society. In its place, a world filled with chaos, anarchy, and disaster would quickly develop. Can it be true? Is the collapse of civilization just around the corner? Are we being denied the terrible facts? Let's see.

One of the biggest problems that faces us in a world without oil is that the human population is growing at an incredible rate. No one doubts that issues need to be dealt with when it comes to the matter of overpopulation. It is, indeed, a very serious issue—one that is an undeniable threat to our future as a species. Only so much space, and so many resources, exist that one day, we will reach the point at which the Earth can no longer adequately sustain the human population. When—rather than if—that day comes, we will very likely see worldwide chaos and anarchy as the starving, desperate millions raid stores, peoples' homes, and do just about anything and everything they can do to stay alive, so yes, a problem exists; it's a huge problem but one that a lot of people don't even give much thought to. However, the Controllers certainly do give the subject a great deal of thought. They have done so for many years, and they continue to do so. Their focus is on finding a way to provoke a sudden, massive cut in the numbers. In bleak terms, they are primed and ready to cull what they term as the herd.

If you think all of this amounts to nothing but fear-mongering conspiracy fodder, you would be wrong—very wrong. Undoubtedly, our future might be extremely bleak after the world's population has doubled. The mainstream is now quickly picking up on this global problem and warning of what might soon be around the corner. The United Kingdom's *Guardian* newspaper has highlighted the issues that face us and cannot be ignored. The *Guardian* stated in 2012: "Fresh water is crucial to human society—not just for drinking, but also for farming, washing and many other activities. It is expected to become increasingly scarce in the future, and this is partly due to climate change."

The *Guardian* continued and revealed something very disturbing: namely, that when it comes to the matter of so-called regional groundwater, little is understood about how extensive—and expansive—those reserves of freshwater are or, in a worst-case scenario, are *not*. This is particularly worrying because around half of all the water used by the human race on a daily basis comes from regional groundwater. If those reserves dry up—and dry up much faster than anticipated—then civilization could easily and quickly collapse upon itself. Water is the one thing we cannot live without. No water means deaths on an unimaginable level—aside, of course, for those who may be

Recently, fresh water shortages have caused the city of Cape Town, South Africa, to ration supplies for its citizens. Growing populations and climate change are making water a serious factor for the future of humanity.

preparing for that day. The Controllers, of course. They may be dicing with death, too, by hoping that a global catastrophe will allow them to change the course of the human race—a radically shrunken human race.

Echoing the words of the *Guardian* newspaper is Melanie McDonagh, a journalist with the *Spectator*. Her conclusions are grim, concerning, and extremely thought-provoking. McDonagh focused her attention on the work of Anne and Paul Ehrlich. Their research into this field of worldwide disintegration led to the release of a 2013 article, which was published by the Royal Society. The title of the article was presented as a question. It was, and still is, an important and potentially life-changing question: "Can a Collapse of Global Civilization Be Avoided?"

One would hope that such a thing can be avoided, but things are not looking too good for us. The Ehrlichs pointed out that not only are we faced with massive overpopulation issues, but we are getting through precious commodities at an incredible and disturbing rate, and in doing so, we are changing the environment. Yes, global warming is a reality, regardless of what some might say otherwise. In simple terms, we may well be screwed or, as Prince Charles—the heir to the British Monarchy—put it, we are recklessly engaging in what amounts to "an act of suicide on a grand scale."

This is doubtless. Right now, the human population is current at around seven and a half billion. If things don't change by 2050, say Anne and Paul Ehrlich, that figure will have reached around nine and a half billion. That will mean two billion more people than now will be digging ever deeper into a limited supply of essentials, such as water, oil, land, and food. The conclusion of the pair is that the only outcome—as they see things right now, at least—will be complete collapse, all across the world.

To demonstrate just how incredibly the number of people on the planet is growing, take note of the following: It was in the very earliest years of the nineteenth century that the world's population finally reached one billion. It was not until around 1930 that the population was doubled to two billion. By the dawning of the sixties, three billion of us were on Earth, four billion by the midseventies, and five billion by the late eighties. As the twenty-first century began, the number was six billion. In 2013, we hit seven billion. You may not like—or even be prepared for—what is to come next. Current estimates are that 2024 will roughly be when the Earth finds itself buckling under the weight of eight billion people. By 2040, we'll be at nine. Get the picture? It's one that everyone should be concerned about.

It's very hard to say whether or not we can do anything about this. If draconian laws were put into place that limited families—in every country on the planet—to just one child, even that would not have an appreciable effect on population levels for years, and what if people chose to have more than one child? Are millions of pregnant women going to be thrown into jail or be forced to have abortions? Another issue is also at play: fuel. Specifically, oil.

One year after the Ehrlichs' report was published, *USA Today* revealed something that everyone should be concerned about—not so much for us but certainly for our children and grandchildren: namely, that fossil fuels, such as oil, may run out by the 2060s—and by run out, we are not talking about having to ration oil and gas. We're talking about no more oil. No more gasoline. Ever. Goodbye to the world we know it.

Gas 2, who have been at the forefront of demonstrating why "green cars" are so important to our future survival, provide the following words on those estimates for what may occur in the 2060s: "These estimates are actually 1.1% more than last year, thanks in part to growing estimates of American shale oil. Of course keep in mind that the oil industry is regularly growing or shrinking estimated energy reserves, with California's Monterey Shale having its reserves downgraded some 96%. There's also suspicion that countries like Saudi Arabia are outright lying about how much crude they actually have left. So yeah. Skepticism."

Current estimates are that 2024 will roughly be when the Earth finds itself buckling under the weight of eight billion people.

Gas 2 suggests that when the-you-know-what hits the proverbial fan in full-on fashion, some nations around will be "caught flat-footed." That is putting matters mildly, to say the very least. Undoubtedly, massive drops in the water supply will be bad enough. Add to that no fuel—just abandoned cars, trucks, and bikes on highways that no one else uses because they *can't* use them—and what you have is something far beyond "flat-footed." A global emergency of unprecedented proportions will occur: people will turn on one another, looting homes and killing neighbors, all for just a few pints of water and a tank of gas. You think it couldn't happen? When matters are really down to the wire and personal survival is the name of the game, people will do just about anything and everything to stay alive. The end of civilization could come with rapid, astonishing speed.

Now we come to the heart of the cover-up—as conspiracy theorists see it, at least.

A great deal has been said—much of it extremely controversial—regarding the High Frequency Active Auroral Research Program, which is better known as HAARP and that, before it was shut down in 2014, was based on U.S. Air Force land close to Gakona, Alaska. The official line of the U.S. Navy's Office of Naval Research and the Naval Research Laboratory—in combination with the Defense Advanced Research Projects Agency (DARPA)—is that HAARP's role was to "analyze the ionosphere and investigate the potential for developing ionospheric enhancement technology for radio communications and surveillance purposes." Is that really it, though? If not, how did the program tie in with the issue of mass control? Let's see. The public face of HAARP appears to be very different from the behind-closed-doors face.

Undoubtedly, a significant portion of HAARP's work did indeed revolve around researching the ionosphere—chiefly in relation to issues relative to coming up with more and more advanced ways to enhance communication—and surveillance, too. HAARP was also responsible for undertaking new ways of monitoring changes in the weather and keeping a close check on the ozone layer in terms of determining if and when any fluctuations occur in it. Of course, all of this work was highly valuable in terms of scientific and technological advancement, but are we being told the full story? Many conspiracy theorists suggest that no, we are not being given the complete picture; HAARP just might have had another agenda: a covert agenda.

Antenna arrays like this one were used by HAARP to research the ionosphere around our planet, as well as to monitor changes in weather patterns.

Researchers of the controversy suggest that because the HAARP program was so inextricably tied to the military, there must be more to the program than initially meets the eye. Certainly, the Navy played a major role in the entire HAARP issue. This makes a great deal of sense, particularly with regard to the aforementioned issue of communication. The ionosphere begins thirty-plus miles above the Earth's surface, and it's a fact that if and when anomalies occur in the ionosphere, they can indeed significantly provoke issues in terms of communication—lost signals and disturbances to communications are typical, hence the reason why HAARP played a leading role in the goal to fully understand the nature of the ionosphere.

Undoubtedly, the idea that HAARP had a nefarious agenda—as well as its regular mandate—is one that the employees of the program were fully cognizable of. In the face of countless allegations of conspiracy and cover-up, HAARP staff issued the following statement, which was designed to lay matters to rest. Of course, it didn't achieve its goal at all, with many conspiracy theorists believing that it amounted to nothing but an attempt to deflect interest away from the HAARP facility. Nevertheless, let's see what HAARP's personnel had to say, despite what many claimed were nothing but lies: "Inter-

Haiti was devastated by an earthquake in 2010, and some people believe that it was a disaster instigated by the HAARP project.

est in ionosphere research at HAARP stems both from the large number of communication, surveillance and navigation systems that have radio paths which pass through the ionosphere, and from the unexplored potential of technological innovations which suggest applications such as detecting underground objects, communicating to great depths in the sea or the earth, and generating infrared and optical emissions."

Those who doubt that this was all that HAARP was engaged in point fingers in the direction of what has become known as "weather control." Why would those on the HAARP program want to have had the ability to manipulate the weather, though? What would have been the goal? Let's take a look.

We'll begin with an event that occurred on January 12, 2010. That was the date on which Haiti—a country that is situated on the Caribbean island of Hispaniola—was pummeled to a disastrous degree by a landscape-changing earthquake. More than a quarter of a million people would lose their lives before it was all over. It was a terrible tragedy—but was that all it was? Could more have been to it than just the work of Mother Nature? One of the first groups to suggest that HAARP had played a decisive role in the Haitian earthquake was Ahrcanum, whose work is dedicated to the study of some of the more inflammatory conspiracy theories in our midst. Their research on the HAARP–earthquake angle pretty much ensured that a great deal of interest and commentary would quickly follow. It did. The conspiracy was a complex one, to be sure.

It was suggested that Haiti had been deliberately targeted by HAARP essentially for a highly nefarious reason. Conspiracy theorists quickly pointed to the fact that in the immediate aftermath of the terrible disaster, the U.S. military descended upon Haiti ostensibly to provide as much help as possible; we're talking about supplies of food, clean water, and much-needed medical supplies and emergency personnel. Nothing was wrong with that at all. Not everyone, though, saw things quite like that. At the Ahrcanum website, an intricate conspiracy theory was developing—and it was developing quickly, too. Those who were following the thread commented that perhaps the earthquake was deliberately engineered to provide the American military with a reason to create a massive U.S. presence on the island of Hispaniola, but why would HAARP—or those behind the scenes giving out the orders—want to, as Ahrcanum believed, take control of Haiti? The answer to that question revolves around what is arguably the world's most precious commodity next to water: oil. It's something we simply cannot do without.

It's a little-known fact that Haiti has an abundance of oil. In fact, "abundance" is putting things mildly in the extreme. The island is absolutely teeming with oil, near-endless oil. Presently, the figure is around three million barrels of what is termed offshore oil. In fact, the Greater Antilles—which cover not just Haiti but also Jamaica, the Cayman Islands, Cuba, and Puerto Rico—is estimated to be the "home" of around 140 million barrels of oil and 160 billion cubic feet of gas. They are figures accurately determined back in 2000 by the U.S. Geological Survey (USGS). Today, some believe that those figures may actually be even higher: almost a million barrels of oil and a trillion cubic feet of gas. Clearly, this is an incredible amount of two of the most important things almost no one can do without.

What did any of this have to do with HAARP, though? Well, as startling as it may sound, as well as having the ability to monitor the ionosphere, HAARP's technology allowed its employees to monitor the Earth's subsurface, too, particularly its mineral content. In essence, HAARP had the ability to seek out those places on the planet that have massive quantities of oil—specifically those reserves located underground and/or under the oceans. Conspiracy theorists quickly pointed to the fact that both Afghanistan and Iraq have massive oil reserves—and both were invaded in the early 2000s and, essentially, annexed in the process. Was the same done to Haiti? Those same theorists say "Yes."

Of course, when it came to Iraq and Afghanistan, the U.S. government did see justification for invading both countries, but what do you do when you are faced with a nation that has gigantic oil reserves but that poses no military threat at all? We're talking about Haiti. The conspiracy grew and grew with suspicions that HAARP technology had been deliberately targeted at Haiti to provoke the quake and then, in the immediate aftermath of the event, offer what appeared to be a helping hand but which, in reality, amounted to a plan to grab Haiti's oil if and when supplies dwindle elsewhere in the world to drastic degrees. The idea that just a scenario might come to fruition is not at all out of the question.

Many people worry that the oil reserves are declining more quickly than most people realize or could even guess. Sadad al-Husseini, a geologist who served as the head of the Saudis' Aramco company, believes that the oil supplies will peak in the near future but that after that, they will shrink—and in a fast, catastrophic fashion. This is not a mere conspiracy theory. For example, the bleak scenario ahead of us was laid out in a February 2005 U.S. Department of Energy document. Its title: "Peaking of World Oil Production: Impacts, Mitigation, and Risk Management." The most eye-opening—and worrying—section of the document states: "The peaking of world oil production presents the U.S. and the world with an unprecedented risk management problem. As peaking is approached, liquid fuel prices and price volatility will increase dramatically, and, without timely mitigation, the economic, social, and political costs will be unprecedented."

Now let's move on to the issue of HAARP and Japan.

> Conspiracy theorists quickly pointed to the fact that both Afghanistan and Iraq have massive oil reserves—and both were invaded in the early 2000s....

Few people will forget the catastrophic disaster that hit Japan in near-apocalyptic form in March 2011. It was on the eleventh of the month that a huge earthquake, which led to the creation of a veritable tsunami with churning, racing waters rising in excess of one hundred feet, caused significant damage to the Fukushima 1 and Fukushima 2 nuclear power plants. More than twelve thousand people lost their lives as a result of the calamity. Following the disaster, around twenty thousand American troops, an armada of U.S. Navy ships, and in excess of one hundred military planes all descended upon the area under what was termed Operation Tomodachi—a word meaning "friend" in Japanese.

In the same way that conspiracy theories surfaced suggesting that the Haitian disaster had been secretly orchestrated by HAARP, so such theories were applied to Japan, too. Once again, the specter of oil soon raised its head. Studies undertaken in the first decade of the twenty-first century showed that Japan had around three hundred million barrels of oil. Its reserves were even more: around 120 million barrels.

It's worth noting, too, what the *New York Times* had to say about Japan's huge amount of oil way back in 1922. On February 21 of that year, in an article titled "Experts Say Japan Has 300 Years' Oil," it was reported: "Considering her actual requirements, it appears that Japan is more fortunate than most nations in the possession of oil reserves in the future. Japan possesses much more oil than her propagandists have tried to make the world believe she has."

While the HAARP–oil conspiracy theory is simply that—a theory—the fact is that the oil is indeed on a notable decline. Of the twenty richest oil fields on the planet, nine of them are already declining. That's around 50 percent—and it won't get better. In fact, matters are destined to get only worse.

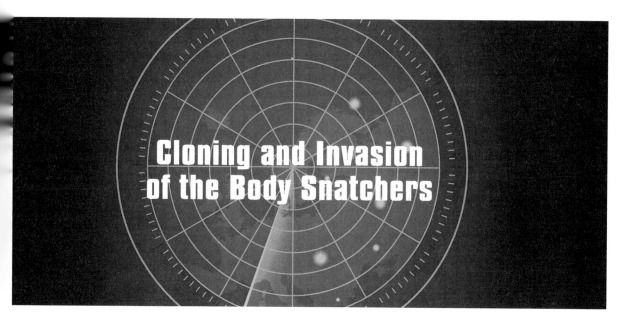

Cloning and Invasion of the Body Snatchers

In 1954, a sci-fi novel titled *The Body Snatchers*, written by Jack Finney, appeared in serial form in *Colliers Magazine*. In the following year, 1955, it surfaced in full-length book form. Then, in 1956, it was made into a classic and excellent piece of big-screen paranoia: *Invasion of the Body Snatchers*, starring Kevin McCarthy. A pretty good remake appeared in 1978, with Donald Sutherland taking the lead role. A not-bad version—*Body Snatchers*—hit the cinemas in 1993, and a downright awful version was unleashed in 2007: *The Invasion*.

Most people know the general plot of the story, even if they haven't seen the film: the Earth is being invaded by hostile extraterrestrial entities. However, the takeover of the planet doesn't occur in a laser-guns-blazing, *Independence Day*-style assault. Indeed, not even a single UFO is in sight—just a bunch of curious-looking flowers that are springing up all over the place. Things quickly progress, albeit not in a good fashion. People are quietly, systematically, and one by one being replaced by identical clones of themselves, which are grown in giant-sized pods. The clones, however, are cold, emotionless monsters, and when they spring to life, the person whose appearance they have adopted dies.

Why am I mentioning all this? Well, as incredible as it may sound, some of the more extreme fields of conspiracy theorizing believe that we are being replaced.

Back in the mid to late 1990s, several British-based UFO investigators (from the now defunct newsstand publications of that era, *UFO Magazine* and *UFO Reality*) were given the details of a bizarre story that, they were assured by their Deep Throat-like sources, was absolutely true. The tale went that late one night, at some point around 1991 or 1992, a number of animal rights activists broke into Porton Down, Wiltshire, England—one of the most secretive installations in the United Kingdom, whose work focuses to a very significant degree on matters of a chemical and biological nature. If a real-life zombie apocalypse ever erupts, no one should be surprised if it begins at Porton Down.

When the activists were actively searching for all the many and varied animals they were intent on freeing—mice, rats, monkeys, and so on—they entered a room filled with dozens of approximately eight-foot-long containers, all carefully positioned on sturdy tables and all containing seemingly lifeless, or sleeping, duplicates of famous, then-current British politicians. The terrified activists fled Porton Down, never to return. Of course, the outlandish tale has never been verified, and as for the activists, not a single one has gone on the record.

It must be said, too, that stories of people going into the "wrong room" and coming across something terrifying are commonplace within Forteana. I very well remember being told a highly disturbing story—probably around

A view of a field at Porton Down, a secret English Military of Defense facility where research has been conducted. Research into what is anyone's guess.

1995 or 1996—of someone who took a wrong turn in a British hospital years earlier and entered a room filled with dozens of people—from babies to adults—all exhibiting hideous and impossible deformities. Again, no proof, or a name, was ever forthcoming.

In the late 1970s and throughout the 1980s, "crashed UFO" researcher Leonard Stringfield was given dozens of accounts of military personnel going down the wrong corridor, opening the wrong door, and seeing alien bodies, cryogenically preserved in missile-like containers. They were warned to never, ever reveal what they had seen. Clearly, then (to me, at least), the Porton Down story is simply a piece of entertaining folklore of very similar proportions.

On the matter of politicians being replaced, one of the most hilarious things I ever heard was that you can easily tell which ones are clones. Want to know the secret? Well, here it is: When a politician gets elected, if he or she breaks the promises they made before they were elected, that's a definite signal that they have been replaced. No, it's not, actually. Politicians make and break promises for one single reason: they're politicians! That's what they do, and the voters fall for it time and again. No need to invoke weird tales of duplicates, whether originating in outer space or from the dark depths of a secret, government lab.

Is it possible that something along the lines of *Invasion of the Body Snatchers* could really happen? Well, as strange as it might sound, a technology really does exist that could, in effect, allow for duplicates of us to be created. It's called cloning—and, as it develops, it's a subject that is going down dangerously controversial avenues. It's possible that, one day, the tried-and-tested fashion for having a baby—a fashion that has worked very well for millions of years—will be no more. Incredibly, could it be the case that our children will be "designed" and even "grown"? Might we be able to create clones of ourselves?

On January 8, 2017, the *Guardian* newspaper revealed what it had learned on the latest news in the fields of designing babies: "Novelist Kazuo Ishiguro, whose 2005 novel, *Never Let Me Go*, described children produced and reared as organ donors, last month warned that thanks to advances in gene editing, 'we're coming close to the point where we can, objectively in some sense, create people who are superior to others.'"

The *Guardian* asserted that even if such a situation does occur, then the likelihood is that it will not lead to the "engineering" of the populace but, instead, it will be a means to have people sign up for the programs—thereby increasing profits of the respective companies involved rather than radically changing society. The *Guardian* urges restraint on all fronts when it comes to this specifically controversial area of research. Nevertheless, not everyone is convinced that we will find ourselves heading down a road to a definitive

A Stanford University professor of law, Henry Greely specializes in social, ethical, and legal issues involving genetics, stem cell research, and neuroscience. As a bioethicist, he has lectured on the dangers of creating a "superman."

nightmare. For example, a bioethicist named Henry Greely is of the opinion that the idea of creating a "superman," or what he terms a "split in the species," is unlikely. More correctly, he doesn't see such a situation coming to fruition soon, mainly because "we don't know enough" or, rather, we don't know enough yet—but, perhaps, one day, we will know.

Certainly, the *Guardian*'s term "modified babies" should be enough to ensure that we never go down a path that sees us becoming something less than we are—something that can be controlled and regulated. Of course, everyone should encourage medical advances, but turning significant portions of the human population into subservient, unquestioning slaves is hardly what the vast majority of people would term a positive prospect.

Nevertheless, the *Guardian* does admit that "every new advance puts a fresh spark of life into Huxley's monstrous vision." Certainly, the warnings and concerns of Kazuo Ishiguro are all too real. Undoubtedly, many of Ishiguro's deep concerns were prompted by what is known as CRISPR-CAS9. It's a process that falls under the admittedly sinister-sounding title of "gene editing." It was a process that came into being in 2012. Yes, it was created to, essentially, find ways to eradicate so-called "mutant genes" that can wreak havoc in the human body and lead to severe illness and death. In that sense, the process is a positive one. On the other hand, however, and as is always the case in such situations, the possibility of crossing the line and abusing the science and technology involved cannot be ruled out. What we are faced with, then, is a definitive double-edged sword, which offers a future free of disease, but if misused, the technology may take us down a path in which only nightmares can be found.

The fact that we may already be heading down that dark path is not just a theory. For example, since 2012, CRISPR-CAS9 has been used in China to, ahem, "modify" human embryos. So far, the results of such tinkering and tampering with the natural order has produced nothing but mixed results. The United Kingdom is getting onboard with CRISPR-CAS9, too: the United Kingdom's Francis Crick Institute has been issued a license to allow it to use CRISPR-CAS9 on two- to three-day-old human embryos chiefly to try to understand some of the reasons why miscarriages occur during pregnancy.

The biggest problem with all this is not just the fact that the technology exists and is ripe for manipulation of a sinister kind. No; the major issue revolves around the fact that throughout the world, hard and definitive legislation does not exist to prevent scientists from going down the roads they have no business going down. Since it's an area that is filled with definitive unknowns, it's equally unknown how exactly we should proceed. Of course, that is all understandable, but it's also an issue that needs far more research—specifically to ensure that one hundred years from now, we are not all under the control of crazed scientists whose mandate is to create a superior class of people and an inferior one. The rise of a real master race? Don't bet against it. Even the *Guardian*, which sees the positive aspects of the technology, admits that unchecked developments might push us down "a path towards non-therapeutic genetic enhancement."

Let's see what other media outlets have to say about all of this.

In January 2015, the BBC immersed itself in the domain of "designer babies." It warned that experts in the field of advanced genetics were coming to a stark realization that society needs to "be prepared" for what the future may bring. One of those was Dr. Tony Perry, one of the foremost people in the field of cloning. When he stated that we're no longer talking about "H. G. Wells territory," he meant that science fiction was rapidly becoming science fact. It's hardly surprising that cries to curb certain programs, until the implications of such research could be fully ascertained, were heard just about here, there, and everywhere.

Dr. Perry most definitely knows what he is talking about. He was, for example, one of the very first people to successfully clone other animals, such as pigs and mice. Writing in the publication *Scientific Reports*, said the BBC, Dr. Perry "details precisely editing the genome of mice at the point DNA from the sperm and egg come together."

He further explained: "We used a pair of molecular scissors and a molecular sat-nav that tells the scissors where to cut. It is approaching 100% efficiency already, it's a case of 'you shoot you score.'"

Two years later, in 2017, *The Blaze* turned its attention to these controversies,

Nazi leader Adolf Hitler dreamed of creating a superhuman Aryan race to rule over mankind. Is genetic engineering leading us down that same dangerous path?

too. They noted too that a group within the National Academy of Sciences and National Academy of Medicine was "advocating for 'germ-line modification' of human babies in certain narrow circumstances to prevent the birth of children with serious diseases." *The Blaze* got to the crux of the matter in lightning speed, noting that the biggest worries concerned the abuse of technology "for modifying the germ-line—or inherited DNA—of human beings because it could lead to 'designer babies' with pre-selected eye color, physical strength or even intelligence."

One of those who urged caution on the introduction of such science—a form of science that could easily, one day, be turned against us by the Controllers—was Dr. Marcy Darnovsky, whose concerns *The Blaze* noted. A "liberal policy advocate" based out of the Center for Genetics and Society, Dr. Darnovsky said at the dawning of the twenty-first century that a very real possibility existed that such technology could "significantly exacerbate socio-economic inequality." The result may well see only the rich having designer babies—something which would widen the chasm between "the upper and lower classes."

In February 2017, *Industry Leaders* said: "Organizations like 23andMe and GenePeeks, Inc. are receiving backlash from the media and from organizations dealing with reproductive issues."

That backlash came from the aforementioned Dr. Marcy Darnovsky of the Center for Genetics and Society. She was very vocal on this particular issue and said: "It would be highly irresponsible for 23andMe or anyone else to offer a product or service based on this patent. It amounts to shopping for designer donors in an effort to produce designer babies. We believe the patent office made a serious mistake in allowing a patent that includes drop-down menus from which to choose a future child's traits."

Industry Leaders added: "Eventually, 23andMe succumbed to the pressure and wrote off its inheritance calculator service in fertility treatments."

It is not just the scientific and medical communities that are aware of the growing controversies and dangers surrounding designer babies and the manipulation of the human species. The U.S. government's National Human Genome Research Institute has been careful to detail the technology at work as well as what may be around the corner. The NHGRI says of the process of cloning and genetic manipulation that three different types of artificial cloning exist: gene cloning, reproductive cloning, and therapeutic cloning. Gene cloning produces copies of genes or segments of DNA. Reproductive cloning produces copies of whole animals. Therapeutic cloning produces embryonic stem cells for experiments aimed at creating tissues to replace injured or diseased tissues. Gene cloning, also known as DNA cloning, is a very different process from reproductive and therapeutic cloning. Reproductive and therapeutic cloning share many of the same techniques but are done for different purposes.

The National Human Genome Research Institute adds that despite several highly publicized claims, human cloning still appears to be fiction. They are certain—or fairly certain— that no one has cloned human embryos. The NHGRI notes that back in 1998, scientists in South Korea claimed to have successfully cloned a human embryo but said that the experiment was interrupted very early when the clone was just a group of four cells. In 2002, Clonaid, part of a religious group that believes humans were created by extraterrestrials, held a news conference to announce the birth of what it claimed to be the first cloned human, a girl named Eve. However, despite repeated requests by the research community and the news media, Clonaid never provided any evidence to confirm the existence of this clone or the other twelve human clones it purportedly created.

In 2004, states the National Human Genome Research Institute, a group led by Woo-Suk Hwang of Seoul National University in South Korea, published a paper in the journal *Science* in which it claimed to have created a cloned human embryo in a test tube. However, an independent scientific committee later found no proof to support the claim and, in January 2006, *Science* announced that Hwang's paper had been retracted.

From a technical perspective, says the NHGRI, cloning humans and other primates is more difficult than in other mammals. One reason is that two proteins essential to cell division, known as spindle proteins, are located very close to the chromosomes in primate eggs. Consequently, removal of the egg's nucleus to make room for the donor nucleus also removes the spindle proteins, interfering with cell division. In other mammals, such as cats, rabbits, and mice, the two spindle proteins are spread throughout the egg, so removal of the egg's nucleus does not result in loss of spindle proteins. In addition, some dyes and the ultraviolet light used to remove the egg's nucleus can damage the primate cell and prevent it from growing.

Gene cloning is a carefully regulated technique that is largely accepted today and used routinely in many labs worldwide. However, both reproductive and therapeutic cloning raise important ethical issues, especially as related to the potential use of these techniques in humans.

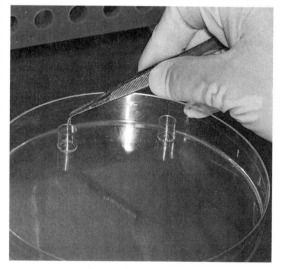

A lab technician works on cloning genes in vitro in this photo. Cloning techniques such as plant cuttings have actually been used for years in agriculture; it's just the techniques that have advanced.

Reproductive cloning would present the potential of creating a human that is genetically identical to another person who has previously existed or who still exists. This may conflict with long-standing religious and societal values about human dignity, possibly infringing upon principles of individual freedom, identity, and autonomy. However, some argue that reproductive cloning could help sterile couples fulfill their dream of parenthood. Others see human cloning as a way to avoid passing on a deleterious gene that runs in the family without having to undergo embryo screening or embryo selection.

Therapeutic cloning, while offering the potential for treating humans suffering from disease or injury, would require the destruction of human embryos in the test tube. Consequently, opponents argue that using this technique to collect embryonic stem cells is wrong, regardless of whether such cells are used to benefit sick or injured people.

The National Human Genome Research Institute is not alone in addressing such matters. Christopher A. Pynes, for example, of Western Illinois University, notes: "The U.K. has a clear prohibition on reproductive human cloning, but works to keep laws current with and relevant to technological advances. The EU supports funding for embryonic stem cell research, but has banned human cloning. The USA has a complex mix of state and federal regulations and interlocutors often conflate the cloning issues with the abortion debate, which gives rise to strong objections to both types of cloning and to stem cell research."

The staff members of the NCSL—the United States' National Conference of State Legislatures—state: "Fifteen states have laws pertaining to human cloning. The issue was first addressed by California legislature, which banned reproductive cloning, or cloning to initiate a pregnancy, in 1997. Since then Arkansas, Connecticut, Indiana, Iowa, Maryland, Massachusetts, Michigan, Rhode Island, New Jersey, North Dakota, South Dakota, and Virginia have enacted measures to prohibit reproductive cloning."

The NCSL also notes that Arizona and Missouri have measures that address the use of public funds for cloning, and Maryland prohibits the use of state stem cell research funds for reproductive cloning and possibly therapeutic cloning, depending on how one interprets the definition of human cloning in the statute. Louisiana also enacted legislation that prohibited reproductive cloning, but the law expired in July 2003.

The NCSL continues that Arkansas, Indiana, Iowa, Michigan, North Dakota, and South Dakota laws extend their prohibitions to therapeutic cloning, or cloning for research purposes. Virginia's law also may ban human cloning for any purpose, but it may be open to varying interpretations because the law does not define the term "human being," which is used in the definition of human cloning. Rhode Island law does not prohibit cloning for research, and California and New Jersey human cloning laws specifically permit cloning for the purpose of research.

Jonathan Moreno, an ethicist, is highly concerned about all this. He states: "We know from farm animals that they've had problems with their neurological systems, that they've had tumors, that they've had problems of premature aging. So we don't really know what the health consequences are going to be."

What all of this tells us is that as our science, technology, and medical knowledge all advance—possibly even at exponential rates—we are going to be faced with awkward, disturbing, and challenging situations. If it's down to the medical community to do the right thing, one hopes they will do exactly that. If, however, the Controllers get their hands on the technology, it's not at all impossible that we'll see a situation in which the human race as we know it may not exist in fifty or one hundred years. As sinister and as disturbing as it most assuredly sounds, different tiers of people—those who wield the power and those genetically "modified" to do their work—could very possibly exist. It's up to everyone to ensure that we don't fall into that situation, and if we do, it's also up to us to turn the tables on the Controllers for the sake of everyone.

Zombie Conspiracies

Is a real-life zombie apocalypse just around the corner? Does the U.S. government know what looms on the horizon? It may sound unlikely to many, but that doesn't mean it won't happen. Granted, the scenario might not directly mirror the scenarios played out in the likes of *The Walking Dead*, *Night of the Living Dead*, and *28 Days Later*, but the possibility of at least some kind of apocalypse occurring is not at all impossible.

Make mention of the words "alien abduction," and most people will have at least some degree of understanding of the term. Since the early 1960s, countless individuals—all across the world—have made astonishing claims to the effect that they have been kidnapped and experimented upon in bizarre fashion by emotionless, dwarfish entities sporting large, bald heads and huge, black, insectlike eyes. Those same alleged alien entities have become famously known as the Greys. Their helpless and terrified victims are the abductees.

A wealth of theories exists to try to explain what may be afoot when darkness sets in and the creepy Greys surface from their dark, hidden lairs. While the skeptics and the debunkers prefer to relegate everything to the realms of nightmarish dreams, sleep disorders, hoaxing, and fantasy, not everyone is quite so sure that is all that is going on.

Many UFO researchers believe that the spindly Greys are on a significant and serious evolutionary decline and that to try to save their waning species, they secretly harvest DNA, blood, cells, eggs, sperm, and much more from the human race. The sheer nerve of it all! They then use all of this acquired material in sophisticated gene-splicing-style programs to boost their waning bodies and repair their weakened immune systems. However, a much darker theory exists than that. It's a theory that's downright menacing.

Many so-called alien abductees—usually when placed in hypnotic states and regressed to the time of the presumed otherworld experience—describe the Greys implanting into their bodies, or under the surface of their skin, small, metallic devices. We are talking here about what have become infamously known as alien implants. If such an astonishing and controversial claim has even a nugget of truth to it, then what might be the purpose of these sinister actions? The answer to that question is not necessarily a positive one.

Some flying saucer sleuths have suggested that the devices allow the aliens to secretly track the movements of the abductees throughout their entire lives—thus permitting their extraterrestrial captors to find them and extract even more and more cells and DNA, no matter where the people live or where they might move. A mind-blowing variant on this controversial theory suggests that the implants are put in place to control the minds of the abductees. Here is where things become decidedly sinister and zombielike.

Alien Greys might be implanting abductees with devices that, at a later time, would be turned on to make them mind-controlled slaves to their will.

Imagine, if you will, millions of people, all across the planet, implanted with highly sophisticated devices fashioned on another world very different from ours. Imagine, too, that the day finally comes when E.T.—a definitively hostile and deceptive creature very far removed from Steven Spielberg's highly annoying and sickly sweet E.T.—decides to take over the planet.

However, the aliens don't do so via a massive show of force or by pummeling our cities and landscapes with terrible, futuristic weaponry in *Independence Day*-style. No; instead, they get the abductees to do their dirty work for them. Talk about taking the easy way out.

One day, those researchers who adhere to this particular theory believe, all of those millions of currently dormant implants will be "switched on." For all intents and purposes, each and every one of the abductees will then suddenly become a mind-controlled slave to the alien hordes.

In this scenario, we will wake one morning to frightful scenes of utter carnage on the streets as the zombified abductees follow their preprogrammed assignments in violent and crazed fashion—but it won't be occurring just here or there. It will be everywhere. It will be on your very doorstep. It will be on the doorsteps of all of us.

The world will be plunged into utter chaos as the implanted—rather than the infected—do their utmost to wipe out the rest of us for their extraterrestrial masters. When the war is finally over and humankind has been decimated, the aliens will take over a planet that will be largely free of us but in a fashion that leaves the Earth utterly intact.

In view of the above, should you, one day, encounter groups of alien abductees roaming the cities, it might be wise to follow that one word that so often gets shouted, in fear-filled tones, in just about every zombie movie at some point or another: "Run!"

Within the controversial field of UFO research, surely very few things are more menacing than the sinister Men in Black—a subject the U.S. government has secretly investigated for decades. In the highly successful trilogy of MIB movies, starring Will Smith and Tommy Lee Jones, the dark-suited ones are portrayed as the secret agents of an equally secret government agency that is doing all that it can to keep the lid solidly on the alien presence on Earth. The Men in Black were not created by, or for, Hollywood, however. Indeed, the MIB movies were based on a comic book series of the same name, which, in turn, was inspired by genuine encounters with these macabre characters dating back to the latter part of the 1940s.

The real Men in Black are very different from their movie counterparts, however. They are far less like government agents and far more like definitive zombies in terms of both their appearances and their actions. In other words, the image that Smith and Jones portray on-screen is just about as far as you can get from the much darker, gruesome reality of the situation.

Despite what many might think or assume, the real MIB do not chiefly force their way into the homes of witnesses to UFO activity. Most of those who have encountered the MIB note a very curious fact: When the Men in Black make their calls on those who have seen or who investigate UFOs—calls that usually occur late at night and long after the sun has set—they loudly knock on the door. Then, when the door is duly opened by the owner, who usually reacts with a mixture of fear and astonishment, they patiently wait to be invited in.

Very few people need to be told that this action of not entering a person's home until specifically invited uneasily parallels the lore surrounding yet another undead monster that feeds upon the living: the grotesque, bloodsucking vampire. Then is the matter of the attire of the MIB. They curiously wear the typical black suits and fedora-style hats that were chiefly in vogue in the 1940s and 1950s, but it's their unsettling physical appearance that matters most of all. They seldom exceed five feet, five inches in height, they are very often thin to the point of near-emaciation, and their skin is described as being not just white but milk-white and very sickly looking.

As for those suits, they're not the cool, chic, expensive types worn by the likes of agents J and K in the films. Rather, they are sometimes described as being crumpled, creased, and badly fitting. Interestingly, I have three cases on file—two from the United States and one from the United Kingdom, all three from the 1960s—where the MIB projected a distinct and distasteful odor described as being musty and dirtlike, which provoked one of the witnesses to speculate that the MIB had been underground for a significant period of time, possibly even in nothing less than … a grave.

Rather notably, and very closely echoing the data immediately above, the late John Keel—the author of the acclaimed book *The Mothman Prophecies*—called this particular breed of MIB "the cadavers." Keel said, and I quote him word for word: "These are people who look like they've been dead a long time. Their clothes hang on them; their flesh is pasty white and they look like maybe somebody's dug them up from a cemetery. This cadaverous type has turned up in strange places: England and Sweden. I saw one in the early '60s. They're very elusive when you approach them, and hurry away. And they do have a habit of turning up in UFO areas and following UFO investigators around."

Filmmaker George Romero is often credited for founding the zombie movie genre with his 1968 thriller *Night of the Living Dead*.

We should not, of course, consider the Men in Black to be literal shambling or fast-running zombies of the cinematic variety in the sense of them trying to violently and physically devour us after becoming infected with a mysterious virus, but the fact is that some witnesses to the MIB have developed deep and disturbing suspicions that their mysterious visitors in black were feeding psychically on their bodily energy, leaving them feeling weak, nauseated, dizzy, and not unlike a diabetic in full-on crashing mode.

Are hostile space zombies in our very midst? If so, are they bleeding us dry—so to speak—and living and thriving on our life forces? Don't bet against it, particularly so if, late one night, you hear a loud, slow, and deliberate knocking on your door. The outcome of such a visit may not quite be so savagely akin to encountering the reanimated dead of George Romero's *Night of the Living*

Dead; of the 1964 movie, *The Last Man on Earth*; or of *The Walking Dead*. In a roundabout and highly alternative fashion, however, it might not be that far off, either.

It may intrigue many to learn that a medical condition called Walking Corpse Syndrome actually exists. For the sufferers, however, it's an absolute nightmare and no joke at all. WCS is officially known as Cotard's Syndrome. It's a condition steeped in mystery and intrigue. Very disturbingly, Cotard's Syndrome causes the victim to believe that he or she is dead or that their limbs are no longer living or even theirs. The condition takes its name from one Jules Cotard, a French neurologist who died in 1889 from diphtheria. He spent much of his career studying and cataloging cases of Walking Corpse Syndrome. Not only do those affected by WCS believe they are dead, they also fall into spirals of psychosis and fail to take care of their personal appearances.

One of the most disturbing cases of Walking Corpse Syndrome surfaced out of the United Kingdom in May 2013. A man, referred to by the medical community only as "Graham," found himself descending into a deeply depressed state to the point where he ultimately came to believe he was literally a member of the walking dead club. As Graham's condition rapidly worsened and as he actually spent his days and nights wandering around graveyards, his family was forced to seek medical treatment. For a while, Graham became convinced that his brain was clinically dead or was "missing" from his skull. Fortunately, treatment finally brought Graham back to the world of the living.

New light was soon shed on the nature of Cotard's Syndrome as a result of a connection to Zovirax, generally used in the treatment of herpes-based conditions, such as cold sores. Although Zovirax is known for having a small number of side effects, studies revealed that approximately 1 percent of people prescribed Zovirax developed psychiatric conditions, including Cotard's Syndrome. Intriguingly, most of those taking Zovirax and who experienced Walking Corpse Syndrome were suffering from renal failure at the time.

Studies undertaken by Anders Helldén of the Stockholm, Sweden-based Karolinska University Hospital, and Thomas Linden, based at the Sahlgrenska Academy in Gothenburg, Sweden, have uncovered remarkable, albeit unsettling, data on this curious phenomenon. Their case studies included that of a woman who was prescribed Zovirax after having a bout of shingles. When the drug took hold of the woman, who also happened to have renal failure, she began to act in crazed and concerned fashion, believing—or suspecting—that she was dead. When given emergency dialysis to cope with the effects of kidney failure, her strange beliefs began to fade—to the point where she finally came to accept that she was not dead after all. For hours, however, she remained convinced that "my left arm is definitely not mine."

French neurologist Jules Cotard specialized in strokes and described "Cotard's Syndrome," a condition in which a patient believes they are dead.

The *Independent* said of this strange saga:

The woman ran into a hospital in an extremely anxious state, author of the research Anders Helldén from the Karolinska University Hospital in Stockholm said. After receiving dialysis, the woman explained that she had felt anxious because she had been overwhelmed by a strong feeling that she was dead. Within a few hours her symptoms began to ease, until she felt that she was "pretty sure" she wasn't dead, but remained adamant her left arm did not belong to her. After 24 hours, her symptoms had disappeared. Blood analysis later revealed that acyclovir, which can normally be broken down in the body before being flushed out by the kidneys, can leave low levels of breakdown product CMMG in the body. Blood tests of those who had Cotard's symptoms showed much higher levels of CMMG. All but one of those tested also had renal failure.

Midway through November 1989, a document—prepared by a still unknown source—was circulated to a number of researchers within the field of ufology, including the late Leonard Stringfield, who investigated numerous crashed UFO-themed accounts up until his death in 1994. The document detailed the alleged landing—or crash-landing—of a UFO in the rural community of Carp, Ontario, Canada. Although some talked of the entire issue as being a hoax, Stringfield felt the case was either (a) genuine or (b) "an orchestrated disinformation ploy" designed to "muddy the waters." Pertinent parts of the document are detailed below:

Canadian and American Security Agencies are engaged in a conspiracy of silence to withhold from the world the alien vessel seized in the swamps of Corkery Road, Carp, in 1989. UFO sightings in the Ontario region had intensified in the 1980's, specifically around nuclear power generating stations. On November 4, 1989 at 20:00 hrs., Canadian Defense Department radars picked up a globe shaped object traveling at a phenomenal speed over Carp, Ontario. The UFO abruptly stopped, and dropped like a stone.

Canadian and American Security Agencies were immediately notified of the landing. Monitoring satellites traced the movements of the aliens to a triangular area, off Old Almonte and Corkery Roads. The ship had landed in deep swamp near Corkery Road. Two AJ–64 Apaches and a UH–60 Blackhawk headed for the area the following night. The helicopters carried full weapon loads. They were part of a covert American unit that specialized in the recovery of alien craft.

Flying low over Ontario pine trees, the Apache attack choppers soon spotted a glowing, blue, 20 meter in diameter sphere. As targeting lasers locked-on, both gunships unleashed their full weapon loads of eight missiles each. All sixteen were exploded in proximity bursts ten meters downwind from the ship. The missiles were carrying VEXXON, a deadly neuroactive gas which kills on contact. Exposed to air, the gas breaks down quickly into inert components. Immediately after having completed their mission, the gunships turned around, and headed back across the border.

Now the Blackhawk landed, as men exploded from its open doors. In seconds, the six-man strike-team had entered the UFO through a seven meter hatchless, oval, portal. No resistance was encountered. At the controls, three dead crewmen were found. With the ship captured, the United States Air Force, Pentagon, and Office of Naval Intelligence were notified. Through the night, a special team of technicians had shut down and disassembled the sphere. Early the next morning, November 6, 1989, construction equipment and trucks were brought into the swamp. The UFO parts were transported to a secret facility in Kanata, Ontario.

As a cover story, the locals were informed that a road was being built through the swamp. No smokescreen was needed for the military activity as Canadian forces regularly train in the area. Although someone anonymously turned in a 35mm roll of film, it was received by the National Research Council of Canada, in Ottawa. The film contained several clear shots of an entity holding a light. At this time, the photographer is still unidentified. The humanoids were packed in ice and sent to an isolation chamber at the University of Ottawa. CIA specialists performed the autopsies. Three reptilian, fetus-headed beings, were listed as CLASS 1 NTE's (Non-Terrestrial Entities). Like others recovered in previous operations, they were muscular, grey-white skinned humanoids.

The ship was partially reassembled at the underground facility in Kanata. Unlike previous recoveries, this one is pure military. Built as a "Starfighter," it is heavily armed and armored. In design, no rivets, bolts, or welds were used in fastening, yet when reconstructed, there are no seams. The UFO itself is made up of a matrixed dielectric magnesium alloy.

Things then get even stranger as the issue of so-called alien implants rears its head. The document states:

All individuals implanted by the aliens are classified as zombies. The zombies have been programmed to help overthrow Mankind in the near future. When China finishes with Israel, it will invade Europe. At the same time, Chinese space-based bacteriological weapons will be launched at the Arctic. The winds will carry the diseases into Russia and North America. In days, hundreds of millions will be dead: the survivors will have to deal with the Chinese, the aliens, and the Zombies.

The aliens want an all-out war so that the human resistance would be minimal, when they invade. They tried this same tactic once before with Nazi Germany. Most of the scientific advances we have today came from German science which was based on alien technology. Had Hitler won the war, the Earth would have become a concentration camp in order to depopulate the continents for the aliens. Data aboard the sphere explained why the aliens are so comfortable on our world. They preceded man on the evolutionary scale by millions of years; created with the dinosaurs. Some 65 million years ago, an interdimensional war destroyed most of their civilization, and forced them to leave the Earth. Now, they have chosen to reclaim what was once theirs.

The alien forces with their Chinese and Arab allies will attack within the next five years. Waiting longer than that would make it impossible, even for the aliens, to reverse the ecological damage inflicted on the Earth by man.

True, hoax, or—as Leonard Stringfield suspected—disinformation? I know where I stand on it, and it's neither truth nor disinformation! Garbage, in my view. Of course, the references to Hitler and concentration camps make me suspect that some extreme right-wing nut played a part in all this. Finally, guess what? The aliens did not "attack within the next five years" after all. Further proof of the over-the-top nature of this pile of steaming you-know-what!

If you think that the concept of the jerky, slow-moving zombies is a relatively modern one, then it is very much a case of time to think again. Within Chinese culture and folklore, tales of such abominations date back centuries. In China, the zombie is known as the jiang-shi. It is just about as deadly and terrifying as its Haitian and western counterparts. Jiang-shi translates into English as "stiff corpse" for very good reason: the movements and gait of the Chinese undead are not at all dissimilar to the zombies of George A. Romero's *Night of the Living Dead.*

In China, the jiang-shi is a creature with a seemingly never-ending case of rigor mortis. Most people are familiar with the concept of this postdeath condition: when a person dies, the body significantly stiffens. This is due to a now permanent lack of oxygen, which prevents the body from producing Adenosine triphosphate, a molecule significantly involved in the regulation of the human metabolism.

As the metabolic system finally comes to an irreversible halt, the process of rigor mortis quickly begins. Many people, however, are unaware that rigor mortis is not a permanent condition. While it typically sets in just a few hours after death, within a day or so, its effects have completely vanished, and the body is as supple in death as it was in life. For the jiang-shi, however, rigor mortis never, ever goes away, something that ensures the creature retains a stiff, robotic gait at all times, just like Romero's infamous ghouls. Notably, the jiang-shi has another zombie parallel: like its cine-

The Chinese version of the zombie is called a jiang-shi, or "stiff corpse," a horrifying creature on the hunt for people's Qis.

matic counterpart, the jiang-shi feeds on humans. Whereas the walking and running undead need human flesh to fuel their bodies, the jiang-shi is fueled by the very essence of what makes us human: the human soul.

Chinese tradition tells of the soul being the container of a powerful energy, which the average jiang-shi craves, that is known as Qi. The average zombie may be quite content to eat its prey while they are still alive and fighting for their lives, but the jiang-shi is first required to slaughter its victim before the act of devouring Qi can begin in earnest. In the same way that two kinds of zombies exist—the Haitian, mind-controlled type and the rabid, infected type of the movies—so, too, are two groups of jiang-shi. One is a freshly dead person who reanimates extremely quickly, perhaps even within mere minutes of death taking place. The other is an individual who rises from the grave months, or even years, after they have passed away but who displays no inward or outward evidence of decomposition.

As for how and why a person may become a jiang-shi, the reasons are as many as they are varied: being buried prematurely, dabbling in the black arts, and, rather interestingly, getting hit by lightning can all result in transformation from a regular human to a jiang-shi. On this latter point of lightning, electricity has played a significant role in the resurrection of the dead in the world of fiction, most noticeably in Mary Shelley's classic novel of 1818, *Frankenstein*.

Another way of transforming into a jiang-shi is one that zombie afi-cionados will definitely be able to relate to: when a person is killed and their Qi is taken, the victim also becomes a jiang-shi. What this demonstrates is that the jiang-shi's act of stealing energy is very much the equivalent of the zombie delivering an infectious bite.

Also, just like most zombies of movies, novels, and television shows, most jiang-shis don't look good in the slightest. Although the jiang-shi typi-cally appears relatively normal when it first reanimates—in the sense that decomposition is not in evidence—things soon change, and not for the better. The walking, jerky corpse of the jiang-shi begins to degrade significantly, the rank odor of the dead becomes all-dominating, and the flesh begins to hang, turning an unhealthy-looking lime color as it does so.

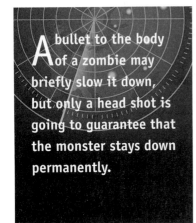

A bullet to the body of a zombie may briefly slow it down, but only a head shot is going to guarantee that the monster stays down permanently.

Killing a jiang-shi can be just as difficult as putting down a cinematic zombie. A bullet to the body of a zombie may briefly slow it down, but only a head shot is going to guarantee that the monster stays down permanently. It's very much the same with the jiang-shi: the trick is in knowing what actually works best. The jiang-shi cannot abide vinegar, which acts as the equivalent of a deadly poison. While actual-ly managing to pour significant amounts of vinegar into the mouth of a fero-cious jiang-shi may prove to be far more than tricky, it is said to work at a rapid rate.

Smearing the skin of a jiang-shi with the blood of a recently dead dog will also put a jiang-shi to rest, although exactly why is a very different matter. Mind you, providing it worked, would you even care why? No, you probably would not. You would simply be glad to be alive!

In the 1997 movie *Conspiracy Theory*, Mel Gibson's character—a para-noid cab driver named Jerry Fletcher, who has been the subject of strange mind-control experiments—states that a good conspiracy theory is one that can never be proved. The very same thing can be said about one of the most controversial of all the zombie-based conspiracies currently in circulation.

It suggests that right now, classified research of a highly controversial nature is being undertaken to try to create a terrible cocktail. It is claimed to be one based around a mutated version of the rabies virus, one that will, in the near future, be unleashed upon enemy forces and cause them to attack each other in violent, homicidal fashion. They won't be literally dead, but trying to tell the difference between the real-life infected and those of television and cinema will be no easy task in the slightest.

Could it be true? Are dark forces really at work, trying to create a virus that will mimic—as closely as conceivably possible—the effects of a real zombie apocalypse? If so, who are the perpetrators? In true, tried, and tested conspiratorial fashion, vague references to "them" and "they" are all that we get from those slightly (and occasionally significantly) unusual characters who are absolutely chomping at the bit to see a real zombie apocalypse erupt all around us.

Well, I'm sorry (no, actually, I'm not), but references to "them" and "they" are simply not good enough for me. If something like a *28 Days Later*-style "rage virus" is about to break out all around us, then I want to see far more than mere vague references. I want hard facts.

Unfortunately, within the realms of those who think that TV's finest show *The Walking Dead* is actually nonfiction, facts don't exist—only Internet rumors. However, let's give them the benefit of the doubt and see what is being said by those who just can't wait to excitedly scream: "Shoot him in the head!"

Certainly, rabies radically transforms the character and actions of an infected individual to a radical degree. Its name is highly apt, too: it is a Latin term meaning nothing less than "madness." Rabies spreads from animal to animal via bites that penetrate the skin and provokes inflammation in the brain, as Ozzy Osbourne almost learned to his cost when he very unwisely bit the head off a bat at a Des Moines, Iowa, gig in 1982.

Left untreated, disturbing characteristics develop anywhere from weeks to months after infection, including violent outbursts, manic behavior, aggression, and a fear of water. Death usually occurs from within forty-eight hours to two weeks after the first symptoms surface. Despite the assumption that rabies is on the way out, this is far from the case. Tens of thousands of people still die from this terrible condition every year, chiefly in Africa and Asia.

Disturbingly, most animals on the planet can fall victim to infection, too. Fortunately, vaccinations and care have kept levels of rabies to a minimum in the Western world. Indeed, between 1996 and 2013, only forty-five cases of human infection occurred in the whole United States. All of the victims had been bitten overseas prior to their return to the United States

Rumors among conspiracy theorists suggest that a rage-instilling, highly infectious, airborne version of rabies is, right now, being developed. It will not quickly kill the infected individuals, however. Instead, their lives will

Rabies is a frightening and deadly disease that people often associate with bites from animals like dogs or bats, but what if an airborne strain of rabies were developed?

be prolonged, albeit in violent, murderous, rage-filled states. That might seem like an ideal weapon to release on enemy troops and then sit back and watch as they tear each other to pieces.

What happens when the wind blows hard and weaponized, airborne rabies—mutated into something even more nightmarish—begins to spread far and wide, outside of the confines of the battlefield, though? Will we be faced with a veritable army of rabid, infected killers, indiscriminately murdering and infecting everyone that crosses their paths?

It's highly unlikely—in the extreme, to say the absolute very least—that exposure to radiation could provoke any kind of violent, cannibalistic, zombielike behavior. The possibility that a returning spacecraft might unwittingly unleash hazardous extraterrestrial materials on our planet, however, is not at all an impossibility. In fact, dealing with just such a potentially catastrophic event has already been planned for. In a fictional format, at least, such a scenario was famously presented in the 1969 book *The Andromeda Strain* (which was written by Michael Crichton of *Jurassic Park* and *Congo* fame) and in the subsequent 1971 movie spin-off of the same name. Although zombies do not appear in either the novel or the film, pretty much everything else does.

An American space probe—as it returns to planet Earth and crashes in the wilds of Arizona—unleashes a lethal virus of extraterrestrial origins. Matters soon escalate in ominous, doomsdaylike fashion: the U.S. government struggles to find an antidote, the virus threatens to wipe out the entire human race, and ... well, you get the apocalyptic picture.

While *The Andromeda Strain* is just a highly entertaining story of disturbing and thought-provoking proportions, it does, rather incredibly, have its real-life counterparts. According to *Article IX of The Treaty on Principles Governing the Activities of States in the Exploration and Use of Outer Space, Including the Moon and Other Celestial Bodies*, which was collectively signed in Washington, London, and Moscow on January 27, 1967, and was entered into force on October 10th of that year: "In the exploration and use of outer space, including the Moon and other celestial bodies, States Parties to the Treaty shall be guided by the principle of co-operation and mutual assistance and shall conduct all their activities in outer space, including the Moon and other celestial bodies, with due regard to the corresponding interests of all other States Parties to the Treaty."

The document continues: "States Parties to the Treaty shall pursue studies of outer space, including the Moon and other celestial bodies, and conduct exploration of them so as to avoid their harmful contamination and also adverse changes in the environment of the Earth resulting from the introduction of *extraterrestrial matter* and, where necessary, shall adopt appropriate measures for this purpose."

It becomes very clear from studying the available data of that particular era that officials were indeed concerned about a deadly—albeit admittedly theoretical—alien virus running wild on the Earth and provoking a worldwide pandemic—which just might escalate to the point where it could possibly wipe out each and every one of us. However, what if that same pandemic didn't just kill us but provoked something along the lines of a real-life zombie apocalypse? No, we are not talking about a *Night of the Living Dead*-style scenario involving radiation and the recently deceased but something far more akin to the scenario that played out in the movies *28 Days Later* and *28 Weeks Later*.

In combined fashion, the films tell of how the United Kingdom becomes overwhelmed by what is known as the "Rage Virus." The infected are not the dead returned from the grave, however. Rather, as a result of infection from a virus that spreads incredibly quickly, an untold number of British people are transformed into deranged, psychotic killers. Although, thankfully, the "Rage Virus" is merely fictional, we should consider the following....

In the mid-1980s, the first signs of a terrifying condition began to surface in the heart of the British countryside. It was a condition that targeted cattle and made them behave in distinctly zombielike fashion before finally killing the animals in a deeply distressing fashion. Its official name is Bovine Spongiform Encephalopathy. Unofficially, but far more infamously, it is known as Mad Cow Disease.

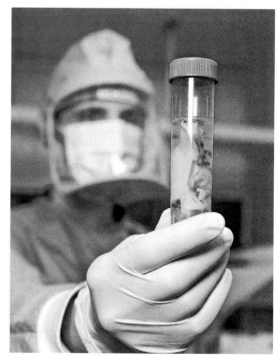

BSE is caused by a prion—a protein-based agent that attacks and affects the normal function of cells. Worse still, just like the fictional zombie virus of so many movies, prion-inducing BSE is utterly unstoppable and incurable. By 1987, the British government recognized that it had not just a problem on its hands but a major problem, too. Not only that, the government acted in wholly unforgivable fashion by secretly putting the beef industry, the economy, and profits way ahead of public safety.

In the same way that, in typically fictional format, infected people feed upon the uninfected survivors of the zombie apocalypse, very much the same can be said about the origins of BSE: it was spread by cows eating cows. To the horror of the British public—who had previously, and utterly outrageously, been kept in the dark by the government, who had cov-

A scientist holds up a vial containing a bovine brain sample infected with bovine spongiform encephalopathy, or mad cow disease, a deadly contagion resulting from proteins called prions.

ered up the facts—it was finally revealed by the government that, for years, the discarded remains of millions of cattle that had been put to death in British slaughterhouses had been ground to a pulp and used to create cattle feed. It was, for the animal kingdom at least, *Soylent Green* come to hideous reality. That's when the problems started.

It quickly became very easy to spot a zombie cow: they shuffled rather than walked, their personalities began to change, they exhibited behavior that varied from confusion to outright rage, and they quickly became unmanageable under normal circumstances. As the crisis grew, an even more terrifying development surfaced: the infection jumped to the human population in the form of what is termed Creutzfeldt-Jacob Disease, or CJD, which can also provoke sudden outbursts of rage. The utterly panicked British government took the only option it felt was available.

With close to an estimated two hundred thousand cattle infected, officialdom decided to play things safe by systematically wiping out no fewer than 4.4 million cows all across the nation. While such actions were seen as horrific, they were also perceived as necessary to ensure that chaos and death did not spread even further. For some, however, it was all too little and too late.

Although the cannibalizing process was brought to a halt by the government in the late 1980s, around two hundred British people have since died from what is termed variant CJD (or vCJD), the result of eating BSE-contaminated meat. On top of that, the significant increase in Alzheimer's disease in the United Kingdom in recent years has given rise to the highly disturbing theory that many of those presumed to have Alzheimer's have been misdiagnosed. They may be suffering from vCJD.

Well, wouldn't an autopsy show evidence of vCJD? Yes, it would, if the brain of the deceased individual was examined carefully. Indeed, studying the brains of the dead, or testing the blood, are the only sure ways to fully confirm vCJD, but here's the thing: most people suspected of having Alzheimer's are not tested for vCJD. If a person has been diagnosed with Alzheimer's, then their death is usually attributed to complications arising from the disease rather than anything strange or suspicious.

In other words, in most patients where an Alzheimer's diagnosis has already been put forward, no autopsy is done. I know this, as my own mother died of Alzheimer's. Since she had been diagnosed with the disease, an autopsy was not perceived as being necessary after her death to check for something else that might have led to similar symptoms. Thus, with a lack of large-scale autopsying of presumed Alzheimer's victims, we have no real way of knowing exactly how many may have been misdiagnosed.

Here, we see the disastrous damage that a condition of wholly terrestrial origins can provoke across an entire nation—and, more importantly, how that same condition can significantly affect the minds of both people and animals. Perhaps something of extraterrestrial origins could do far worse. Preparing for the sudden surfacing of an alien-originated pandemic may not mean that government officials are also secretly anticipating that a *28 Days Later*-like apocalypse will be far behind. On the other hand, nothing suggests that they haven't secretly pondered just such a possibility....

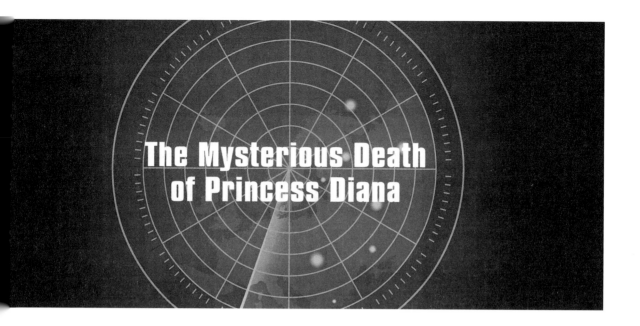

The Mysterious Death of Princess Diana

When Diana, Princess of Wales, was killed in a car crash in Paris, France, on August 31, 1997, the world was shocked—but was Diana's death nothing more than a tragic accident? Not everyone is quite so sure. Indeed, a wealth of material links Diana's death to the secret activities of certain clandestine, powerful groups. *Vigilant Citizen* provides the following:

> Similarly to the Virgin Mary, Diana had (and still has) legions of followers, worshiping her giving nature and her maternal energy. In other words, she seems to fulfill the almost inherent need in human beings to worship a female goddess, giver of life and filled with compassion. The media has been a key actor in the creation of this icon by documenting every detail of her fairytale wedding, her troubled marriage, her humanitarian activities and, finally, her untimely death. Was Diana picked and groomed to become a sort of a "modern day Goddess" to ultimately be sacrificed, in accordance with ancient pagan practices? This might sound preposterous to the average *National Inquirer* reader, but not to the connoisseur of the occult practices of the world elite. Furthermore, numerous clues and symbols have been placed by this group to subtly commemorate the occult nature of Lady Di's death.

Vigilant Citizen continues:

> The city of Paris was built by the Merovingians, a medieval dynasty which ruled France for numerous generations. Before converting to Christianity, the Merovingian religion was a mysterious brand of paganism. The Pont D'Alma Tunnel was a sacred site dedicated to the Moon Goddess Diana, where they used to practice ritual

sacrifices. During those ceremonies, it was of an utmost importance that the sacrificed victim died inside the underground temple. The assassination of Diana was a reenactment of this ancient pagan tradition.

As for who, exactly, the Merovingians were, James Wiener provides this:

Mythologized and circumscribed for over 1500 years, the Merovingians were a powerful Frankish dynasty, which exercised control [over] much of modern-day France, Germany, Switzerland, Austria, and the Low Countries. During the Early Middle Ages, the Merovingian kingdoms were arguably the most powerful and most important polities to emerge after the collapse of the Western Roman Empire, blending Gallo-Roman institutions with Germanic Frankish customs.

IlluminatiWatcher expands on this issue:

The Merovingian dynasty worshiped the goddess Diana, and the murder of Princess Diana is a ritual sacrifice to the goddess Diana.

The ex-wife of Prince Charles of England, Princess Diana was an immensely popular public figure whose tragic death has initiated considerable speculation.

To believe this, we must believe that the Merovingian dynasty secretly retained power up to present day, which isn't too far of a stretch. If the British royal family can continue to hold a position of power over the citizens simply because they have a "superior" blood, perhaps France has Merovingian bloodlines in positions of power unknown to the citizens.

Intriguing words, to say the very least. While Princess Diana's tragic death made worldwide news, another affair that also involved Diana occurred.

For years, rumors circulated to the effect that Princess Diana was the subject of intense surveillance by the United Kingdom's intelligence agencies—MI5, MI6, and the Government Communication Headquarters (GCHQ), the latter being the United Kingdom's equivalent of the United States' National Security Agency. Some of those rumors were vindicated in the latter part of 1998. It was in December of that year that the NSA went on record as stating that it had around one thousand pages of classified material on the princess, none of which the NSA was willing to relinquish and place into the public domain. It's hardly surprising that, with this revelation, the United Kingdom's media covered the story extensively. Staff at the *Daily Mirror* newspaper ran a sensational story that began as follows: "America's spy chiefs admitted last night they snooped on Princess Diana for years—and learned some of her most intimate love secrets." U.S. media got on the story, too.

The *Washington Post* chose to avoid the sensational aspects of the revelations and instead focused on the withheld NSA files. From the *Post*, we have this: "In denying the request, the NSA disclosed existence of a 1,056-page Diana file and reported that Fort Meade, where the agency is located, had produced 39 'NSA-originated and NSA-controlled documents,' totaling 124 pages." The *Post* added that the material was denied release due to the fact that "their disclosure could reasonably be expected to cause exceptionally grave damage to the national security," adding: "The giant spy agency, Maryland's largest employer, has been the subject of intense controversy in Britain and across Europe since a report released in January by the European Parliament concluded that 'within Europe, all e-mail, telephone and fax communications are routinely intercepted by the United States National Security Agency.'"

The most amazing development came in 2000, however.

It is very likely that more than a few of those documents held by the NSA were concentrated on certain materials collated by Mohamed Al-Fayed, who is the father of Diana's boyfriend, the late Dodi Fayed, and a lawsuit filed by Al-Fayed in 2000 in the U.S. District Court for the District of Columbia. The lawsuit begins as follows:

> This is an action under the Freedom of Information Act ... for the expedited processing and disclosure of agency records pertaining to the deaths of Princess Diana and Dodi Fayed, and events and individuals associated with the tragedy, that were improperly withheld from plaintiffs Mohammed Al Fayed and Punch Limited by defendants Central Intelligence Agency, the National Security Agency, the Defense Intelligence Agency, the United States Departments of Defense, Justice and State, the Federal Bureau of Investigation, the Executive Office of United States Attorneys, the Immigration and Naturalization Service and the United States Secret Service.

We are then told:

> On August 31, 1997, at approximately 12:25 A.M. local time, an automobile carrying Diana Frances Spencer, Princess of Wales, and Dodi Al Fayed crashed into the thirteenth pillar in the tunnel under the Place d'Alma in Paris, France. Princess Diana and Dodi Al Fayed were killed along with the automobile's driver,

Henri Paul, a French security officer at the Ritz Hotel. Bodyguard Trevor Rees-Jones was the sole survivor. Shortly after the tragedy, Premier Juge d'instruction Herv Stephan, a French investigating magistrate, instituted an investigation. On or about January 29, 1999, it was announced that the investigation had ended and concluded that the tragedy was caused by drunk driving by Henri Paul, excessive speed and a dangerous stretch of road. Nine photographers and a press motorcyclist were placed under formal investigation—a step immediately before being formally charged—for manslaughter and failing to render aid to accident victims. On or about September 3, 1999, Judge Stephan dismissed all charges against the photographers and motorcyclist. The decision to formally end the investigation is presently under appeal by Al Fayed, and judicial proceedings are scheduled for September 2001.

Matters got even more controversial; the lawsuit referred to the controversial story of a man named Richard Tomlinson. The lawsuit states:

> Richard Tomlinson, 37, is a former MI6 (British foreign intelligence service) officer who served from September 1991 through April 1995. On or about August 28, 1998, Tomlinson informed investigating magistrate Herv Stephan that Henri Paul, the chauffeur killed in the tragedy, had been on the MI6 payroll for at least three years. He also revealed that the death crash resembled a MI6 plot to kill Yugoslavian President Slobodan Milosevic in Geneva.

This is the Alma tunnel, where Princess Diana met her awful fate while speeding away in her limousine, paparazzi in hot pursuit.

> In or around September 1998, Tomlinson traveled to the United States on board a Swiss Air Flight in order to appear on a NBC television program to discuss his recent revelations. Upon arrival at John F. Kennedy International Airport in New York, Tomlinson was escorted off the plane by United States government officials and detained for several hours. He was never permitted to enter the United States, and instead was placed back on a plane to Europe. Upon information and belief, the United States government prevented Tomlinson from entering the United States at the request of MI6 or other British government officials.

Oswald LeWinter, 70, has claimed to be a former United States intelligence operative for more than two decades. He has been linked to several high profile controversies here in the United States and Europe, all of which involved allegations of intelligence connections and specifically the CIA. These controversies have included LeWinter providing what apparently turned out to be disinformation regarding "October Surprise," which involved allegations that individuals associated with Ronald Reagan's presidential campaign delayed the release of American hostages in Iran in order to defeat President Jimmy Carter; claims by LeWinter that the CIA was involved in the 1986 assassination of former Swedish Prime Minister Olof Palme; his appearance in a 1994 documentary on the bombing of Pan Am Flight 103 entitled The Maltese Double Cross in which LeWinter claimed that the CIA knew that Libya was not responsible for the terrorist attack; and a 1998 attempt, more fully described below, to sell fraudulent CIA documents concerning the deaths of Princess Diana and Dodi Al Fayed.

In his book *October Surprise* (1991), Professor Gary Sick describes LeWinter as an "intelligence operative," who was a "graduate of University of California at Berkeley and had a master's degree in English literature from San Francisco State. He spoke German and English, but he had also acquired a working knowledge of Hebrew, Persian, and French, and some Urdu." Sick stated LeWinter "had served with U.S. forces in Vietnam and also claimed long experience with various U.S. and Israeli intelligence agencies." Upon information and belief, LeWinter previously formally maintained a relationship with the CIA, at least to the extent he provided information to the Agency during the 1970s. The CIA presently maintains in its possession records that confirm a relationship, as well as information pertaining to the fraud attempt described below.

In a lengthy section of the document titled "The Effort to Defraud Mohamed Al Fayed," the strange story is told of a series of controversial documents that surfaced not long after the death of the Princess of Wales, documents that were purported to be official, leaked from the U.S. government about the secret surveillance of Diana:

> In late 1997 or early 1998, Keith Fleer ("Fleer"), a prominent California attorney, George Williamson ("Williamson"), an independent journalist, Pat Macmillan ("Macmillan") and LeWinter—the latter two are both alleged former CIA agents—participated in an enterprise to sell forged documents purportedly stolen from the CIA that indicated MI6—the British foreign intelligence agency—had plotted to murder Princess Diana and Dodi Al Fayed. Other individuals who are alleged to have played a role in the

scheme include Linda Tumulty, who is tied to the late film producer Alan Francovich, and another former CIA operative named Thompson.

LeWinter, Macmillan, and other associates apparently forged the documents and planned to misrepresent them as genuine to induce potential buyers to purchase the documents. Along with Williamson, who was also aware that the documents to be sold were not authentic, LeWinter, Macmillan, and their colleagues agreed that a sale of the forged documents to a tabloid newspaper should be arranged. The participants in the scheme anticipated a sale price of over $1 million.

Upon information and belief, at the suggestion of Gaby Leon (phonetic), an individual who allegedly formerly worked for the Argentine Secret Service, Williamson was advised to contact Fleer, an entertainment attorney in Los Angeles, for advice on the sale of the documents and to serve as a broker for their sale.

In their course of discussions, Fleer noted that Al Fayed had offered a reward of up to $20 million for information concerning the deaths of his son and Princess Diana and he suggested that they should approach Al Fayed in lieu of a tabloid and offer him the information for $20 million. Fleer stated that he knew one of Al Fayed's attorneys in Washington, D.C. and would make the necessary approaches to him. Upon information and belief, Fleer was to receive 5% of any monies obtained through the sale of the alleged CIA documents.

On or about March 24, 1998, Fleer contacted Douglas Marvin ("Marvin"), Al Fayed's legal representative in Washington. Marvin, in turn, put Fleer in contact with John Macnamara ("Macnamara"), Al Fayed's chief of security. In a series of telephone conversations over the first two weeks of April 1998, between Fleer and Macnamara, Fleer stated that he had been approached by reliable individuals with credible information that the deaths of Dodi Al Fayed and Princess Diana were not accidental but in fact were the product of a carefully planned assassination carried out at the behest of British intelligence with the knowledge and acquiescence of Buckingham Palace. Fleer indicated that his immediate contact was Williamson, an investigative reporter, and that several "principals" were also involved.

According to Fleer, Williamson had connections with CIA sources who had been reliable in the past. Those CIA employees, Fleer stated, would be prepared to disclose their information concerning the deaths of Dodi Al Fayed and the Princess, provided that Al Fayed would provide them with the financial security and assistance to "take measures to protect themselves"—a price of $20 million. Fleer indicated that, while it was unlikely that the CIA employees would agree to testify in any manner, they could provide authentic and sufficiently detailed CIA documentary evidence to prove the involvement of British intelligence agencies in the assassination plot. Fleer also stated that the CIA sources knew that a CIA operative in Europe had been contacted by someone within the British intelligence agency MI6. The British agent indicated that an assassination team was being compiled and asked for assistance. The CIA employee subsequently cabled for instructions and received in return a telex indicating that the CIA was not to become involved directly but that the agent could give British intelligence the name of a contact with a Mossad-affiliated "K team" operating out of Switzerland.

In addition to the telexes from and to the CIA operative, Fleer indicated that the CIA sources could and would supply Al Fayed with a relevant intelligence collection report and a medical document indicating that the Princess was pregnant at the time of her death. Fleer also indicated that there was a report of the results of an internal CIA investigation into the agency's involvement with the assassination of Dodi Al Fayed and Princess Diana, but that this document could only be obtained through a "seven figure" cash payment.

On or about April 8, 1998, Fleer requested that Macnamara arrange for the wire transfer of $25,000 "expense money" so that Al Fayed's representatives and the "principals" could meet in a foreign country to arrange for the inspection of the CIA documents and their subsequent sale to Al Fayed.

Given that alleged classified information was being offered for sale, on or about April 13, 1998, Al Fayed's representatives contacted and began cooperating with officials from the FBI and the CIA.

Mohamed Al-Fayed, the father of Dodi Al Fayed, has maintained that his son and Princess Diana were targeted by Britain's MI6.

From here on, all actions taken by Al Fayed's representatives were done so with the approval and supervision of law enforcement and intelligence officials of the United States government.

On or about April 13, 1998, Fleer requested that Macnamara send the $25,000 via wire transfer to the account of Garland and Loman, Inc., a New Mexico company with an affiliate in Juarez, Mexico, at the Western Bank, 201 North Church Street, Las Cruces, New Mexico 88001. Fleer explained in a subsequent call to Macnamara that the Western Bank would contact Williamson when the funds were received. The FBI directed Al Fayed's representatives to wire the money from a bank in the District of Columbia so that criminal jurisdiction would lie with the United States Attorney's Office for the District of Columbia. Macnamara was told that at the very least the transmittal and receipt of the funds would constitute wire fraud, even if nothing else came of the intended transaction to sell the documents.

On or about April 14, 1998, with the approval of U.S. law enforcement authorities, Marvin ordered the wire transfer of $25,000 from a NationsBank branch in Washington, D.C. to the Garland & Loman account. FBI, CIA and EOUSA officials were all aware of the ongoing events.

Upon information and belief, Williamson traveled to the Garland and Loman premises in New Mexico to withdraw the $25,000 wire transfer with the intent to use those funds to finance and further the sale of the forged documents to Al Fayed. Williamson subsequently traveled to London, England and disbursed some or all of the $25,000 to his co-conspirators; including, but not limited to, LeWinter.

On or about April 14, 1998, following confirmation from Williamson that the $25,000 wire transfer had been received, Fleer informed Macnamara that the meeting to exchange the documents for payment was to take place in Vienna, Austria. Fleer stated that in Austria, Al Fayed's representatives would meet with four "principals," who would offer for sale two CIA telexes and a doctor's certificate that Princess Diana was pregnant at the time of her death. Fleer emphasized that the internal CIA investigative report on the circumstances of the crash would not, however, be provided at the Vienna meeting because "they" had yet to procure it.

With the intent to render the proceeds of the sale difficult or impossible to trace, and in an effort to conceal their source, Fleer instructed Macnamara during their conversation on or about April

14, 2000, that he should arrange to have the $15 million negotiated purchase price (having been reduced from $20 million) for the documents deposited at the Austrian bank Kredit Anstalt in a Sparbuch, an anonymous, bearer passbook account. Fleer stated that the passbook was to be handed over to the "principals" at the Vienna meeting as payment for the documents.

On or about April 20, 1998, Macnamara received a telephone call in Austria from Williamson, who stated that he was at the Hilton Hotel, New York City. Williamson confirmed that he dealt regularly with the "principals" supplying the documents and that he served as their go-between. He also stated that the "principals" would be present in Vienna and that at least one of them, whose identity remains unknown, had traveled from the United States to meet with Al Fayed's representatives. At an initial meeting, Al Fayed's representatives would be shown at least one of the CIA telexes dealing with the assassination of Dodi Fayed and Princess Diana, and that a serving member of the CIA would be on hand to authenticate the document. Additionally, Williamson also stated that the $25,000 wired by Macnamara had been spent and that "nobody's cheating on you."

Following additional negotiations concerning the time, place, and format of the Vienna meeting, Macnamara received two telephone calls from an unknown individual on his mobile phone discussing the mechanics of the document exchange and setting a meeting for April 22, 1998, 2:00 P.M. at the Hotel Ambassador, 1010 Vienna, Neuer Markt 5. Macnamara was to sit on the Kartner Strasse side, where he would be approached by one of the "principals." With the approval of United States and Austrian law enforcement authorities, Macnamara followed the instructions that had been given to him regarding the planned rendezvous.

At approximately 2:30 P.M. local time, a man (later identified as LeWinter) approached Macnamara and identified himself as an ex-CIA agent who was in Vienna with six CIA and Mossad agents to deal with "the business." LeWinter spoke to Macnamara for approximately one half hour, briefing him on the provenance of the CIA documents, and indicated that there had been a meeting in London between an MI6 operative named Spelding and a CIA agent named Harrison, who was attached to the United States Embassy in London. At that meeting, Spelding asked Harrison for the CIA's assistance in assassinating Dodi Al Fayed, who had formed a close relationship with Princess Diana. Harrison allegedly cabled CIA headquarters in Langley, Virginia for instructions and was informed via telex that the CIA would not become involved but could refer the British to the Mossad "K team" in Geneva. LeWinter indicated to Macnamara that these two telexes were for sale, and he also gave a brief description of the CIA investigative report that could be obtained, including a reference in that report to Princess Diana's pregnancy.

At the conclusion of their meeting at the Hotel Ambassador, LeWinter provided a telephone number and requested Macnamara to call him there under the name George Mearah at 5:00 P.M. Law enforcement personnel working with Macnamara traced the telephone number to the Hotel Stadt Bamberg, where they confirmed that the hotel had as a guest an American named Oswald LeWinter who matched Mearah's description.

By arrangement, and with the approval of United States and Austrian authorities, Macnamara met with LeWinter later that after-

This memorial placed outside a London Harrods store includes what looks like an engagement ring that Dodi Al Fayed may have been planning to give to Princess Diana.

noon at the Ambassador Hotel. Following further discussions with Macnamara, LeWinter was taken into custody at the Ambassador Hotel by Austrian law enforcement officials. On information and belief, two associates (one of which has apparently been identified as Thompson) of LeWinter who were nearby evaded capture. In fact, it turns out that one of the individuals who assisted LeWinter during his time in Vienna was Karl Koecher, a Czechoslovakian intelligence operative who had infiltrated the CIA as a "sleeper" agent during the 1970s. After more than a decade of spying on the United States, Koecher was arrested and ultimately exchanged in a spy trade for Soviet dissident Anatoly Shcharansky on February 11, 1986. Upon information and belief, Koecher and LeWinter became acquainted while serving in prison together in New York State.

It's worth noting that even if the papers were bogus in nature, more than a bit of effort had been used to make them look like the real thing. One, for example—of June 17, 1997—looked just like the real deal. Its title was: "DOMESTIC COLLECTION DIVISION Foreign Intelligence Information Report Directorate of Intelligence WARNING NOTICE—INTELLIGENCE SOURCES AND METHODS INVOLVED REPORT CLASS: TOP SECRET." It stated:

1. Relationship initiated between Diana POW and Dodi aF according to reliable intel sources in November 1996. Intimacy begins shortly after they meet. (Report filed).

2. Reliable source reports Palace seriously disturbed by liaison. PM considers any al Fayed relationship politically disastrous. [The Duke of] Edinburgh sees serious threat to dynasty should relationship endure. Quote reported: "Such an affair is racially and morally repugnant and no son of a Bedouin camel trader is fit for the mother of a future king," Edinburgh. (Report filed).

3. Request from highest circles to DEA attaché UK for 6 on Dodi re: Cocaine. See File forwarded to UK embassy DC. (Copy filed).

4. United States liaison to MI6 requested by David Spedding for assistance in providing permanent solution to Dodi problem. Blessing of Palace secured (Twiz filed).

5. WHuse [White House] denies Spedding request. Harrison authorized only to arrange meeting for MI6 representative with K-Team Geneva. (Twiz on file).

6. Meeting in Geneva reportedly successful (Report filed).

7. al Fayed Mercedes Limo stolen and returned with electronics missing. Reliable intel source confirms K-team involved. Source

reports car rebuilt to respond to external radio controls. (Report filed).

8. COBGeneva reports that on May 28, 1997 heavily weighted Fiat Turbo.

Here is a thought-provoking, final angle to all of this. In summer 1999, journalists Duncan Campbell and Stuart Millar said that "LeWinter has since claimed, during two meetings with the Harrods head of security, that although the papers shown to Mr. Fayed were forgeries, they were copies of real documents held by the CIA."

Real, fake, or somewhere in between? We may never know.

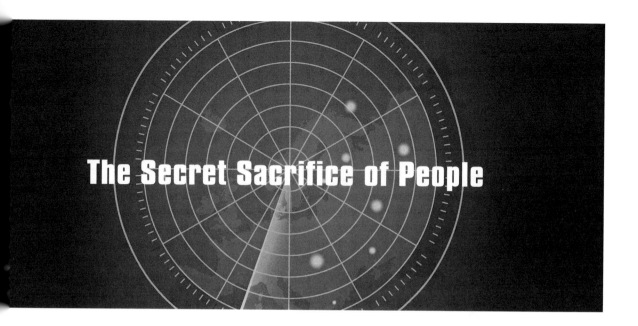

The Secret Sacrifice of People

Filey Brigg is an impressively sized, rocky peninsula that juts out from the coast of the Yorkshire, England, town of Filey. Local folklore suggests that the rocks are actually the remains of the bones of an ancient sea dragon. Unlikely, to say the least, but the story may have at least a basis in reality. In all likelihood, the story takes its inspiration from centuries-old sightings of giant monsters of the sea that called the crashing waters off Filey Brig their home. One person who was able to attest to this was Wilkinson Herbert, a coast guard, who, in February 1934, had a traumatic, terrifying encounter with just such a sea dragon at Filey Brigg. It was—very appropriately—a dark, cloudy, and windy night when Herbert's life was turned upside down.

The first indication that something foul and supernatural was afoot came when Herbert heard the terrifying growling of what sounded like a dozen or more vicious hounds. The growling, however, was coming from something else entirely. As he looked out at the harsh, cold waves, Herbert saw—to his terror—a large beast, around thirty feet in length, and equipped with a muscular, humped back and four legs that extended into flippers. For a heart-stopping instant, the bright, glowing eyes of the beast locked onto Herbert's eyes. Not surprisingly, he said: "It was a most gruesome and thrilling experience. I have seen big animals abroad but nothing like this."

Further up the same stretch of coastland is the county of Tyne and Wear, and in the vicinity of the county's South Shields is Marsden Bay, an area that is overflowing with rich tales of magic, mystery, witchcraft, and supernatural, ghostly activity. Legend tells of a man named Jack Bates (a.k.a. "Jack the Blaster") who, with his wife, Jessie, moved to the area in 1782. Instead of setting up home in the village of Marsden itself, however, the Bates family decided that they would blast a sizeable amount of rock out of Marsden Bay and create for themselves a kind of grotto-style home.

It wasn't long before local smugglers saw Jack's cavelike environment as the ideal place to store their goods—which led Jack to become one of their number. It was a secret, working arrangement that existed until the year of Jack the Blaster's death in 1792. The caves were later extended to the point where they housed, rather astonishingly, a fifteen-room mansion. Today, the caves are home to the Marsden Grotto, one of the very few "cave pubs" in Europe.

Mike Hallowell is a local author-researcher who has uncovered evidence of a secret cult in the area that extends back centuries and which engages in controversial and dangerous activities. It all began with the Viking invasion of the United Kingdom in the ninth century and their beliefs in a violent, marauding sea monster known as the Shoney. Since the Shoney's hunting ground ranged from the coast of England to the waters of Scandinavia and the monster had a reputation for ferociousness, the Vikings did all they could to placate it. That, primarily, meant providing the beast with certain offerings. We're talking, specifically, about *human* offerings.

> The crews of the Viking ships would draw straws, and he who drew the shortest straw would be doomed to a terrible fate.

The process of deciding who would be the creature's victim was a grim one: The crews of the Viking ships would draw straws, and he who drew the shortest straw would be doomed to a terrible fate. He would first be bound by hand and foot. Then, unable to move, he would have his throat violently slashed, after which the body of the unfortunate soul would be tossed into the churning waters, with the hope that the Shoney would be satisfied and would not attack the Vikings' longships, as they were known. Sometimes, the bodies were never seen again. On other occasions, they washed up on the shore of Marsden, hideously mutilated and savagely torn to pieces.

Incredibly, however, this was not a practice strictly limited to the long-gone times when the Vikings roamed and pillaged in marauding fashion. Mike Hallowell was able to determine that belief in the Shoney never actually died out. As a result, the last such sacrifice was rumored to have occurred in 1928. Hallowell's sources also told him that the grotto's caves regularly, and secretly, acted as morgues for the bodies of the dead that the Shoney tossed back onto the beach, following each sacrifice.

Now the story becomes even more disturbing. As a dedicated researcher of the unknown, Hallowell began to dig ever deeper into the enigma of Marsden's dragon cult and even contacted local police authorities to try to determine the truth of the matter—and of the murders too, of course. It was at the height of his research that Hallowell received a number of anonymous phone calls sternly and darkly warning him to keep away from Marsden and its tale of a "serpent sacrifice cult" and verbally threatening him as to what might happen if he didn't. To his credit, Hallowell pushed on, undeterred by the Men in Black-like threats, and although much of the data is circumstantial, Hallowell has made a strong case that such a cult still continues its dark activities—possibly in other parts of the United Kingdom, too.

February 14, 1945, was the date of a still unresolved murder in rural England that bore all the hallmarks of death at the hands of a secret society. Some suggested that a band of witches were the culprits and others a secret sect of druids. The victim was a farm worker, seventy-four-year-old Charles Walton, found dead with nothing less than a pitchfork stuck out of his chest. He was a resident of a small, picturesque village in Warwickshire, England, called Lower Quinton. Walton had lived in the village all his life in a pleasant, old cottage that stood across from the local church. It was a scene not unlike what one might expect to see on *Downton Abbey* or in the pages of a Jane Austen novel. Until, that is, murder, mayhem, and a secret cult came to Lower Quinton.

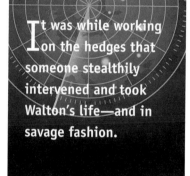

It was while working on the hedges that someone stealthily intervened and took Walton's life—and in savage fashion.

So far as can be ascertained, no one in the village had a grudge against Walton; he was known to all of the locals. He was an affable but quiet sort and—somewhat intriguingly—had the ability to entice wild birds to eat seeds from his hands. He was also said to have the power to reduce a wild, aggressive dog to a man's best friend simply by speaking to it. On top of that, he had expert knowledge of local folklore and legend. Rumors suggest that perhaps Walton's slightly uncanny "powers" had ensured him a place in a secret witchcraft cult, which he ultimately fell out of favor with and, as a result, paid the ultimate price: namely, his life.

What is known for sure is that on the day in question—Valentine's Day, no less—Walton was busily trimming hedges on what was known as Hillground: a large field at the foot of the Meon Hill. His tools were a hook and a pitchfork. It was while working on the hedges that someone stealthily intervened and took Walton's life—and in savage fashion. When his body was stumbled on by a shocked local, all hell broke loose in the small village. He was lying dead on the grassy ground, with the pitchfork pinning him to the ground and the hook having pierced his throat in savage and violent fashion. On top of that, a large cross had been cut into his chest.

It should be noted that Meon Hill has, for centuries, been associated with supernatural activity: sightings of blazing-eyed, black dogs—not unlike the terrible beast in Sir Arthur Conan Doyle's *The Hound of the Baskervilles*—have been reported. Satan himself is said to have kicked a large rock from the top of the hill to the bottom of it with the intention of flattening Evesham Abbey.

Such was the strange and sinister nature of Walton's death that the investigation wasn't just left in the hands of the local "bobbies." None other than Scotland Yard's finest detectives were soon on the case, and they weren't just on the case—they took over the entire investigation, under the control of Detective Inspector Robert Fabian. Despite an extensive investigation and suspicions that the guilty party was a man named Albert Potter—who was employing Walton on the day he met his grisly end—the matter was never resolved to the satisfaction of the police, and the mystery remained precisely that: a mystery.

It's worth noting, however, that Detective Inspector Fabian later said of his investigation of the affair: "One of my most memorable murder cases was at the village of Lower Quinton, near the stone Druid circle of the Whispering Knights. There a man had been killed by a reproduction of a Druidical ceremony on St. Valentine's Eve."

He also offered the following memorable words: "I advise anybody who is tempted at any time to venture into Black Magic, witchcraft, Shamanism—call it what you will—to remember Charles Walton and to think of his death, which was clearly the ghastly climax of a pagan rite. There is no stronger argument for keeping as far away as possible from the villains with their swords, incense and mumbo-jumbo. It is prudence on which your future peace of mind and even your life could depend."

It should also be noted that within Lower Quinton, the village folk are still very reluctant to speak about the decades-old affair. Tony Smith, the landlord of the village's College Arms pub, told the BBC: "I can't talk to you about that. After 17 years of running this place I know there are some things we don't talk about. Talking about it would upset people and there's no sense in alienating people in a small village like this. There are no relatives of Charles Walton left in the village and people that might have known what happened are all dead or gone."

A Mrs. Wakelon, who ran the village store, was equally reluctant to say much to the BBC: "People don't talk about it; it's a closed subject. Those that know about it are gone, except one who's in hospital and another that's in a nursing home. All the others have gone or passed away."

The manager of the local post office—who was only willing to be referred to by the BBC as Joyce—spoke in a similar vein and tones: "No one will talk to you about it. The family have all gone now, anyway. There are none of the Walton family left here now. I have no answers to your questions."

Death by pitchfork, rumors of a witchcraft cult, and a village still living in uneasy and closed-mouth fashion—the memories of the murder of Charles Walton show no signs of fading away anytime soon.

Summer 1969 was a strange period in the quest for the truth behind the legend of the Loch Ness Monster. It was a decidedly alternative period, too, given that information surfaced on a secret "dragon cult" operating in the vicinity of the huge loch. In early June, three American students paid a visit to Loch Ness. The purpose of their visit was to visit Boleskine House, an old hunting lodge (which burned down in 2015) that had once been owned by one of the key players in the world of secret societies. We're talking about none other than Aleister Crowley.

It was while walking around a centuries-old cemetery that stands close to where Boleskine House stood that they came across a strangely decorated piece of cloth: a tapestry, one might say. It was roughly four feet by five feet and was wrapped a large sea snail shell. It was covered in artwork of snakes and words that were soon shown to have been written in Turkish. One of the words translated as "serpent," which was a most apt description for the beast of Loch Ness. Rather notably, Turkey has its very own lake monster, which is said to dwell in the waters of Lake Van. More was to come, though; the tapestry found by the three students was adorned with images of lotus flowers. In ancient Chinese folklore, dragons had a particular taste for lotus flowers to the extent that in lakes where dragons were said to reside, the people of China would leave such flowers on the shores as a means to appease the violent beasts.

Of the several other people who had the opportunity to see and examine the tapestry in June 1969—in fact, only mere hours after it was found—one was a near-full-time Nessie seeker named Frederick "Ted" Holiday. He couldn't fail to make a connection between the Loch Ness Monster and the dragon- and serpent-based imagery. On top of that, the matter of the lotus flowers led Holiday to conclude that all of this was evidence of some kind of clandestine "dragon cult" operating in the area. The fact that Holiday knew all too well that Aleister Crowley was linked to all manner of secret societies was yet another reason that led Holiday to suspect the presence of a dragon cult in the area. As he began to dig even further into the story, Holiday uncovered rumors of alleged human sacrifice in the wooded areas surrounding Loch Ness as well as attempts by the secret group to try to "invoke" supernatural serpents from the dark waters of the loch.

The mysterious group in question, Holiday believed, was said to worship Tiamat, a terrifying Babylonian snake goddess, or sea dragon, who was revered as much as she was feared chiefly because of her murderous, homicidal ways. She mated with Abzu, the god of freshwater, to create a number of supernatural offspring, all of dragon- and serpentlike appearance. Then were the dreaded Scorpion Men, equally hideous offspring of Tiamat that were, as their name suggests, a horrific combination of man and giant arachnids. The legend goes that Abzu planned to secretly kill his children but was thwarted from doing so when they rose up and slayed him instead. Likewise, Tiamat was ultimately slaughtered by the god of storms, the four-eyed giant known as Marduk.

If, however, one knew the ways of the ancients, one could still call upon the power and essence of Tiamat—despite her death—as a means to achieve power, wealth, influence, and sex. Such rituals were definitively Faustian in nature, however (as they almost always are), and the conjurer had to take great heed when summoning the spirit form of Tiamat, lest violent, deadly forces might be unleashed. It was highly possible, thought Holiday, that the monsters seen at Loch Ness were manifestations of Tiamat, in some latter-day incarnation, specifically provoked to manifest by that aforementioned cult.

> If, however, one knew the ways of the ancients, one could still call upon the power and essence of Tiamat—despite her death—as a means to achieve power, wealth, influence, and sex.

Nothing was ever conclusively proved, but the entire situation left a bad taste in Holiday's mouth, made him deeply worried for his own safety, and eventually convinced him that the legendary creature of Loch Ness was itself supernatural in nature.

In September 2001, an investigation began into one of the United Kingdom's most mysterious—and still unresolved—murders. It all revolved around the shocking killing of a young boy who was suspected of being the victim of a mysterious and deadly cult. The date was September 21 when the body of a child was found in London's River Thames near where today the reconstruction of Shakespeare's Globe Theater can be found. To say that the child's "body" was found would, however, be something of an exaggeration. All that was recovered was the poor child's torso; his arms, legs, and head were missing. On top of that, his body was drained of blood. The police wasted no time in trying to get to the bottom of the mystery, which caught the attention of practically the entire U.K. population and the media.

It quickly became clear to the police that this was not a case of murder as such. Rather, it was a disturbing example of full-blown sacrifice. All of the child's limbs had been removed with what was obviously surgical expertise, and his stomach contents included the calabar bean, which is native to Africa. Notably, if ingested, the calabar bean can provoke seizures, respiratory failure, and even death. Very oddly, the boy's stomach also contained clay particles that were peppered with gold dust. The shocking story was widely reported by the United Kingdom's press amid rumors that perhaps an African secret society had killed the young boy—who the police dubbed "Adam."

Forensic analysis of Adam's remains revealed that they contained close to three times higher than normal levels of lead and copper—which suggested that Adam originated in West Africa and almost certainly in Nigeria. That theory was bolstered even further when it was determined that the calabar bean particles found in Adam's stomach were of a kind that were only found in Nigeria's Edo State. The investigation was led by Detective Constable Will O'Reilly and Commander Andy Baker. In quick time, they were able to determine that the shorts that were still attached to Adam's waist were available in only two countries: Austria and Germany. In addition, the investigators were positive that this was indeed a case of human sacrifice.

One of those brought into the investigation was Dr. Richard Hoskins of Bath University, an authority on African voodoo cults and their practices. He said:

> Adam's body was drained of blood, as an offering to whatever god his murderer believed in. The gold flecks in his intestine were used to make the sacrifice more appealing to that god. The sacrifice of animals happens throughout sub-Saharan Africa and is used to empower people, often as a form of protection from the wrath of the gods. Human sacrifice is believed to be the most "empowering" form of sacrifice—and offering up a child is the most extreme form of all.

Within West African witchcraft cults, it is not at all uncommon for the victims' amputated limbs to be used as a form of medicine. The eyes, fingers, and sexual organs are also utilized as magical charms.

Despite the overwhelming mystery surrounding the case, a breakthrough was finally made. It all revolved around a woman named Joyce Osagiede. A citizen of Nigeria, she was detained at Scotland's Glasgow Airport by immigration officers partly because she was acting in a highly erratic fashion. Significantly, she claimed knowledge of "extreme religious ceremonies" that her husband was involved in. Detective Constable O'Reilly and Commander Baker wasted no time in checking out the woman's story. They discovered something notable.

Osagiede and her children were temporarily housed in a Glasgow apartment in which the team found a pair of shorts identical to those that Adam was wearing at the time of his death. Osagiede was also found to have lived for a while in Germany, where such shorts, the police had confirmed, were available. However, it was also discovered that Osagiede was in Hamburg, Germany, at the time of Adam's murder, so although she may very well have known something of the grisly affair, she certainly wasn't the murderer. British authorities quickly deported her back to Nigeria. That was not the end of the matter, however.

Years later, Osagiede decided to come clean on what she knew—or, rather, on what she claimed she knew. While living in Germany, asserted

Osagiede, she took care of a young Nigerian boy whose mother was about to be sent back home, German authorities having refused to give her permission to stay. Osagiede added that she later handed the boy over to a man only known as Bawa, who was prepared to take him to London, England. Osagiede even had a name for the child: Ikpomwosa. She was certain that whatever cult Bawa was attached to, "they used [Ikpomwosa] for a ritual in the water."

However, problems exist with this story. Osagiede has also claimed that the boy's name was Patrick Erhabor. She later maintained that Bawa was actually one Kingsley Ojo, a bogus asylum seeker who arrived in the United Kingdom in 1997. Ojo denies any involvement in the death of the child, and the police have found nothing that might suggest any involvement on his part. Nevertheless, as the BBC noted:

> Ojo, who used three different identities, was arrested in London in 2002 by officers investigating the Adam case. In his flat they found in a plastic bag, a mixture of bone, sand and flecks of gold very similar to a concoction found in the dead boy's stomach. There was also a video marked "rituals" which showed a B-movie in which an actor cuts off the head of a man. Ojo said the video and mixture belonged to other people in the house and detectives could not establish a link between him and the Adam case. In 2004, he was sentenced to four-and-a-half years in prison for people smuggling. While in prison he contacted officers and offered to help with the inquiry. But investigators concluded he was wasting police time and he was deported to Nigeria.

The police's latest word on this horrific saga: "The investigation remains ongoing and any new information provided to the team will be thoroughly investigated."

Strange Twenty-First-Century Deaths

This book demonstrates that the New World Order is determined to control the pharmaceutical industry and its profits as well as ensuring that as many people as possible are hooked on mind-numbing drugs. Of course, if faced with a threat from the field of alternative health care, it is not at all out of the question that the New World Order might take steps to ensure that those who offer alternative health treatments are taken out of circulation—as in permanently. Disturbingly, that is exactly what we are seeing: holistic doctors are dying at an alarming rate. Let's see what people are saying of this affair.

On July 29, 2015, *Health Impact News* ran an article titled "Is the U.S. Medical Mafia Murdering Alternative Health Doctors Who Have Real Cures Not Approved by the FDA?" It stated:

> On June 19, 2015, Dr. [Jeffrey] Bradstreet reportedly shot himself in the chest after his offices were raided by U.S. FDA agents and State of Georgia law enforcement agents. Three days before his death, agents exercised a search warrant to gather information about the use of GcMAF with autistic patients in his clinic. Human GcMAF holds great promise in the treatment of various illnesses including cancer, autism, chronic fatigue and possibly Parkinson's. Since 1990, 59 research papers have been published on GcMAF, 20 of these pertaining to the treatment of cancer.

Freedom Outpost, in October 2015, offered the following from writer Tim Brown:

> Back in July, I reported that five holistic doctors had met untimely and suspicious deaths within 30 days and that five more were still

missing. Within days of that report, two more doctors were also found dead under suspicious circumstances, which made 7 inside of a month. Now, within the span of 90 days, eleven doctors have been found dead under suspicious circumstances, and just prior to the writing of this article a twelfth holistic doctor, Marie Paas, was found dead due to an apparent suicide.

Moving into 2016—specifically February—*Natural News* posted a news story with the title of "Wave of Holistic Doctor Deaths Continues, as Florida Chiropractor Suddenly Dies Despite Being 'Hearty and Healthy.'" The following is an excerpt from the article, which was the work of staff writer Julie Wilson:

> A wave of mysterious deaths continues to plague practitioners in the field of holistic medicine, including chiropractors, herbalists and other alternative healers, with the latest fatality involving a licensed chiropractor who also worked as a full-time teacher. Dr. Rod Floyd, Associate Professor and Faculty-Clinician with the Palmer College of Chiropractic at the Port Orange, Fla. campus, had just celebrated he and his wife's 37th wedding anniversary, when he abruptly passed away in his home late last month.

"50 Holistic Doctors Have Mysteriously Died in the Last Year, But What's Being Done about It?" That was the eye-catching title of an article that appeared at *Truth Theory* in June 2016. The story was intriguing and high-lighted thirty-four deaths within the previous year. They said: "We'll let you be the judge on whether or not the untimely demise of many of these practi-tioners is fate or suspect. What matters most is that if these doctors were killed because they're practicing true medicine, the injustice is uncovered and the parties responsible pay for their crimes."

Snopes.com took a different approach and stated: "As of March 2015, there was an estimated range of 897,000 to just over 1,000,000 doctors in the United States, and per every 100,000 people (of all vocations) each year, approximately 821 die. Going by those numbers alone, between 6,500 and 8,200 medical doctors will statistically die of myriad causes in any given year."

Are we seeing the sinister murder of holistic doctors on a large scale by the New World Order, or are people assuming that's the case as a result of looking for threads and links that may not be relevant? In time, we may know for sure.

Healthy Protocols noted in 2013:

> The death of Andrew Moulden is shrouded in mystery. Some sources say he had a heart attack and others say he committed sui-cide. A colleague of Dr. Moulden who wishes to remain anony-mous reported to Health Impact News that he/she had contact

with him two weeks before he died in 2013. Dr. Moulden told our source and a small number of trusted colleagues in October of 2013 that he was about to break his silence and would be releasing new information that would be a major challenge to the vaccine business of big pharma. He was ready to come back. Even though he had been silent, he had never stopped his research. Then, two weeks later, Dr. Moulden suddenly died. Dr. Moulden was about to release a body of research and treatments, which could have destroyed the vaccine model of disease management, destroyed a major source of funding for the pharmaceutical industry, and at the same time seriously damaged the foundation of the germ theory of disease.

In 2014, *The Telegraph* reported:

A Cambridge Professor has made the astonishing claim that three scientists investigating the melting of Arctic ice may have been assassinated within the space of a few months. Professor Peter Wadhams said he feared being labelled a "looney" over his suspicion that the deaths of the scientists were more than just an "extraordinary" coincidence. But he insisted the trio could have been murdered and hinted that the oil industry or else sinister government forces might be implicated. The three scientists he identified—Seymour Laxon and Katherine Giles, both climate change scientists at University College London, and Tim Boyd of the Scottish Association for Marine Science—all died within the space of a few months in early 2013. Professor Laxon fell down a flight of stairs at a New Year's Eve party at a house in Essex while Dr Giles died when she was in collision with a lorry when cycling to work in London. Dr Boyd is thought to have been struck by lightning while walking in Scotland. Prof Wadhams said that in the weeks after Prof Laxon's death he believed he was targeted by a lorry which tried to force him off the road. He reported the incident to the police.

Interestingly, microbial matters at the Arctic were areas that all three were working on.

IWB, in August 2014, revealed the following:

Glenn Thomas, a leading consultant in Geneva, an expert in AIDS and, above all, Ebola Virus, was on board the Boeing 777 Malaysia Airlines cut down on the border between Ukraine and Russia. Glenn Thomas was also the coordinator of the media and was involved in the investigations that were bringing to light the issue of trial operations of Ebola virus in the laboratory of biological weapons at the hospital in Kenema. Now that this workshop was closed by order of the Government of Sierra Leone, more details emerge about the interests that [are] hidden behind its management. Bill and Melinda Gates have connections with biological weapons labs located in Kenema, the epicenter of the epidemic of Ebola developed from the hospital where they were doing clinical trials on humans for the development of its vaccine, and now, following the opening of an informal survey, it appears the name of George Soros, through its Foundation, is funding the laboratory of biological weapons.

Steve Quayle, who has carefully studied the mysterious wave of deaths that have occurred in the last decade and a half, posted this in 2015, a breaking story on yet another death:

> Alberto Behar, Robotics expert NASA at the JPL died instantly when his single-engine plane nosedived shortly after takeoff Friday from Van Nuys Airport. He worked on two Mars missions and spent years researching how robots work in harsh environments like vol-

International investigators, such as these men from the Netherlands and Austria, were permitted to analyze the crash site where the Malaysia Airlines plane went down in 2014, killing all passengers, including an important Ebola virus researcher.

canoes and underwater. As part of the NASA team exploring Mars with the Curiosity rover, Behar was responsible for a device that detected hydrogen on the planet's surface as the rover moved.

47-year old NASA Scientist Alberto Behar helped to prove that there had once been water on Mars according to the *Daily Mail* story published to announce his recent death in a plane crash that happened on Friday in LA, California. While plane crashes do happen and scientists do die, Behar's name has now been added to a very long list of scientists and astronomers who have met their untimely ends prematurely, leading us to ask, did Behar know something that "they" don't want the rest of society to find out?

In late March 2002, the Rickenbaugh family of Denver, Colorado—Kent, Caroline, and son Bart—were wiped out when their aircraft plunged to the ground close to Centennial Airport. Also killed was sixty-three-year-old Steven Mostow. It turns out that Mostow was at the forefront of research into highly infectious diseases at the University of Colorado's Health Sciences Center. Notably, on several post-9/11 occasions, Mostow briefed the U.S. Intelligence Community on the latest developments in the field of what is termed bioterrorism. Coincidence or something more, on the same day that Mostow and his passengers were killed on that ill-fated flight, on the other side of the Atlantic, a man named David Wynn-Williams died after being hit by a car. He had done work for NASA, specifically looking at how viruses could exist in the most extreme of all environments. Moving on to 2003....

> At the time of his death, Burghoff was deeply studying the possibility of terrorists attacking cruise ships.

On July 18, the body of Dr. David Kelly was found in woods near his home. Kelly was not your average doctor. He had been the British Ministry of Defense's chief scientific officer, the senior adviser to the Proliferation and Arms Control secretariat and to the Foreign Office's Non-Proliferation Department. Not only that, but Kelly held the prestigious position of senior adviser on biological weapons to the United Nations' biological weapons inspections teams (Unscom) from 1994 to 1999. Roughly four months later, Robert Leslie Burghoff was killed. He was a forty-five-year-old scientist who lost his life due to the actions of a hit-and-run driver in Braeswood, Texas. At the time of his death, Burghoff was deeply studying the possibility of terrorists attacking cruise ships. He prepared several papers on that very subject for U.S. Intelligence, none of which have surfaced into the public domain via the terms of the Freedom of Information Act.

July 3, 2004, was the date of yet another death that was seen as being potentially suspicious in nature—not just by conspiracy theorists but also by elements of the U.K. government and Intelligence Community. It was on that day that Dr. Paul Norman of Salisbury, Wiltshire, England, was killed. His light plane slammed into the ground in the English county of Devon. You may not be at all surprised to know that Dr. Norman had ties to British Intelligence and to the field of deadly viruses. Indeed, he was the chief scientist for chemical and biological defense at the British Ministry of Defense's laboratory at Porton Down, Wiltshire—a highly secure, and deeply secret, installation that is at the forefront of the U.K. government's work in the fields of bacteriology and chemical warfare. The site was sealed off due to the fact that the pilot was someone of great significance to the defense of the United Kingdom. The crash was the result of a tragic accident, the media was informed.

One month later, Professor John Clark, head of the science laboratory that created Dolly, the "cloned" sheep, was found hanging by the neck in his vacation home. Clark led the Roslin Institute in Midlothian, Scotland, one of the world's leading animal biotechnology research centers, and played a crucial role in creating the transgenic sheep that earned the institute worldwide fame.

Just like the years from 2001 to 2004, working in the field of deadly viruses in 2005 was far more hazardous than it usually was. On January 7, a retired research assistant professor at the University of Missouri—Jeong H. Im, primarily a protein chemist—was knifed to death, his corpse found in the trunk of a torched car in a local parking garage. Witnesses talked of seeing a man in a ski mask fleeing the area, but nothing of substance was ever confirmed.

May 2005 also proved to be deadly. David Banks, an Australian scientist in the employ of Biosecurity Australia, lost his life in a plane crash in Queensland. At the time, he was undertaking a "survey for the Northern Australia quarantine strategy." It was just an accident, said the Australian authorities.

Some people may say that if one looks closely at any community, one can find that threads and leads that suggest what appear to be mysterious deaths may actually not be anything of the sort. Of course, that's not at all impossible. On the other hand, though, one can say with a fair degree of certainty that it's most unusual to see such a large number of people wiped off the face of the planet in a field that, up until 2001, was not exactly known for its multiple, regular deaths of a very controversial kind. Also, let's not forget that many of these cases eerily mirror what was afoot in the United Kingdom from the early 1970s to the start of the 1990s.

As for the second decade of the twenty-first century, we're still seeing a wealth of mysterious deaths of scientists and doctors.

The New World Order is clearly determined to create a world bank of a kind never before seen, which will control and hold the savings of everyone on the planet. What might happen to those in the banking community who dare to go against this dangerous plot? They might pay with their lives. It looks like that may already be happening.

In 2016, the *Free Thought Project* informed its readers:

In 2015 there was a popular "conspiracy theory" floating around the internet after a rash of mysterious "suicides" by high profile banking professions. What once looked like wild speculation is now beginning to resemble a vast criminal conspiracy connected to the Libor [London Inter-Bank Offered Rate] interest-rigging scandal. Over forty international bankers allegedly killed themselves over a two-year period in the wake of a major international scandal that implicated financial firms across the globe. However, three of these seemingly unrelated suicides seem to share common threads related to their connections to Deutsche Bank. These three banker suicides, in New York, London, and Siena, Italy, took place within 17 months of each other in 2013/14 in what investigators labeled as a series of unrelated suicides.

Financial regulators in both Europe and the U.S. in 2013 began a probe that would ultimately become known as the Libor scandal, in which London bankers conspired to rig the London Interbank Offered Rate, which determines the interest banks charged on mortgages, personal and auto loans. The scandal rocked the financial world and cost a consortium of international banks, including Deutsche Bank, about $20 billion in fines.

One of those who died under unusual circumstances, in March 2013, was David Rossi, a fifty-one-year-old communications director at the world's oldest bank, Italian Monte dei Paschi di Siena. It was verging on disaster as a result of massive losses in the financial crisis of 2008. He fell to his death on March 6, 2013. The *New York Times* said of Rossi's death:

A devastating security video shows Rossi landing on the pavement on his back, facing the building—an odd position more likely to occur when a body is pushed from a window. The footage shows the three-story fall didn't kill Rossi instantly. For almost 20 minutes, the

The Montei dei Paschi bank in Siena, Italy, the world's oldest, still-operating bank (pictured), was on the verge of a huge financial scandal when its communications director died mysteriously.

banker lay on the dimly lit cobblestones, occasionally moving an arm and leg. As he lay dying, two murky figures appear. Two men appear and one walks over to gaze at the banker. He offers no aid or comfort and doesn't call for help before turning around and calmly walking out of the alley. About an hour later, a co-worker discovered Rossi's body. The arms were bruised and he sustained a head wound that, according to the local medical examiner's report, suggested there might have been a struggle prior to his fall.

This is from *Wall Street on Parade* in April 2014:

It doesn't get any more Orwellian than this: Wall Street mega banks crash the U.S. financial system in 2008. Hundreds of thousands of financial industry workers lose their jobs. Then, beginning late last year, a rash of suspicious deaths start to occur among current and former bank employees. Next we learn that four of the Wall Street mega banks likely hold over $680 billion face amount of life insurance on their workers, payable to the banks, not the families. We ask their Federal regulator for the details of this life insurance under a Freedom of Information Act request and we're told the information constitutes "trade secrets."

Clearly, powerful figures do not want the media too close to uncovering the truth of this dark and deadly aspect of the banking business. Powerful figures within the New World Order? Who else?

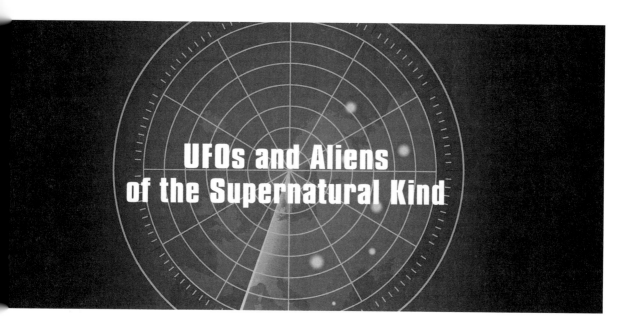

UFOs and Aliens of the Supernatural Kind

A s we saw in the first chapter of this book, in late 2017 the *New York Times* revealed the startling story of a secret program within the Pentagon that had been clandestinely investigating UFO sightings for a number of years, including reports from U.S. military pilots. One of those who played a key role in the creation of the project was Democratic senator Harry Reid. In December 2017, it was revealed that Reid had a controversial belief with regard to UFOs: namely, that the UFO phenomenon was not extraterrestrial in nature and origin but, rather, that it was a mystery of supernatural or occult proportions. It's a theory that, as we shall now see, has been the subject of highly classified U.S. government programs dating back decades.

Back in January 2007, I interviewed a man named Ray Boeche. He has an interesting background, as he is both a priest and a former state director with MUFON, the Mutual UFO Network. At the time in question, I was thinking about writing a book on the infamous Rendlesham Forest UFO event of December 1980 (which plays a role in the chapter of this book on the theory that holograms played a significant role in the 9/11 events). I already knew that Boeche had spoken to a couple of government insiders who had shared some pretty bizarre and amazing data with him on the incident. It was data that suggested that at least a significant portion of the affair may have revolved around the use of sophisticated holograms rather than anything extraterrestrial.

As I continued to chat with Boeche, however, he told me something that I found even more intriguing. Boeche revealed that his insider sources said they were attached to a classified program within the military intelligence–government world that was seeking contact with what they termed

"Non-Human Entities," or NHEs for short. At first, the group suspected that the entities were extraterrestrial. As time went on, however, that theory was replaced by a far more controversial one. The group came to believe that they were dealing with nothing less than demonic entities from a realm of the supernatural, but apparently, that didn't stop the group from trying to contact and interact with them.

Reportedly, as a result of the group trying to work with demons, various deaths occurred in the program (Boeche told me that his sources personally showed him graphic photos of some of the dead) as well as ill health and bizarre runs of bad luck. It was as if the entire project was cursed. In fact, that is exactly what some of the members of the group came to believe. When Ray told me all of this, I found it far more fascinating than the Rendlesham idea, so I decided to dig further into what was clearly a much stranger story, interviewing Boeche at length and seeking out other sources, too. Most of the information I uncovered on this group—which used the nickname of "The Collins Elite" (I still don't know its real name)—was published in my 2010 book, *Final Events*.

U.S. senator Harry Reid of Nevada once admitted in an interview with journalist George Knapp that some people in government believed the UFO phenomenon had supernatural connections.

I don't personally think that the NHEs are literal demons, but I do believe that they are dangerous and manipulative entities from other realms of existence. However, for me, the most notable and fascinating aspect of all this was the fact that some element of the U.S. government was (and still is) covertly funding the group, primarily those in government who adhere to the "satanic UFO" angle. You may well ask, then, why am I mentioning all of this right now? I'll tell you.

In December 2017, Las Vegas, Nevada-based investigative journalist George Knapp spoke with Reid, who had retired as senator in January of that year. In the interview, Knapp brought up the matter of "satanic UFOs" and "fear based on religious beliefs" in relation to the Intelligence Community and UFOs. Knapp then addressed the matter of the UFO phenomenon being "evil." Reid was clearly awkward about addressing this issue for the media, but he did somewhat grudgingly admit that people in the U.S. government believed that UFOs had supernatural, rather than extraterrestrial, origins.

With all of this in mind, let's now see how the whole story of Ray Boeche, the U.S. government, and the phenomenon of supernatural UFOs and paranormal aliens occurred.

Boeche believes that the UFO phenomenon has supernatural—rather than extraterrestrial—origins. In November 2001, he met two physicists working on a classified program buried deep in the heart of the Department of Defense. The story told to Boeche revolved around attempts on the part of the people in that same program to contact what they termed "Non-Human Entities." Some of us might call them aliens. Others, though, might suggest they are demons; certainly, this latter theory was endorsed widely within the U.S. government. I interviewed he extensively about the story. If the story is true and Boeche was not the subject of a disinformation program, it's mind-blowing and horrifying. He said:

> I found it interesting because they had contacted me at work; and I have no idea how they tracked me down there. But, they wanted to know if we could get together and have lunch to discuss something important. I met them for a brief period of time on that first meeting, and then they said: "We'd like to get together and have a longer conversation." I arranged a time and it was quite a lengthy discussion, probably three and a half hours. And that's how it all came about.

> After both meetings, when I was able to verify that the men held the degrees they claimed to hold, and were apparently who they claimed to be, I was intrigued and excited at the possibility of having stumbled on a more or less untouched area which could be researched. But I was also cautious in terms of "why me?"

> I had no way of knowing before our face-to-face meeting if there was any legitimacy to this at all. I wasn't given any information at all before our meeting, just the indication that they were involved in areas of research I would find interesting, and that they had some concerns they wished to discuss with me. Both men were physicists. I'd guess they were probably in their early-to-mid fifties, and they were in a real moral dilemma. Both of them were Christians and were working on a Department of Defense project that involved trying to contact the NHEs. In fact, this was described to me as an "obsessive effort." And part of this effort was to try and control the NHEs and use their powers in military weapons applications and in intelligence areas, such as remote-viewing and psychotronic weapons.

> They came to believe that the NHEs were not extraterrestrial at all; they believed they were some sort of demonic entities. And

that regardless of how benevolent or beneficial any of the contact they had with these entities *seemed* to be, it always ended up being tainted, for lack of a better term, with something that ultimately turned out to be bad. There was ultimately *nothing* positive from the interaction with the NHE entities. They felt it really fell more under the category of some vast spiritual deception instead of UFOs and aliens. In the course of the whole discussion, it was clear that they really viewed this as having a demonic origin that was there to simply try and confuse the issue in terms of who they were, what they wanted, and what the source of the ultimate truth is. If you extrapolate from their take that these are demons in the biblical sense of the word, then what they would be doing here is trying to create a spiritual deception to fool as many people as possible.

From what they told me, it seemed like someone had invoked something and it opened a doorway to let these things in. That's certainly the impression they gave me. I was never able to get an exact point of origin of these sorts of experiments, or of their involvement, and when they got started. But I did get the impression that because of what they knew and the information that they presented, they had been involved for at least several years, even if the project had gone on for much longer. They were concerned that they had undertaken this initially with the best of intentions, but then as things developed they saw a very negative side to it that wasn't apparent earlier. So, that's what leads me to think they had a relatively lengthy involvement.

Most of it was related to psychotronic weaponry and remote viewing, and even deaths by what were supposed to be psychic methods. The project personnel were allowed to assume they had somehow technologically mastered the ability to do what the NHEs could do: remote-viewing and psychotronics. But, in actuality, it was these entities doing it all the time, or allowing it to happen, for purposes that suited their deception. With both psychotronic weapons and remote-viewing, I was told that the DoD had not really mastered a technology to do that at all; they were allowed by the NHEs to think that this is what they had done. But the NHEs were always the causal factor.

They showed me a dozen photos of three different people—four photos of each person, who had apparently been killed by these experiments. These were all post-mortem photographs, taken in-situ, after the experiments. The areas shown in all of the photographs were like a dentist's chair or a barber's chair, and the bodies were still in those positions, sitting in the chairs. Still there, with EEG and EKG leads coming off of them. They were all wired. It was a very clinical setting, and there was no indication of who they were. It was a very disturbing sort of thing. And I'm thinking in the back of my mind: if these are real, who would they have gotten for these experiments? Were they volunteers? Were they some sort of prisoners? I have no idea. Were they American? Were they foreign? There was no way to tell.

They had read some of my stuff, and they knew that I'd become a pastor and that I had a Christian viewpoint from which I could examine these things. And they were concerned morally and ethically that they had allowed themselves to be duped into doing this research, and it had taken such a turn. My concern was always that: why come to me? Who am I? I can't do anything for you. I'm happy to evaluate it as best I can, but if you have this concern, why not go to a Christian leader with a lot more clout and public visibility than I've got? But that was their reason: they were aware of the research I had done on a lot of things, that I could approach it from a Christian viewpoint, and that it was more of a moral dilemma for them. They wanted the information out there. But, to me, I have to think: is any of this accurate? On one hand, is this a way to throw disinformation out? But, on the other hand, I think that even if they wanted to just spread disinformation, they could have done it with someone a lot more influential than me.

I've been involved in this since 1965 and this is the most bizarre stuff I've ever run across. I didn't know what to make of it then and I don't know what to make of it now.

It's very important to note that Ray Boeche's story does not stand alone. In fact, quite the opposite; more than a few threads collectively demonstrate that certain projects, programs, and think tanks within the U.S. government have addressed this matter for decades. Dan T. Smith is an interesting character, a man whose father was Harvard economist Dan Throop Smith, the Treasury Department's number-one tax advisor during the Eisenhower administration. Researcher Gary Bekkum said of Smith: "His personal meetings have included former and present representatives of the U.S. government intelligence community and their political associates, like Chris Straub, a former member of the Senate Select Committee on Intelligence."

Researcher Vince Johnson, who had the opportunity to speak with Smith about his ufological views and insider contacts, stated:

> According to Smith, UFOs are primarily a psychological/metaphysical phenomenon which are both preparing us and pressuring us to develop our own psi abilities. Not that UFOs are a single type

of entity; Smith asserts that there are "powers and principalities" at work—presumably supernatural entities like angels and demons.

[Smith] reported that his governmental sources "hinted at" an eschatological emergency…. When I asked why the CIA was interested in eschatology, he replied that the ramifications of the eschaton event represented a serious threat to national security, and thus, fell into the purview of the intelligence agencies. Smith also revealed that the eschatological issues he raised related directly to the biblical prophecies of the Book of Revelation.

Back in 2009, I met with a certain elderly Dr. Mandor, who had invited me to his run-down home. Infinitely paranoid and deeply disturbing, Mandor had apparently been at the forefront of a quasi-official U.S. government project tasked, in the early 1980s, with determining the truth behind the "alien abduction" phenomenon. To say that Mandor was obsessed with the world and lore of the Middle Eastern Djinn is not an understatement. Mandor, who believed the so-called "Grey" aliens of UFO lore were literal djinn, was also obsessed with trying to call forth and command djinn—surely a goal of definitively crackpot proportions—but Mandor was apparently not the only member of this project who had a pressing desire to summon up supernatural entities hellbent on tormenting the human race. This story, too, does not stand alone.

One explanation of the origins of the Greys is that they are actually djinn, demons of paranormal origin.

In an April 8, 2014, article at *Mysterious Universe*—titled *Did the CIA Possess Djinn Infested Jewelry?*—Jesse Woldman notes: "One site I came across advertised a second-hand ring, for around $500. What I found particularly interesting was its description. It was claimed that the ring had been worn by 'a very successful CIA Agent' who had used the Djinn contained inside to be promoted quickly within her department and enjoy many positive experiences in both her personal and professional life."

For those who are not familiar with the djinn, they are ancient, supernatural creatures who, according to the Qur'an, are made of "smokeless fire" and are typically hostile, manipulative, and even deadly. They can, however, be benevolent, too, when the mood takes them.

Woldman also notes of this CIA/secondhand ring story: "This wacky item reminded me of rumors I'd heard previously about how the US Government did indeed have a relationship with Djinn and other entities, in an effort to try to harness these little-understood powers for Military gain."

Jumping back in time, the DoD—or, at least, some within it—had, as far back as 1972, concluded that what has become known as Hell was not a fiery pit overseen by Satan but some form of extradimensional realm inhabited by dark entities with a profound hatred of the human race and who "farm" our "soul energy" upon death for reasons that were hypothesized and suspected but never ultimately proved. The story came from a well-known professor who shared the story with me at the height of my research into the story of Ray Boeche. The scenario was not at all like that in the trilogy of *Matrix* movies, starring Keanu Reeves. Indeed, the only major differences were that (a) in the movies, we are milked by machines, whereas in the minds of certain players in the Pentagon, it was extradimensional entities that were doing the milking; and (b) in *The Matrix*, it's our bodies that are being used, but for the DoD, it was our life force, our soul.

Having been "slightly more than gently nudged not to speak on this" with colleagues, the media, friends, and family, the professor was asked if he would be willing to prepare a detailed report for the group on his knowledge of, and extensive research into, three specific issues: theories pertaining to the nature of the human soul, the concept and agenda of demons, and the role played by fallen angels with respect to deception as described in the Bible.

He agreed and was given a telephone number where the pair could always be reached. Six weeks or so later, his report completed, the professor placed his call, and the two men duly came back again. They thanked him for his time and, having handed over his paper, which ran to around 130 double-spaced pages, he received a "very nice" payment for his efforts, courtesy of Uncle Sam.

Given the clandestine nature of the experience, the professor somewhat wryly titled the document "To Whom It May Concern." Before the two men left, they asked him if he would be willing to speak on the subject of his paper for the group. Nothing ultimately ever came of this offer, however, even though the professor was both quite agreeable and open to the idea of presenting a lecture on the nature of his report.

Then is the matter of a CIA program known as Operation Often. Investigative writer Brent Swancer reveals that the project was designed to understand, exploit, and militarize the worlds of the occult and the supernatural. He says:

> The accusation was first put forth by British investigative journalist and author Gordon Thomas who wrote

Hell was not a fiery pit overseen by Satan but some form of extradimensional realm inhabited by dark entities with a profound hatred of the human race....

the 2007 book *Secrets and Lies*, and who claims that a Dr. Sidney Gottlieb, chief of the CIA's Technical Services Branch and also known as the "Black Sorcerer" due to his expertise with poisons, used the program to "explore the world of black magic and harness the forces of darkness and challenge the concept that the inner reaches of the mind are beyond reach."

It's worth noting that while yes, Thomas did indeed reveal interesting and relevant data in his 2007 book, he was actually looking into the Often controversy years before that. For example, back in 1988, Thomas's *Journey into Madness* was published by Bantam Press. Its subtitle: *Medical Torture and the Mind Controllers*. The book contains five pages on Operation Often. It also includes a quote taken from an Often memo, so it would appear that Thomas's knowledge of the operation probably dated back to at least the mid-eighties. Maybe even earlier than that.

Swancer adds: "It is unclear just how much of this is true and how much of it is pure conspiracy theory. Although it is known that the U.S. did in fact pursue mind control experiments with its MKUltra program, the real extent of how deep the rabbit hole goes is still rather a mystery. Did any of the offshoots and subprograms actually look into the occult and utilizing magic to any extent, and if so what results did they achieve, if any?"

It's highly likely that a great deal of truth to all this exists. Why should we think that? Well, because when we go looking, we find other examples that seem to suggest a more-than-passing interest in the occult on the part of government agencies. In 1994, Dr. Nelson Pacheco—a principal scientist with the Supreme Headquarters, Allied Powers, Europe (SHAPE), Technical Center—and Tommy Blann wrote a book with the title of *Unmasking the Enemy*. It was a look at the "aliens are really demons" controversy. The pair noted something that may interest those of you who might want to try to uncover more on Operation Often.

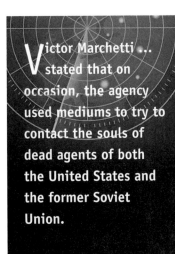

Victor Marchetti ... stated that on occasion, the agency used mediums to try to contact the souls of dead agents of both the United States and the former Soviet Union.

Pacheco and Blann stated in their book: "The CIA began infiltrating séances and occult gatherings during the 50s.... A memo dated April 9, 1953, refers to a domestic—and therefore illegal—operation that required the planting of a very specialized observer at a séance in order to obtain a broad surveillance of all individuals attending the meetings."

Victor Marchetti, the author of *The CIA and the Cult of Intelligence*, stated that on occasion, the agency used mediums to try to contact the souls of dead agents of both the United States and the former Soviet Union. Marchetti was careful to note that he never came across anything that suggested such experiments worked, but the important thing in all this is that Marchetti confirmed a link between the CIA operations and what we might term paranormal activity. Also of relevance is the legendary occultist, Aleister Crowley, who died in 1947.

The United Kingdom's Freedom of Information Act has shown that MI5 (the Brits' equivalent of the United States's FBI) had at least some degree of interest in the "Great Beast," as Crowley was famously known. It's all very much thanks to the research of Richard B. Spence, of the International Spy Museum, that we know this. Spence has said of Crowley: "He was such a disreputable and even evil character in the public mind that arguably no responsible official would think of employing him. But the very fact that he seemed such an improbable spy was perhaps the best recommendation for using him."

While knocking on the doors of MI5 (so to speak), Spence learned, in 2003, that MI5 had had a file on Crowley that had been destroyed back in the 1950s. Spence continued to investigate and found references to additional papers on Crowley. Those records were said to have been destroyed, too. In other words, we know that an MI5–Crowley connection exists, but we don't know how extensive (or not) it was. On one hand, maybe Crowley was secretly employed by MI5 as a spy. On the other hand, perhaps, the files were opened because MI5 considered Crowley to be a subversive or, at the absolute extreme end of theorizing, just possibly someone in MI5 wanted to know if occult phenomena could be weaponized—which is, basically, what Operation Often's staff were trying to determine.

Whatever the full story of Operation Often and the far-less-than-clear saga of Aleister Crowley and MI5, when we add all of that to the revelations of Pacheco and Marchetti, what we see is a definite interest in the world of the occult on the part of intelligence agencies. How far that interest has gone, though, is anyone's guess.

What all of this demonstrates is that interest in the world of the supernatural—and its connections to the issues of alien life and UFOs—dates back a very long time and, as the December 2017 revelations of former senator Harry Reid make clear, that interest still continues.

The 9/11 Controversy

September 11, 2001, will go down as one of the worst days in the history of the United States of America, if not *the* worst. In terms of tragedy and outrage, it is equaled only by the terrible events of December 7, 1941, when Japanese forces attacked Pearl Harbor, Hawaii, killing nearly twenty-five hundred Americans in the process. In shockingly quick progression—and with equally shocking ease—nineteen al-Qaeda terrorists seized control of four large passenger planes and, essentially, turned them into the equivalents of missiles. On the morning of September 11th, United Airlines Flight 175 and American Airlines Flight 11 slammed, respectively, into the South and North Towers of New York's World Trade Center. Another American Airlines plane, Flight 77, hit the Pentagon, and United Airlines Flight 93 hurtled to the ground outside of Shanksville, Pennsylvania, when a number of passengers attempted to wrestle control of the plane from the hijackers. Some suspected that the plan of the hijackers was to target none other than the White House itself. Before the day was over, a nation was stunned to its core, and almost three thousand people had lost their lives.

Although the United States had been subjected to terror attacks in the past, none equaled the levels of horror that 9/11 provoked. They were attacks that, near-singlehandedly, prompted the invasions of both Iraq and Afghanistan, as the George W. Bush administration sought to bring the guilty parties to justice and prevent any future similar events from occurring. It wasn't just horror and outrage that resulted from 9/11; the events also ensured the rapid development of a wide and varied body of conspiracy theories, all suggesting that the story told to the public and the media—that the attacks were the work of al-Qaeda—was very wide of the mark.

Rather oddly, given that Osama bin Laden made no bones about his hatred of the West, and the United States in particular, he denied any involvement in the attacks of September 11, 2001, at all—until 2004. Precisely why the one man who, more than any other, wished to do significant harm to the United States would deny his involvement in committing the worst atrocity on U.S. soil since 1941 makes very little sense. In terms of the propaganda value and of instilling fear in the minds of American citizens, bin Laden should have been all over 9/11 from day one. The fact that he was not is something many have failed to realize and, even more, do not understand.

Also of interest is the matter of how less than two dozen men, armed with nothing more than box cutters, were able to kill thousands of Americans, destroy both of the Twin Towers, and cause major damage to the Pentagon. It's almost as if the terrorists were *allowed* to carry out their deadly actions while the authorities looked the other way and turned a blind eye. Maybe, that's precisely what did occur. Let's begin with the events at the World Trade Center.

Steve Alten is a best-selling author, probably most widely known for his controversial novel *The Shell Game*, a 2009 story that tells of the next 9/11-style event on U.S. soil. Alten makes no bones about the fact that he has major suspicions that we have not been told the real story of what happened on September 11, 2001. In a foreword to his novel, Alten correctly notes that on the morning of 9/11, then-Vice President Dick Cheney oversaw a series of war games that, in Alten's opinion, "purposefully diverted all of our jet fighters away from the Northeastern Air Defense Sector (NEADS) where the four hijackings took place, sending them over Alaska, Greenland, Iceland, and Canada."

Alten also significantly noted: "One of these exercises, *Vigilant Guardian*, was a hijack drill designed to mirror the actual events taking place, inserting twenty-two false radar blips on the FAA's radar screens so that flight controllers had no idea which blips were the hijacked aircraft and which were the war game blips."

The result: mass confusion over what was real and what was not and a lack of adequate military defense at the time when the Twin Towers were struck.

Then is the matter of certain highly suspicious stock trading that went on in the immediate days before the attacks, which led to vocal assertions from the conspiracy-minded that those engaged in the trading secretly knew of what was about to hit the United States. Most of the activity revolved around the very two airlines whose planes were used in the attacks: American Airlines and United Airlines.

Allen M. Poteshman, of the *Journal of Business*, said of this curious state of affairs: "A measure of abnormal long put volume was also examined and seen to be at abnormally high levels in the days leading up to the attacks. Consequently, the paper concludes that there is evidence of unusual option

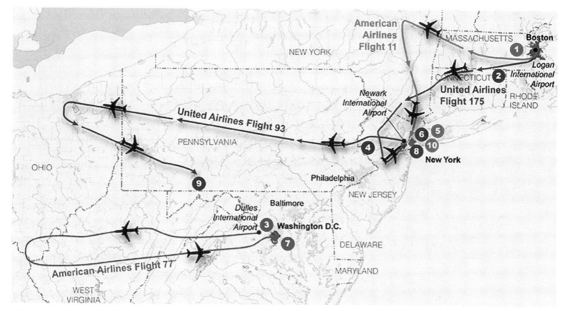

This map shows the flight paths the four planes hijacked by terrorists took on September 11, 2001. Two crashed into the Twin Towers in New York City, one into the Pentagon, but a fourth crashed into the Pennyslvania countryside after passengers bravely attacked the pilots.

market activity in the days leading up to September 11 that is consistent with investors trading on advance knowledge of the attacks."

It wasn't just airlines that were experiencing abnormal stock-based activity right before 9/11. The world of insurance did, too. Both Morgan Stanley and Citigroup Inc., experienced massive increases in trading from September 8 right up until the time of the attacks. Indeed, Citigroup Inc.'s trading was in excess of *forty times* its normal level. Citigroup stood to pay out millions in insurance claims from the World Trade Center attacks. Morgan Stanley had their offices *within* the World Trade Center. One of the United States' leading defense companies, Raytheon, saw trading leap more than five times its normal approximate level on September 10.

Also on the matter of advance knowledge of 9/11 is a curious, and downright surreal, story that has a link to none other than *The X-Files*. Although Mulder and Scully were the focus of just about every episode, from time to time, they received significant help in their efforts to uncover the truth of a number of cosmic conspiracies from a trio of eccentric conspiracy theorists. They were John Byers, Melvin Frohike, and Richard Langly, who published the *Magic Bullet Newsletter*. The three characters became better known as the Lone Gunmen. Such was the enthusiasm that the show's fans had for Langly, Frohike, and Byers, in early 2001, they were given their very own short-lived series. The name of the series surprised no one: *The Lone Gunmen*.

The first episode aired on March 4, 2001. Its title was *Pilot*. The plotline was chillingly similar to the events that went down on 9/11. In the show, a computer hacker takes control of a Boeing 727 passenger plane and flies it toward the World Trade Center with the specific intention of crashing the plane into one of the Twin Towers. It's only at the very last moment that the Lone Gunmen are able to hack the hacker and avert disaster and death for those aboard the plane and those inside the World Trade Center.

The story gets even more intriguing: the hacker is not just some random, crazy guy. It's all the work of a powerful group buried deep within the U.S. government. The secret plan, had it worked, was to put the blame for the World Trade Center attacks on one or more foreign dictators who are "begging to be smart-bombed" by the U.S. military. It should be stressed that no evidence exists that the creators of *The Lone Gunmen* had any advance knowledge of 9/11. It is worth noting, however, that the media was deeply reluctant to address the storyline of *Pilot* and its parallels to 9/11—not to mention that the episode had its premiere broadcast in Australia just *thirteen days* before the events of September 11th occurred.

One of those who commented on this odd state of affairs was Christopher Bollyn. He said: "Rather than being discussed in the media as a prescient warning of the possibility of such an attack, the pilot episode of *The Lone Gunmen* series seemed to have been quietly forgotten. While an estimated 13.2 million Fox TV viewers are reported to have watched the pilot episode … when life imitated art just six months later on 9/11, no one in the media seemed to recall the program."

Frank Spotnitz was one of the executive producers of *The Lone Gunmen*. He said: "I woke up on September 11 and saw it on TV and the first thing I thought of was *The Lone Gunmen*. But then in the weeks and months that followed, almost no one noticed the connection. What's disturbing about it to me is, you think as a fiction writer that if you can imagine this scenario, then the people in power in the government who are there to imagine disaster scenarios can imagine it, too."

Robert McLachlan was the director of photography on *The Lone Gunmen*. He had words to say, too: "It was odd that nobody referenced it. In the ensuing press nobody mentioned that [9/11] echoed something that had been seen before."

Jeffrey King, who has carefully studied the 9/11 events, asked: "Is this just a case of life imitating art, or did [the production company] know something about the upcoming attacks? Was this an attempt to use the highly visible platform of the first episode of a new series (and a spin-off from the very popular *X-Files*) to make enough people aware of the scenario that it would become too risky to implement? Or was it just one of those ideas that was 'in the air' at the time, an expression of the zeitgeist?"

King had more to impart: "Great and traumatic events always seem to be preceded by certain foreshadowings [sic], like the upstream standing waves that form behind a rock in the streambed. Perhaps this is just another in the endless string of odd synchronicities surrounding the events of 9/11, peculiar juxtapositions of events that must eventually strain the credulity of even the most devoted coincidence theorist, though no single one rises to the level of a smoking gun."

Then is the matter of the speed, and ease, with which the Twin Towers fell to the ground. Many people claimed that the ways in which the South and North Towers collapsed were far less consistent with what one could expect from aircraft collisions and far more consistent with the likes of a carefully controlled demolition—and those people were not all conspiracy theorists.

It should be noted that when the towers were constructed, they were specifically designed to survive a direct strike from an aircraft the size of a Boeing 707. They were also built to withstand winds of up to 160 miles per hour. Instead, both towers did not continue to stand. Quite the opposite: they crumbled to the ground, causing even more terror and death for the people of New York. The South Tower fell just short of an hour after it was hit, while the North Tower stood for just one hour and forty-two minutes.

One person who carefully studied the data suggesting that the towers were brought down in definitive demolition style was Steven Jones, a physics professor at Brigham Young University. In 2005, Jones helped to establish an organization called Scholars for 9/11 Truth. Jones suffered for his cause: after publishing his theories that the collapse of the Twin Towers was caused by explosives, he was placed on leave by the university. He responded by retiring on January 1, 2007. It was Jones's theory that the specific type of substance used was likely to have been nano-thermite, used by the military in explosives.

"I am electing to retire so that I can spend more time speaking and conducting research of my choosing," said the professor as he bid the university goodbye.

Global Research noted:

The massive core columns—the most significant structural feature of the build-

The World Trade Center is shown here in March 2001, just a few months before it was destroyed by airplanes piloted by terrorists.

ings, whose very existence is denied in the official 9/11 Commission Report—were severed into uniform 30-foot sections, just right for the 30-foot trucks used to remove them quickly before a real investigation could transpire.

There was a volcanic-like dust cloud from the concrete being pulverized, and no physical mechanism other than explosives can begin to explain how so much of the buildings' concrete was rendered into extremely fine dust. The debris was ejected horizontally several hundred feet in huge fan shaped plumes stretching in all directions, with telltale "squibs" following the path of the explosives downward.

These are all facts that have been avoided by mainstream and even most of the alternative media. Again, these are characteristics of the kind of controlled demolitions that news people and firefighters were describing on the morning of 9/11.

It's important to note that it was not just the North and South Towers that fell on 9/11. A third tower, completely untouched by the aircraft that plowed into the towers, also collapsed. It was Tower 7 of the World Trade Center complex. Dylan Avery, who directed the 9/11-themed film *Loose Change*, said: "The truth movement is heavily centered on Building 7 and for very good reason; a lot of people are very suspicious about what went down that day."

The BBC noted: "Avery points out that Tower 7 housed some unusual tenants: the CIA, the Secret Service, the Pentagon and the very agency meant to deal with disasters or terrorist attacks in New York—the Office of Emergency Management. And some people think Tower 7 was the place where a 9/11 conspiracy was hatched."

The official explanation, the BBC noted, was that "ordinary fires" were to blame for the fall of Tower 7 but, the BBC also said, this "makes this the first and only tall skyscraper in the world to have collapsed because of fire."

Then is the theory that, as per the claims surrounding the December 7, 1941,

7 World Trade Center collapsed just like its sisters, the Twin Towers, but it was never struck by an airplane. Why and how was it destroyed, then? Many suspect this strongly supports the idea that the towers were deliberately taken out by the U.S. government.

attack on Pearl Harbor, 9/11 was allowed to happen to justify an invasion of the Middle East. Michael Meacher was the British government's environment minister from 1997 to 2003. His words, as a senior official of the government, did not go by unnoticed. They were picked up widely:

> [I]t is clear the US authorities did little or nothing to pre-empt the events of 9/11. It is known that at least 11 countries provided advance warning to the US of the 9/11 attacks. Two senior Mossad experts were sent to Washington in August 2001 to alert the CIA and FBI to a cell of 200 terrorists said to be preparing a big operation. The list they provided included the names of four of the 9/11 hijackers, none of whom was arrested.

> It had been known as early as 1996 that there were plans to hit Washington targets with airplanes. Then in 1999 a US national intelligence council report noted that "al-Qaida suicide bombers could crash-land an aircraft packed with high explosives into the Pentagon, the headquarters of the CIA, or the White House."

> Fifteen of the 9/11 hijackers obtained their visas in Saudi Arabia. Michael Springman, the former head of the American visa bureau in Jeddah, has stated that since 1987 the CIA had been illicitly issuing visas to unqualified applicants from the Middle East and bringing them to the US for training in terrorism for the Afghan war in collaboration with Bin Laden. It seems this operation continued after the Afghan war for other purposes. It is also reported that five of the hijackers received training at secure US military installations in the 1990s.

September 11 Secrets

Of the four aircraft that were involved in the 9/11 attacks, three succeeded in reaching their intended targets: United Airlines Flight 175 and American Airlines Flight 11 slammed into the Twin Towers of the World Trade Center, and American Airlines Flight 77 hit the Pentagon. The one exception was United Airlines Flight 93, which failed to reach its target—which may have been the White House, although this is, admittedly, speculation. Instead, it crashed in a field near Shanksville, Pennsylvania. Although Flight 93, a Boeing 757, could hold almost two hundred passengers, fewer than forty were onboard when, at 8:42 A.M. on the morning of September 11th, the plane took to the skies from Newark International Airport, New Jersey, under the control of Capt. Jason Dahl. Forty-six minutes later, the plane was under siege.

Terrorists had control of the plane. Each and every one of them had practically breezed their way through security. They were Ziad Jarrah, Saeed al-Ghamdi, Ahmed al-Nami, and Ahmed al-Haznawi. Only the latter was subjected to a high degree of screening, but it was a screening that raised no red flags whatsoever. All four men were sitting in first class, which made it relatively easy for them to invade the cockpit with speed.

It was just a couple of minutes before 9:30 A.M. that the hijackers launched their attack on the cockpit, which occurred after the Twin Towers had already been hit. Although United Airlines staff members sent messages to their crews, Capt. Dahl did not receive the message until just mere minutes before the hijack began. A study of the cockpit recordings retrieved after the crash showed that the hijackers successfully breached the cockpit and overpowered the crew, possibly critically injuring, or killing, Capt. Dahl in the process.

A few moments later, a voice, coming from the cockpit, echoed around the plane: "Ladies and gentlemen: this is the captain. Please sit down and keep remaining seated. We have a bomb on board. So sit."

Not surprisingly, the frantic passengers and flight attendants quickly phoned friends and family and, in doing so, learned of the attacks on the World Trade Center. They soon learned, too, of the attack on the Pentagon, which occurred just minutes after the hijacking of Flight 93. As a result, the passengers formulated a plan to try to wrestle the plane out of the hands of the terrorists. The recordings reveal a wealth of confusion, shouting, screaming, and moaning, all of which graphically demonstrated the nightmarish, terrifying situation onboard the plane. Friends and family were told that the pilots were dead or dying, that men with bombs strapped to their bodies were in the cabin, and that the hijackers were supposedly going to return to the airport to make their demands known to U.S. authorities.

When a group of passengers attempted to storm the cockpit—by ramming the door with the food and drink cart—the hijackers knew their time

This is the field in Somerset County, Pennsylvania, where Flight 93 crashed in 2001. It is believed the terrorists were taking the plane to Washington, D.C., and that brave passengers thwarted the attempt at the cost of their own lives.

was short, as the black box data showed. Instead of continuing on to their destination of San Francisco, California, or heading back to Newark, they first put the plane through a violent series of maneuvers to specifically try to knock the passengers off their feet. When that failed to work and the passengers continued, the hijackers chose to end things there and then. Shortly after 10:00 A.M., the plane crashed into the ground between Shanksville and Indian Lake, Pennsylvania. No one survived the impact.

Although no definitive proof exists, it has been suggested that some of the passengers may have made it into the cockpit and managed to prevent the hijackers from continuing on with their mission to hit whatever their intended target was.

In terms of the conspiracy theories that surround the events of September 11, 2001, the most enduring, when it comes to Flight 93, is that the plane was not deliberately crashed by the hijackers or as a result of a confrontation between the hijackers and the passengers but was blasted out of the skies by a U.S. military aircraft.

On September 15, *CBS 58 News* reported: "Federal investigators said on Thursday they could not rule out the possibility that the United jet was shot down. 'We have not ruled out that,' FBI agent Bill Crowley told a news conference when asked about reports that a U.S. fighter jet may have fired on the hijacked Boeing 757. 'We haven't ruled out anything yet.'"

Then, in November, journalist William Bunch spoke with the mayor of Shanksville, Ernie Stuhl, on the issues surrounding the crash of Flight 93. Bunch reported:

> Ernie Stuhl is the mayor of this tiny farming borough that was so brutally placed on America's psychic map on the morning of Sept. 11, when United Airlines Flight 93 slammed nose-down into the edge of a barren strip-mine moonscape a couple of miles outside of town. A 77-year-old World War II veteran and retired Dodge dealer, he's certainly no conspiracy theorist.
>
> And, when you ask Stuhl for his theory of what caused the jetliner to crash that morning, he will give you the prevailing theory— that a cockpit battle between the hijackers and burly, heroic passengers somehow caused the Boeing 757 to spiral out of control. "There's no doubt in my mind that they did put it down before it got to Washington and caused more damage," he said.
>
> But press the mayor for details, and he will add something surprising.
>
> "I know of two people—I will not mention names—that heard a missile," Stuhl said. "They both live very close, within a couple of hundred yards. This one fellow's served in Vietnam and he says

he's heard them, and he heard one that day." The mayor adds that based on what he knows about that morning, military F-16 fighter jets were "very, very close."

In April 2009, writer Paul Joseph Watson reported:

A woman who claims she was stationed at Fort Meade on September 11, 2001, has given an explosive interview about how she personally heard military commanders make the decision to shoot down United Airlines Flight 93 on 9/11.

A person using the pseudonym Elizabeth Nelson [said] that she personally heard officials agree on the order to shoot down Flight 93. The decision was apparently made because the plane was flying in a no-fly zone near to Camp David and heading toward *Site R*, a military facility known as the "backup Pentagon."

Nelson stresses that at no time was there any talk of "hijackers," and the plane was shot down purely because communication had been lost and standard operating procedure mandated that the plane be intercepted and destroyed.

Christopher Bollyn, of *American Free Press*, said:

Susan McElwain, a local teacher, also reported seeing a white "military" plane at the scene of the crash before witnessing an explosion. Ms. McElwain told *The Daily Mirror* what she saw:

"It came right over me, I reckon just 40 or 50 feet above my minivan," she recalled. "It was so low I ducked instinctively. It was traveling real fast, but hardly made any sound. Then it disappeared behind some trees. A few seconds later I heard this great explosion and saw this fireball rise up over the trees, so I figured the jet had crashed. The ground really shook. So I dialed 911 and told them what happened. I'd heard nothing about the other attacks and it was only when I got home and saw the TV that I realized it wasn't the white jet, but Flight 93."

None of this proves that Flight 93 was shot down, and the fact that some of the data has been offered anonymously weakens the case. Nevertheless, whatever the truth of the matter, the claim that Flight 93 was brought down by the U.S. military continues to endure.

Only minutes after Flight 93 was hijacked, the crew and passengers of American Airlines Flight 77 suffered a near-identical fate. They, too, found themselves hijacked and on a course with death. Just like Flight 93, the aircraft involved was a Boeing 757. It was piloted by Capt. Charles Burlingame and left Washington Dulles International Airport for Los Angeles International Airport, California, at 8:20 A.M. on the morning of 9/11. It was around twenty to twenty-five minutes into the flight that terror broke out across the plane: a group of five men took control of the aircraft. The ringleader was Hani Saleh Hasan Hanjour, a Saudi Arabian who possessed a commercial pilot's certificate, which gave him significant skills when it came to directing the 757 into the Pentagon.

Much of what happened on board the plane remains a mystery to this very day—chiefly because the cockpit voice recorder was so badly damaged in the fiery crash that nothing of any use was ever recovered. What is known for certain is that air traffic controllers lost contact with Capt. Burlingame and his crew at 8:50 A.M. Given that the first attack on the World Trade Center had already occurred, it was clear to ground control that something serious was going on and almost certainly a hijacking. A couple of people—including Barbara Olson, the wife of U.S. Solicitor General Theodore Olson—managed to contact family and confirmed that the plane had been hijacked by men armed with knives. Barbara Olson told her husband that everyone—including the crew—had been ordered to the rear of the plane. The hijackers now had complete control of the cockpit.

Only minutes after Flight 93 was hijacked, the crew and passengers of American Airlines Flight 77 suffered a near-identical fate.

Hanjour, a skilled pilot, took his plane toward Washington, D.C., on a course for the Pentagon. Somewhat incredibly, he managed to not only aim the huge 757 at the Pentagon but actually managed to fly low and horizontal right into the building at a speed of more than five hundred miles an hour. So low was the plane, it actually destroyed a number of street-level lampposts as it smashed directly into its target. The result was complete chaos and devastation: everyone on board—six crew members, fifty-three passengers, and all five hijackers—was killed, as were 125 people in the Pentagon. It was almost a miracle that more Pentagon employees didn't lose their lives, since the aircraft penetrated the building by more than three hundred feet and sent a massive fireball into the skies above.

Mike Walter, a *USA Today* writer, witnessed the terrible event: "I looked out my window and I saw this plane, this jet, an American Airlines jet, coming. And I thought, 'This doesn't add up, it's really low.' And I saw it. I mean it was like a cruise missile with wings. It went right there and slammed right into the Pentagon."

Terrance Kean, who lived nearby, said that he saw a "very, very large passenger jet ... plow right into the side of the Pentagon."

Despite all the evidence suggesting that the plane had been hijacked and crashed into the Pentagon—something confirmed by Kean, Walter, and others—a controversial conspiracy soon took shape: that the Pentagon was not hit by a hijacked aircraft at all but by a missile.

The account that Flight 77 hit the Pentagon is troublesome because the plane wreckage seems to have disappeared. Some say the large plane was a cover for the actual attack by an F-16.

Maj. Gen. Albert N. Stubblebine, the commanding general of the United States Army Intelligence and Security Command from 1981 to 1984, said:

> I saw a photograph taken by one of the sensors on the outside of the Pentagon. Now, all of the sensors had been turned off, which is kind of interesting—isn't it? That day, why would all of the sensors around the Pentagon be turned off? That's strange. I don't care what the excuse is. That's strange.
>
> There happened to be one that apparently did not get turned off. And in that picture, coming in, flying into the Pentagon, you see this object, and it obviously hits the Pentagon. When you look at it, it does not look like an airplane. Sometime later, after I'd gone public, that imagery was changed. It got a new suit around it that now looked like an airplane. But, when you take the suit off, it looks more like a missile—not like an airplane.

The website *911review.com* noted that, in 2002, a theory was advanced suggesting:

A Boeing 757 did indeed swoop down toward the west block of the Pentagon, but disappeared into a blinding pyrotechnic display, making it appear that it had crashed into the building, while in fact it had cleared the facade, overflown the Pentagon, and then banked sharply to land at Reagan National Airport, whose runways are only about two miles away from the Pentagon. As the jetliner was disappearing into the fireball, a small attack jet, such as an F-16, approached from a different trajectory and crashed into the wall, producing, in combination with a missile, the damage to the facade and interior.

This theory has the advantage over other no-757-crash theories that it is consistent with the many credible eyewitness reports of a jetliner. However, it neither explains the eyewitness statements that the plane collided with the building, nor the lack of a single eyewitness statement supporting the idea that a 757 overflew the Pentagon and then landed at the nearby National airport. Also, the theory raises questions about the fate of the passengers of Flight 77.

On the tenth anniversary of 9/11, Britain's *Guardian* newspaper reported in its summary of the conspiracy theories that had risen over the past decade:

> A French author, Thierry Meyssan, had a bestseller—*9/11: The Big Lie*—within months of the attacks by claiming the Pentagon was destroyed by a missile and aircraft parts were brought to the scene to fake the crash. It is a theory supported by Dean Hartwell who claims in his books—*Planes without Passengers: The Faked Hijackings of 9/11* and *Osama bin Laden Had Nothing to Do with 9/11*—to have uncovered documentary evidence that two of the hijacked flights never took off and the other two landed safely in secret.

The *Guardian* asked quite reasonably, then, what happened to those who we are assured died on all four aircraft on the morning of September 11, 2001? According to Hartwell:

> The people who got on the planes were simply pawns. They were, whether wittingly or unwittingly, directed to show up at the airport terminal just to show people who were watching that there were passengers. They were simply agents and they were given new identities. The government wanted to fake plane attacks to scare the public. We saw horrible images on television that were designed to provoke us into supporting wars in Afghanistan and Iraq.

It's also important to remember that we saw images of normal, everyday Washington, D.C., residents assuring us that they saw a Boeing 757 hit the Pentagon.

As with the killings of the Kennedy brothers, John and Robert, the death of Martin Luther King Jr., and the events at Pearl Harbor in 1941, it's most unlikely that the conspiracy theories surrounding 9/11 will fade away anytime soon. Many have said they shouldn't fade away, since they tell the truth of what really happened.

Michael Lerner, a political activist, rabbi, and the editor of *Tikkun* magazine, gets the last words:

> I would not be surprised to learn that some branch of our government conspired either actively to promote or passively to allow the attack on 9/11. For those who watched the reactionary political uses made of this tragedy, it's easy to conjure up a variety of possible conspiratorial motives that would have led the president, the vice president, or some branch of the armed forces or CIA or FBI or other "security" forces to have passively or actively participated in a plot to re-credit militarism and war.

Undoubtedly, the most controversial theory of all for what happened on September 11, 2001, is that no aircraft were involved. Not a single one. Welcome to the world of holograms. A growing number of conspiracy theorists firmly believe that what everyone assumed were real aircraft were, instead, highly sophisticated holograms. It's not just those aforementioned conspiracy theorists who believe that not a single aircraft was involved in the 9/11 events. One of them is Morgan Reynolds. He is none other than the former chief economist within the Labor Department under the George W. Bush administration. He is very vocal in his belief that aircraft were not responsible for the thousands who died on September 11th. He says that "digital composing" only made it appear that way. He firmly stated: "There were no planes, there were no hijackers. I know, I know, I'm out of the mainstream, but that's the way it is."

Then there is David Shayler. A former employee of the United Kingdom's MI5 (which is the U.K. government's equivalent of the FBI) caused a sensation in the late 1990s when he blew the whistle on multiple secrets held by MI5. As a result, Shayler fled to France, where he stayed until the summer of 2000, when he returned to the United Kingdom of his own volition. Incredibly, Shayler got off very lightly, spending only weeks in jail. As for his views on 9/11, Shayler says that "the only explanation is that they were missiles surrounded by holograms made to look like planes. Watch footage frame by frame and you will see a cigar-shaped missile hitting the World Trade Center."

Does such highly sophisticated hologram-style technology really exist? Well, that very much depends on who you ask. Certainly, no shortage of such claims exists, as we shall now see.

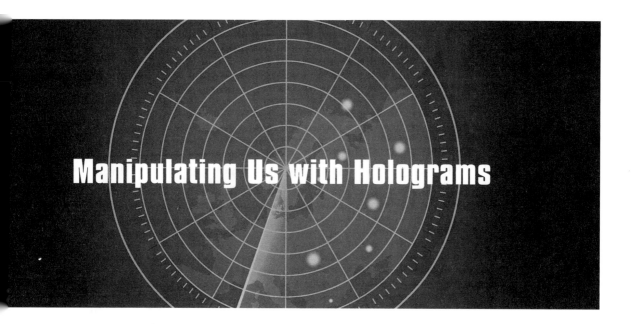

Manipulating Us with Holograms

Over the years, many UFO researchers have sought to find the answers to a strange incident that occurred in Rendlesham Forest, Suffolk, England, in the latter part of December 1980. An official report prepared by Charles I. Halt, Lt. Col., USAF, deputy base commander of the Royal Air Force Bentwaters base. Halt wrote the following:

1. Early in the morning of 27 Dec 80 (approximately 0300L) two USAF security police patrolmen saw unusual lights outside the back gate at RAF Woodbridge. Thinking an aircraft might have crashed or been forced down, they called for permission to go outside the gate to investigate. The on-duty flight chief responded and allowed three patrolmen to proceed on foot. The individuals reported seeing a strange glowing object in the forest. The object was described as being metallic in appearance and triangular in shape, approximately two to three meters across the base and approximately two meters high. It illuminated the entire forest with a white light. The object itself had a pulsing red light on top and a bank(s) of blue lights underneath. The object was hovering or on legs. As the patrolmen approached the object, it maneuvered through the trees and disappeared. At this time the animals on a nearby farm went into a frenzy. The object was briefly sighted approximately an hour later near the back gate.

2. The next day, three depressions 1.5 inches deep and 7 inches in diameter were found where the object had been sighted on the ground. The following night (29 Dec 80) the area was checked

for radiation. Beta/gamma readings of 0.1 milliroentgens were recorded with peak readings in the three depressions and near the center of the triangle formed by the depressions. A nearby tree had moderate (0.05–0.07) readings on the side of the tree toward the depressions.

3. Later in the night a red sun-like light was seen through the trees. It moved about and pulsed. At one point it appeared to throw off glowing particles and then broke into five separate white objects and then disappeared. Immediately thereafter, three star-like objects were noticed in the sky, two objects to the north and one to the south, all of which were about 10 degrees off the horizon. The objects moved rapidly in sharp, angular movements and displayed red, green and blue lights. The objects to the north appeared to be elliptical through an 8–12 power lens. They then turned to full circles. The objects to the north remained in the sky for an hour or more. The object to the south was visible for two or three hours and beamed down a stream of light from time to time. Numerous individuals, including the undersigned, witnessed the activities in paragraphs 2 and 3.

UFO researchers consider the Rendlesham Forest affair to be one of the most significant UFO cases of all time, but is that really the case? Some say "No." What they do say is that the whole affair was a sophisticated experiment, one designed to fool the airmen who encountered the "craft" into thinking they were encountering something extraterrestrial when, in reality, it was a hologram drive ruse, one designed to see the extent to which the human mind could be fooled.

Of the many UFO researchers who have studied the Rendlesham Forest affair, one is Ray Boeche. He is a longtime UFO investigator and priest whose work in the field of UFOs is also referenced elsewhere in the pages of this book, much of it relative to Boeche's conclusions that the true UFO phenomenon is supernatural in nature. It's not monsters we're focusing on in this chapter, though. Rather, it's the issue of what went down in Rendlesham Forest close to forty years ago.

In November 1991, Ray Boeche had the opportunity to meet with two physicists working on a classified program for the U.S. Department of Defense. It was a program that had a direct tie to the Rendlesham Forest event of December 1980. I spoke to Boeche on this very issue back in 2007, and he detailed what he learned from his two informants. Boeche stated:

I found it interesting that they would mention Rendlesham at the meeting. They said there was a sense that this was maybe, in some sense, staged. Or that some of the senior people there were more

An artist's recreation of the strange, triangular objects encountered by patrolmen at RAF Woodbridge.

concerned with the reaction of the men—how they responded to the situation, rather than what was actually going on. That this was some sort of psychotronic device, a hologram, to see what sort of havoc they can wreak with people. But even if it was a type of hologram, they said it could interact with the environment. The tree marks and the pod marks at the landing site were indications of that. But how can you have a projected thing like a hologram that also has material, physical capabilities? They wouldn't elaborate on this.

Was a part of the Rendlesham Forest incident tied to the advancing technology of holograms? Yes, it seems so, but, as will now become apparent, far more is to the case than that.

Within the field of conspiracy theorizing, few greater controversies exist than Project Blue Beam. Allegedly, it is the brainchild of a secret group of powerful figures in, among many others, NASA, the United Nations, the Bilderbergers, the Trilateral Commission, and the Vatican. Project Blue Beam, so the story goes, will be at the forefront of a program to create a new society dominated by martial law and an iron-fisted world government.

How might such a government come about? By faking the Second Coming of Jesus Christ, specifically by using sophisticated, hologram-type technology to project huge images of the Son of God across the skies of the United States, Canada, Australia, and much of Europe. Other parts of the world will see massive images of Buddha, of Allah, of Krishna, of Mohammed, and of multiple other gods depending on the regions, the people and their cultures, and the beliefs of the relevant nations.

In mere days, however, each and every one of those images will merge into one far more sinister and terrifying image: that of the Antichrist, who will inform the people of Earth that not a single one of the world's religions has the correct version of events. Only that of this nightmarish entity is the accurate version. As a result, the entire human race will be expected to bow down and worship the Antichrist.

Such a thing will result in worldwide chaos, disorder, and anarchy—which the people behind Project Blue Beam shrewdly know only all too well. With the world plunged into states of fear and mayhem, this terrible ruse will then allow the United Nations to coordinate a planetwide program to

The east gate at RAF Woodbridge, where the incident took place, but was it actually a UFO incident, or was it a holographic fraud?

enslave the Earth's entire population. The story is as fantastic as it is terrifying, but is it true?

The source of the Project Blue Beam story was Serge Monast, a journalist from Montreal, Quebec, Canada. Although Monast began his career in regular journalism, by 1994, he was focused almost exclusively on conspiracy theories, including matters relative to Masonic-based conspiracy theories and matters relative to the one-world government scenario. It was at this time that Monast claimed to have uncovered massive amounts of secret information on Project Blue Beam and how it would be utilized to enslave all but that aforementioned elite. The fact that Monast died in December 1996 of a heart attack at the age of just fifty-one has led to suspicions that he was murdered by agents of this dangerous program. The reason: to prevent Monast from blowing the whistle, big-time, on the project.

The Watcher Files notes:

> The infamous NASA Blue Beam Project has four different steps in order to implement the new age religion with the antichrist at its head. We must remember that the new age religion is the very foundation for the new world government, without which religion the dictatorship of the new world order is completely impossible. I'll repeat that: Without a universal belief in the new age religion, the success of the new world order will be impossible! That is why the Blue Beam Project is so important to them, but has been so well hidden until now.

> [It] involves a gigantic "space show" with three-dimensional optical holograms and sounds, laser projection of multiple holographic images to different parts of the world, each receiving a different image according to predominating regional national religious faith. This new "god's" voice will be speaking in all languages.

David Openheimer, who has studied the Project Blue Beam claims, says:

> The "system" has already been tested. Holographic projections of the "CHRIST IMAGE" have already been seen in some remote desert areas. These have only been reported in tabloid papers, so they are instantly rendered moot. They can also project images of alien craft, aliens, monsters, angels—you name it. Computers will coordinate the satellites and software will run the show-and-tell.

> Holography is based on very nearly identical signals combining to produce and image, or hologram, with depth perception. This is equally applicable to acoustic (ELF, VLF, LF) waves as it is to optical phenomena.

> Specifically, the "show" will consist of laser projections of multiple holographic images to different parts of the planet, each receiving

different images according to the predominating regional religious faith. Not a single area will be excluded. With computer animation and sound effects appearing to come from the depths of space, astonished followers of the various creeds will witness their own returned Messiah in spectacularly convincing lifelike realness.

Time may tell if Project Blue Beam plays a role in the looming New World Order. Let us sincerely hope it does not.

If you think that such a thing could not be achieved, it may be time to reassess your position. It was attempted way back in the early 1960s. Born in 1908, Maj. Gen. Edward Geary Lansdale served with the U.S. Office of Strategic Services during the Second World War. Then, in 1945, he was transferred to HQ Air Forces Western Pacific in the Philippines, and in 1957, he received a posting to the Office of the Secretary of Defense, working as deputy assistant to the SoD for what were vaguely, but intriguingly, termed as Special Operations.

> Certainly, no such Cold War-era operation got more special (and weird) than one that Lansdale pretty much singlehandedly coordinated. It was one, truly, of biblical proportions.

Certainly, no such Cold War-era operation got more special (and weird) than one that Lansdale pretty much singlehandedly coordinated. It was one, truly, of biblical proportions. Indeed, it was designed to try to convince the leadership and the people of Cuba of two startling things: (a) that the Second Coming of Jesus Christ had arrived; and (b) that he was a big fan of the United States of America! Yep, I kid you not....

Contained within the pages of a November 20, 1975, document titled *Alleged Assassination Plots Involving Foreign Leaders, Interim Report of the Select Committee to Study Government Operations with Respect to Intelligence Activities* is a fascinating statement from one Thomas A. Parrott, who served with the CIA for twenty-four years and who held the prestigious position of assistant deputy director for national intelligence programs. Commenting on some of Lansdale's more bizarre operations that were prompted by religion, ancient mythology, and legend, Parrott noted to the committee:

> I'll give you one example of Lansdale's perspicacity. He had a wonderful plan for getting rid of [Fidel] Castro. This plan consisted of spreading the word that the Second Coming of Christ was imminent and that Christ was against Castro who was anti-Christ. And you would spread this word around Cuba, and then on whatever date it was, that there would be a manifestation of this thing. And at the time—this was absolutely true—and at the time just over the horizon there would be an American submarine that would

surface off of Cuba and send up some star-shells. And this would be the manifestation of the Second Coming and Castro would be overthrown.

Star shells, for those who may be wondering, are, essentially, pyrotechnic flares of the military designed to fill the skies at night with bright and widespread illumination. The ambitious plan that Lansdale had in mind, though, involved much more than just dazzling the Cubans with mere flares. The feasibility was also looked into of using a U.S. Navy submarine to project images of Jesus Christ onto low-lying clouds off the coast of the Cuban capital of Havana.

The plan also involved—at the very same time—the crew of a U.S. military plane, camouflaged by the clouds and with its engine significantly muffled, using powerful loudspeakers to broadcast faked messages from an equally faked Christ to the people of Cuba, ordering them to overthrow their government and renounce communism. Executed properly, such a highly alternative operation might very well have convinced the Cubans that Jesus Christ himself really was calling—and he was not bringing good news for Fidel Castro. Ultimately, while the whole thing was seen as undoubtedly ingenious in nature, it was also viewed as an operation that had a very big chance of failing catastrophically.

If the Cubans got word that a U.S. submarine was in the very immediate area and took successful military action against it, the disastrous cost to American lives might have far outweighed anything that the operation could have achieved. Thus, this strange, biblical charade of the Cold War was shelved.

Of course, this begs a very important, significant, and troubling question: if any sort of Second Coming really does occur at some point in the future of the human race, how will we know if it has its origins in Heaven or the murky and mysterious world of officialdom? Maybe we actually won't know. Perhaps those in power see the ingenious exploitation of religion as the ultimate tool of warfare, manipulation, and overwhelming control.

A Controversy-filled Act

The events of September 11, 2001—coupled with the anthrax attacks that occurred shortly afterward—provoked terror, fear, and feelings of deep paranoia and angst within the American population. They also provoked something else: the rapid passing of what became known as the Patriot Act. It was—and still, to this very day, remains—without doubt one of the most controversial pieces of legislation ever put into place by government officials. Very few people doubted that, post–9/11, America needed to create new policies and programs to combat terror-driven attacks on the nation and its people. For many, however, the controversial content of the Patriot Act was seen as being way over the top and something that had the excessive ability to take away the rights, freedoms, and everyday existences of American citizens—and to do so with shocking speed, if it was so deemed necessary.

It was on October 24, 2001—only a month and a half after 9/11 forever changed the United States—that Congress passed the act. It was not an act that everyone in government was happy about, however. The vote was 357 to 66 in the House. Twenty-fours later, in the Senate, things were very different: 98 to a dissenting 1. Like it or not, the Patriot Act was now a reality and one that was here to stay.

Given that the Patriot Act was designed to help lessen the potential for terror attacks on the United States and on its overseas interests, why did it so quickly become the target of critics? The answer is as simple as it is disturbing: the act allowed for widespread monitoring of U.S. citizens in ways that had never before been used. It allowed for extreme measures to be taken—all in the name of national security—to keep the nation safe, and, said the critics, could be enforced to try to turn America into a nation of Orwellian proportions. One does not have to be a conspiracy theorist to see how such a sorry state of affairs could, one day, come to pass.

Included in the Patriot Act are clauses that allow government agencies and personnel to (a) access someone's home without their permission or even their knowledge; (b) hold individuals in prison-style facilities indefinitely; and (c) dig through e-mails, phone calls, and personal bank records—all without any need for permission from a court or a judge. Particularly chilling: the Patriot Act gives the government carte blanche access to the reading habits of each and every U.S. citizen and resident. It does so by allowing government agencies to record the title of every single book taken out of a library, to note who is borrowing the book, and to store their physical address in relevant data banks. It should be noted that while many—even within government and in the court system—have argued loudly and soundly that all of this is outrageously unconstitutional, it has not made a single bit of difference. Although certain changes were made to the legislation in 2005, the Patriot Act continues to stand as an example of the kind of thing that would have given the likes of the aforementioned George Orwell nightmares.

Let's not get ahead of ourselves, though. Let's see how the act came to be and how and why its very existence has created such a furor.

Only eight days after the attacks on the World Trade Center and the Pentagon, new legislation was presented to Congress by the Department of Justice. It was a bill entitled the Anti-Terrorism Act. It was also a bill that introduced Congress to the Patriot Act. It's an act whose very title has meaning. "Patriot" stands for *Provide Appropriate Tools Required to Intercept and Obstruct Terrorism*. In one sense, that was all well and good, since the act would clearly help in the fight against those who wish to do us harm. It was, however, the negative impact that the tools used in the fight could have on American society that concerned so many. Indeed, the Anti-Terrorism Act swept aside pre-existing acts designed to protect the rights of each and every U.S. citizen, including the Bank Secrecy Act, the Electronic Communications Privacy Act, the Money Laundering Control Act, and the Foreign Intelligence Surveillance Act.

President George W. Bush is shown here shortly after signing the Patriot Act into law. Many felt it gives the U.S. government too many powers to snoop into citizens' private lives.

One of the most outrageous aspects of the story of the Patriot Act is how it came to be so easily passed and why only one dissenter existed, Senator Russell Feingold of Wisconsin. Put simply, and astonishingly, the overwhelming majority who voted to enact the new legislation did not read it prior to agreeing to its creation. Worse still, solid indications exist that it was deliberately made difficult for senators to see the bill before passing it.

Alex Jones wrote: "Congressman Ron Paul (R-Tex) told the *Washington Times* that no member of Congress was allowed to read the first Patriot Act that was passed by the House on October 27, 2001. The first Patriot Act was universally decried by civil libertarians and Constitutional scholars from across the political spectrum." Jones also noted that William Safire, writing for the *New York Times*, detailed the first Patriot Act's powers by saying that "President [George W.] Bush was seizing dictatorial control."

Jones continued:

> The secretive tactics being used by the White House and Speaker [Dennis] Hastert to keep even the existence of this legislation secret would be more at home in Communist China than in the United States. The fact that Dick Cheney publicly managed the steamroller passage of the first Patriot Act, insuring that no one was allowed to read it and publicly threatening members of Congress that if they didn't vote in favor of it that they would be blamed for the next terrorist attack, is by the White House's own definition terrorism. The move to clandestinely craft and then bully passage of any legislation by the Executive Branch is clearly an impeachable offense.

At the same time that critics of the act were trying to reign in its abilities, however, government personnel were trying to make it even more powerful.

This scenario was further noted by Michael Moore in his 2004 documentary, *Fahrenheit 9/11*. Congressman John Conyers makes an incredible statement in the movie on the matter of those who did or did not read the act before passing it. In Conyers' very own words: "We don't read most of the bills: do you really know what that would entail if we read every bill that we passed?"

Faced with such an extraordinary and mind-numbing statement—that major congressional figures do not read the bills they may be asked to pass, bills that can have significant bearing on the entire American population— it's hardly surprising that the Patriot Act made an almost effortless transition from concept to reality. The passing of the law did not, however, stop numerous attempts to have the act modified and curtailed. At the same time that critics of the act were trying to reign in its abilities, however, government personnel were trying to make it even more powerful.

The Benjamin Franklin True Patriot Act and the Protecting the Rights of Individuals Act were among the bills that sought to cap the capability of the Patriot Act to intrude into, and limit, the rights of U.S. citizens and residents. It's a sign of power that those who wanted the act passed yielded, since neither bill had any bearing on the power of the Patriot Act—they both failed. The government responded in 2003 by creating what was known as the Domestic Security Enhancement Act, which, in essence, was an outgrowth of, and an amendment to, the original Patriot Act. When copies were leaked to the media, it caused a sensation, despite assertions from officialdom that it was nothing more than a concept for change, rather than a literal soon-to-be-in-place plan.

It was specifically thanks to the Center for Public Integrity that the document (draft or otherwise) surfaced. The CPI notes: "The Center for Public Integrity was founded in 1989 by Charles Lewis. We are one of the country's oldest and largest nonpartisan, nonprofit investigative news organizations. Our mission: To serve democracy by revealing abuses of power, corruption and betrayal of public trust by powerful public and private institutions, using the tools of investigative journalism."

In the first week of February 2003, the CPI acquired the document, which contained two key amendments: the government planned to (a) increase its ability to intrude into the lives of American citizens, and (b) make it more and more difficult for courts to deny the instigation of the amendments. It is, almost certainly, due to the actions of the CPI—who quickly posted the document to their website—that the "draft" was pulled.

Had it gone through in its original form, it would have allowed for (a) the collection of DNA from people suspected of having terrorist links—even if wholly unproven, (b) the legal ability to undertake so-called search-and-surveillance overseas without any kind of court order needed, and (c) extensions and modifications to the death penalty.

Slate.com has demonstrated that the change in presidency—from George W. Bush to Barack Obama—made very little difference to the power of the Patriot Act: "Sen. Obama voted to reauthorize the Patriot Act in 2005, a decision he defended on the campaign trail in 2008 with the caveat that some provisions contained in Section 215, like allowing the government to go through citizens' library records, 'went way overboard.' But in 2011 President Obama signed a bill to extend the Patriot Act's sunset clause to June 1, 2015—with Section 215 intact in its 2005 form."

Today, the Patriot Act continues to stand just as it has since 2001. Coming soon to a library near you....

Endless Surveillance

If, prior to 2013, someone were to ask you for your thoughts on Edward Snowden, you would almost certainly reply: "Who?" Indeed, his family, friends, and work colleagues aside, Snowden was unknown. Just about completely. That all changed—and changed radically—in the summer of 2013. That was when the shocking story of the National Security Agency's top-secret program of widespread surveillance came tumbling out into the public domain. It created shock waves that are still reverberating right now. Not only was Snowden suddenly the most talked-about man on the planet, he was also—in many quarters—public enemy number one.

As Snowden revealed, unbeknownst to just about everyone (the National Security Agency aside, of course), the NSA was spying not just on foreign nations but on U.S. citizens, too—as in just about each and every one of them—potentially, anyway. Landlines, cell phones, e-mail, Facebook, Twitter, and Skype: they had all been penetrated by the NSA, very often with the witting, subservient, and unforgivable help of those same companies. The data collection process was so mind-bogglingly huge that it would likely have had even George Orwell himself shaking his head in disbelief, except for just one thing: this was all too real. Control had just reached an entirely new level.

The response to Snowden's revelations was interesting and thought-provoking. For some people, Snowden is the definitive American hero: someone who succeeded in demonstrating to the American people and to the world at large that the NSA is an agency run riot in its goal to place the entire United States under electronic surveillance. For others, however, he is a man who has massively jeopardized U.S. national security and placed our troops in danger. Calls were even made for not just his lifelong incarceration but for his execution, too, as the ultimate traitor. For many people, however, Snowden falls somewhere between both camps. Before we get to the matter of what, precisely, Snowden revealed, let us take a look at the man's background.

Edward Snowden was born in 1983 in North Carolina, and he is someone who has had an intriguing, albeit turbulent, life. Although he is constantly and near-consistently referred to as an "NSA whistleblower," Snowden has proved, in his thirty-something years, to have been way more than that. It's interesting to note that practically the entire Snowden family has had significant links to officialdom. Snowden's mother, for example, works for the U.S. District Court. His grandfather, Edward J. Barrett, held a senior position in the Federal Bureau of Investigation, and his father served in the Coast Guard. It was, then, perhaps inevitable that Edward Snowden would also gravitate to a government job—and he did, several of them, actually. His work for the government, however, was of a far more covert, secret, and sensitive nature compared to those of his family.

When he was barely into his twenties, Snowden was in the U.S. Navy Reserve. Until, that is, he had a very serious accident: both of his legs were broken, and he was forced to find another career. In 2005, Snowden held a position of sensitivity at the Center for Advanced Study of Language. Evidently, Snowden was seen as a potentially valuable asset to U.S. Intelligence, as in the following year, 2006, he signed up with none other than the CIA, where he was employed in the agency's Global Communications Division. He stayed with the CIA until 2009. That is something that many people who are only aware of the basics of the Snowden affair don't realize: namely, that Snowden wasn't just someone who took a job with the NSA and then blew a massive whistle. No. In reality, he had been plugged into the world of secret government intelligence-based programs for years.

Former CIA employee and computer specialist Edward Snowden now lives in exile outside the United States after he let the cat out of the bag as to how U.S. citizens are being spied on by the NSA.

Later in 2009, Snowden gained employment with Dell, Inc., but this was far from being an everyday job, as one might expect. Dell has secret contracts with a large number of U.S. government, military, and intelligence agencies. It was as a result of this little-known fact that Snowden—while still with Dell—was offered a position at a National Security Agency facility in Japan, specifically in Fussa, Japan (a city in the western part of the Tokyo metropolitan area), where much of his daily work revolved around combatting the threats posed by computer hackers.

By 2011, Snowden was on the move again—this time back to the United States. He was still with Dell but now also for the CIA. A year later, he headed off to Hawaii. This is where, and specifically when, things began to change for Snowden. The dutiful employee began to change, and the infamous whistle-blower was molded into shape. It was while he was in Hawaii that Snowden saw something that shocked and outraged him. He began to see how the NSA was increasingly violating the Constitution of the United States, engaging in widespread surveillance of not just terrorists and those who were a threat to the nation but of the American people, too. The NSA, Snowden found out, was watching an untold number of individuals whose daily activities had no bearing upon national security or the defense of the nation and the free world at all, so having been exposed to a secret world that George Orwell would have had nightmares about, Snowden decided to do something about it: he blew the whistle in a way that ensured that himself, the NSA, and the issue of personal privacy would never again be quite the same.

The nature of the information Snowden was in possession of, and how he came to be in possession of it, surfaced bit by bit, piece by piece. So far as can be ascertained, it was around one month after he started working in Hawaii that Snowden started to download massive amounts of documentation that detailed the many shocking violations of law that Snowden wished to expose. The actual number of documents that Snowden accessed, downloaded, and released to the press, as well as others that still have yet to surface, was estimated in some media and government quarters to be close to a quarter of a million.

Then, in late May 2013, Snowden flew to Hong Kong. Given his actions, Snowden—who may have been reckless but certainly no fool—knew all too well that it would not be long at all before the authorities were on his tail, so the very last place he needed to be was Hawaii. It was while he was in Hong Kong that Snowden quietly told journalist Glenn Greenwald (of *Guardian US*) and film producer-director Laura Poitras of what was afoot in the top-secret world of the National Security Agency. It was in early June that the story finally broke. The NSA's massive programs of surveillance were wide open, and Edward Snowden was a household name.

It is hardly surprising that when even the smallest snippets of information first surfaced in the world's media, U.S. authorities were determined to stop Snowden in his tracks. Indeed, he faced (at the very least) a three-decades-long prison term for violating the terms of the Espionage Act, and his passport was revoked. Seeing what was in the cards for him, Snowden hit the road, so to speak. Where did he go? To none other than Moscow, Russia—specifically, the Sheremetyevo International Airport. Despite initial concerns on Snowden's part that he would not be allowed to stay—because of certain visa issues—his fears were soon eased when he was given a 365-day period of asylum. That was then extended to a three-year period of asylum.

Snowden remains in Russia to this day, although on February 10, 2017, the Russian government stated that it was pondering the idea of extraditing Snowden to American authorities as a ploy to curry favor with newly elected President Donald Trump.

With Snowden's life, history, background, and motivations revealed, what, exactly, did Snowden reveal? It had to have been something of massive, controversial proportions, right? Yes, right.

Undoubtedly, the most inflammatory revelations revolved around something that quickly became a major talking point in both the media and government. It was known as PRISM, which stands for Planning Tool for Resource Integration, Synchronization, and Management. Basically, PRISM is a highly sophisticated program that both collects and stores electronic data on a massive scale. We have to "thank" President George W. Bush for pushing PRISM through via the terms of (a) the Protect America Act of 2007, which was implemented on August 5th of that year; and (b) the FISA Amendments Act of 2008—FISA standing for Foreign Intelligence Surveillance Act. Collectively, the acts permit the gathering of electronic data from countless sources—and, in the process, protects those same sources from prosecution.

What outraged so many was who, precisely, the sources were that Snowden knew of and blew the whistle on. They included Sprint, Yahoo, AT&T, Facebook, YouTube, Verizon, Google, Skype, Microsoft, Apple, and Paltalk—and that was just the top of the long list. In no time at all, the world realized the implications of all this: the National Security Agency practically had carte blanche to wade through the e-mails, photos, instant messages, Skype conversations (both audio and video), texts, file transfers, voice mail messages, and live conversations by phone and Internet of every U.S. citizen and resident without hardly a concern for the law or matters relative to personal privacy.

If all the NSA had been up to was diligently spying on the activities of potential or known terrorists, others who wish to do us harm, and those who are possible threats to the security of the nation, very few people would likely have any complaints. In fact, just about everyone would rightly say that such actions were wholly warranted. However, as the Snowden revelations showed, that's not what was, or still is, going on. American hospitals, universities, private corporations, and even libraries were targeted, as were bank records, doctor–patient files, and more. In a mind-numbing piece of Orwellian fiction come to life, it was revealed that the reason why libraries were targeted was because the NSA was carefully, and systematically, creating a database of material on the reading habits of the entire U.S. population.

Glenn Greenwald, the journalist who broke the story of Snowden, said that the NSA's employees "listen to whatever emails they want, whatever telephone calls, browsing histories, Microsoft Word documents. And it's all done with no need to go to a court, with no need to even get supervisor approval on the part of the analyst."

Of course, the National Security Agency's people were not going to allow all of this to be said without having its say—and have their say, they most assuredly did. In the first week of June 2013, James Clapper, who was the director of national intelligence, admitted that yes, the NSA was working with the likes of Facebook and Google, but he clarified this by stating that the program only targeted overseas individuals and groups that were potentially threatening to the United States.

Clapper had more to say:

> *The Guardian* and *The Washington Post* articles refer to collection of communications pursuant to Section 702 of the Foreign Intelligence Surveillance Act. They contain numerous inaccuracies. Section 702 is a provision of FISA that is designed to facilitate the acquisition of foreign intelligence information concerning non-U.S. persons located outside the United States. It cannot be used to intentionally target any U.S. citizen, any other U.S. person, or anyone located within the United States. The unauthorized disclosure of information about this important and entirely legal program is reprehensible and risks important protections for the security of Americans.

This statement was made on the back of another statement from Clapper on March 13, 2013, when he said that the NSA wasn't "wittingly" collecting data on hundreds of millions of Americans. It turned out that this was all nothing but a bald-faced lie; the Snowden files showed that the NSA was doing exactly that. Clapper said when caught: "I responded in what I thought was the most truthful, or least untruthful manner by saying no."

Journalist Glenn Greenwald is known for the series of stories he did for *The Guardian* about Edward Snowden and government surveillance programs.

"Least untruthful" is a phrase that should send chills up the spines of just about everyone and anyone who cares about the truth, government control, and personal privacy.

On June 7, 2013, President Obama weighed in on the matter of Edward Snowden and his revelations:

> What you've got is two programs that were originally authorized by Congress, have been repeatedly authorized by Congress. Bipartisan majorities have approved them. Congress is continually briefed on how these are conducted. There are a whole range of safeguards involved. And federal judges are overseeing the entire program throughout. You can't have 100 percent security and then also have 100 percent privacy and zero inconvenience. You know, we're going to have to make some choices as a society.

More and more stories and revelations were on the horizon just waiting to be unleashed. In March 2014, in a feature written by Glenn Greenwald and Ryan Gallagher, it was said:

> Top-secret documents reveal that the National Security Agency is dramatically expanding its ability to covertly hack into computers on a mass scale by using automated systems that reduce the level of human oversight in the process.

> The classified files—provided previously by NSA whistleblower Edward Snowden—contain new details about groundbreaking surveillance technology the agency has developed to infect potentially millions of computers worldwide with malware "implants." The clandestine initiative enables the NSA to break into targeted computers and to siphon out data from foreign Internet and phone networks.

> The covert infrastructure that supports the hacking efforts operates from the agency's headquarters in Fort Meade, Maryland, and from eavesdropping bases in the United Kingdom and Japan. GCHQ, the British intelligence agency, appears to have played an integral role in helping to develop the implants tactic.

What was, almost certainly, the biggest and most disturbing revelation hit the world's media in July 2014: the *Washington Post* discovered from information provided by Snowden that around 90 percent of those secretly watched by the NSA had no ties to matters of a national security nature at all. They were, as the newspaper simply put it, "ordinary Americans." Snowden, then, was right all along.

The newspaper's investigative team said: "Some 160,000 emails and instant-messages and 7,900 documents from 11,000 online accounts, gathered by the NSA between 2009 and 2012, have been examined by the *Washington Post*, which alleges that nine out of ten of the account holders were not the intended targets."

The story continued that the information gathered provides a startling insight into the lives of ordinary Americans but is not of any intelligence value. For the most part, the electronic data that was under the scrutiny of the NSA revolved around "love and heartbreak, illicit sexual liaisons, mental-health crises, political and religious conversions, financial anxieties and disappointed hopes."

They were, as the newspaper simply put it, "ordinary Americans." Snowden, then, was right all along.

No greater example in the modern era of the ways and means by which we are controlled exists than the still ongoing saga of Edward Snowden. Many might say—or assume—that the Snowden story is far more focused on surveillance than it is on control, but think about it: knowing that they are possibly being listened to by the National Security Agency (and possibly by who knows how many other agencies of the government, too) may make many people fearful of airing their views on government via their cell phones, landlines, and the likes of Skype, so, in other words, yes, the Snowden affair is about surveillance—primarily, at least—but the unfortunate side effect is that knowing we are being listened to has had an adverse effect on the part of many to say what they really think of the world today. The result of all this? People stay quiet—not because of a particular law or mandate but out of fear and concern for their own safety. In that sense, the effects and potential blowbacks of surveillance on a massive scale *do* control us, and they *do* dictate what we say, or what we prefer not to say, on social media or on our phones.

Finally, when any mention is made of Edward Snowden, it inevitably conjures up imagery of one of the most important novels of all time: George Orwell's *Nineteen Eighty-Four*. Although ostensibly a satire, Orwell's book, which was published in 1949, is actually a chilling story of a world plunged into a state of dystopia of the very worst kind possible. In the book, the world of 1984 is one in which the iron fist of the government is all-dominating. People live in constant states of fear. Paranoia is rampant. The human population lives under the control of a ruthless regime. Propaganda, indoctrination, lies, and alternative facts are the combined order of the day.

In 2017, sales of *Nineteen Eighty-Four* soared in the immediate wake of White House counselor Kellyanne Conway's absolutely chilling comments about those aforementioned "alternative facts." Thankfully, just the fact that Orwell's book was once again in the news meant that a large number of people had, and still have, significant worries about the possibility that *Nineteen Eighty-Four* could become a reality.

Secrets of the Philadelphia Experiment

Undoubtedly, when it comes to the issues of control and conspiracy, just about the biggest doozy of all is that which revolves around what is known as the Montauk Project. It's a complicated saga that is filled with tales of mind control, time travel, government cover-ups, secret experiments, and much more, and it's all focused around a certain facility located on Long Island, New York. It's a story that has its origins in the 1940s and an incredible series of classified programs run by the U.S. Navy but which didn't start to surface publicly until the 1950s.

It was in 1955 that a highly controversial book on flying saucers was published. The author was Morris Ketchum Jessup, and the title of his book was *The Case for the UFO*. It was a book that, for the most part, highlighted two particular issues: (a) how gravity could be harnessed and used as an energy; and (b) the source of power of the mysterious flying saucers that people were seeing in the skies above. It wasn't long after the book was published that Jessup was contacted by a man who wrote him a number of letters that detailed something astounding. The man was one Carlos Allende, a resident of Pennsylvania.

Allende's letters were as long as they were rambling and almost ranting, but Jessup found them oddly addictive. Allende provided Jessup what he—Allende—claimed were top-secret snippets of a story that revolved around nothing less than invisibility—the type achieved, in fictional formats, at least, in the likes of *The Invisible Man* movie of 1933, starring Claude Rains. It wasn't just invisibility that Allende had on his mind; it was teleportation, too, of the kind that went drastically wrong for Jeff Goldblum's character, Seth Brundle, in 1986's *The Fly*.

Jessup read the letters with varying degrees of amazement, worry, fear, and incredulity. That's hardly surprising, given the nature of the alleged events. Allende's tale went that it was at the Philadelphia Naval Yard in October 1943 when the U.S. Navy reportedly managed to bring both teleportation and invisibility into the real world. According to Allende, the ship in question—the DE 173 USS *Eldridge*—vanished from Philadelphia and then very briefly reappeared in Norfolk, Virginia, after which it returned to the Philadelphia Naval Yard. How did Allende know all this? He told Jessup that he was onboard a ship whose crew were monitoring the experiment, the USS *Andrew Furuseth*. In one of his letters that detailed his own claimed sighting of the *Eldridge* vanishing from view, Allende wrote that he watched "the air all around the ship turn slightly, ever so slightly, darker than all the other air. I saw, after a few minutes, a foggy green mist arise like a cloud. I watched as thereafter the DE 173 became rapidly invisible to human eyes."

Allende's story was, to be sure, incredible, but the important thing was: was it true?

It sounded like an amazing hoax, but something about the story just made Jessup suspect that this was not a joke at all. The more that Allende related the growing aspects of the tale, the more and more Jessup was reeled in. Allende told him that while the experiment worked—in terms of achieving both teleportation and invisibility—it had terrible, adverse effects upon the crew. Many of them had gone completely and utterly insane and lived out the rest of their lives in asylums for the insane. Some vanished from view and were never seen or heard from again. Others were fused into the deck of the ship, flesh and metal combined into one. Agonizing deaths were the only inevitabilities for these poor souls.

Jessup knew, with the stakes being so potentially high, that he had to dig into the story further—and he did precisely that. Jessup was able to confirm that Allende was indeed on the *Andrew Furuseth* at the time. That was

The USS *Eldridge* is pictured here in 1944, shortly after an experiment to make it invisible was supposedly conducted, although the U.S. Navy denies any such thing happened.

good news. Things got downright fraught for Jessup, however, when, practically out of the blue, Jessup was contacted by the U.S. Navy; they had received—anonymously—a copy of Jessup's book, *The Case for the UFO*. It was filled with scrawled messages written in pen and included numerous data on the events that allegedly went down in the Philadelphia Naval Yard in 1943. The Navy insisted on a meeting with Jessup. That was not good. When the meeting went down and Jessup was shown the annotated copy of his book, he was amazed to see that the annotations were the work of Carlos Allende. Jessup—worried about an official backlash—spilled the beans, revealed all he knew, and then went on his way. As for the Navy, it had dozens of copies of the annotated version made. Why? No one, even to this day, is too sure. That was not quite the end of it, though; in 1959, Jessup was found dead in his car in a Florida park. For the UFO research community of the day, Jessup's death was viewed through highly suspicious eyes and with a lot of justification, too.

In the late 1970s, the story of the incident in Philadelphia was picked up again by researchers Bill Moore and the late Charles Berlitz. The result: their 1979 book *The Philadelphia Experiment*. One of the more interesting things that the pair uncovered was a newspaper clipping titled "Strange Circumstances Surround Tavern Brawl." It reads as follows:

> Several city police officers responding to a call to aid members of the Navy Shore Patrol in breaking up a tavern brawl near the U.S. Navy docks here last night got something of a surprise when they arrived on the scene to find the place empty of customers. According to a pair of very nervous waitresses, the Shore Patrol had arrived first and cleared the place out—but not before two of the sailors involved allegedly did a disappearing act. "They just sort of vanished into thin air … right there," reported one of the frightened hostesses, "and I ain't been drinking either!" At that point, according to her account, the Shore Patrol proceeded to hustle everybody out of the place in short order.

> A subsequent chat with the local police precinct left no doubts as to the fact that some sort of general brawl had indeed occurred in the vicinity of the dockyards at about eleven o'clock last night, but neither confirmation nor denial of the stranger aspects of the story could be immediately obtained. One reported witness succinctly summed up the affair by dismissing it as nothing more than "a lot of hooey from them daffy dames down there," who, he went on to say, were probably just looking for some free publicity. Damage to the tavern was estimated to be in the vicinity of six hundred dollars.

While the story is certainly a controversial one, in the 1990s, it was given a degree of support thanks to a man named George Mayerchak. For a period of time in 1949, Mayerchak—a sailor—was a patient at the Philadelphia Navy Hospital getting over a bad case of pneumonia. It was while Mayerchak was in the hospital that he heard very weird tales of the top-secret experiment that, at the time, occurred six years earlier. Tales of the vanishing sailors and the invisible ship abounded, as did the story of the barroom brawl and the men who disappeared into states of nothingness. Mayerchak said, though, that rather than having completely vanished, they "flickered" on and off, like a light bulb—which surely would have been a bizarre thing to see.

Further amazing testimony came from Harry Euton. He confided in Bill Moore that, having a top-secret clearance during the Second World War, he, Euton, was directly involved in the highly classified experiment. Reportedly, it was an experiment designed to shield U.S. ships from being picked up by Nazi radar systems. Something went wrong, though, explained Euton, who said that the ship became invisible. As he looked down and couldn't see any sign of the ship, Euton felt instantly nauseous and reached out for a nearby cable, which he knew was there and which he could feel but couldn't see. Euton, too, confirmed that several of the men vanished—never to be seen again—and that the surviving crew didn't look as they did normally, curious words that Euton preferred not to expand upon. All of which brings us to Montauk.

> Reportedly, it was an experiment designed to shield U.S. ships from being picked up by Nazi radar systems. Something went wrong....

The story continues that due to the fact that (a) we were at the height of the Second World War when the Philadelphia Experiment occurred and (b) no one fully understood how terribly wrong the experiment had gone, a decision was made to put the whole thing on hold until such a time when the hostilities with the Nazis were over and normality had returned to the world. It was, Montauk researchers say, in 1952 that tentative steps were taken to resurrect the Philadelphia Experiment for a whole new team of scientists. Supposedly, though, the U.S. Congress—fearful of opening what may have been a definitive Pandora's box—got very cold feet and axed the program. That didn't end matters, however. The U.S. military was determined to push on and funded the classified program in a very alternative way: by using a massive stash of gold that had been secured from the Germans when the war came to its end in 1945.

The money was now available. The scientific team was eager and ready to go. The Montauk project was about to begin. Reportedly, things began at the Brookhaven National Laboratory, situated on Long Island and under the control of the Atomic Energy Commission, later taken over by a powerful and shadowy elite that worked out of the Montauk Air Force station, also on Long Island. It's said by Montauk investigators that today, the research into time travel, invisibility, mind control, and much more is still going not so much at the old base but a hundred feet below it in fortified bunkers. How much of this can be confirmed? Can any of it be confirmed? These are important and crucial questions.

Undoubtedly, such a military facility did exist on Long Island. Even as long ago as the latter part of the eighteenth century, the area was noted for its ability to provide the military with the perfect lookout spot for potential enemy navies attempting to invade via the waters of the Atlantic Ocean, such as the Brits at the height of the War of Independence. In the First World War, the military was using the area to keep watch for any and all potential German troops that might try to launch an assault. It was in 1942, however, that things really began to take off big-time. It was a direct result of the terrible attack on Pearl Harbor, Hawaii, by the Japanese in December 1941 that plans were initiated to create what was initially termed Camp Hero. It was ingeniously camouflaged as a pleasant little fishing port. In reality, it was one of the most strategically positioned military facilities in the entire country. When the war was over, the base became largely inoperative—that is, however, until it became clear that the Soviets were going to be the next big threat. Camp Hero was soon reopened as Montauk Point, followed by the Montauk Air Force Station. The base was said to have been closed for good in 1978 at the orders of then-President Jimmy Carter. Montauk theorists, however, suggest that the work continued way below the old base—regardless of the fact that nothing at all was afoot on the surface as the 1980s loomed on the horizon.

Yes, a military facility certainly was at Montauk, then—and it was a place that, at various points in time, was integral to the arsenal of the Air Force. Let's see what else can be verified.

Pictured here is a gun casement at Camp Hero State Park. The park is located on part of Montauk Air Force Station.

It may come as a surprise to many to learn that the U.S. Navy of today does not deny that something may have happened at the Philadelphia Naval Yard in late 1943. They don't—you may already have guessed—endorse the tales of invisible sailors and a teleporting ship. Rather, the Navy believes that the legends were born out of legitimate programs, which became sensationally distorted over time.

Due to the fact that they are often contacted by people wanting to know about the Philadelphia Experiment, the U.S. Navy has a couple of user-friendly information sheets available, both of which outline what the Navy believes to have been the origins of the experiment. It's worth taking a look at both information sheets, as they provide data that suggests more than one answer to the riddle—from their perspective, at least. In its first document on the controversial affair, the Navy states the following:

> Allegedly, in the fall of 1943 a U.S. Navy destroyer was made invisible and teleported from Philadelphia, Pennsylvania, to Norfolk, Virginia, in an incident known as the Philadelphia Experiment. Records in the Archives Branch of the Naval History and Heritage Command have been repeatedly searched, but no documents have been located which confirm the event, or any interest by the Navy in attempting such an achievement.

> The ship involved in the experiment was supposedly the USS *Eldridge*. The Archives has reviewed the deck log and war diary from *Eldridge's* commissioning on 27 August 1943 at the New York Navy Yard through December 1943. The following description of *Eldridge's* activities are summarized from the ship's war diary. After commissioning, *Eldridge* remained in New York and in the Long Island Sound until 16 September when it sailed to Bermuda. From 18 September, the ship was in the vicinity of Bermuda undergoing training and sea trials until 15 October when *Eldridge* left in a convoy for New York where the convoy entered on 18 October. *Eldridge* remained in New York harbor until 1 November when it was part of the escort for Convoy UGS-23 (New York Section). On 2 November the convoy entered Naval Operating Base, Norfolk. On 3 November, *Eldridge* and Convoy UGS-23 left for Casablanca where it arrived on 22 November. On 29 November, *Eldridge* left as one of escorts for Convoy UGS-22 and arrived with the convoy on 17 December at New York harbor. *Eldridge* remained in New York on availability training and in Block Island Sound until 31 December when it steamed to Norfolk with four other ships. During this time frame, *Eldridge* was never in Philadelphia.

> A copy of *Eldridge's* complete World War II action report and war diary coverage, including the remarks section of the 1943 deck log,

is held by the Archives on microfilm, NRS-1978-26. The original file is held by the National Archives.

Supposedly, the crew of the civilian merchant ship SS *Andrew Furuseth* observed the arrival via teleportation of the *Eldridge* into the Norfolk area. *Andrew Furuseth's* movement report cards are in the Tenth Fleet records in the custody of the Modern Military Branch, National Archives and Records Administration, (8601 Adelphi Road, College Park, MD 20740–6001), which also has custody of the action reports, war diaries and deck logs of all World War II Navy ships, including *Eldridge*. The movement report cards list the merchant ship's ports of call, the dates of the visit, and convoy designation, if any. The movement report card shows that *Andrew Furuseth* left Norfolk with Convoy UGS-15 on 16 August 1943 and arrived at Casablanca on 2 September. The ship left Casablanca on 19 September and arrived off Cape Henry on 4 October. *Andrew Furuseth* left Norfolk with Convoy UGS-22 on 25 October and arrived at Oran on 12 November. The ship remained in the Mediterranean until it returned with Convoy UGS-25 to Hampton Roads on 17 January 1944. The Archives has a letter from Lieutenant Junior Grade William S. Dodge, USNR, (Ret.), the Master of *Andrew Furuseth* in 1943, categorically denying that he or his crew observed any unusual event while in Norfolk. *Eldridge* and *Andrew Furuseth* were not even in Norfolk at the same time.

The Office of Naval Research (ONR) has stated that the use of force fields to make a ship and her crew invisible does not conform to known physical laws. ONR also claims that Dr. Albert Einstein's unified field theory was never completed. During 1943–1944, Einstein was a part-time consultant with the Navy's Bureau of Ordnance, undertaking theoretical research on explosives and explosions. There is no indication that Einstein was involved in research relevant to invisibility or to teleportation.

The Philadelphia Experiment has also been called "Project Rainbow." A comprehensive search of the Archives has failed to identify records of a Project Rainbow relating to teleportation or making a ship disappear. In the 1940s, the code name RAINBOW was used to refer to the Rome–Berlin–Tokyo Axis. The RAINBOW plans were the war plans to defeat Italy, Germany, and Japan. RAINBOW V, the plan in effect on 7 December 1941 when Japan attacked Pearl Harbor, was the plan the United States used to fight the Axis powers.

Some researchers have erroneously concluded that degaussing has a connection with making an object invisible. Degaussing is a process in which a system of electrical cables are installed around the circumference of ship's hull, running from bow to stern on both sides. A measured electrical current is passed through these cables to cancel out the ship's magnetic field. Degaussing equipment was installed in the hull of Navy ships and could be turned on whenever the ship was in waters that might contain magnetic mines, usually shallow waters in combat areas. It could be said that degaussing, correctly done, makes a ship "invisible" to the sensors of magnetic mines, but the ship remains visible to the human eye, radar, and underwater listening devices.

After many years of searching, the staff of the Archives and independent researchers have not located any official documents that support the assertion that an invisibility or teleportation experiment involving a Navy ship occurred at Philadelphia or any other location.

The Navy expands on the story with its second report on the matter:

Over the years, the Navy has received innumerable queries about the so-called "Philadelphia Experiment" or "Project" and the alleged role of the Office of Naval Research (ONR) in it. The majority of these inquiries are directed to the Office of Naval Research or to the Fourth Naval District in Philadelphia. The frequency of these queries predictably intensifies each time the experiment is mentioned by the popular press, often in a science fiction book.

The genesis of the Philadelphia Experiment myth dates back to 1955 with the publication of *The Case for UFO's* by the late Morris K. Jessup.

Some time after the publication of the book, Jessup received correspondence from a Carlos Miguel Allende, who gave his address as R.D. #1, Box 223, New Kensington, Pa. In his correspondence, Allende commented on Jessup's book and gave details of an alleged secret naval experiment conducted by the Navy in Philadelphia in 1943. During the experiment, according to Allende, a ship was rendered invisible and teleported to and from Norfolk in a few minutes, with some terrible after-effects for crew members. Supposedly, this incredible feat was accomplished by applying Einstein's "unified field" theory. Allende claimed that he had witnessed the experiment from another ship and that the incident was reported in a Philadelphia newspaper. The identity of the newspaper has never been established. Similarly, the identity of Allende is unknown, and no information exists on his present address.

In 1956 a copy of Jessup's book was mailed anonymously to ONR. The pages of the book were interspersed with hand-written comments which alleged a knowledge of UFO's, their means of motion, the culture and ethos of the beings occupying these UFO's, described in pseudo-scientific and incoherent terms.

Two officers, then assigned to ONR, took a personal interest in the book and showed it to Jessup. Jessup concluded that the writer of those comments on his book was the same person who had written him about the Philadelphia Experiment. These two officers personally had the book retyped and arranged for the reprint, in typewritten form, of 25 copies. The officers and their personal belongings have left ONR many years ago, and ONR does not have a file copy of the annotated book.

Personnel at the Fourth Naval District believe that the questions surrounding the so-called "Philadelphia Experiment" arise from quite routine research which occurred during World War II at the Philadelphia Naval Shipyard. Until recently, it was believed that the foundation for the apocryphal stories arose from degaussing experiments which have the effect of making a ship undetectable or "invisible" to magnetic mines. Another likely genesis of the bizarre stories about levitation, teleportation and effects on human crew members might be attributed to experiments with the generating plant of a destroyer, the USS *Timmerman*. In the 1950's this ship was part of an experiment to test the effects of a small, high-frequency generator providing 1,000hz instead of the standard 400hz. The higher frequency generator produced corona discharges, and other well known phenomena associated with high frequency generators. None of the crew suffered effects from the experiment.

Verifiable data exists that the U.S. military, in the 1940s, was exploring the issue of invisibility.

ONR has never conducted any investigations on invisibility, either in 1943 or at any other time (ONR was established in 1946). In view of present scientific knowledge, ONR scientists do not believe that such an experiment could be possible except in the realm of science fiction.

Of course, the fact that the Navy initially claimed that nothing was to the story but now provides two very different explanations has some researchers of the case rolling their eyes and shaking their heads—and the story does not end there. Verifiable data exists that the U.S. military, in the 1940s, was exploring the issue of invisibility. One such program was code-named "Yahootie." The plan was to create an airplane that could not be visually seen. The plan revolved around strategically placed lights and mirrors on the planes, which were designed to reflect the skies in which the plane was flying. Of course, this would not have amounted to literal invisibility, but it does show that some degree of invisibility was an issue on the minds of the military when the experiment was said to have occurred in Philadelphia in 1943. If nothing else, this brief aside is definitive food for thought.

Now we come to the most controversial aspect of this entire story: namely, the work that is said to have taken place at Montauk in the field of teleportation. Although no such official documentation on this fringe topic has ever surfaced from the archives of Montauk, the fact that the U.S. military has indeed taken a keen interest in the subject is not in doubt at all. We know this, as the U.S. Air Force—under the terms of the Freedom of Information Act—released a startling document on the subject into the public domain. Its title: *The Teleportation Physics Study*. It was the work of Eric W. Davis of Las Vegas, Nevada's Earp Drive Metrics—a company secretly contracted by the Air Force Research Laboratory.

In his report for the Air Force, Davis wrote: "This study was tasked with the purpose of collecting information describing the teleportation of material objects, providing a description of teleportation as it occurs in physics, its theoretical and experimental status, and a projection of potential applications."

Interestingly, Davis appears to imply that he knew of other research in this particular field. He wrote that it was known to him that "anomalous teleportation has been scientifically investigated and separately documented by the Department of Defense." Again, no smoking gun exists here, but this is yet another example of intriguing research of the type said to be far more advanced at Montauk.

Joe Nickell is a senior research fellow at the Committee for Skeptical Inquiry. His conclusion about the "Montauk Monster" was that it was likely a waterlogged raccoon that had lost its fur.

One of the truly strangest, many have said wholly outrageous, allegations that has been made within conspiracy-themed research circles is that Montauk has a connection to the United States's most famous of all monsters: Bigfoot. The claim is that top-secret research is afoot deep below the old base to create Tulpa-style versions of the Bigfoot. That's to say that monsters conjured up in the imagination can then be projected outwardly and given some degree of quasi-independent life in the real world. *Weird U.S.* notes that on one occasion, one of those attached to the secret experiments—a man named Duncan Cameron—envisioned in his mind "a large, angry, powerful Sasquatch-like" entity that "materialized at Montauk and began destroying the base in a rage. It utterly decimated the place, tanking the project and disconnecting it from the past. As soon as the equipment harnessing people's psychic power was destroyed, the beast disappeared."

Still on the matter of Montauk and mysterious creatures....

Joe Nickell is a senior research fellow of the Committee for Skeptical Inquiry (CSI) and "Investigative Files" columnist for *Skeptical Inquirer*. A former stage magician, private investigator, and teacher, he is author of numerous books, including *Inquest on the Shroud of Turin* (1998), *Pen, Ink and Evidence* (2003), *Unsolved History* (2005), and *Adventures in Paranormal Investigation* (2007).

He notes: "In July 2008, the carcass of a creature soon dubbed the 'Montauk Monster' allegedly washed ashore near Montauk, Long Island, New York. It sparked much speculation and controversy, with some suggesting it was a shell-less sea turtle, a dog or other canid, a sheep, or a rodent—or even a latex fake or possible mutation experiment from the nearby Plum Island Animal Disease Center."

The strange saga of the admittedly very weird beast was one that caught the attention of not just national, but international, media. This was hardly surprising, since the animal appeared to have a beaklike face, large claws, and a doglike body. While the controversy rolled on for a long time and provoked deep rumors about what "the government" was doing, an answer to the riddle finally came, as Dr. Darren Naish noted:

> Is the carcass that of a dog? Dogs have an inflated frontal region that gives them a pronounced bony brow or forehead, and in contrast the Montauk monster's head seems smoothly convex. As many people have now noticed, there is a much better match: Raccoon *Procyon lotor*. It was the digits of the hands that gave this away for me: the Montauk carcass has very strange, elongated, almost human-like fingers with short claws.

Finally is the matter of time travel. For years, rumors have circulated to the effect that the alleged missing sailors from the USS *Eldridge* were not rendered invisible but were flung into the future: our present. While this remains the most controversial aspect of the various claims about Montauk and of course has yet to be proved, it is also an issue that has some supportive data. Dr. David Lewis Anderson of the Anderson Institute, which is based out of New Mexico, states that many years ago, he worked on a highly classified program that was focused on time travel. The location was the U.S. Air Force's Flight Test Center at the California-based Edwards Air Force Base.

Perhaps, one day, we will know for sure the true story of Montauk. The revelations may prove to be amazing.

Fahrenheit 451 Coming Soon?

In 1953, Ray Bradbury's classic novel *Fahrenheit 451* was published. Bradbury's book is a grim one, indeed. Its title comes from the fact that Fahrenheit 451 is the temperature at which paper burns. Why is that so relevant to the story? Well, in case you don't already know, read on. The world of *Fahrenheit 451* is acutely different from the one that we live in today. It's very much dystopian in nature (although we are getting there). The population is kept in check with an iron fist and almost all books are banned—but they are not just banned, they are burned, too. As to who, exactly, undertakes the burning, it's the nation's firemen. The firemen of the future are very different from those of today. Their job is to seek out books and torch them—hence the title of Bradbury's novel. All of which brings us to the matter of the new movie version, which was released in 2018 on the HBO channel.

Running at just under two hours, it stars Michael B. Jordan as a fireman—Guy Montag—who comes to realize that something is wrong with the world and society. Something *very* wrong. His senior officer is Capt. John Beatty (played by Michael Shannon), a man who goes about his business of burning in definitive "just following orders" fashion. As does Montag, for a while.

As is the case with Bradbury's novel, we are not specifically told when the movie is set, although it's clearly more than a few decades from now, after the United States has been ravaged by two civil wars, which led to the deaths of millions of Americans. Surveillance of the population is never-ending. Drones surf the skies in routine fashion. Schoolkids are taught that (a) books are dangerous, (b) that—several books aside—they should be avoided at all costs, and (c) that nothing good can come from reading a book. On top of that, much of the population is medicated with mood-altering drugs, which screw with their memories to significant degrees. Plus, most of the movie is set at night, which adds to the bleak atmosphere.

In one of those "it would be funny if it wasn't so disturbing" situations, it's the norm for everyone to have their equivalent of Amazon's Echo in their homes. Alexa of the future, however, is far more like Hal 9000 from Stanley Kubrick's *2001: A Space Odyssey*. "Her" name is Yuxie. Highly advanced artificial intelligence of just about the worst kind possible, Yuxie is a dangerous spy in the home who clearly cannot be trusted. Montag learns this, to his cost, as he becomes more and more disillusioned by the endless burning of books and the harsh treatment that those who dare to still read books (who are known as "Eels") are given.

In one particularly chilling part of the movie, Capt. Beatty tells Montag that by the time he has grandchildren, the kids of that era won't even have any concept of what a book is. We also learn that of the approximately six thousand languages that once existed, only sixty now remain. The clear implication is that one day, just one worldwide language will exist, which would, of course, be grim and tragic in the extreme (the jackbooted elements of today's society would probably not have a problem with it, though). Diverse cultures, independent nations, and history will all soon be gone—or will they? The answer is in both the novel and the movie.

The late, great sci-fi author Ray Bradbury wrote a story about a future society that burned books, *Fahrenheit 451*.

Fahrenheit 451 is, of course, just fiction, but watching the movie, and comparing it to the ways and means by which widespread surveillance is becoming the norm—and how the erosion of privacy is growing—it's hard not to think deeply on what the world might be like fifty or more years from now. Maybe even less, as we shall now see.

Without a doubt, the creepiest part of the Patriot Act was that which was alluded to earlier—namely, the government's legal and wide-reaching ability to monitor the reading habits of every single American citizen. This relates to what are termed national security letters, or NSLs. They are, essentially, subpoenas that are used "to protect against international terrorism or clandestine intelligence activities." That is 100 percent correct. The fact is, though, that such NSLs can—and have been— used by the Controllers on more than a few occasions. The reasons are far from positive. In fact, they are downright disturbing.

Such NSLs can permit agencies to demand access to—and with potential imprisonment for those who do not comply—bank account data, e-mail history, address books, telephone numbers (both called and received), and books bought, borrowed, and read. All of this falls under Section 215 of the Patriot Act. In a decidedly hazy fashion—which conveniently allows for widespread interpretation on the part of those who employ it—the act notes that certain "tangible things" may be accessed, such as "books, records, papers, documents, and other items."

Four years after the Patriot Act was passed, Library Connection—a Connecticut-based body—joined forces with the American Civil Liberties Union (ACLU) to highlight and curtail the government's ability to monitor the average reading matter of the average American: "Librarians need to understand their country's legal balance between the protection of freedom of expression and the protection of national security. Many librarians believe that the interests of national security, important as they are, have become an excuse for chilling the freedom to read."

The ACLU elaborated on this by accurately demonstrating that the Patriot Act has actually made it much easier for agencies of the government, the military, and the Intelligence Community to seize and study our most private files, paperwork, and data. The long list includes even what are termed "third-party" files. We're talking about our private medical records, our university- and college-based records, and even our online purchases of books—as well as the books we borrow from our local libraries, the latter two issues being those central to this particular chapter.

Surveillance orders, notes the ACLU, "can be based in part on a person's First Amendment activities, such as the books they read, the Web sites they visit, or a letter to the editor they have written."

Slate.com has aired its concerns on the matter of the Patriot Act, too: "Post-Patriot Act, third-party holders of your financial, library, travel, video rental, phone, medical, church, synagogue, and mosque records can be searched without your knowledge or consent, providing the government says it's trying to protect against terrorism."

As for the situation in more recent years, in May 2011 at *Wired*, Spencer Ackerman said: "You think you understand how the Patriot Act allows the government to spy on its citizens. Sen. Ron Wyden says it's worse than you know.... Wyden (D-Oregon) says that powers they grant the government on their face, the government applies a far broader legal interpretation—an interpretation that the government has conveniently classified, so it cannot be publicly assessed or challenged."

In Senator Wyden's own words: "We're getting to a gap between what the public thinks the law says and what the American government secretly thinks the law says. When you've got that kind of a gap, you're going to have a problem on your hands."

April Glaser of *Future Tense* highlighted the concerns and developments in this Orwellian saga:

> Librarians were among the first to raise concerns about the Patriot Act while it was being debated in Congress. The American Library Association was a signatory on the earliest coalition-led opposition to what became the Patriot Act, which passed in October 2001. Within a few months, a University of Illinois survey found that 85 libraries had been contacted with government requests— and that's likely a low figure, considering that Patriot Act requests came with a gag order.

Glaser notes that back in 2005, a group of librarians based in Connecticut took their case to court after a national security letter was issued to them in an effort to obtain what is known as "patron data." In effect, the group said not just "No" but "Hell, no!" They quite rightly saw matters as being wholly outrageous, particularly in view of the fact that all of this, in theory, could be undertaken without any kind of judicial review or an authorized warrant. Thankfully, sense was seen on this particularly Orwellian affair. Such was the outrage that the American Library Association, also in 2005, filed in the Supreme Court in an effort to get rid of this outrageous piece of spying of the deeply personal variety.

While it might not be burning books to control reading behavior, the government *does* have an interest in what you read, and the Patriot Act allows them to snoop on you and your books.

On October 14, 2015, *The Hill* informed its readers: "Librarians are warning that a cybersecurity bill about to hit the Senate floor could help the government spy on people using library computers. On Wednesday, the head of the country's largest advocate for libraries urged senators to oppose the 'privacy-hostile' bill known as the Cybersecurity Information Sharing Act (CISA)."

The Hill also noted that libraries were warning fellow staff how a new "cybersecurity bill" was in danger of taking away yet further civil liberties within libraries. The warning was focused on how the government was pushing to have the ability and the permission to access library-based computers used by their customers. In other words, it's not enough to have your laptop monitored or your iPhone, but now, even computers that you don't own but which you might use when, perhaps, you are out of town.

This also came from *The Hill*: "'As Sens. Wyden, [Rand] Paul and [Bernie] Sanders have courageously pointed out in opposition to it, the Cybersecurity Information Sharing Act would dramatically over-share the personal information of tens of millions of Americans who depend upon library computer networks, and could function, as a practical matter, as a new warrantless surveillance tool,' [Sari] Feldman [the president of the American Library Association] said."

In November 2016, the United Kingdom's *Guardian* newspaper stated the following:

> Public and private libraries are reacting swiftly to the election of Donald Trump, promising to destroy user information before it can be used against readers and backing up data abroad. The New York Public Library (NYPL) changed its privacy policy on Wednesday to emphasize its data-collection policies. Last week, the NYPL website stated that "any library record or other information collected by the Library as described herein is subject to disclosure pursuant to subpoena, court order, or as otherwise authorized by applicable law."

On January 6, 2016, writer Brian Tashman—in an article for *Rightwingwatch.com* titled "Ben Carson: Government Should Spy on Classrooms and Libraries"—said:

> In a meeting with *The Des Moines Register*'s editorial board today, Ben Carson defended his proposal to crack down on political bias on college campuses by saying that the Department of Education should have the power to secretly monitor classrooms and libraries to root out and uncover potential bias. He said that the same surveillance could also root out inefficiencies in federal government agencies. Carson, ironically, then railed against the "craziness" of "safe zones" on campus that try to "shelter" students from offensive language. He has regularly claimed that the "P.C. Police" wants to restrict "the freedom of speech [and] the freedom of expression." In the meeting, Carson again wildly misrepresented an incident at Florida Atlantic University to justify his position.

The Des Moines Register got on this story, too, and stated:

> Ben Carson suggested on Wednesday that the Department of Education and other government agencies should secretly enter classrooms, libraries and other government offices to track instances of political bias and inefficiency. Carson, a Republican presidential candidate, was responding to a question from *The Des Moines Register*'s editorial board regarding prior statements he's made calling

for federal monitoring of colleges and universities for political bias. "Basically, when complaints are heard, you know, from students or from other faculty members, you would go in and investigate," Carson said. "You can do that rather surreptitiously."

All of this growing desire on the part of the government to intrude on our reading habits is as worrying as it is obscene. Could a real-life version of *Fahrenheit 451* be just around the corner? Don't bet against it.

Further Reading

"25 Marconi Scientists, 1982–88." http://projectcamelot.org/marconi.html. 2014.

"1977 Senate Hearings on MKULTRA." http://www.druglibrary.org/Schaffer/history/e1950/mkultra/index.htm/. 2014.

"9/11 Attacks." http://www.history.com/topics/9-11-attacks. 2014.

Ackerman, Spencer. "There's a Secret Patriot Act, Senator Says." http://www.wired.com/2011/05/secret-patriot-act/. May 25, 2014.

Adachi, Ken. "Chemtrails." http://educate-yourself.org/ct/. 2014.

Adams, Mike. "The United Nations 2030 Agenda Decoded." http://www.naturalnews.com/051058_2030_Agenda_United_Nations_global_enslavement.html. September 4, 2015.

"The Alleged Secret Underground Alien Base in Dulce, New Mexico." *Curiosity Makes You Smarter.* https://curiosity.com/topics/the-alleged-secret-underground-alien-base-in-dulce-new-mexico-curiosity/. 2018.

Allen, Joseph. "The White God Quetzalcoatl." https://www.nephiproject.com/white_god_quetzalcoatl.htm. 2002.

Alten, Steve. *The Shell Game.* Springville, UT: Sweetwater Books, 2009.

"Animal Mutilation." http://vault.fbi.gov/Animal%20Mutilation. 2014.

"Annual Report of the Board of Regents of the Smithsonian." http://www.jasoncolavito.com/smithsonian-giant-reports.html. 2018.

Andrews, Steve. "David Icke and the Reptilian Conspiracy." https://exemplore.com/ufos-aliens/David-Icke-and-the-mystery-of-the-Reptilians. April 19, 2017.

Ansary, Alex. "Mass Mind Control through Network Television." http://rense.com/general69/mass.htm. December 29, 2005.

"Are They Dangerous?" http://www.bfro.net/gdb/show_FAQ.asp?id=659. 2014.

Associated Press. "9/11 Conspiracy Theorist to Leave Brigham Young." http://www.washingtonpost.com/wp-dyn/content/article/2006/10/21/AR2006102100635.html. October 22, 2006.

Ausiello, Michael. "The Sept. 11 Parallel 'Nobody Noticed' ('Lone Gunmen' Pilot Episode Video)." http://www.freerepublic.com/focus/news/703915/posts. June 21, 2002.

Austin, Jon. "New Shock Claim JFK Was 'Murdered by CIA' Days after Demanding UFO Files and NASA Visit." http://www.express.co.uk/news/science/631341/New-shock-claim-JFK-was-murdered-by-CIA-days-after-demanding-UFO-files-and-NASA-visit. January 4, 2016.

Axe, David. "Luis Elizondo, Director of the Pentagon's Aerospace ID Program, Says Some UFOs Still 'Defy Explanation.'" https://www.thedailybeast.com/luis-elizondo-former-director-of-the-pentagons-aerospace-id-program-says-some-ufos-still-defy-explanation. December 17, 2018.

Ball, Philip. "Designer Babies: An Ethical Horror Waiting to Happen?" https://www.theguardian.com/science/2017/jan/08/designer-babies-ethical-horror-waiting-to-happen. January 8, 2017.

Banias, M. J. "Chicago's Current Mothman Flap 'A Warning,' Says Expert." http://mysteriousuniverse.org/2017/06/chicagos-current-mothman-flap-a-warning-says-expert/. June 7, 2017.

"Barcode Everyone at Birth." http://www.bbc.com/future/story/20120522-barcode-everyone-at-birth. November 18, 2014.

Barker, Gray. *M.I.B.: The Secret Terror among Us.* Clarksburg, WV: New Age Press, 1983.

———. *They Knew Too Much About Flying Saucers.* NY, University Books, Inc., 1956.

Beckley, Timothy Green. *The UFO Silencers (Special Edition).* New Brunswick, NJ: Inner Light Publications, 1990.

Beckley, Timothy Green, and John Stuart. *Curse of the Men in Black*. New Brunswick, NJ: Global Communications, 2010.

Begich, Nick, and Jeane Manning. *Angels Don't Play This HAARP*. Anchorage, AK: Earthpulse Press, 1995.

Bell, Rachel. "The Death of Marilyn." http://www.crimelibrary.com/notorious_murders/celebrity/marilyn_monroe/index.html. 2014.

Bender, Albert. *Flying Saucers and the Three Men*. New York: Paperback Library, 1968.

"Benjamin Franklin True Patriot Act." https://en.wikipedia.org/wiki/Benjamin_Franklin_True_Patriot_Act. 2016.

Berlitz, Charles, and William L. Moore. *The Philadelphia Experiment*. St. Albans, UK: Granada Publishing, 1979.

Bishop, Greg. *Project Beta*. New York: Paraview-Pocket Books, 2005.

Bishop, Jason III. "The Dulce Base." Sacred Texts. http://www.sacred-texts.com/ufo/dulce.htm. 2017.

Bitto, Robert. "The Flying Saucer Crash at Coyame: A Mexican Roswell?" http://mexicounexplained.com/flying-saucer-crash-coyame-mexican-roswell/. September 5, 2016.

Blackburn, Lyle. *Lizard Man: The True Story of the Bishopville Monster*. San Antonio, TX: Anomalist Books, 2013.

———. *The Beast of Boggy Creek: The True Story of the Fouke Monster*. San Antonio, TX: Anomalist Books, 2012.

"Bohemian Grove." http://bohemiangroveexposed.com/. 2016.

Bollyn, Christopher. "Did Rupert Murdoch Have Prior Knowledge of 9-11?" http://www.bollyn.com/did-rupert-murdoch-have-prior-knowledge-of-9-11-2. October 3, 2003.

———. "Eyewitnesses Saw Military Aircraft at Scene of Flight 93." http://www.bollyn.com/eyewitnesses-saw-military-aircraft-at-scene-of-flight-93-2. July 15, 2005.

Bowe, Rebecca. "NSA Surveillance." https://www.theguardian.com/world/2013/jul/04/restore-the-fourth-protesters-nsa-surveillance. July 5, 2013.

Bradbury, Ray. *Fahrenheit 451*. New York: Simon & Schuster, 2012.

Bragalia, Anthony. "UFO Researcher Demands 'Alien Metal' Test Results from Government, Files Uunder the Freedom of Information Act." https://www.ufoexplorations.com/researcher-demands-alien-metal-test. December 2017.

"Brain Washing, Social Control and Programming—Why You Should Kill Your Television." http://www.wakingtimes.com/2014/02/26/brain-washing-social-control-programming-kill-your-television/. February 26, 2014.

Branton. "The Dulce Book." *Whale*. http://www.whale.to/b/dulce_b.html. 2017.

"A Brief History of the Underground." https://tfl.gov.uk/corporate/about-tfl/culture-and-heritage/londons-transport-a-history/london-underground/a-brief-history-of-the-underground. 2018.

Brown, Tim. "12 Holistic Doctors Have Now Died within a Little Over 90 Days." http://freedomoutpost.com/12-holistic-doctors-have-now-died-within-a-little-over-90-days/. October 13, 2015.

Bunch, William. "Flight 93: We Know It Crashed But Not Why." http://whatreallyhappened.com/WRHARTICLES/flight_93_crash.html. November 15, 2001.

Carrasco, David. *Quetzalcoatl and the Irony of Empire: Myths and Prophecies in the Aztec Tradition*. Boulder, CO: University Press of Colorado, 2001.

Central Intelligence Agency. "Mars Exploration, May 22, 1984." https://www.cia.gov/library/readingroom/document/cia-rdp96-00788r001900760001-9. 2018.

———. "Noah's Ark." https://www.cia.gov/library/readingroom/docs/DOC_0000839386.pdf. 2018.

"Chemtrail Conspiracy Theory." http://moonconspiracy.wordpress.com/chemtrail-conspiracy-theory/. 2014.

"Chemtrails." http://www.sheepkillers.com/chemtrails.html. 2014.

"Chemtrails Killing Organic Crops, Monsanto's GMO Seeds Thrive." http://www.geoengineering-watch.org/chemtrails-killing-organic-crops-monsantos-gmo-seeds-thrive/. May 23, 2014.

"Chemtrails—Spraying in Our Sky." http://www.holmestead.ca/chemtrails/response-en.html. 2014.

"CIA Report on Noah's Ark." http://www.jasoncolavito.com/cia-report-on-noahs-ark.html. 2016.

Coleman, Loren, and Patrick Huyghe. *The Field Guide to Bigfoot and Other Mystery Primates*. San Antonio, TX: Anomalist Books, 2006.

Collins, Tony. *Open Verdict: An Account of 25 Mysterious Deaths in the Defense Industry*. London, UK: Sphere Books, 1990.

Committee on Biological Warfare, March 28, October 16, October 19, and October 22, 1947.

A Concise Compendium of the Warren Commission Report on the Assassination of John F. Kennedy. New York: Popular Library, 1964.

Cooper, Helen, Ralph Blumenthal, and Leslie Kean. "Glowing Auras and 'Black Money': The Pentagon's Mysterious U.F.O. Program." https://www.nytimes.com/2017/12/16/us/politics/pentagon-program-ufo-harry-reid.html. December 16, 2017.

Cope, Alec. "The Commercial That Shows What TV Does to Your Brain." http://www.collective-evolution.com/2014/11/19/this-is-what-tv-can-do-to-your-brain/. November 19, 2014.

Coppens, Philip. "Report from Iron Mountain." http://philipcoppens.com/ironmountain.html. 2016.

Corbett, James. "Lone Gunmen Producer Questions Government on 9/11." http://www.corbettreport.com/articles/20080225_gunmen_911.htm. February 25, 2008.

Cowan, Alison Leigh. "Four Librarians Finally Break Silence in Records Case." http://www.nytimes.com/2006/05/31/nyregion/31library.html?_r=0. May 31, 2006.

Dakss, Brian. "John Lennon Remembered." http://www.cbsnews.com/news/john-lennon-remembered-08-12-2005/. December 8, 2005.

"Death Line." https://www.rottentomatoes.com/m/death_line/. 2018.

Denison, Caleb. "Samsung Smart TVs Don't Spy on Owners." http://www.digitaltrends.com/home-theater/samsung-tvs-arent-spying-eavesdropping-listening/. February 9, 2015.

Doc Conjure. "Miriam Bush—Repost for the 65th Anniversary of the Roswell Crash." http://thedemoniacal.blogspot.com/2012/06/miriam-bush-repost-for-65th-anniversary.html. June 20, 2012.

Downes, Jonathan. *Monster Hunter*. Woolfardisworthy, UK: CFZ Press, 2004.

"DREADED WILD MEN Strike Fear into Indian Children." *Lethbridge Herald*, March 3, 1934.

Duffy, Jonathan. "Bilderberg: The Ultimate Conspiracy Theory." http://news.bbc.co.uk/2/hi/uk_news/magazine/3773019.stm. June 3, 2004.

"Edward Snowden: Leaks That Exposed US Spy Program." http://www.bbc.com/news/world-us-canada-23123964. January 17, 2014.

"Edward Snowden: Timeline." http://www.bbc.com/news/world-us-canada-23768248. August 20, 2013.

"Everything You Need to Know about PRISM." http://www.theverge.com/2013/7/17/4517480/nsa-spying-prism-surveillance-cheat-sheet. July 17, 2013.

"FBI Does Not Rule Out Shootdown of Hijacked 757 over Pennsylvania." http://www.rense.com/general13/penn.htm. September 13, 2001.

Federal Bureau of Investigation. "Bacteriological Warfare in the United States." 2018.

———. "Ernest Hemingway File." 2018.

———. "Errol Flynn File." 2018.

———. "George Van Tassel." 2016.

———. "John Lennon." 2018.

———. "Marilyn Monroe File." 2018.

"Fifth Annual Report of the Bureau of Ethnology." http://www.jasoncolavito.com/smithsonian-giant-reports.html. 2018.

"Flight 93." http://www.history.com/topics/flight-93. 2014.

"Flight 93 Hijacker: 'Shall We Finish It Off?'" http://www.cnn.com/2004/US/07/22/911.flight.93/. July 23, 2004.

Flock, Elizabeth. "Bohemian Grove: Where the Rich and Powerful Go to Misbehave." https://www.washingtonpost.com/blogs/blogpost/post/bohemian-grove-where-the-rich-and-powerful-go-to-misbehave/2011/06/15/AGPV1sVH_blog.html. June 15, 2011.

"The Flying Saucer (1950)." https://www.imdb.com/title/tt0042469/. 2018.

Fuller, John G. *The Interrupted Journey*. New York: The Dial Press, 1965.

Gallagher, James. "'Designer Babies' Debate Should Start, Scientists Say." http://www.bbc.com/news/health-30742774. January 19, 2015.

"GAO Report on Roswell, NM UFO Crash." https://fas.org/sgp/othergov/roswell.html. July 28, 1995.

Garrison, Jim. *On the Trail of the Assassins*. London: Penguin Books, 1988.

Global Research. "9/11 Theologian Says Controlled Demolition of World Trade Center Is Now a Fact, Not a Theory." http://www.globalresearch.ca/9-11-theologian-says-controlled-demolition-of-world-trade-center-is-now-a-theory/1129?print=1. October 21, 2005.

Graham, Robbie. "UFOs and Disney." http://silverscreensaucers.blogspot.com/2011/07/ufos-and-disney-behind-magic-kingdom.html. July 29, 2011.

Greenberg, Andy. "How the NSA Could Bug Your Powered-Off iPhone, and How to Stop Them." https://www.wired.com/2014/06/nsa-bug-iphone/. June 3, 2014.

Griffin, Andrew. "iPhone Has Secret Software That Can Be Remotely Activated to Spy on People, Says Snowden." http://www.independent.co.uk/life-style/gadgets-and-tech/news/iphone-has-secret-software-that-can-be-remotely-activated-to-spy-on-people-says-snowden-9991754.html. January 21, 2015.

Griffin, Andrew W. "Riders on the Storm (Strange Days Have Tracked Us Down)." http://www.red dirtreport.com/red-dirt-grit/riders-storm-strange-days-have-tracked-us-down. August 15, 2017.

Guest, E. A. "The Other Paradigm." *Fate*, April 2005.

Hagopian, Joachim. "The Evils of Big Pharma Exposed." http://www.globalresearch.ca/the-evils-of-big-pharma-exposed/5425382?print=1. March 7, 2016.

Howard, Clark. "Your Smart TV Could be Spying on You." http://www.clark.com/your-smart-tv-spying-you. February 10, 2015.

"Illuminati: Order of the Illumined Wise Men." http://www.bibliotecapleyades.net/esp_sociopol_illuminati.htm. 2016.

Illuminati Watcher. "Illuminati Symbolism of Princess Diana's Death in Selena Gomez 'Slow Down' Video." http://illuminatiwatcher.com/illuminati-symbolism-of-princess-dianas-death-in-selena-gomez-slow-down-video/. July 22, 2013.

"In Search of Quetzalcoatl." http://www.unexplained-mysteries.com/column.php?id=147918. February 26, 2009.

"The John Lennon FBI Files." http://www.lennonfbifiles.com/. 2014.

Keel, John. *The Mothman Prophecies*. New York: Tor Books, 1991.

Keith Jim. *Black Helicopters II*. Lilburn, GA: IllumiNet Press, 1997.

———. *Black Helicopters over America*. Lilburn, GA: IllumiNet Press, 1994.

Kennedy, Sequoyah. "Amazon Alexa Says Chemtrails Are a Real Government Conspiracy." http://mysteriousuniverse.org/2018/04/amazon-alexa-says-chemtrails-are-a-real-government-conspiracy/. April 23, 2018.

King, Jeffrey. "The Lone Gunmen Episode 1: Pilot." http://www.plaguepuppy.net/public_html/Lone%20Gunmen/The_Lone_Gunmen_Episode_1.htm. 2014.

King, Jon. "Did the CIA Murder John Lennon?" http://www.consciousape.com/2012/10/08/did-the-cia-murder-john-lennon/. October 8, 2012.

"The Kingman, Arizona UFO Crash." http://www.prufon.net/2012/12/the-kingman-arizona-ufo-crash.html. December 30, 2012.

Knox, Olivier. "Intelligence Chief Clapper: I Gave 'Least Untruthful' Answer on U.S. Spying." http://news.yahoo.com/blogs/the-ticket/intel-chief-clapper-gave-least-untruthful-answer-u-164742798.html. June 10, 2013.

Korkis, Jim. "Ward Kimball and UFOs." http://www.mouseplanet.com/9720/Ward_Kimball_and_UFOs. August 24, 2011.

Lardinois, Frederic. "U.S. Government: Reports about PRISM Contain 'Numerous Inaccuracies.'" http://techcrunch.com/2013/06/06/u-s-government-reports-about-prism-contain-numerous-inaccuracies/. June 6, 2013.

"Lee Harvey Oswald." http://jfkassassination.net/russ/jfkinfo4/jfk12/defector.htm#OSWALD. 2014.

Lee, Timothy B. "Here's Everything We Know about PRISM to Date." http://www.washingtonpost.com/blogs/wonkblog/wp/2013/06/12/heres-everything-we-know-about-prism-to-date/. June 12, 2013.

Lendman, Stephen. "'The True Story of the Bilderberg Group' and What They May Be Planning Now." http://www.globalresearch.ca/the-true-story-of-the-bilderberg-group-and-what-they-may-be-planning-now/13808. June 1, 2009.

Loeb, Saul. "The Pentagon's Secret Search for UFOs." https://www.politico.com/magazine/story/2017/12/16/pentagon-ufo-search-harry-reid-216111. December 16, 2017.

Lowe. Keith. *Tunnel Vision*. New York: MTV Books, 2001.

Mantle, Philip. *Alien Autopsy Casebook*. Middlesex, UK: Healing of Atlantis, 2010.

"Mark Chapman: The Assassination of John Lennon." http://www.crimeandinvestigation.co.uk/crime-files/mark-chapman—the-assassination-of-john-lennon. 2014.

McDonald, Hugh. *Appointment in Dallas*. New York: Zebra, 1975.

McGowan, Kathleen. "The Mystery of the Versailles Time Slip." http://www.kathleenmcgowan.com/the-mystery-of-the-versailles-time-slip/. 2013.

McGreal, Chris. "September 11 Conspiracy Theories Continue to Abound." http://www.theguardian.com/world/2011/sep/05/september-11-conspiracy-theories. September 5, 2011.

Meacher, Michael. "This War on Terrorism Is Bogus." http://www.theguardian.com/politics/2003/sep/06/september11.iraq. September 6, 2003.

Meek, James Gordon. "FBI Was Told to Blame Anthrax Scare on Al Qaeda by White House Officials." www.nydailynews.com/news/national/2008/08/02/2008-08-02_fbi_was_told_to_blame_anthrax_scare_on_a.html. August 2, 2008.

Mitchell, Alanna, Simon Cooper, and Carolyn Abraham. "Strange Cluster of Microbiologists' Deaths under the Microscope." *Globe and Mail*, May 4, 2002.

Moon, Peter. *The Montauk Project*. Sky Books, 1992.

"News Gathering Is Illegal under New Patriot Act II." http://www.democraticunderground.com/discuss/duboard.php?az=view_all&address=104x4899596mber. September 27, 2005.

Openheimer, David. "What Is the Blue Beam Project?" http://www.bibliotecapleyades.net/sociopolitica/esp_sociopol_bluebeam04.htm. April 16, 2000.

Organic Consumers Association. "Food for Thought—Several Dozen Microbiologists & Scientists Dead under 'Suspicious Circumstances.'" http:// www.organicconsumers.org/corp/suspicious012805.cfm. January 27, 2005.

Pilkington, Mark. "Plane Truth on the Conspiracy Trail." http://archive.today/NFCOW. 2014.

Pittman, Ross. "9/11 Must See." http://consciouslifenews.com/911-prove-airplane-hit-pentagon-major-general-albert-stubblebine/. September 11, 2014.

"Princess Diana's Death and Memorial: The Occult Meaning." http://vigilantcitizen.com/vigilantreport/princess-dianas-death-and-memorial-the-occult-meaning/. 2016.

"Project Blue Beam." http://www.thewatcherfiles.com/bluebeam.html. 2016.

Randles, Jenny. *Breaking the Time Barrier*. New York: Paraview–Pocket Books, 2005.

Redfern, Nick. *Close Encounters of the Fatal Kind*. Wayne, NJ: Career Press, 2014.

———. "Conspiracies of the Sex Pistols Kind." http://mysteriousuniverse.org/2015/06/conspiracies-of-the-sex-pistols-kind/. June 12, 2015.

———. *Final Events*. San Antonio, TX: Anomalist Books, 2010.

———. Interview with Frank Wiley, June 3, 2004.

———. Interview with Jonathan Downes, June 11, 2011.

———. Interview with Mac Tonnies, July 7, 2009.

———. Interview with Mac Tonnies, March 14, 2004.

———. Interview with Mac Tonnies, September 9, 2006.

———. Interview with Ray Boeche, January 22, 2007.

———. Interview with Timothy Green Beckley, July 15, 2009.

———. *Men in Black*. Bracey, VA: Lisa Hagan Books, Bracey, 2015.

———. *The Black Diary*. Bracey, VA: Lisa Hagan Books, 2018.

———. *The Zombie Book*. Detroit, MI: Visible Ink Press, 2015.

"Reform the Patriot Act." https://www.aclu.org/reform-patriot-act. 2014.

"Report of Air Force Research Regarding the Roswell Incident." http://www.strangemag.com/reviews/reportofairforceresearch.html. 2014.

"Report of Scientific Advisory Panel on Unidentified Flying Objects Convened by Office of Scientific Intelligence, CIA January 14–18, 1953." http://www.cufon.org/cufon/robert.htm. 2014.

"Report of Scientific Advisory Panel on Unidentified Flying Objects Convened by Office of Scientific Intelligence, CIA. January 14–18, 1953." http://www.cufon.org/cufon/robert.htm. 2016.

"Report of the Select Committee on Assassinations of the U.S. House of Representatives." http://www.archives.gov/research/jfk/select-committee-report/. 2014.

Roberts, Scott Alan. *The Secret History of the Reptilians*. Pompton Plains, NJ: New Page Books, 2013.

Roller, Emma. "This Is What Section 215 of the Patriot Act Does." http://www.slate.com/blogs/weigel/2013/06/07/nsa_prism_scandal_what_patriot_act_section_215_does.html. June 7, 2013.

Roosevelt, Theodore. *The Wilderness Hunter*. New York: Putnam, 1906.

"Royal Western Counties Hospital Starcross." http://discovery.nationalarchives.gov.uk/details/r/0fd8d2fb-cfd3-442e-934a-66ce68535b5e. 2018.

Seaburn, Paul. "Ex-Pentagon Official Reveals New Info on UFOs and Aliens." https://mysteriousuniverse.org/2017/12/ex-pentagon-official-reveals-new-info-on-ufos-and-aliens/. December 20, 2017.

———. "Navy Ships Stalked for Days by UFOs." http://mysteriousuniverse.org/2018/05/navy-ships-stalked-for-days-by-ufos/. May 30, 2018.

Seale, Avrel. *Monster Hike*. San Antonio, TX: Anomalist Books, 2017.

Shain, Michael. "LA Jazz Singer's Book Deal to Reveal Her Sex Life with Aliens." *New York Post*, June 3, 1998.

Shapiro, Joshua. "The Montauk Project and the Philadelphia Experiment." http://www.v-j-enterpris es.com/montauk.html. 2016.

Singh, Manish. "Samsung Lied." http://betanews.com/2015/02/19/samsung-lied-its-smart-tv-is-indeed-spying-on-you-and-it-is-doing-nothing-to-stop-that/. February 19, 2015.

Steiger, Brad. *Conspiracies and Secret Societies*. Detroit, MI: Visible Ink Press, 2013.

Strieber, Whitley. *Warday*. New York: Warner Books, 1984.

Stringfield, Leonard. *Situation Red: The UFO Siege*. London: Sphere Books, 1978.

Sauer, Gerald. "A Murder Case Tests Alexa's Devotion to Your Privacy." https://www.wired.com/2017/02/murder-case-tests-alexas-devotion-privacy/. February 28, 2017.

Sauver, Mike. *Who Authored the John Titor Legend?* Big Swerve Press, 2016.

Siddique, Haroon. "Pentagon Admits Running Secret UFO Investigations for Five Years." https://www.theguardian.com/world/2017/dec/17/pentagon-admits-running-secret-ufo-investigation-for-five-years. December 17, 2017.

Sutton, William Josiah. *The Illuminati 666*. Fort Oglethorpe, GA: Teach Services, 1996.

Taylor, Porcher III. "Ararat Anomaly." http://www.noahsarksearch.com/porcher.htm. January 9, 1996.

Thomas, Gordon. "Microbiologists with Link to Race-Based Weapon Turning Up Dead." *American Free Press*. http://www.americanfreepress.net/08_09_03/Microbiologists_With/microbiologists_with.html. August 9, 2003.

———. "The Secret World of Dr. David Kelly." http://www.rumormillnews.com/cgi-bin/archive.cgi?noframes;read=35765. August 21, 2003.

Thomas, John P. "Is the U.S. Medical Mafia Murdering Alternative Health Doctors Who Have Real Cures Not Approved by the FDA?" https://healthimpactnews.com/2015/is-the-u-s-medical-mafia-murdering-alternative-health-doctors-who-have-real-cures-not-approved-by-the-fda/. 2016.

Thomas, Kenn. *Maury Island UFO*. Lilburn, GA: IllumiNet Press, 1999.

Thomas, Kenn, and Jim Keith. *The Octopus*. Portland, OR: Feral House, 1996.

"Timeline for American Airlines Flight 77." http://www.npr.org/templates/story/story.php?storyId=1962742. June 17, 2004.

Tonnies, Mac. *After the Martian Apocalypse*. New York: Paraview-Pocket Books, 2004.

———. *The Cryptoterrestials*. San Antonio, TX: Anomalist Books, 2010.

Torres, Noe, and Ruben Uriarte. *The Coyame Incident*. Edinburg, TX: Roswell Books, 2014.

Treiman, Daniel. "A 9/11 Conspiracy? 'I Would Not Be Surprised,' Says Tikkun Editor." http://forward.com/articles/10024/a-govt-conspiracy-i-wouldnt-be-surprised-sa/. February 6, 2007.

"A True Account of Alien Abduction." http://www.ufocasebook.com/trueaccountofalienabduction.html. 2007.

U.S. Air Force. *The Roswell Report: Case Closed*. U.S. Government Printing Office, 1997.

———. *The Roswell Report: Fact versus Fiction in the New Mexico Desert*. U.S. Government Printing Office, 1994.

U.S. Department of the Interior, U.S. Fish and Wildlife Service. "Are We Ready for 'Bigfoot' or the Loch Ness Monster?" http://www.bfro.net/gdb/show_article.asp?id=304. December 21, 1977.

"Vast Majority of NSA Spy Targets Are Mistakenly Monitored." http://www.louisiana.statenews.net/index.php/sid/223558101/scat/b8de8e630faf3631/ht/Vast-majority-of-NSA-spy-targets-are-mistakenly-monitored. July 6, 2014.

Vorhees, Josh. "Obama Defends NSA Surveillance: 'Nobody Is Listening to Your Telephone Calls.'" June 7, 2013.

Watson, Paul Joseph. "Military Whistleblower Claims She Witnessed Flight 93 Shootdown Order." http://www.prisonplanet.com/military-whistleblower-claims-she-witnessed-flight-93-shoot-down-order.html. April 8, 2009.

"What Hit the Pentagon?" http://911review.com/attack/pentagon/hypothesis.html. December 21, 2012.

"Why Was John Lennon's Doorman on CIA Payroll?" http://www.rumormillnews.com/cgi-bin/archive.cgi/noframes/read/86959. May 27, 2006.

Young, Kenny. "Jackie Gleason and the Pickled Alien." http://www.theblackvault.com/casefiles/jackie-gleason-and-the-pickled-alien-by-kenny-young/. May 25, 2015.

Zero, Keith. "Arizona Wilder: Revelations of a Mother Goddess." http://reptilian-facts.blogspot.com/2014/02/arizona-wilder-revelations-of-mother.html. February 18, 2014.

Zetter, Kim. "How to Keep the NSA From Spying through Your Webcam." https://www.wired.com/2014/03/webcams-mics/. March 13, 2014.

INDEX

Note: (ill.) indicates photos and illustrations.